G000155889

GUIDE TO
CHRISTIAN LIVING

GUIDE TO
CHRISTIAN LIVING

A New Compendium of Moral Theology

GEORGE V. LOBO, S. J.

Christian Classics, Inc.
Westminster, Maryland 21157

1989

Fifth Printing, 1989

© 1982 by
Theological Publications in India
St. Peter's Pontifical Seminary
Bangalore, India

ISBN: 0-87061-092-9

Printed in the United States of America

Contents

Contents

Contents

Preface

Among all the theological disciplines, perhaps moral theology has felt the impact of the conciliar renewal most. There has been a mass of excellent literature calling for a synthetic presentation. At the same time, a more flexible and dynamic ethic based on the Gospel values of love and freedom, while it has undoubtedly deepened the Christian life of many, has also caused not a little confusion in the minds of many. There are endless discussions on burning issues like contraception and abortion which often do not end in any satisfactory conclusion because the general principles for ethical decision are not clear. There is also a polarization between conservatives and progressives which leaves the neutral observer puzzled. This book is written with an eye to clarifying the basic issues in Christian ethics in an age of secularism and pluralism.

Although it can be taken as a treatise on general moral theology, this book is addressed to a wider audience than students of theology. It is meant to be a guide to Christian living in the spirit of Vatican II. It seeks to transcend the unfortunate dichotomy between moral and spiritual theology, as the Council clearly wanted when it spoke of moral theology as "the Christian vocation of the faithful, and their obligation to bring forth fruit in charity for the life of the world."

While discussing the basic principles of Christian ethics, the main preoccupation has been to discover an approach to moral decision that would safeguard all the moral values in a given situation. The broad orientations for moral guidance today have been brought out in several places. Special attention has been given to the question of moral absolutes, as it is central to ethical discourse now.

The ecumenical spirit, common preoccupations and a shared respect for the Word of God have brought Catholic and Protestant moral theology closer. Hence an effort has been made to have a dialogue with the theologians of the Reformed tradition. The strong influence of Protestant ethical writers on current Catholic moral theology has been brought out.

The development of human sciences has had a powerful impact on ethics. If morality is looked upon as a dimension of personality development, moral theology clearly must utilize the findings of these sciences. Thus, especially the topics of conscience and the human act have been discussed in the light of modern psychology. In dealing with matters like human rights, the Indian situation has been kept in mind; in fact, the need for going beyond a bourgeois individualistic ethic, especially in poor countries, has been pointed out at every step.

As the bibliography on the subject runs to thousands of items, the references have had necessarily to be selective. With a few exceptions, English works alone have been cited, although the treatment has been inspired by works in other languages.

I am indebted to a galaxy of writers for many valuable insights. Here I would like to mention only two. First, Josef Fuchs, S.J., under whose enlightened guidance I did my doctoral studies in Rome. Then Bernard Häring, C.SS.R., who has made the greatest single contribution to the renewal of Catholic moral theology. I would also like to thank many friends without whose encouragement and help it would not have been possible to complete this large work.

Vidya Jyoti   *George V. Lobo, S.J.*
Institute of Religious Studies   Professor of Christian Ethics
23, Raj Nivas Marg, Delhi-110 054

Abbreviations of Vatican II Documents

LG   Dogmatic Constitution on the Church, *Lumen Gentium*

SC   Constitution on the Sacred Liturgy, *Sacrosanctum Concilium*

GS   Pastoral Constitution on the Church in the Modern World, *Gaudium et Spes*

OT   Decree on Priestly Formation, *Optatam Totius*

PC   Decree on the Renewal of Religious Life, *Perfectae Caritatis*

GE   Declaration on Christian Education, *Gravissimum Educationis*

DH   Declaration on Religious Freedom. *Dignitatis Humanae*

IM   Decree on the Instruments of Social Communication, *Inter Mirifica*

Acknowledgements

Scripture quotations have been taken from *The Holy Bible, Revised Standard Version, Catholic Edition,* London, Catholic Truth Society, 1966.

The Documents of Vatican II have been cited from the edition of Walter M. Abbot, New York, Guild Press, 1966.

CHAPTER I

Moral Theology down the Ages

1. THE MORAL TEACHING OF THE BIBLE

The moral teaching of the Old Testament is essentially linked with the historical covenant of Sinai. It is the expression of the holiness of the people chosen by Yahweh and consecrated to His service. The law given to Israel was to be a preparation for the fulfillment of the promises made by God to His covenanted people. The Pentateuch places the moral ideals and laws of Israel in the context of the history of God's dealings with His people. The prophets recognize the authority of the Torah and expound its innermost demands. The doctrine of the Wisdom writers is enlightened by the Torah. After the exile, Ezra, by his cultic and moral reforms, sought to bring the life of the surviving community into conformity with the "book of the law of Moses" (most probably some version of the Pentateuch). From that time, Judaism assumed the distinctive characteristic of strict adherence and fidelity to the law.

But, unfortunately, Judaism largely succumbed to the deviation of legalism. The elaborate temple worship tended to become an empty ritual for many. There was also the tendency to set all precepts—moral, cultic and civil—on the same plane. As a result, the law became more and more the preserve of canonists and was so overloaded with minutiae that it turned into an insupportable burden. There was also the danger of seeking justification, not from the gracious gift of God, but from the meticulous observance of the law.

The New Testament restores and deepens the dialogical nature of morality. All the precepts are completely unified and taken up into the "new commandment" of love. Christ comes to "fulfill" the law. In

1

the Sermon on the Mount, He makes more exacting demands than those of the law, but at the same time breathes a spirit of freedom unknown to the Pharisees. His moral teaching is situated within the totality of the Good Tidings of salvation, announcing that the Kingdom of God is at hand and calling man to conversion from sin to God. The sacrificial love of Jesus is to be the basis and measure for the love of a Christian.

Paul emphasizes that man is justified, not by the works of the law, but by faith in Jesus Christ, and hence is freed from the constraint of the law. This does not imply antinomianism, but a subjection to the higher law of charity. The grace of the Holy Spirit, poured out into our hearts, enables us to fulfill the demands of the Gospel with spontaneity and freedom.

The moral teaching of the New Testament is not a systematic version of Christian morality. Here the new life of grace and the imperative of love are insistently proclaimed. The very person of the Lord, who is "the Way, the Truth and the Life," is proposed as the supreme exemplar to be imitated and followed. The perspective of the final consummation at the Lord's Second Coming is constantly placed before the mind. Still, under the present circumstances, practical problems like eating meat sacrificed to idols, the Christian's relation to civil authorities and so on, are tackled, not from a casuistic angle, but in the light of the basic Gospel and the Christian mystery. The way fornication is condemned is typical of the New Testament moral teaching: "Shall I take the members of Christ and make them members of a prostitute?" (1 Cor. 6:15), asks Paul. Likewise, the main vices (catalogues of sin) are characterized as modes of behavior that exclude one from the Kingdom (cf. 1 Cor. 6:9ff).

2.   THE PATRISTIC PERIOD (UNTIL 700)[1]

The main preoccupation of the Fathers was to transmit faithfully the revelation of the Word of God. They do not distinguish between dogma and morals. They propose Christianity as the paschal mystery of Christ to be lived. Following biblical tradition, and differing from Greek and Roman moral philosophy, they stress the religious source and sanction of moral laws.

The *Didache* (c. 90) groups moral teaching according to the Essenian scheme of the Two Ways: that of Salvation and that of Perdition.

St. Ignatius of Antioch (+ 200) develops the Johannine and Pauline ideal of life in Christ. The Christian is a "temple of God," "a Christ-bearer," who follows Christ unconditionally even unto death.

The apologists like Justin Martyr (+ 165) defend the ideal of Christian virtue based on the new life in Christ against the background of pagan vices.

The comments of early Fathers like Tertullian, St. Clement of Alexandria, Origen and St. Cyprian on burning issues such as cooperation in the official pagan worship or the fashioning of idols by Christian craftsmen should be of enlightenment even today. Their stand regarding a lewd theater and fashions, cruel circuses or military service in the pagan army is based on the principle of "being in the world, but not of the world" (cf. Jn. 17:14–16). They do not hesitate to integrate what is best in pagan thought with the Christian moral ideal. They do not find much difficulty in this, since they recognize that, wherever there are authentic moral values, there Christ, the divine teacher, is at work—the pagans having gathered up genuine truths as "so many seeds strewn about by the Logos." They also have to tackle inner problems like obedience to ecclesiastical authority, readiness for martyrdom, reconciliation of apostates and public sinners. We start to notice a beginning of casuistry in handling some of these problems.

The martyr (literally, "witness") is said to realize fully the ideal of the following of Christ. Virginity, as a witness of faith and love, is seen as an anticipation of the eschatological fulfillment and as a substitute for martydom. This is especially true when persecution ceases. A strong asceticism, or "spirituality of the desert," also develops.

In the *Mystagogic Catecheses* of St. Cyril of Jerusalem (+ 386) and similar works, moral instruction is entirely derived from the sacred mysteries. Actually, such instruction was given on the occasion of baptismal initiation and the celebration of the other sacraments. Thus morality appears clearly as flowing from the baptismal life in Christ. This pastoral and liturgical approach needs to be revived today.

The *De Officiis* of St. Ambrose (+ 397), reflecting somewhat the Stoic philosophy, can be considered as the first systematic work of moral theology. While not hesitating to accept what is good in the Stoa, he brings out the specific nature and superiority of the Christian moral ideal.

St. Augustine (354–430) is easily the most influential of the Fathers for later thinking. For St. Augustine, Christian morality is the way toward loving union with God, the eternal Beatitude. He has elaborately treated of subjects like marriage, virginity, truth and the theological virtues. More than that, he has penetrated those doctrinal truths that are the basis of Christian morality: grace and freedom, faith and good works, divine love and concupiscence, the Kingdom of God and the Kingdom of Satan, and the divine vision as the term of Christian moral life. His famous sayings, like "Love and do what you will," have been matter for reflection all through the centuries. While freely accepting the good points of Platonists and Stoics, he corrects and perfects their vision through a massive use of Scripture. A man of deep feeling and experience, he has given his works a profound psychological dimension and has stressed the importance of "motive" and of "the discerning of conflicting spirits" in moral life. His Manichaean background, from which he was not able to free himself entirely, has left a great deal of ambiguity in his treatment of sexual ethics and has had an unfortunate effect on succeeding writers down to our times.

The work of St. Gregory the Great (+ 604) is quite influential and thoroughly practical. In his well-known work *Moralia in Job,* he stresses the importance of the moral imperative as distinct from the kerygma, thereby foreshadowing much of later moral thinking in the Church.

3.   THE LATENT PERIOD (700–1100)

This period is rather barren, there being little creative activity. Materials from the Fathers are collected and arranged for practical use.

Elements of some importance may be gathered from the sermons and decrees of popes, councils and bishops which react against the many abuses of the disturbed times and thus try to maintain the purity of the Christian moral ideal.

A remarkable development of the period is the appearance of *Libri Penitentiales* (Penitential Books), which had considerable influence on the later evolution of moral theology. While in the early centuries we hear mostly of canonical penance or the public rite of ecclesiastical reconciliation that was utilized rarely, a new private penitential discipline was introduced by the Irish monks in the seventh century. This later spread throughout the Western Church. In order to help the confessors, special books containing detailed lists of sins together with the corresponding scale of penances to be imposed were prepared. The various species of sins were distinguished down to the least detail. This system of tariff-penances was very mechanical, and so it would be idle to look for much moral insight in these pragmatic aids which had their own utility for an insufficiently educated clergy in a crude age.

4. THE HIGH MIDDLE AGES (1100–1300)

There is a rebirth of theology as a whole with its beneficial effect on moral reflection. *Libri Sententiarum* (Books of Sentences), supplementing scripture commentaries, collect aphorisms from the Fathers. These books are commented on and soon develop into theological summas. They do not distinguish a special branch of moral theology, but take up moral themes in connection with the treatment of God, creation and fall, incarnation and sacraments. "For them, the whole of theology is indivisible doctrine on God, and on man only in the sight of God; in all its truths it is the 'teaching of wisdom'; this means that by their very nature all revealed truths are to be studied in theology so as to stimulate fruitfully our faith and our love."[2] For St. Bonaventure (+ 1274), for instance, theology exists "to serve contemplation and to make us holy; however, its first purpose is to make us holy."[3]

St. Thomas Aquinas (1223–1274), who is the most brilliant light of the epoch, presents a magnificent and unified conception of the whole of theology. After having treated of God in Himself in Part I of his *Summa Theologica,* he exposes man's movement toward God in Part II, followed by Christ as man's way to God in Part III. Thereby, his moral teaching is entirely theocentric and Christocentric. Christian life consists in realizing the image of God in man by following Christ through the sacramental life of grace.

St. Thomas maintains a balance between revelation and natural reason. He makes the best of pagan thought, especially the *Nicomachean Ethics* of Aristotle, but integrates it into the Christian vision drawn from Scripture and the Fathers. The man-centered moral goal of the Greeks is transformed into the beatific vision or communion in the knowledge and love of God, the Father of Jesus Christ. He systematically treats of general moral theology in I-IIae and special moral theology in II-IIae. We shall come back to his striking statement: "That which is primary in the New Law and wherein all its efficacy is based is the grace of the Holy Spirit."

Another feature of the period is the treatment of moral questions by canonists following the leadership of Gratian's *Decree* (1140), which is the first major collection of Church laws. The canonists have contributed many moral insights, especially regarding justice and marriage. But their intervention will produce a lasting confusion between the moral law imprinted in the heart of man and positive canon law—a confusion which is yet to be completely dissipated. Due to the prevailing "voluntarism" of the times, Christian morality was often reduced to "wilful" laws of God looked upon as the supreme (and arbitrary) legislator.

Meanwhile, in order to meet the needs of confessors, penitential and pastoral summas originating from the Irish penitential books were evolved. These *Summae Confessorum* are not moral treatises but a kind of *vade mecum* providing ready information to the priest on moral norms, canonical regulations, liturgical prescriptions, as well as pastoral instruction on the sacraments. They are an advance on the older penitentials but are far from coming up to the standard of moral theology and have little relation to the expositions of the great Scholastic writers of the time.

5. THE RENAISSANCE PERIOD (1300–1600)

Gradually the *Summae Confessorum* became more and more developed. Their exposition became systematic, often arranged under key words after the manner of encyclopedias.

Meanwhile, moral theological reflection was enriched by a number of commentaries on Part II of the *Summa Theologica* of St. Thomas. These were affected by the Renaissance and thus acquired a naturalistic flavor, the biblical tradition receding more and more into the background.

The nominalistic current initiated by Duns Scotus and William Ockham stressed the importance of the individual moral act with its concrete circumstances more than the observance of universal rules or the cultivation of virtues. This led to the development of casuistry, which had its good and bad points. On the one hand, the personal element in morality was rightly stressed; but, on the other hand, morality was in danger of being atomized into isolated acts.

This problem, as we shall see later, is of great current importance. The depreciation of the objective order in nominalism also led to voluntarism, which in turn developed into legalism. This accentuated the influence of the jurists, morality being more and more reduced to the juridical element with its dry casuistry. Morality and human legislation were thought of on the same legal model: "Law is the will of the legislator pure and simple; sin would be concerned with the mere breach of the law."

Those with a more spiritual bent developed an ascetical and mystical theology. Here is the origin of the divorce between classical moral theology, supposedly meant for ordinary people, and a "spiritual" theology meant for a superior class of Christians.

In the sixteenth century, the Spanish Dominicans of Salamanca wrote commentaries on the *Summa* of St. Thomas in which they attempted a synthesis between the great orientations of Thomism and the

penchant for concrete data of the nominalists. Some of these (like
Francis de Vitoria, known as the founder of Western international law)
addressed themselves to problems of justice and international law arising
from rapid economic expansion and the conquest of vast territories by
Christian powers. They sought to introduce an element of humanity, if
not the Gospel spirit, into the horrible process of colonialism.

6. CLASSICAL MORAL THEOLOGY (1600–1960)

At the turn of the century, the great Jesuit theologians, like Gabriel
Vasquez and Francis Suarez, wrote commentaries on St. Thomas which
already show an independence of thought. Some produced monumental
works: for instance, Thomas Sanchez, *De Matrimonio;* Leonard Les-
sius, *De Justitia et Jure;* and De Lugo, *De Justitia.*

The great movements of the Reformation and Counter-Reformation
did not produce the ferment in Catholic moral theology that might have
been expected. Still, the desire of the Council of Trent for a thorough-
going pastoral "care of souls" had to be met. In order to prepare the
clergy for this work, several authors, beginning with John Azor (1603),
prepared a new type of *Institutiones Morales* somewhere between the
speculative theological summas used in the universities and the extant
summas for confessors.

They contained fundamental moral theology, treatment of the commandments of God and the Church, regulations concerning the admin-
istration of the sacraments and ecclesiastical penalties. This format, in
which the divorce between moral and dogmatic theology was substantially sealed, continued in the manuals of moral theology that lasted till
Vatican II.

These systematic works provided a ready reference to all possible
"cases of conscience." The whole effort was concentrated on preparing
confessors who could help penitents in an accurate examination of
conscience and the confession of mortal sins "according to their number
and species," as required by Trent. In spite of their several undoubted
merits, they were largely responsible for the legalistic, minimalistic and

casuistic trends in Catholic moral theology that dominated the scene until Vatican II.

Meanwhile, the question of individual conscience came up for discussion. The laudable goal of making room for subjective factors in determining moral imputability often degenerated into laxism. From the legitimate view held by many that a doubtful moral law as such does not bind in conscience (doctrine of probabilism), all kinds of subtleties were invented to discover some doubt and thus to excuse from the obligation of most laws. Casuistry divorced from solid doctrine often degenerated into sophistry and laxism. More than one manualist competed for the title of Prince of Laxists, although Antonine Diana seems to have won the palm by "solving" more than 20,000 cases! Popes Alexander VII and Innocent XI had to condemn a long list of propositions as "at least scandalous and pernicious in practice."

A strong rigoristic reaction was not slow in coming. This was led by the Jansenists, who exaggerated the weakness of fallen nature and sought to protect it by a wall of security. The apparently laxist doctrine of probabilism was countered by one of probabiliorism, affirming that between two probable opinions one must always choose the safer course by adopting the more probable one.

St. Alphonsus Liguori, the founder of the Redemptorists and patron of moral theologians, proposed a via media of equiprobabilism, balancing the claims of law and liberty. Though this theory by itself did not resolve the question, his several works are characterized by an acute pastoral sense. His *Theologia Moralis* is a guide to prudent moral discernment. Though it might look dry, it must be read together with his other pastoral and spiritual works, which breathe spiritual unction. While many of his predecessors were contending between different options regarding the probability of a law, he pointed out the need for going beyond the mechanical application of the law whether in a laxist or rigoristic sense.

The influence of St. Alphonsus produced a lull in the storm and sowed the seed for a more adequate moral theology that would take long to germinate and fructify. Meanwhile, the majority of manualists continued with their casuistic approach.

The legalism of the manualists was balanced by the spiritual writings of the French School of the seventeenth and eighteenth centuries, led by de Bérulle, Olier and Lallemant, who made a remarkable contribution to Catholic spirituality. But, unfortunately, their influence was restricted to a small group of the devout.

At the same time, philosophers like Descartes, Spinoza, Leibnitz and Kant developed ideological currents that would prove a challenge to all morality based on revealed religion.

7. EARLY EFFORTS AT RENEWAL

Rationalistic movements like the Enlightenment (*Aufklärung*) as well as the French Revolution contributed their share to the ferment of ideas. Since a merely negative stance would not save the situation, discerning minds like John Michael Sailer (1751–1832) and John Baptist Hirscher (1788–1865) promoted an evangelistic renewal of moral theology which would be less legalistic and more imbued with the spirit of the Gospel. Instead of being satisfied with tracing the frontiers of what is right and what is wrong, or of what is gravely or lightly sinful, they tried to set forth the ideal of Christian life.

This work was carried forward by the Tübingen School, which stressed the dynamic character of Christian morality. Starting from the gift of grace, it described the response to which man is called and the continuous struggle with the forces of evil. It acknowledged the value of casuistry but limited it to a narrow sphere of strict duties circumscribed by laws, while an immense area of free decision lay open. It elaborated a Christian personalism based on love. It explained how true freedom is the possibility of loving what is most exalted through the union of the human will with the transcendent will of God.

While the use of the manuals continued till very recently, several theologians were influenced by the Tübingen School and were helped by the revival of authentic Thomism. Thus Joseph Mausbach (1861–

1931), who wrote a standard treatise generally according to the accepted plan, seeks to free moral theology from its canonical accretions and expounds its doctrinal foundations. He makes the glory of God the supreme norm of morality. Though he follows the practical order of the commandments, he in fact expounds a positive theology of Christian virtues.

Otto Schilling (1874–1956) maintains that charity is the formal principle of moral theology. He pays special attention to social problems.

The work of Fritz Tillmann (1874–1953) merits special attention since he began his career as an exegete. Basing himself on the Word of God, he presents Christian morality as imitation of Christ and tries to overcome the dichotomy between a morality of minimum requirements and an asceticism meant only for the perfect. For him the ethics of the Sermon on the Mount is binding on all the faithful. Still, he does not bring out sufficiently the relationship between interior union with the Lord through grace and the sacramental mysteries. The work of Tillmann will later be deepened by Scripture scholars like Rudolf Schnackenburg and Ceslaus Spicq.

Emile Mersch (+ 1940), taking his starting point from the Mystical Body of Christ, has brought out the communitarian dimension of Christian morality.

Theologia Moralis of Arthur Vermeersch, first published in 1935 and arranged according to virtues instead of commandments, already shows the impact of the renewal. Jacques Leclercq, by his critique of classical manuals, and Odon Lottin, by his historical studies, have played an important part in the renewal. Gerard Gilleman (1952) has developed the Thomistic concept of charity being the "form" of all virtues and proposed a blueprint of moral theology based on the "new commandment."

The publication of the first German edition of *The Law of Christ* by Bernard Häring in 1954 greatly spurred on the movement of renewal. He brings out the personal and dialogical character of Christian life.

The sacraments are treated, not merely as objects of regulations, but as means of personal encounter with the Lord. He stresses the importance of the *kairos,* the unique call of God to each person in his particular situation. In this work, as well as in his other prolific writings, he discusses in detail the important problems of our time, always bringing fresh insights. While he has thoroughly imbibed the biblical tradition, he also manifests a certain influence of value ethics of phenomenologists like Max Scheler. He may not always be fully logical or consistent in matters of detail, but it has rightly been said: "Häring, more than anyone else, has helped to change the attitude and orientation of moral theology."[4]

Josef Fuchs is one of the most profound and careful thinkers who have provided a solid basis for current renewal. He has masterfully exposed Catholic natural law ethics and the concept of the fundamental option underlying particular moral decisions.

Some of the great contemporary dogmatic theologians, like Karl Rahner, because of the comprehensiveness and vitality of their thought, could not but touch on the basic themes of Christian morality. Hence their contribution to the renewal of moral theology cannot be neglected.

All the efforts of these pioneers were crowned by the teaching of the Second Vatican Council, especially in its Pastoral Constitution on the Church in the Modern World, *Gaudium et Spes.* The Council asked for renewal and in specific areas itself provided the basic orientations. Almost twenty years after the Council, many have yet to grasp its teachings, while others have misunderstood them and made the process of renewal more difficult. The present work is meant to be a contribution to the renewal of moral theology and Christian life in the light of the Council teaching and current thought.

———o———

Notes to Chapter I

1. Cf. F. Bourdeau and A. Danet, *Introduction to the Law of Christ,* Cork, Mercier, 1966, pp. 45–59; Vernon J. Bourke, *History of Ethics,* Garden City, NY, Doubleday, 1968; Bernard Häring, *The Law of Christ,* Westminster, MD, Newman Press, Vol. I, 1961, pp. 3–33; *New Catholic Encyclopedia,* New York, McGraw-Hill, 1967, Vol. IX, 1117–1122; C. Henry Peschke, *Christian Ethics,* Alcester & Dublin, Goodliffe Neale, 1975, pp. 43–64.
2. Bernard Häring, *op. cit.,* p. 11.
3. *Commentaria in IV Libros Sententiarum, Proemium, Q. 3, Opera Theologica Selecta,* Firenze, Quaracchi, 1934, p. 11.
4. Charles E. Curran, *A New Look at Christian Morality,* Notre Dame, Fides, 1968, p. 157.

CHAPTER II

The Renewal of Moral Theology

1. CRITIQUE OF THE OLDER APPROACH

The sixties were marked by strong criticism of the older manualistic approach to moral theology. It must be noted that many critics did not seem to have examined the teaching of the manualists in depth but were moved by impatience to make hasty judgments or to swing to the opposite extreme. Still, as many of the points of criticism had their validity, we shall examine some of them.[1]

a) *Preoccupation with sin.* The whole emphasis seemed to be on avoiding sin and thus escaping punishment. Hence there was a negative and pessimistic note which incurred the label "manuals of spiritual pathology."

The concentration on sin and its species historically arose because the manuals were the direct successors of the *Summae Confessorum* that were meant to aid the confessor in his role as judge. Though there were some indications of the remedies for sin, his role as spiritual guide did not receive adequate attention. This was partly due to the conception that the fulness of Christian perfection was meant for the clergy and the religious, while the laity generally were supposed to be satisfied with observing the commandments. There is now need for realizing the sublime vocation to sanctity of all the faithful and hence the corresponding role of the confessor in leading them on to attain it. Besides, moral theology is not only a preparation for confessors, but is the unfolding of the Christian call to perfection and of the way to achieve it. However, the reality of sin as the radical obstacle to holiness should not be lost sight of.

b) *Excessive casuistry* or the preoccupation with determining the minimum requirements of the law in particular sets of circumstances. This should not be overdone. The positive ideal of the Christian vocation and its demands cannot be determined merely by a casuistic solution to a whole series of problems. It needs a much more positive approach. Still, a certain amount of training in the art of casuistry is useful. If people want to act as responsible Christians, they must learn how to decide whether a particular action is according to the divine will. Vague feelings about what is right and wrong do not manifest maturity and moral refinement. There is need for spiritual discernment as well as the application of general moral principles to particular circumstances.

The mysterious core of the personality comes into play in moral decision. Still, an enlightened formation in casuistry can help in mature judgment because it can help discern the moral values of the concrete data involved.

c) *Multiplicity of laws* while the fundamental law of love is neglected. This was customarily treated in a separate chapter that was given minor attention. Indeed, the primacy of charity in Christian morality needs to be restored. But we must not oppose law and love. Law, rightly understood, is the expression of the will of the loving God who invites us to a response of love. Moral obligation is not an arbitrary constraint, but the demand of love. If the value of law is unduly depreciated, the way is open to arbitrary conduct. As Edward Schillebeeckx puts it: "One who has studied history must come to the bewildering conclusion that humanity has suffered unspeakably under 'subjectively good' actions and that therefore 'subjectively good morality' cannot be the final word."[2] It is not enough to have a right intention; but we must responsibly tend toward objective rectitude of action in order to fulfill the divine will and thereby achieve true human perfection.

The law directly expresses only the minimum demands of morality. But this is no reason to belittle its significance. As Ford and Kelly affirm: "The world would be a paradise if all the commandments were kept."[3]

d)   *Confusion between the moral law and positive Church law*. Canon law has its own importance for the well-being of the Church, but it should be carefully distinguished from moral theology lest the sanctity of the divine law be obscured by the imperfections of human legislation. In the interpretation of canon law itself, "the mystery of the Church should be kept in mind."[4]

e)   *Overemphasis on abstract principles* to the neglect of concrete circumstances and personal response. The manuals have spoken about some factors that diminish imputability, like violence, fear, passion. However, the recent findings of psychology call for a revision of the classical treatise on human acts. Such findings can serve, not only to assess the imputability of sinful acts, but also to enrich and deepen the understanding of free will and responsibility. They should be of great help in developing an integrated personality.

The relationship between universal moral principles and personal response is one of the chief problems now under discussion. There is need for a proper balance in this matter, as we shall see later.

f)   *Too much reasoning* divorced from revelation. This can be rectified by deepening the scriptural foundations of Christian moral life. Still, all the norms of morality cannot be derived immediately from Scripture. Besides, Scripture itself teaches the value of human nature and the gift of reason which God has given to man. It clearly speaks of the conscience or "the law written in the heart of man."

A fully adequate exposition of Christian morality would have to dwell on the mysteries of Christianity as revealed in the Word of God. But this poses the practical problem of distinction of disciplines and the need for avoiding large-scale overlapping.

g)   The rationalistic approach also led to the *tendency toward self-righteousness* or "justification by works." It should be noted that moral theology as a separate discipline arose during the decadent period of Scholasticism and as a negative reaction against the Reformers, who overstressed the aspect of faith. Now, fortunately, with the return to Scripture and the emphasis on the gratuitous gift of the Holy Spirit, the balance is being restored.

h) *Social obligations neglected.* Indeed, there was too much concentration on individual rectitude. Till the great encyclicals of recent popes, beginning with *Rerum Novarum* of Leo XIII, there was too much individualism in moral theology. But even afterwards, the manuals did not change their perspective significantly, perhaps because social justice was treated as a separate discipline. Now it is becoming clear that the whole of moral theology should bring out the social dimensions of the Christian life.

2. MORAL THEOLOGY ACCORDING TO VATICAN II

In the Decree on Priestly Formation, the Council asks that students in dogmatic theology should learn how the mysteries of salvation "are interconnected and be taught to recognize their presence and activity in liturgical actions and in the whole life of the Church. Let them learn of revelation, to apply eternal truths to the changing conditions of human affairs, and to communicate such truths in a manner suited to contemporary man."[5] Here dogmatic theology itself is given a dynamic orientation toward life which precludes an artificial separation of theological disciplines.

The Council goes on to say that "other theological disciplines should also be renewed by livelier contact with the mystery of Christ and the history of salvation. *Special attention needs to be given to the development of moral theology.* Its scientific exposition should be more thoroughly nourished by spiritual teaching. It should show the nobility of the Christian vocation of the faithful, and their obligation to bring forth fruit in charity for the life of the world."[6]

In the light of these directions and other texts of Vatican II, we can trace the general lines of renewal of moral theology according to the mind of the Council.[7]

Moral theology should be:

a) *Theocentric.* Not mere self-perfection, but the manifestation of the glory of God and sharing in His life is the goal of Christian life. The Christian God is essentially the God of revelation, who communicates Himself to man. Morality is the response to God's call out of love. The dialogical pattern of invitation-response should clearly appear.

The divine Spirit dwelling within us moves us, not only to direct this or that action to God, but to surrender to the Father our heart, our entire self. "It does not matter whether the moral act is an explicit expression of love of God, or any other act of our life. For, in every good moral act, we seek to produce not only this or that good, but we seek to express our whole selves as persons, self-yielding, self-surrendering to God; that is to say, we seek to love."[8] This happens even when we are not aware of it in a reflex way. Even the agnostic or professed atheist, if he be of good will, is able to perceive the real God in the depths of the self as a "horizon," as a "ground of his being," even though he may deny the concept of God in his explicit consciousness.

b) *Christocentric.* The Council asks that the person of Christ and our being-in-Christ be the center and focus of moral theology. Since it is in and through Christ that God invites man, it is only in and through Him that man can respond to this call. The consideration of man as man, or the "order of creation," is not to be neglected. But this "natural law" aspect must be seen only as a dimension of the fullness and richness of the relationship of man-in-Christ with God. There is also the need of emphasizing the action of the indwelling Spirit of Christ in us. It is He who awakens in us the desire to be conformed to Christ and to discover the genuine ways of expressing our life in Christ.

Moral theology explicitly deals with the way of life following from the Christian's being-in-Christ. But since all men are called in Christ, His Spirit is working in the non-Christian invisibly. Hence, however different at times the outlook and convictions of non-Christians may seem to be, they too are called to share in Christian morality.

c) *Ecclesial.* Christ is present to us and is acting in us today in and through the Church, which is His visible extension. His salvific work is directed toward building up His Mystical Body. Even at the secular level, the corporate destiny of mankind is very much in the forefront of man's preoccupation today. Hence it is all the more necessary that the communitarian dimension of Christian life be emphasized. We should go beyond a mere individualistic morality of isolated acts and concern for individual perfection to a vision of building up the human community, of which the Church is called to be the leaven. The place of the magisterium in guiding moral reflection must be understood in this context.

d) *Biblical.* The Word of God is authoritative in matters of faith and of morality, which is the living out of the demands of faith. However, we must always be careful to discern whether a particular scriptural injunction is essential moral teaching, normative for all times, or relevant only to the particular situation or to a certain stage in salvation history.

When the Council asked that moral theology should be ''more thoroughly nourished by scriptural teaching,'' it meant that the fundamental orientation and conception of morality should be derived from Scripture. This does not mean that every concrete moral norm can be immediately drawn from scriptural texts. Scripture shows the overall context of Christian morality—the covenant of love between God and His people. It provides the basic attitudes that should characterize Christian life—for instance, openness to the saving Word of God in Christ, and love of neighbor as a sign of love of God. Many important themes of moral life, like law, sin, conscience, sexuality and poverty are treated in the Bible. But Scripture does not provide ready-made answers to the complex problems of modern life.[9]

Needless to say, one should not seek to prove an assertion from isolated texts, neglecting their context and the literary genre in which they are expressed. Hence, a moral theologian cannot dispense with scientific exegesis. He should avoid the extremes of fundamentalism, which is too prone to a literal interpretation, and of excessive erudition, which gets lost in technical details to the detriment of vital knowledge. To a large extent, he will have to rely on professional exegetes for the spadework in interpreting the Word of God.

e) *Sacramental.* In the past, much of the moral theology course was devoted to liturgical regulations and marriage law. While most of this matter is better transferred to other disciplines, moral theology should develop the sacramental dimension of the Christian life. The sacraments are powerful signs by which we encounter God through Christ in His Church. The progressive sacramental incorporation into the ecclesial community brings about a gradual transformation into Christ. The gratuitous character of Christian sanctity as opposed to self-justification through the mere observance of the law will then be brought into focus. The aspect of worship should be given its central place in Christian living. The consciousness of the cultual character of the whole of moral life should be emphasized. The role of the laity as active participants in the worshipping community should bring out their role in the life of the Church.

The liturgical community must be seen as a loving and serving community. Hence the common participation in worship is a call to service in daily life, especially of the poor.

f) *Personalistic.* Vatican II exalts the dignity of the human person, "subject and goal of all social institutions." This points to the importance of personal conscience and to the need for developing the personal dimension of the moral law.

The personalistic and existentialist currents of modern thought are a help in presenting the basic Christian moral message, provided one is not misled by its excesses.[11]

There is need for understanding the human person as a whole. "It remains each man's duty to preserve a view of the whole person, a view in which the values of the intellect, will, conscience and fraternity are pre-eminent."[12] Instead of the dichotomy between body and soul, we must consider, according to biblical anthropology, the physical, psychic and spiritual dimensions of man, in both their individual and social aspects.

The social is not something added to man. The human person is essentially social. Today, especially, there is need for emphasizing the social aspects of morality, since the person finds his fulfillment in society and is impeded from attaining perfection through adverse social factors.

Hence the data of social sciences can be very useful in understanding ethical behavior. However, care should be taken not to conclude from statistical data to moral norms.

Modern psychology has uncovered the factors that foster or inhibit free moral response. Its valuable insights should be used to evaluate moral responsibility and to promote full personal growth. The English writer Galsworthy once said: "To teach Johnny Latin, it is more important to know Johnny than to know Latin." This is especially true with respect to moral education. However, undue psychologizing, which reduces all morality to psychological analysis, should be avoided.

g) *Ecumenical.* For a long time, Catholic and Protestant moral thought had gone along separate paths. Now there is a rapprochement. The more scriptural and theocentric presentation of Reformed moral thought has already had its useful impact on Catholic moral theology. Protestants, on the other hand, are rediscovering the importance of human values in Christian ethics. It is refreshing to note that many Catholic and Protestant writers are at home with each other's thought. Slowly a consensus is growing on important issues, although the differences are still significant. The recent publication of *Protestant and Roman Catholic Ethics* by James M. Gustafson[13] is likely to prove a landmark in ecumenical dialogue in this important area.

There is also the need for trying to achieve a wider understanding between the ethical systems of different religions. For a Christian who realizes the universality of the Gospel message, there should be no question of opposing Christian ethics, say, to Hindu ethics. Just as the

Gospel message was expressed in Aristotelian terms by St. Thomas, there should also be a similar possibility of expressing it in Hindu terms. For this we have still to go a long way. Indian Christians would need to be much more familiar with the Gospel message and Hindu thought, and at the same be liberated from a Western problematic which is also becoming increasingly difficult. Still, it is heartening to note that some beginnings have been made in recent monographs and briefer studies.

The ethical dialogue has to be extended to unbelievers. The adoption of the Universal Declaration of Human Rights by the United Nations and the publication of various medical ethics codes by the World Medical Association are signs that such a dialogue is possible.

Notes to Chapter II

1. John C. Ford and Gerald Kelly, *Contemporary Moral Theology,* Vol. I, Westminster, MD, Newman Press, 1958, pp. 80–103.
2. *God and Man,* London, Sheed and Ward, 1956.
3. *Op. cit.,* p. 96.
4. Vatican II, *O.T.,* art. 16.
5. *Ibid.*
6. *Ibid.*
7. Josef Fuchs, *Human Values and Christian Morality,* Dublin, Gill and MacMillan, 1970, ch. 1 and 2; Enda McDonagh, *Moral Theology Renewed,* Dublin, Gill, 1965, pp. 13–30.
8. Josef Fuchs, *op. cit.,* p. 62.
9. Cf. Edouard Hamel, "L'usage de l'Écriture sainte en théologie morale," *Gregorianum.* 47 (1966), 53–85.
10. *GS,* art. 25.
11. Cf. Karl Rahner, *Mission and Grace,* 3 vols., London, Sheed and Ward, 1964–66; Bernard Häring, *Morality Is for Persons,* New York, Farrar, Straus and Giroux, 1971.
12. *GS,* art. 61.
13. Chicago and London, University of Chicago Press, 1978.

CHAPTER III

The Morality of the Old Testament

1. COVENANT MORALITY

The Bible is the normative Word of God as it is the divinely inspired and authorized account of God's self-communication to man. The Christian community has to remain ever faithful to it. But, on the other hand, the Scriptures cannot be understood properly except within the faith community from which they were derived. The long history of community reflection on the Word of God should not be neglected. The opposite extremes of a naive biblical fundamentalism and of ecclesiasticism must be avoided.

The specific content of biblical morality, especially in the Old Testament, may be largely time-conditioned. Consequently, the external details of biblical injunctions might not always literally apply to the considerably changed conditions today. So we must try to discover what is distinctive about the biblical approach to morality. As William Barclay puts it: "The one thing that the Christian ethic is all about is personal relationships. It is about the relationships between man and man, and man and woman, and man and woman and God; and personal relationships don't change."[1]

In examining the moral message of the Bible, the growth in Israel's reflection must be noticed. The laws and customs recorded in the Bible bear the mark of the long and involved process by which the diverse tribes were knit into the people of Israel. Like any other ancient nation, Israel discovered its code of behavior experientially from the daily demands of life, but always with reference to its special relationship with Yahweh, the God of the covenant. Every stage of its sacred history contains, more and more clearly, the ideal conduct of men in the salvific design of God. The traditions of Israel, as described in the Bible, are traditions of faith, based especially on the call of Abraham and the covenant of Sinai. As the significance of the covenant becomes clearer, the moral ideal also becomes more luminous.

Thus, what is primary in biblical revelation as a source of morality is, not the explicit directions it contains, but the framework or structure in which they are set. This is, above all, the covenant (*berith* in Hebrew; *diatheke* in Greek), in which God reveals Himself by entering into personal relationship with His people. If Israel enjoys His special favor, it must also respond to this initiative in its whole way of life. God's self-giving demands a corresponding human response.

When this gift aspect of the covenant and the significance of law as the call to personal response are forgotten, so that the fulfillment of the law is made into a human claim against God, then the law becomes, in Pauline language, a source of sin instead of grace.

2.   THE TORAH IN THE LIFE OF ISRAEL

In the central exchange between God and man in the Old Testament revelation, the Law or Torah appears as the pattern of life appropriate to God's people. The Torah has a religious more than a juridical significance. Derived from the root *yarah*, meaning "to cast," it originally meant the divine response obtained by divination. For the Hebrews, it came to mean the sum of regulations which ordered the whole life of Yahweh's faithful.

It was customary among the ancient peoples of the East to give a religious character to their laws by attributing them to the gods. Thus the famous lawgiver Hammurabi refers his knowledge of truth and justice to the god Shamah and invokes all the gods of Babylon to punish those who break his code. But the law of Israel is unique inasmuch as it is founded on the historical covenant of Sinai, which gives rise to the people of God as such (cf. Ex. 19:5–6) and at the same time endows it with the rule of life that it promises to observe for ever (cf. Ex. 24:7–8).

The Sinaitic pact is renewed at critical moments in Israel's history: by Joshua at Sichem, at the inauguration of the temple of Jerusalem (cf. 1 Kgs. 8); by Josiah (cf. 2 Kgs. 23:1–3; 2 Chr. 34:29–31). The ritual of these renewals includes a solemn reading of the law and the uttering of "blessings" and "curses." Deut. 31:10–13 speaks of a reading every seventh year during the Feast of the Booths.

The compilers of Israel's traditions systematically insist on referring the whole legislation to the events of the life of Moses: Sinai, the march through the desert, Gades and the plains of Moab. The experience of Sinai serves as the chief inspiration (cf. Deut. 4:9–20; 5:1–31). No other lawgiver—not even the great monarchs like David and Solomon, reformers like Ezechiel and Josiah, or restorers like Nehemiah and Esdras—ever dares to place his name by the side of Moses. For the people of God there can be no law that is not Mosaic because its whole basis depends upon the covenant of Sinai, of which Moses is the mediator. It is not the human qualities of Moses as leader that are stressed but his role as an inspired prophet speaking in the name of Yahweh. It is not his literary activity that matters but his historic role as mediator of the covenant.

Biblical ethic was not for a few privileged people; nor was it restricted to some spheres of life. It involved every man, and concerned every action. God's will had to be performed in every detail of life.

The core of biblical morality is the decalogue, which expresses the perennial moral law or the basic exigencies of the moral life. However, Israel felt the need to spell out the obligations of the covenant people regarding its cultual life and the socio-political organization. These are found mainly in: a) the Code of Alliance (Ex. 20:22–23:33), which elaborates the laws Israel has to observe as its covenant obligations; b) the Ritual Covenant (Ex. 34:17–27), which is a religious collection dealing with the prohibition of images, with festivals and offerings; c) Deuteronomy 12–26, which is an extensive compilation including many prescriptions from a) and b) and where law appears clearly, not only as a code of obligations, but also as a gift from Yahweh; d) the Holiness Code (Lev. 17–27), which is a compilation of religious and cultic prescriptions—including a series of moral prescriptions in Ch. 19 as well as extensive regulations concerning marriage and sexuality; e) and the Priestly Code (Lev. 1–7; 11–15; Num. 28–29), which contains directions for priests concerning sacrifice, ritual purity and festivals. Law is placed in a historical context; i.e., the origin of an institution is attached to some event.

3.   THE DECALOGUE

The full text of the moral decalogue is found in Ex. 20:2–17 and Deut. 5:6–21.[2] The Exodus text is older, though it is later in literary fixation. It should be placed in the whole enveloping context of Chapters 20 to 24. Chapter 19 narrates the arrival of the Israelites at Sinai and the conclusion of the covenant. In an astounding theophany (19:16–25), God gives the decalogue as a condition of the alliance (20:2–17). This is followed by the more extended Code of Alliance (20:22–23:19). The pact is sealed by a sacrifice (Ch. 24). Since the covenant is to make Israel "a kingdom of priests and a holy nation" (19:6), a series of ordinances concerning worship are given (Ch. 25–31). While Moses tarries on the mountain, the people, wishing to have a more accessible god whom they could manipulate and who should not make radical ethical demands on them, fashion for themselves a golden calf (32:1–6). Angered by their apostasy, Moses smashes the tables of the law, but implores God's pardon on the people (32:7–34). God renews the covenant, but the reiterated commandments are presented as the cultic decalogue (34:14–26).

In Deuteronomy, the decalogue is inserted into the second introductory exhortation to keep the law (Ch. 5–11) and is followed by the covenant scene of Sinai and an exhortation to love Yahweh.

a)   In Ex. 20:11, the motivation for the Sabbath observance is the example of God, who completed the work of creation in six days and rested on the seventh, thus sanctifying if (cf. Gen. 1:1–2). In Deut. 5:14, the motive is connected with liberation from Egypt and is humanitarian. The Israelite is to allow his servants to rest from work, remembering that he was freed from the slavery of Egypt by the wonderful intervention of God.

b) In the prohibition of coveting, in Ex. 20:17, the wife is included in the neighbor's "house" (in the comprehensive sense of family and property). But in Deut. 5:21, the wife is mentioned first apart from "house" (meaning *dwelling* only). This is a sign that the Deuteronomy text is a development, a rereading in view of the changing social conditions and deeper theological insights. In Christian times, the distinction between wife and material possessions is carried further by breaking up the last commandment into two distinct ones in most versions.

With the exception of the law concerning the Sabbath and that forbidding graven images, the decalogue is an immediate expression of the moral law written in the heart of man. As such, its demands are accessible to human reason. Still, the conscience of man is obscured in many matters. Hence, the morality of the Old Testament does not present itself as mere human wisdom to be acquired by the light of reason, but as founded on divine revelation. It integrates the ethical traditions of the surrounding peoples, but also opens up entirely new perspectives. Law in the Bible belongs to the order of salvation. It is essentially *religious* and appeals exclusively to God, Creator and Saviour. It is a positive institution given to man as a grace linked to the events of Sinai. It opens the way for the restoration of fallen man by the light it sheds on the demands of his being.

The meaning of the decalogue can be best determined from the *context of its revelation,* from its being bound up with the Passover, the double central event of salvation history in the Old Testament—the liberation from the bondage of Egypt, and the covenant of Sinai. The decalogue is revealed in the context of a theophany, a manifestation of the true nature of Yahweh. While the other gods make their demands primarily in terms of cult requirements, Yahweh above all demands special relationships.

a) *Context of Liberation.* The commandments are prefaced by the words: "I am Yahweh, your God, who brought you out of the land of Egypt, out of the house of bondage" (Ex. 20:2; Deut. 5:6). The Word of God does not start with a law, but with the proclamation of the good news of liberation. The God who calls Israel is not an abstraction or an anonymous vital force, but the living and personal God who reveals Himself by His power and goodness. Through the revelation of His name, *Yahweh,* God renders Himself present to Israel and, addressing her in the second person, inaugurates an intimate dialogue.

Yahweh announces Himself, first of all, as the God of freedom, the one who summons Israel out of slavery. "The Hebrew discovery of God (or God's revelation of Himself to them) begins in their recognition that man historically is a slave, and enslaved by his own preference. The true God reveals himself as He who summons him to the painful business of being free."[4] The decalogue reveals that the worship of any other god is slavery. To pay homage to the forces of nature, to the spirit of a particular place or group, or anything that is too powerful for man to understand or control, is to submit to slavery and degradation.

Thus the decalogue is a *gift,* a charter of liberty, a bill of rights. In Egypt there was no law properly speaking for the Israelites, but only the arbitrary orders of tyrannical masters. Now, because of Israel's liberation, God can ask a free service.[5] So the commandments of the decalogue are not impositions, but *invitations to free service.* The frequent reminders of Israel's slavery in the laws concerning slaves, strangers, etc. (cf. Deut. 15:15; 20:31; 23:5; 24:9,18; 25:7), are not simply incentives to human conduct, but they base the source of obligation on God's saving action. "The decalogue asks nothing from slaves; the human condition of freedom is indispensable to answer the Ten Words."[6]

b) *Context of the Covenant.* The decalogue receives its full significance only from the covenant which God made with Israel. "You have seen what I did to the Egyptians and how I bore you on eagle's wings and brought you to myself. Now, therefore, if you obey my voice and keep my covenant, you shall be my own possession among all peoples, for all the earth is mine'' (Ex. 19:4–5). It should be noted that the covenant is not a bargain or an agreement between two parties on the same level. The whole initiative comes from God.

The service to which God calls is not only free but *loving,* because it is derived from the communion established between God and man. "It is because the Lord loves you, and is keeping the oath which he swore to your fathers, that the Lord has brought you out with a mighty hand and redeemed you from the house of bondage. . . . Know, therefore, that the Lord your God is God, the faithful God who keeps covenant and steadfast love with those who love him and keep his commandments'' (Deut. 7:8–9). The observance of the decalogue is meant essentially to be an act of love. To love God is to respond to His call, to observe the laws that are the expressions of His personal will.

The fundamental imperative of love is well stated in Deut. 6:4: "Hear, O Israel: The Lord our God is one Lord; you shall love the Lord your God with all your heart and with all your soul and with all your might." Again, "You shall therefore love the Lord your God and keep his charge, his statutes, his ordinances, and his commandments always. . . . For, if you will be careful to do all the commandments which I command you to do, loving the Lord your God, walking in his ways and cleaving to him . . ." (Deut. 11:1,22).

Love is not "commanded" in the same sense as an external act. It is awakened by the experience of being loved. The purpose of the commandments is to recall to man his responsibility of removing the obstacles within himself which stand in the way of proper response to God and seeking that which fosters this response. The imperative of love prevents Israel's existence from degenerating into a chaotic and crushing multiplicity of lifeless external performances. Through it, law becomes a transforming force.

The commandments of the decalogue are, then, the *covenant obligation* undertaken by Israel. The Ten Words are the words of the alliance. Consider the people's "Amen": "All that the Lord has spoken we will do" (Ex. 19:8; 24:3). We should also note that the law in

Deuteronomy is already interiorized, although this will be fully achieved only in the New Testament.

c) *Israel's Election.* Antecedent to the faithful response of Israel is the divine initiative, the loving kindness (*hesed*) of God, that has gratuitously chosen Israel and ensures its continued protection. Israel has no inherent merit motivating God's action. "The Lord your God has chosen you to be a people out of all the peoples that are on the face of the earth. It was not because you were more in number than any other people that God set his love upon you and chose you, for you were the fewest of all the peoples, but it is because the Lord loves you and is keeping the oath which he swore to your fathers . . ." (Deut. 7:6–8; cf. 9–14).

The special election of Israel brings with it a terrific responsibility: "You only have I known of all the families of the earth; therefore I will punish you for all your iniquities" (Amos 3:2). It calls for an unconditional obedience: "You shall therefore obey the voice of the Lord your God, keeping his commandments and his statutes, which I command you this day" (Deut. 27:10).

This election, or segregation, is *for a definite purpose.* "The Lord has declared this day concerning you that you are a people for his own possession, as he has promised you, that he will set you high above all nations that he has made, in praise and in fame and in honor, and that you shall be *a people holy to the Lord your God,* as he has spoken" (Deut. 26:18–19).

The gift of the alliance is not meant for self-gratification or to foster exclusiveness but carries with it a responsibility toward other nations. The tables of the law are called "tables of testimony" (Ex. 32:15,18). They are a memorial, the witness of God's saving action, which Israel is to proclaim before the world by faithfulness to the commandments. "He established a testimony in Jacob; and appointed a law in Israel" (Ps. 78:5).

This universal vocation of Israel is stressed by Isaiah: "And many peoples shall come and say: Come, let us go up to the mountain of the Lord, to the house of the God of Jacob, that he may teach us his ways" (2:3). See Deut. 4:6: "Keep them and do them; for that will be your wisdom and your understanding in the sight of the peoples."

"The result of this predilection will be that Israel will be a kingdom of priests, standing before Yahweh in the intimacy of those who serve the sanctuary and as intermediaries between Yahweh and all other nations."[7] Hence the covenant is not a static relationship, but the inner principles of Israel's history directed to actively cooperating with God in the realization of His salvific purpose; and Israel's being termed "holy" is not so much a statement of fact as a program of life. Law in Deuteronomy is the creative and redemptive pattern revealed by God for Israel's existence and mission as His holy people. It prescribes the *manner of life required of the consecrated people.*

The consecration, first of all, calls for a separation from all evil and defilement (cf. laws against idolatry in Deut. 4:15–20; against murder in 19:13; against false witness in 19:19). But, more positively, the decalogue ensures that the whole life of the people in all its spheres is dedicated to God. Such a dedication is truly a communion with God described by such expressions as "to cleave to God" (Deut. 11:22).

d) *Revelation of God's Holiness.*[8] The decalogue is a "tenfold Word of God." It is a channel through which God communicates His divine wisdom to men. Each precept, especially as it is elaborated in Deuteronomy, reveals something of God's infinite sanctity and perfection. It is an affirmation of His nature and absolute power over all creation. The commandments reveal the one transcendent God that cannot be annexed in any way by man—for instance, by the magical use of His name. He is the master of life, of time, of sexual power. He is the Lord of the earth and all its goods.

God desires to see mirrored in His chosen people something of that purity which distinguishes Him from the sinful and unclean ways of men. In asking Israel to be faithful to His commandments, He asks it in some way to imitate Him, "to walk in His ways" (cf. Deut. 11:22; 5:33). This last expression carries with it the overtones and echoes of Israel's desert experience, when Yahweh "went before Israel" exercising His faithful, merciful, saving and educative action.

"You shall be holy, for I, the Lord your God, am holy" (Lev. 19:2; cf. 11:44; 20:7,26; Deut. 14:21). Israel is called to adopt a manner of life intimately related to God. "In willing man's likeness to Himself, God's will in the law becomes a revelation of what He Himself is, no less than of what He wills man to be."[9] This is the ultimate ground of Israelite morality, which entirely surpasses any purely natural or anthropocentric ethic.

e) *Law of the Assembly.* The decalogue is not primarily a code of individual conduct, but the expression of the will of God as regards the *community* of Israel. Since the people as such is delivered from bondage, it should as a community express its gratitude by freely accepting the will of the Liberator.

The covenant of Sinai formed the semi-nomadic tribes into a people whose unity and cohesion was to be maintained and fostered by the observance of the commandments. This demanded separation from the false gods and immorality of the surrounding pagan peoples. "The decalogue creates the society by regulating its internal relationships and gathers all the relationships into relations with Yahweh."[10] The decalogue spells out the implications of Yahweh's self-giving to Israel as His people, not only in terms of response to Yahweh Himself, but also in terms of response to one's fellowmen.

The precepts of the second table, besides expressing fidelity to the covenant God, protect the rights of the community and its members. Their violation, e.g., by murder, is an attack on the covenant, provokes the anger of God and threatens the very existence of the community. It is also the source of contamination. Hence the death penalty prescribed in the Code of Alliance for breaking several of the commandments. One who thus sins grievously places himself outside the order founded by God. The death penalty is more than retribution; it may be called a "radical excommunication," as the community has to be purged from the stain that invites God's wrath and menaces the sanctity and cohesion of the community. "You shall purge the guilt of the innocent blood from Israel, so that it may be well with you" (Deut. 19:13) in the case of murder. "You shall purge the evil from the midst of you" (Deut. 19:19) in the case of false witness. This manifests the sacred character of the decalogue as the law of the "holy people, a royal priesthood." The priestly character of the people to whom the decalogue is given is brought out by the liturgical context in Ex. 24.

We should note here the difference between the Hebrew ethic and the pagan Greek ethic. The latter is individualistic, while the former is governed by an intense awareness of corporate solidarity.

f) *Core of the Mosaic Law.* The decalogue was not intended to be an exhaustive list of the religious and moral duties of the chosen people. But this brief collection of imperatives expresses the fundamental demands of God regarding His covenanted people. It describes what is absolutely displeasing to God.

Its very brevity makes it susceptible of indefinite development and enrichment. It is an *apodictical* law, as opposed to the rest of the Mosaic legislation, which is casuistic. The latter attempts to foresee and regulate all the concrete situations of life, while the decalogue is living and dynamic and hence capable of adaptation to every circumstance. This is a sign that the will of God cannot be adequately formulated in a code, that man should be ever open to new manifestations of the divine will.

Further, the precepts of the decalogue are paranetic—i.e., hortatory to what is presumed to be known and agreed on. Thus the forbidden "killing," etc., had a definite meaning in Israel. The decalogue does not mean to modify that understanding. It does not intend to be an explanatory discourse or moral reasoning. Hence one can hardly use the absolute character of the commandments to foreclose contemporary discussion as to what constitutes murder, theft, and so on.[11]

Because of its intimate link with the covenant, the decalogue was perfectible.[12] It formulated only the most basic duties toward God and other members of the community. In the light of progressive revelation, the conscience of Israel, formed by the prophets, became more and more refined. It began to discover moral implications unsuspected by the first nomadic tribes.

The incisive formulation of the precepts gives the decalogue an incomparable force. Though revealed in a particular context, it is *universal,* transcending the social conditions of the desert people. Founded upon the permanent relationship with God and His people, it is essentially related to the salvific purpose of God and valid for all times and peoples.

The negative formulation of the precepts may appear as a shortcoming. But it shows the absolute and unconditional will of the unique and personal God. The commandments forbid anything that might compromise that relationship. The recently liberated people are warned against forms of slavery that are infinitely more subtle and pernicious than that of Egypt. The negative formulation also gives a greater clarity and more universal character to the precepts. By defining the minimum beyond which one must not wander, it leaves the field open for free determination and for greater adaptation to particular circumstances.[13]

From what we have been saying, we may deduce some catechetical orientations.[14] The decalogue must be presented in the context of salvation history. It is one of the *mirabilia Dei*—that is, a saving act accomplished by a personal God. It is a means of freedom, a more radical deliverance from the subtle slavery of disorderly passions, a passage from sinful inclinations to a fuller life in God. Its relationship with the covenant must be brought out: how each commandment is an aspect of love of God and love of the members of the covenant community. Sin should appear as the breaking of the alliance, more than mere transgression of a law. The aspect of revelation of God and the relationship of created values to God must be investigated. The strong communitarian accent of the decalogue should help in overcoming individualism. The dimension of consecration and worship in the commandments should help in bridging the gulf between worship and life.

4.　SOCIAL JUSTICE IN THE TORAH

The law is particularly designed to protect the widow, the orphan and the poor, who are held especially dear to Yahweh. The Lord is just, and the people must imitate His justice. "For the Lord your God is God of gods and Lord of lords, the great, the mighty, and the terrible God, who is not partial and takes no bribe. He executes justice for the fatherless and the widow, and loves the sojourner, giving him food and clothing. Love the sojourner therefore; for you were sojourners in the land of Egypt" (Deut. 10:17–19). Again, "You shall not pervert justice; you shall not show partiality; and you shall not take a bribe, for a bribe blinds the eyes of the wise and subverts the cause of the righteous. Justice, and only justice, you shall follow, that you may live and inherit the land which the Lord your God gives you" (16:19–20). Judges are asked not to pervert the justice due to the poor (Ex. 23:6).

The destitute have a right to a share in the harvest: "When you reap the harvest of your land, you shall not reap your field to its very border, neither shall you gather the gleanings after the harvest. And you shall not strip your vineyard bare, neither shall you gather fallen grapes of your vineyard; you shall leave them for the poor and for the sojourner; I am the Lord your God" (Lev. 19:9–10). No attempt is to be made to defraud a day laborer of his hire; rather, it should be paid to him promptly: "You shall not oppress a hired servant who is poor and needy. . . . You shall give him his hire on the day he earns it, before the sun goes down, lest he cry against you to the Lord, and it be sin in you" (Deut. 24:14–15; cf. Ex. 19:13).

The millstone, without which the family food could not be prepared, was prohibited as a pledge (Deut. 24:6). If the cloak of a poor man were pledged, it had to be returned before sunset so that the borrower might sleep in it. "If ever you take your neighbor's garment in pledge, you shall restore it to him before the sun goes down; for that is his only covering, it is his mantle for his body; in what else shall he sleep? And if he cries to me, I will hear, for I am compassionate'' (Ex. 22:26–27).

The Israelite may not exact interest from another: "If you lend money to any of my people with you who is poor, you shall not be to him as a creditor, and you shall not exact interest from him" (Ex. 22:25). Deuteronomy explains this by the relationship of brotherhood (23:20). It is not interest as a business transaction that is forbidden, but the exploiting the need of a poor brother.

The law of sabbath rest has a strong humanitarian motive in Deuteronomy. The Israelite should have compassion on the sojourner and slave who are forced to work. He is to remember that he himself was slave in the land of Egypt (Deut. 5:15). All the Israelites must rest on the sabbath day, lest they become slaves to the material order. In the face of Pharisaic legalism, Jesus was to recall the basically humanitarian sense of the law.

Every seventh year was a sabbatical year, when the land was supposed to be allowed to rest in order to show that Yahweh is the supreme master and provider (Lev. 25:2–8). During this year debts were to be remitted. "At the end of every seven years you shall grant a release. And this is the manner of the release: every creditor shall release what he has lent to his neighbor; he shall not exact it of his neighbor, his brother, because the Lord's release has been proclaimed" (Deut. 15:1–2). One is not to hesitate to lend to a poor man because the sabbatical year is approaching (vv. 7–9). If the people are faithful to God's voice, there will be no poor among them (v. 3).

Likewise, every Hebrew slave is to be granted the chance of release in the seventh year of service. Remembering that the Israelites were themselves slaves and have been blessed by God, far from requiring any compensation, they are to let the slave go well provided (vv. 12–15). The idea that slaves are really brothers underlies these provisions.

The law provides that after forty-nine years (or seven sabbatical years) a jubilee is to be proclaimed (Lev. 25:8–17).[15] That year the land is to be left fallow, and each one has the right to recuperate property he has sold. No one is to be forced to alienate his land in perpetuity, "for the land is mine, for you are strangers and sojourners" (v. 23). The Lord alone is sovereign master; man is only the steward of property. The Bible does not subscribe to the doctrine of the absolute right to private property, especially when it is used to exploit the poor.

Some of the above prescriptions, like leaving the land fallow every seventh year, might not have been followed literally. But at least the law represents an ideal of social justice which holds important lessons for our times.

5. THE PROPHETIC MOVEMENT

The prophets are concerned with the people's fidelity to the God who saved them from Egypt. Thus Nathan confronts David with his violation of the commandments on adultery and murder (2 Sam. 12). Elijah, likewise, confronts King Ahab and Jezebel, his wife, for taking possession of Nathan's property in direct violation of the decalogue (1 Kgs. 21).

The example of these pioneers is carried on by the later prophets. Hosea chastises Israel for its moral failure and infidelity to the covenant God: "Hear the word of the Lord, O people of Israel; for the Lord has a controversy with the inhabitants of the land. There is no faithfulness or kindness, and no knowledge of God in the land; there is swearing, lying, killing, stealing, and committing adultery; they break all bounds and murder follows murder" (4:1–2).

The prophets insist on the sincerity of religious practice to be proved by right conduct. The most elaborate and punctilious ceremonial cannot take the place of justice and service of fellowmen. Amos comes out with a poignant outburst against those who concentrate on ritual to the neglect of justice: "I hate, I despise your feasts, and I take no delight in your solemn assemblies. Even though you offer me your burnt offerings and cereal offerings, I will not accept them, and the peace offering of fatted beasts I will not look upon. Take away from me the noise of your songs; to the melody of your harps I will not listen. But let justice roll down like waters, and righteousness like an overflowing stream'' (5:21–24).

This is reechoed by all subsequent prophets. The Lord says through Hosea: ''For I desire steadfast love and not sacrifice'' (6:6). Isaiah is particularly strong in denouncing an empty ritual devoid of significance: ''When you spread forth your hands, I will hide my eyes from you; even though you make many prayers, I will not listen; your hands are full of blood. Wash yourselves clean; remove the evil of your doings from before my eyes; cease to do evil; learn to do good; seek justice, correct oppression; defend the fatherless, plead for the widow'' (1:15–17). ''Is not this the fast that I choose: to loose the bonds of wickedness, to undo the thongs of the yoke, to let the oppressed go free, and to break every yoke? Is it not to share your bread with the hungry, and bring the homeless poor into your house; when you see the naked, to cover him, and not to hide yourself from your own flesh?'' (58:6–7; cf. Jer. 7:8–10; Micah 6:6–8). Recalling the prescriptions of the law, (Lev. 19:35,36; Dt. 25:13–16), the prophets insisted on business morality: to have just weights and measures (Amos 8:4–6; Mic. 6:10–11; Ez. 45:10–12).

The later prophets also contribute to the *interiorization of the law*. Jeremiah formulates the growing experience of Israel as a desire for a new covenant: ''Behold the days are coming, says the Lord, when I shall make a new covenant with the house of Israel and the house of Judah. . . . I will put my law within them, and I will write it upon their hearts; and I will be their God, and they shall be my people. And no longer shall each man teach his neighbor and each his brother, saying, 'Know the Lord,' for they shall all know me'' (31:31–34). There will be no need for external instruction, since knowledge of the law will come from ''knowing the Lord,'' or by intimate union with Him.

For Ezekiel, the transformation is even more profound. Yahweh will change the very heart of man, and the covenant will be effected in total intimacy by the gift of a new spirit, the spirit of Yahweh: "A new heart I will give you, and a new spirit I will put within you: and I will take out of your flesh the heart of stone and give you a heart of flesh. And I will put my spirit within you, and cause you to walk in my statutes and be careful to observe my ordinances" (36:26–27; cf. 11:19–29).

The interiorization of the law is particularly evident in the Psalms, the prayer of Israel. For instance, in Psalm 119 we see how a pious Israelite identifies fidelity to the commandments as seeking Yahweh, so that the law does not appear to him as an external constraint but as an interior delight.

Israel gradually comes to realize that, not reliance on human power, but absolute trust in Yahweh is the way to true security and happiness. Thus the ideal of the *anawim,* or the "poor of Yahweh," who look to Yahweh alone for their fulfillment.[17]

6. WISDOM LITERATURE

This is largely concerned with *the good life.* In the post-exilic period, in the wake of the disillusionment of the high hopes at the return from Babylon, emphasis came to be placed more and more on the problem of everyday living. Many maxims and insights of a secular and extra-Israelite origin were pressed into the service of Israel's faith. Originally, the Wisdom tradition seems to have flowered mainly in court circles, though popular and familiar influences cannot be neglected. It was fashioned through reflection on the experiences of life and the enigmas these posed.[18]

"Avoidance of greed, selfishness or opportunism are important for a young man if he would succeed in life, but motivated by Israel's faith they become expressions of the value of justice, respect for one's neighbor and trust in the God who guides all men."[19] Thus a secular body of literature was assumed into Israel's faith commitment, and this helped in further refining the ethical conscience of the people of God.

Israel recognized that Yahweh alone was truly wise. Wisdom personified is the source of life and nourishment for men. She was present with Yahweh at the creation of the world and, consequently, she knows the secrets of the world, and the ways of God and men. She is the special gift of Yahweh to Israel. By accepting her instruction and guidance, men share in the divine life. In this way natural insights contribute to deepen the awareness and understanding of Yahweh's plan of salvation and His will for the community.

While it surely has a communal dimension, the Wisdom literature is specially preoccupied with the problems of the individual person. Thus it helps in deepening personal values. As it is based on the very nature of man, it is free from any trace of Hebrew particularism.

7. THE SALVIFIC ROLE OF THE OLD LAW

"The law was our custodian (*pedagogus*) until Christ came, that we might be justified by faith" (Gal. 3:24). This statement of Paul directly refers to the rites and observances that occasioned the Judeo-Christian controversy, but it is applicable to the whole religious economy of the Old Testament. The primary function of the law is to educate the people of God in order to dispose it for the Gospel. God had never left men completely to ignorance and impotence as regards morality. He was always speaking to them through their conscience. But the regime of the Old Testament law inaugurates a new stage in salvation history when the final fulfillment is more clearly determined and the moral level of Israel is sensibly raised. The weakness of human judgment is helped by the light of revelation. Human efforts are given a transcendent religious purpose: the accomplishment of the will of God through love. The juridical dispositions are meant to impregnate social relations with the virtues of justice, benevolence, etc., to protect fundamental human values like life, sexuality, etc.

While giving a rule of life in many ways superior to what man could have discovered by his own resources, God also condescends to the concrete situation of the people by adapting Himself to the peculiar mentality of Israel and tolerating certain imperfections and authorizing certain provisional institutions like polygamy. These are not positively approved, but only permitted "because of the hardness of hearts" (Mt. 19:8).

The Old and the New Testaments are often distinguished as if the first inculcates fear, and the second love. It is true that the Old Testament emphasizes fear, not only that inspired by the majesty and holiness of God, but also that of His punishments. In the New Testament, love is obviously the first commandment and resumes all the rest (Mt. 22:37–40 par.; Rom. 13:8–10). But the opposition must not be exaggerated. Religious awe of the Almighty and even fear of His chastisements have their place in the New Testament, while love already appears clearly as a motive of moral life in the Old Testament.

In the Pentateuch, the reward for fidelity to the law seems to be of the temporal order, e.g., "that you may prolong your days in the land which the Lord gives you" (Deut. 4:40; 5:16; 11:9). But something more is implied from the fact that the possession of the promised land is part of Israel's vocation to be the chosen people in order to realize God's purpose. The theme of "life" prefigures the eschatological blessings.

In Ps. 119, the blessing is fully interiorized. Though there is reference to temporal life, the emphasis is on the higher interior life of moral union with God which alone makes life worth living. The precepts of the Lord are the "source of delight" (vv. 16, 24, 35, 47, 143); "honey in the mouth" (v. 103). The Psalmist finds in them freedom of soul (v. 45).

Along with the identification of life with the joyful, liberating fulfillment of the divine will, the vocabulary associated with the promised land is interiorized. The statutes with their "truth" (emet) are the medium of God's salvific presence. In applying to God Himself and to His will the Deuteronomic inheritance, Ps. 119 was carrying out the deepest intention of the former, which was to lead Israel "to love God with all your mind and all your heart and all your might" (Deut. 6:5).

The Old Law was, as such, external. It always carried with it the danger of Pharisaism. From experience, Paul found it a severe task master. But already in the Old Testament, there are anticipations of the economy of grace. For Deuteronomy, as we have seen, the observance of the commandments is an act of love. The prophets call for an interior conversion that cannot be explained merely by social pressures.

———o———

Notes to Chapter III

1. *Ethics in a Permissive Society,* London, Collins, 1971, p. 29.
2. See S. Buckley, "The Decalogue," *Indian Journal of Theology,* 16 (1967), 106–20; Gerhard J. Botterwock, "Form and Growth of the Decalogue," *Concilium,* 5 (1965), no. 1, 33–34.
3. Cf. Paul Tremblay, "Towards a Biblical Catechesis of the Decalogue," *Lumen Vitae,* 18 (1963), 507–529; summary in *Theology Digest,* 1965, 112–15; Albert R. Jonsen, "The Decalogue," *Thought,* 38 (1963), 421–446; Kevin Walsh, "Preaching the Decalogue," *Irish Ecclesiastical Record,* 90 (1958), 419–424; Walther Eichrodt, "The Ten Commandments," *Theology Digest,* 6 (1958), 177–80; Raymond F. Collins, "The Ten Commandments and the Christian Response," *Louvain Studies,* 4 (1971), 308–22.
4. Herbert McCabe, *Law, Love and Language,* London, Sheed and Ward, 1968, p. 116.
5. Cf. the title of an excellent book on the Exodus by Georges Auzou, *From Servitude to Service (De la servitude au service),* Paris, L'Orante, 1961.
6. Georges Auzou, *op. cit.,* p. 288.
7. Albert R. Jonsen, *art. cit.,* pp. 431–39.
8. Cf. T. W. Manson, *Ethics and the Gospel,* New York, Charles Seribner's, 1960, pp. 18–20.
9. Mathew J. Connell, "The Concept of Commandment in the O. T.," *Theological Studies,* 21 (1960), 379.
10. Albert R. Jonsen, *art. cit.,* p. 432.
11. Cf. Richard A. McCormick, "Notes on Moral Theology," *Theological Studies,* 36 (1975), 84–85.
12. Pierre Grelot. *Sens chrétien de l'Ancien Testament,* Tournai, Descleé, 1962, p. 202.
13. Cf. Georges Auzou, *op. cit.,* pp. 282–83.

14. Cf. Paul Tremblay, *art. cit.*, M. P. Butler, "Must We Teach Morality according to the Decalogue?" *Worship*, 37 (1963), 293–300.

15. It is interesting to note that the Hebrew Jubilee is the source of the Holy Year that is celebrated now. One wonders whether the social implication of the observance is clear to many.

16. Cf. F. N. Jasper, "Reflections on the Moral Teaching of the Prophets," *Scottish Journal of Theology*, 21 (1968), 462–76.

17. Cf. Albert Gelin, *The Poor of Yahweh*, Collegeville, Liturgical Press, 1963.

18. Cf. Gerhard von Rad, *Old Testament Theology*, London, Oliver and Boyd, Vol. I, 1962, pp. 418–41.

19. Sean Freyne, "The Bible and Christian Morality," in *Morals, Law and Authority*, ed. by J. P. Mackey, Dublin, Gill and Macmillan, 1969, pp. 11–12.

CHAPTER IV

The Morality of the New Testament[1]

1. THE PROCLAMATION OF THE REIGN OF GOD

In Christianity, as in Judaism, moral instruction is based on the proclamation of the salvific action of God. "The ethical teaching of the New Testament is embedded in a context which consists of a narration of historical facts and the explanation of their religious significance, and the fact gives to Christian Ethics a peculiar character."[2] In the Gospels we find a series of narrative sections showing what Jesus said and did for the people, followed by moral sections. Similarly, Paul in his letters usually gives a theological explanation of some mystery of Christ and then goes on to derive moral conclusions based on this doctrine. Nowhere in the New Testament do we have a closed ethical system nor a piety divorced from moral behavior.

The moral teaching of Jesus is wholly bound up with His religious message, of which the leading idea is the *proclamation of the Kingdom* and its summons to men. "The time is fulfilled, and the kingdom of God is at hand; repent, and believe in the gospel" (Mk. 1:15). The Gospel is not so much good advice as *Good News*. Here there is the announcement of the decisive act of God and a corresponding demand for a response from men. The attitude which one adopts toward this supreme event is of decisive importance for salvation.

The Kingdom has come, but is not yet fully accomplished in "power and glory." The tension between partial fulfillment and the expectancy of the final consummation gives rise to moral urgency. One must prepare oneself for entering into the Kingdom and for sharing in its blessings by following the teaching of Jesus. (Cf. entering into possession of the

inheritance in the Old Testament by obeying God's commandments—
Deut. 4:1; 6:18; 16:20.)

The seriousness of the situation makes it imperative to come to a
decision. Jesus asks for *vigilance.* "Be ready" (Mk. 13:5,9,23,33);
"Watch" (Mk. 13:33,35,37). This is the theme of the "eschatological
discourses" and many of the parables: "Prepare yourselves and show
yourselves worthy to be counted among those who share in the banquet
or marriage feast." Jesus calls for *steadfastness* amidst the trials of this
life.

The salvific action of God in Christ is here and now bestowing
love and demanding love. One can inherit the Kingdom only through
the active service of God and service of neighbor. We should note the
serious "sins of omission" in this context.

The coming of the Kingdom makes the fundamental demand of
metanoia, or radical change of heart. This implies: a) a total attitude
of man; b) turning away from sinful ways; c) resolute turning to God
and answering His call. One must recognize one's sinfulness and give
oneself wholly to God's judgment. There is no room for self-righteousness and presumption. (Cf. the Pharisee vs. the publican in Lk.
18:10 ff; the elder son in Lk. 15.) Humility is an essential precondition
for entry into the Kingdom. Genuine repentance is possible only when
one makes himself small as a child before God (Mt. 18:3).

There is place for outward signs of penance like fasting. But repentance must be expressed in one's whole conduct, especially in loving
works of service.

The predominant note of the message of Jesus is *joy.* But rejection
and obduracy meet with the threat of judgment.

The forgiveness which one receives from the Lord has to be shared
with others. In the parable of the unforgiving servant, we are warned
that, as he who would not forgive his fellow servant was delivered to
the torturers till he should pay all his debts, "so also my heavenly Father

will do to everyone of you, if you do not forgive your brother from your heart'' (Mt. 18:35). In the Lord's Prayer we are taught to say: "Forgive us our debts, as we also have forgiven our debtors" (Mt. 6:12). The Lord presses the matter by repeating: ''For if you forgive men their trespasses, your heavenly Father also will forgive you; but if you do not forgive men their trespasses, neither will your Father forgive your trespasses'' (vv. 14–15).

Faith is the positive side of conversion. ''Repent, and believe in the gospel'' (Mk. 1:15). Faith is a total attitude claiming all of man's faculties, a profound ''Amen'' to God. One who is committed to God's sovereign rule will strive wholeheartedly to fulfill His royal will. There is also the need for a total trust in the salvation which Jesus brings.

Further, Jesus gives the call to ''follow'' Him personally. More than mere imitation, this requires an unconditional acceptance of His Word, sharing in His way of life and destiny. He demands total renunciation of self (Mk. 8:34 par.), even to the point of giving up one's life (cf. Mt.: 34–35 par.).

2. THE SERMON ON THE MOUNT[3]

The moral teaching of Christ is particularly concentrated in the Sermon on the Mount (Mt. 5–7). Christ is conceived as the *new Moses.* As Moses brought the old law from Mount Sinai, so Christ proclaims the new law from a mountain. The Sermon contains much that is demanding, an ideal that goes far beyond anything conceived by Judaism. But it presupposes faith in the risen Lord, who by His Pasch has rescued men from the power of Satan and introduced them to a new life of holiness and grace.

Jesus came, not to abolish the law and the prophets, but to fulfill them, making God's original will fully clear, by reducing the many precepts to the more fundamental demand of love, and by insisting on the claims of the law to the ultimate pitch of its obligation. Jesus has fulfilled the law also in His own person by establishing the new and everlasting covenant, which is now the basis of the new law.

The whole law is now presented in a new and perfect way (Mt. 5:18,19). The frequent "but I say to you" indicates a wholly new understanding of God's will.

Jesus insists on the preeminence of the permanent and basic moral law over mere ritual prescriptions (Mt. 15:1–20; Mk. 7:1–23), of *inner dispositions* over external legality. "Do you not see that whatever goes into a man from outside cannot defile a man? What comes out of a man is what defiles a man. For from within, out of the heart of men, come evil thoughts, fornication, theft . . . All these evil things come from within and they defile a man" (Mk. 7:18–23).

God's commandments apply not only to external actions but also and even more to the inner attitude (Mt. 5:27). The law had condemned murder, but it is necessary to uproot from the heart the anger that leads to murder (v. 22). The law condemned adultery, but adultery itself proceeds from uncontrolled lust of the heart, which must be handled (v. 28). Jesus suggests a drastic remedy: "If your right eye causes you to sin, pluck it out and throw it away" (v. 29).

In discussing the question of the sabbath, Jesus draws attention to the *dignity of man* and the original purpose of the observance against a legalistic interpretation of the commandment to rest. Jesus emphatically declares: "The sabbath was made for man, and not man for the sabbath" (Mk. 2:27). In Deut. 6:14, it is explicitly stated that the sabbath rest was meant to enable the Israelite and his servants to share in God's own rest. By claiming, "The Son of man is Lord of the sabbath also" (Mk. 2:28), Jesus made it clear that He is not accountable to His legalistic opponents for the ultimate ground of His actions.

Jesus Himself went beyond the letter of the law to manifest the goodness of God by healing the man with the withered hand (Mk. 3:1–5 par.). He challenged His opponents: "Is it lawful on the sabbath to do good or to do harm, to save life or to kill?" (v. 4). Again, He disregarded a rigoristic interpretation of the sabbath for the sake of a poor, bent woman whom Satan had bound for eighteen years (Lk. 13:10–16). He paid tribute to her dignity by giving her the title of honor "a daughter of Abraham." Strangely, the legalist, as Jesus ironically points out, did not hesitate to violate the sabbath in order to lift up his own animal that had fallen into a pit! Jesus remarks, "Of how much more value is a man than a sheep!" (Mt. 12:12). Paul rightly interprets the Master's mind by saying: "The written code kills, but the Spirit gives life" (2 Cor. 3:6).

Thus Jesus requires a justice "surpassing that of the Scribes and Pharisees" (Mt. 5:20). While the Pharisees strove to accumulate as many "merits" as possible by a purely external observance of the law, Jesus rejects all such bookkeeping and affirms that the interior disposition is the decisive factor in moral action. He makes the *"heart"* the center of the moral personality (Mk. 7:18). But He certainly does not depreciate the importance of external action. He requires the exact fulfillment of the will of the heavenly Father (Mt. 7:21).

So it should not be too hastily assumed that the provisional character that the New Testament writers attribute to religious customs and observances should also be attached to the moral law itself. See, for instance, the saying of Jesus: "Why do you transgress the commandment of God for the sake of your traditions?" (Mt. 15:3). Jesus is referring to the Pharisaic subterfuge of evading the observance of the commandment "Honor your father and your mother" under the pretext of respecting a ritual prescription.

Jesus condemns the hair-splitting indulged in by the rabbis when it leads to "straining a gnat and swallowing a camel" (Mt. 23:24). They are adept at calculating tithes, but have "neglected the weightier matters of the law, justice and mercy and faith" (v. 23).

Even though Jesus came to lighten the burden of the law (Mt. 11:28–30), He demanded absolute obedience to the holy will of God. Before the exigencies of the Kingdom, everything else must recede into the background (Mt. 6:33), or even be set aside if it becomes a hindrance (Mk. 9:43–47 par.). Jesus asks for a return to the original will of God in matters like divorce (Mt. 5:31–32 par.). He wants brotherly love to extend to every impulse of the heart, so that retaliation becomes unthinkable (Mt. 5:38–42).

Still, what to make of injunctions like "turning the other cheek," "giving the cloak as well," "going another mile as well," "giving to everyone who asks"? (Mt. 5:38–42). Does the average Christian today try to live up to these standards? Can anyone be expected to live up to them? Many explanations have been given for these radical demands.

a)   Some explain them away by referring to what they call "oriental hyperbole," as in the case of the beam in the eye.

b)   According to the Lutheran tradition, the principal function of the law is to bring man to recognize his own sinfulness and helplessness, to become aware that salvation can come, not through the works of the law, but only through faith in Jesus Christ. The radical demands of the Sermon on the Mount would only intensify this pedagogical function of the law.

c)   Among Catholics, there is the tendency to restrict the perfection demanded by these requirements to a few and prescribe only the commandments for the masses.

d)   According to the Interim Ethic Theory of A. Schweitzer, Jesus expected the fulfillment of the Kingdom to come shortly. The ethical teaching of Jesus, proclaimed with that in view, cannot be lived out in the situation when the Parousia is long in coming.

e)   A Pharisaic mentality would try to concentrate on literal conformity to these demands as if they were laws.

However, the demands of the Sermon on the Mount must not be approached in a legalistic spirit which would make them either an impossible burden for many or irrelevant extras for a few. They are best understood through the eschatological tension caused by the coming of Jesus. The Kingdom has already broken forth, but is awaiting its fulfillment. This calls for a continual moral growth. "Where morality is understood as a growing response of love which continually transcends itself as it seeks to meet the real needs of the other, turning the other cheek or letting go one's only cloak can be seen to be possible in a particular situation, while they are always illustrative of the depth of love to which the Christian is summoned."[4]

The ethical teaching of Jesus is a constant reminder of the absolute claim on man of God's call. Jesus indicates the orientation that should always characterize the life of His follower. However, the complexities of life may make conflicting claims on him. "Give to everyone who asks." But there may be a conflict between the need of one's neighbor and of one's family. "Don't strike back." But what if an insane man attacks a child?

Thus the Sermon on the Mount is not so much a collection of concrete norms as a strong appeal to the heart. As Charles H. Dodd puts it, the ethical teaching of the Gospels "is not so much detailed guidance for conduct in this or that situation as a disclosure of the absolute standards which alone are relevant when the Kingdom of God is upon us. These standards, however, are defined, not in general and abstract propositions, but in dramatic pictures of action in concrete situations; and they are intended to appeal to the conscience by way of the imagination."[5]

The startling demands of Jesus are not mere oriental hyperbole. Neither are they prosaic sayings. They are "flashlight pictures of the uncompromising demand which the Kingdom must make upon anyone who would respond to it. . . . This is the kind of thing which at any moment, if you are open to the absolute unconditioned will of God, the Kingdom, or love, can demand of you."[6] The sayings of the Sermon on the Mount do not solve our moral problems, but they transform us.

The *beatitudes,* with which the Sermon on the Mount opens, give the quintessence of the moral message of Jesus. The more primitive form of the beatitudes was probably a Messianic proclamation.[7] Luke presents them in a sapiential perspective, contrasting the promised future happiness with the present poverty and suffering. Matthew relates them in the context of the moral life of those who adhere to the Kingdom; they describe the basic attitudes and dispositions which should characterize the life of the disciple of Jesus.

By declaring the poor and the meek blessed, Jesus is fulfilling the aspirations of the *anawim,* who looked to Yahweh alone for their comfort and happiness.

The beatitudes are not the qualities of a timid soul. They express the heart of one who has been tried in the crucible of adversity and has come out purified by the fire of divine love. Poverty of spirit leads to a hunger and thirst for God's righteousness. Such a person will naturally be ready to be merciful and be a leaven of peace. Instead of persecuting others, he will himself be ready to suffer persecution. It is not a question of bearing adversity with passive resignation. It is a matter of "blessedness." "Rejoice and be glad," says Jesus, "when men revile you and persecute you and utter all kinds of evil against you on my account" (Mt. 5:11–12). Here we are far from the proud self-satisfaction of one who pretends to moral perfection or seeks his satisfaction in domineering. Here we are at the heart of the Gospel message. Should not those who wish to spread the Christian faith concentrate on acquiring this mind, which is the mind of Christ Himself?

"Purity of heart," or sincerity of purpose, has a pride of place in the Sermon on the Mount. Jesus expounds the sixth beatitude by saying: "The eye is the lamp of the body. So, if your eye is sound, your whole body will be full of light; but if your eye is not sound, your whole body will be full of darkness" (Mt. 6:22–23). Jesus emphasizes this especially with respect to almsgiving, prayer and fasting, which were the three traditional acts of piety (Mt. 6:1–18). He plainly speaks out against hypocrisy.

3.   THE GREAT COMMANDMENT[8]

The commandment of the love of God (Deut. 6:5) belongs to the *Shema,* the confession of the monotheistic faith, which was recited daily by pious Jews. Love of neighbor (Lev. 19:8) was also considered a prime duty by the Jews. Yet love has a threefold distinctive note in the message of Jesus.

a)   He revealed the indissoluble *interior bond between the love of God and the love of neighbor*. The first finds its genuine expression in the second (cf. Mt. 22:39). Conversely, brotherly love receives its deepest foundation and support from the love of God, our common Father.

b)   He showed clearly that the *whole law could be reduced to this commandment*. "On these two commandments depend all the law and the prophets" (Mt. 22:40).

c)   *He reinterpreted neighborly love* in an absolute and universal sense. In Lev. 19:8, the command is restricted only to "the children of thy people," though a stranger living among the Israelites was included. Later on, the proselyte who had accepted circumcision was also included. But it did not occur to the Jews in general to extend brotherly love to all men. According to Jesus, no limit is to be set, and one must help a sufferer even when he is a national enemy. The parable of the good Samaritan (Lk. 10:30ff) illustrates the universailty of *neighbor* in the love ethic of Jesus. The neighbor is any person in need, be it a Samaritan, a foreigner or an enemy.

The injunction to love your neighbor "as yourself" does not limit the scope of love. "Rather, the self-love that is sponstaneously and essentially present in everyone should be an unforgettable reminder to us of how far our love for others ought to go."[9]

Jesus specifically demands that our love should extend even to enemies. This is the way to imitate our heavenly Father, whose love is gratuitous. "Love your enemies and pray for them who persecute you, so that you may be sons of your Father who is in heaven; for he makes his sun rise on the evil and on the good, and sends rain on the just and on the unjust. . . . You, therefore, must be perfect, as your heavenly

Father is perfect'' (Mt. 5:44–48). Love of enemies is to be the distinctive note of the disciples of Jesus, as even tax collectors and Gentiles love those who love them.

Jesus gives Himself as the model of fraternal love (Jn. 13:34; 15:12). He has proved His love for us by laying down His life for our sake (Jn. 15:13; Mk. 10:45). He humbled Himself to perform the slave's function of washing the feet of His disciples, thereby giving us an example of self-emptying love.

The great commandment, the core of the ethical teaching of Jesus, is of vital significance for morality. True religion cannot be a self-contained ceremonial system of piety nor a visionary mysticism. One has to express one's love for the all-holy God by the simple path of brotherly love. As John points out: "If any one says, 'I love God' and hates his brother, he is a liar; for he who does not love his brother, whom he has seen, cannot love God, whom he has not seen" (1 Jn. 4:20).

Hence, authentic love of God is found in loving concern for others. Not even worship at the altar can take precedence over this concern. "So if you are offering your gift at the altar, and there remember that your brother has something against you, leave your gift at the altar and go; first be reconciled to your brother, and then come and offer your gift" (Mt. 5:23–24).

The paramount importance of fraternal love is manifested by the fact that it is made the criterion at the final judgment. Each one will be judged by the way he met the needs of his brother (Mt. 25:35ff).

Christian love is not mere emotional reaction, but an attitude of the will. Therefore, it can be commanded and demanded of us. God loves us, not because we are attractive; He makes us lovable by loving us. Hence His love is creative. So also, the Christian is called upon to love even those who seem to be unlovely, the unloving or unlovable, since ultimately his love will also be creative.

4. THE MORAL TEACHING OF THE APOSTOLIC CHURCH

The first Christians did not think that they had received a complete code of morality to deal with every situation. The community of faith had to discover what its moral response should be in the face of emerging problems.

Clearly the words of Jesus had an authoritative value. Occasionally, the Apostles explicitly called upon the "word of the Lord" to answer a particular problem (cf. 1 Cor. 7:10; 9:14). More often, they appealed to the mind of the Master. They did not feel obliged to adhere rigidly to the letter of what the Master might have said. They felt free to interpret, adapt and apply His teachings to new situations, at times with the help of insights from other sources. This was done under the inspiration of the Spirit, through whom the Lord Himself was alive and present with His community (cf. 1 Cor. 7:12,25).

a) *Influence of the Holy Spirit in Moral Conduct.* Indeed, the basic religious experience of the early Church was the outpouring of the Spirit which transformed the dispirited disciples into joyful witnesses and courageous preachers of the Good News (cf. Acts 1:8; 2:29–36). The Spirit was recognized as the real guide of the community and a strong driving force leading to a revolutionary remodelling of the whole of life. According to Paul, "The *Pneuma* as the holy and effective power of God, given to the baptized person and working continually in him, has to overcome the corrupting influence of the *sarx* ('flesh'), human nature inclined to sin."[10] Paul himself says: "We are debtors, not to the flesh, to live according to the flesh—for if you live according to the flesh you will die, but if by the Spirit you put to death the deeds of the body, you will live. For all who are led by the Spirit of God are sons of God" (Rom. 8:12–13; cf. Gal. 5:16ff).

b) *Koinonia Ethic.* The Mosaic law shaped the twelve tribes into the people of God. The new law of charity forms the baptized into the new Israel. "Now the company of those who believed were of one heart and soul" (Acts 4:32; cf. 2:42f).

The concept of *fellowship* was especially fostered in the Pauline churches (cf. 1 Cor. 10–13). Baptism, which gives the Spirit, also introduces the believer into the society of those who are ''in Christ.'' The Spirit builds all into the Body of Christ (cf. 1 Cor. 12:2ff; Rom. 12:4ff; Eph. 4:1–12). In fact, Christian morality, according to Paul, consists in building up the Body of Christ.

The *koinonia* implies, first of all, a common sharing in the riches of the divine life which Christ has brought. ''There is one body and one Spirit, just as you were called to the one hope that belongs to your call, one Lord, one faith, one baptism, one God and Father of us all, who is above all and through all and in all'' (Eph. 4:4–6). But it is also to be translated in terms of practical daily living, particularly in sharing temporal resources (cf. Acts 2:44–45; 4:32–35. Cf. also Rom. 15:25–28 par.).

Hence, the moral doctrine of the New Testament should never be conceived in purely individualistic terms. ''Indeed it is the *koinonia* context and character of Christian ethics that gives ethical sense and substance to the seeking and doing of God's will. For in the *koinonia* and owing to the *koinonia,* man is concretely and inescapably involved in what God is doing in the world.''[11]

c) *Eschatological Perspective.* The early Christians believed that the Pasch of the Lord was the crucial event in history. But they also eagerly awaited the final coming of Christ in majesty. ''The Kingdom of God has come; but it has still to come.'' Due to this tension, Christians were acutely aware that they were living in a unique period of history. The Christian life was to be lived out in the perspective of the Parousia, or final coming of Christ in glory.

In early preaching, the thought of the Parousia was used to stimulate the faithful to holiness of life. ''May the Lord make you increase and abound in love . . . so that he may establish your hearts unblameable in holiness before our God and Father, at the coming of Our Lord Jesus'' (1 Thess. 3:13; cf. 5:23).

The sense of the impending catastrophic end (cf. 1 Cor. 7:20) made everything in the world provisional. As the "form of the world was passing away" (v. 31), only those things that would survive were worthy of attachment. Even so close a human tie as the marriage bond, that acquired a special significance in the mystery of Christ, was relativized, so that virginity attained a special value.

But Paul, who stressed the transient nature of all earthly things, energetically opposed erroneous conclusions from the expectancy of the Parousia. The fact that the Christian is a pilgrim on earth does not exclude or minimize his earthly task. The perspective of fulfillment through the final coming of the Lord should be a stimulus to work, not an excuse for irresponsibility and idleness (cf. 2 Thess. 3:6–12). The Christian has to set his eyes steadfastly on the heavenly fulfillment, but, at the same time, prepare himself for it by helping to liberate creation from its bondage (cf. Rom. 8:21–22). Lively *hope* in the final fulfillment must lead Christians to live in joy and peace.

For John, eternal life is already found by faith in Christ (3:16,36; 5:24; 6:41). Christ has already overcome the "world" by His death. Still, there is a bitter conflict to be waged before the coming of the Parousia, the final consummation.

The delay in the coming of the Parousia does not affect the importance of eschatology for Christian morality. The final events are "a personal summons to vigilance and sobriety, to responsible action in the world, to combat and struggle against the destructive forces of evil and to living hope and joyful confidence."[12]

d) *Deeper Understanding of the Great Commandment.*[13] For Paul, charity is "the bond of perfection" (Col. 3:14). The very vocabulary of Paul is significant. Christ is He who "has loved us," *ho agapesas* (Rom. 8:37; Gal. 2:20). The Christian is one who loves God, *ho agapen* (Rom. 8:28; 1 Cor. 2:9; 8:3). Christian life consists in "walking in love" (Rom. 14:15; Eph. 5:2).

Fraternal charity and the virtues that flow from it are fruits of the Holy Spirit (Gal. 5:22). He who loves his neighbor has *fulfilled* the law. The commandments, "You shall not commit adultery, You shall not kill, You shall not steal, You shall not covet," are summed up in this sentence: "You shall love your neighbor as yourself" (Rom. 13:8–10; cf. Gal. 5:14).

"Charity is the central point around which all the commandments converge to form a unit. The law 'culminates' in love. However varied are the virtues we practice, none has any meaning or can even exist apart from *agape*. Without love they would be empty, lifeless bodies without souls. The essence of Christian morality is love."[14] This is the Pauline basis for the theological thesis that "charity is the form of the virtues."

In his hymn to charity (1 Cor. 12:31—14:1), Paul calls love "the better way." It is greater than all the highly prized charisms. It is the motive force of all genuine virtues. It is the sovereign among the "theological virtues" that alone endure and properly define Christian life. Against all forms of Gnosticism, Paul stresses that it is by the effective love of neighbor that one reaches communion with God.

For John, the relation between the Father and the Son is the type and source of the relation between Christ and His own. We enter into this relationship by observing Christ's commandments. "As the Father has loved me, so have I loved you, abide in my love, just as I have kept my Father's commandments and abide in his love" (15:9–10). The principal commandment of Christ is to love one another "as I have loved you," to the point of "laying down one's life for one's friend" (15:12–13). Effective fraternal love is the criterion of true discipleship (13:35; 1 Jn. 2:10–11).

If one proves one's love by keeping the commandments, one perceives the gift of the indwelling of the Trinity (cf. 14:15–24; 17:23–26; Jn. 1:23–24). Thus one enters into the very mystery of the Trinity.

The disciple's mission is but an extension of the Trinitarian love through union with Christ (17:23–26).

The exercise of the divine gift of charity implies that one is begotten by God and lives in communion with Him who is Love (1 Jn. 4:7–12). "The basis of the obligation to love one another, then, is not laid in moral convenience or an ideal perfection, but in a vital movement which springs from our new nature."[15]

5. LAW AND LIBERTY ACCORDING TO PAUL[16]

Paul is positive in asserting that Christians have been *called to liberty* (cf. Gal. 5:13) and are *"not under the law but under grace"* (Gal. 5:18; Rom. 6:14). Just as a wife is bound to her husband only as long as he lives, so a Christian who has died and is risen with Christ is "dead to the law" and no longer subject to it (Rom. 7:1–6).

This doctrine on Christian liberty, though developed on the occasion of a polemic against the Judaizers who wanted to compel even the Gentile Christians to observe the Jewish law, has a lasting value. Paul means not only the ritual and ceremonial prescriptions of the Mosaic legislation, but also its permanent moral content inasmuch as it is positively proposed.[17]

The law, as expression of God's will, is "good and holy" (Rom. 7:12). It is "spiritual" (v. 14). But it does not by itself justify (Gal. 3:11). It was meant to give life, but in fact "when the commandment came, sin revived and I died" (Rom. 7:9). This is because man is carnal, sold under sin (Rom. 7:12).

A Jew looked for justification from the law. But in fact it has only aggravated his situation. By spelling out God's will, it has denied him the excuse of ignorance (Rom. 7:7f). "The very command which promised life proved to be death to me. For sin, finding opportunity in the commandment, deceived me and by it killed me" (Rom. 7:10–11). The law became "a curse" (Gal. 3:10).

Still, Paul recognizes that "the law was our custodian (*peda-gogue*)[18] until Christ came" (Gal. 3:23). How does it fulfill this role? In other words, why was the law given? Paul ventures the puzzling answer: "because of transgressions" (Gal. 3:19). Stanislaus Lyonnet and many others interpret this to mean that the law was actually meant to provoke transgressions in order to reveal to man his weakness, so that he might look for salvation from the Redeemer.[19] Others find this view inconsistent with divine providence. According to them, the law was, as such, not meant to provoke transgressions, but, in fact, became an occasion of sin because of the weakness of unredeemed man.

In any case, unfortunate man is bound to exclaim: "Who will deliver me from this body of death?" (Rom. 7:24). Paul's answer is: "through Jesus Christ our Lord" (v. 25). He goes on to state the reason: "For the law of the Spirit of life in Christ Jesus has set me free from the law of sin and death" (8:2).

The "law of the Spirit" is not just another code like the law of Moses, less complicated and loftier perhaps, but of the same nature. It is radically different. It is not an external norm of action, but *a new and interior source of spiritual energy*. The basic weakness of the old law consisted precisely in the fact that it did not of itself give grace and hence aggravated the situation of the Israelite. (It is not that God did not give any grace to the people of the Old Testament; but the economy of the old law was, as such, not one of grace. The grace that was given was in view of Christ and was not as abundant as in the New Testament.) By proposing a high moral standard without providing the inner strength to reach it, the law added to the sense of frustration.

The economy of grace was foretold, as we have seen, by the prophets when they spoke of the law "written upon the hearts" (Jer. 31:33) and a "new heart" and a "new spirit" (Ez. 36:26–27). St. Paul alludes to these texts when he tells the Corinthians: "You show that you are a letter from Christ delivered by us, written not with ink but with the Spirit of the living God, not on tablets of stone but on tablets of human hearts" (2 Cor. 3:3).

Christian freedom does not imply amoralism or the breakdown of moral responsibility. Paul warns the Galatians against this grave misunderstanding: "You were called to freedom, brethren; only do not use your freedom as an opportunity for the flesh, but through love be servants of one another" (5:13).[20] The external law constraining from outside is replaced by a movement from within. The Christian, who possesses the Spirit as an active force within him, should "walk by the Spirit and not gratify the desires of the flesh" (v. 16). Only "if you are led by the Spirit, you are not under the law" (v. 18). Such a person bears the "fruit of the Spirit," which is "love, joy, peace, patience, kindness, goodness, faithfulness, gentleness, self-control" (v. 22).

"Against such there is no law." One who fully possesses the Spirit has no need of the law compelling him from without, since he spontaneously and freely fulfills every requirement of the divine will *by the inner dynamism of the Spirit*. He is able to achieve what carnal man seeks in vain: freedom from the dominion of sin. This is the meaning of *Christian liberty*—not licentiousness, but free and loving fulfillment of God's will.

Why, then, does the Church insist on moral precepts and add canon law to them? Paul has provided the answer: "The law is not laid down for the just but for the lawless" (1 Tim. 1:9). If every Christian were wholly "just," i.e., totally filled with the Spirit, there would be no need for any other law. The moral law would be adequately fulfilled by Christian love, and positive (human) law would be superfluous. Thus, the perfect man would surely fulfill the minimum requirements of justice, and a fervent Christian would not have to be commanded to receive communion once a year. So all other laws serve the Christian (as the law of Moses did the Jew), as a "pedagogue" to Christ. They will "not only act as a sort of substitute for the light no longer supplied by the Holy Spirit but will, above all, help him to recognize his condition as a sinner."[21]

It should be noted that everyone of us is to some extent lawless, or "unjust," as long as we are on earth and are led by the Spirit only imperfectly. Hence, the objective moral code as well as human law will always be of help to guide our conscience, to help us not to confuse our own carnal inclinations with the promptings of the Spirit. Consequently, to the extent that man's liberty is imperfect on earth, it needs to be propped up by external guidance. But we should always note the *subsidiary quality* of these precepts and the need for observing them, not in a legalistic fashion as an end in itself, but in a spirit of love, as an expression of the inner dynamism of the Spirit.

"It is true that the Christian who lives according to the Spirit does all that the law commands or can command and far more than the law can command, but our possession of the Spirit in our pilgrim state on earth is imperfect and inchoate only. We have in the Spirit a guarantee and foretaste of the future (Rom. 8:23; 2 Cor. 1:22). Until that future consummation is ours, we shall always need the guidance of external law to ensure true discernment of 'the fruit of the Spirit' from 'the works of the flesh' (Gal. 5:16–26). From this point of view external commandments are not restrictions on Christian liberty but a true safeguard to its exercise."[22]

The law of the Spirit brings inner spontaneity. There is no compulsion, but only an attraction of love. But it does not make things easy. It is very exacting—much more than the letter of the external law, since it calls for a total renouncement of selfishness. "Those who belong to Christ Jesus have crucified the flesh with its passions and desires" (Gal. 5:25).

There is no real contradiction between genuine freedom and obedience, provided this is "obedience of faith" (Rom. 1:5), "not an obedience of a slave but of a son" (cf. Rom. 8:15). The biblical concept of obedience is more "listening" (*shama* in Hebrew; *upakouein* in Greek) than submitting. It is a dynamic openness to God's Word that saves, calls and liberates, rather than imprisonment in fixed structures. That is why Paul, the apostle of freedom, constantly calls the Christian to obedience.

6. THE NEW TESTAMENT AND SOCIAL REVOLUTION

The Kingdom of God is presented as a revolutionary force. Jesus adopts a radically critical attitude toward all existing institutions. They form part of the world that is passing. In purifying the temple of Jerusalem and announcing its destruction, Jesus calls for a worship "in spirit and in truth" (Jn. 4:23). By proclaiming the "beatitude" of the *anawim* and the "woes" of the rich, He has passed judgment on the existing social order with its inbuilt unjust structures. By refusing to bow before the established powers, whether of the Jewish Sanhedrin or the Roman Empire, He has denounced the presumption of absolutism on the part of human authorities. He tells Pilate: "You would have no power over me unless it had been given you from above" (Jn. 19:11).

But does this mean that Jesus was a mere political or social revolutionary? Some have proposed that Jesus belonged to the band of Zealots, who were trying to overthrow Roman rule violently and re-establish Jewish power; or they have compared His activity to that of the Zealots.[23] Others have described him as a social revolutionary. Defenders of the *status quo* answer them by saying that Jesus had nothing to do with political or social activity. He is supposed to have come to establish a purely spiritual Kingdom!

Neither of these positions does justice to the New Testament data. They are both the projection of one's own political option.

On the one hand, there is no doubt that Jesus unambiguously denounced the social evils of His time. Although He came to save all men, He came out clearly in favor of the poor. While He called the poor blessed, He cried "woe" on the rich in a manner that may shock many (cf. Lk. 6:24ff). He condemned the attitude of the rich man who did not positively oppress the poor Lazarus but ignored him, treating him as just part of the scene. He spoke of the difficulty presented by riches for entrance into the Kingdom (Mk. 10:23ff). Hence, the "good Christian" in Latin America who cannot understand what land reform has to do with getting to heaven, does not understand anything about the Gospel.

On the other hand, Jesus did not avoid the company of the rich. He did not preach class warfare. He did not favor violent action to bring about social change. He slipped away from the crowd that wanted to make Him an earthly king (Jn. 6:15). He clarified that His Kingdom is "not of this world" (Jn. 18:36). He made it clear that total human fulfillment will come only beyond this age.

The tension between these aspects of the life and mission of Jesus cannot be ignored. Over-spiritualization and individualization of the Gospel message arose because of the process of Hellenization of Christian thought and is today defended by the vested interests who stand to gain from such a view. Jesus indeed stressed the primary importance of the conversion of hearts without which no change in social and political structures would be of much avail. But the Christ-event is directed to revolutionizing the whole pattern of human behavior and social relationships. The disciple of Christ might be called upon to take an active part in radically changing the social structures in a given situation. Still, the Gospel message makes it clear that no human structure as such can fulfill the aspirations of man. There is need for continually bringing an evangelical critique to bear on every situation, lest a structure brought about by a revolution may turn out to be even more oppressive than the one it replaced.

Paul's attitude toward slavery brings out the nature of the impact of the Gospel on human structures. When the slave Onesimus escaped from his master, Paul could have advised him to disappear in the Roman crowd. He would then have liberated one individual slave, who would become one more plebian in Rome. Instead, Paul restores him to his master, Philemon, but this time, not as a slave, but as a "beloved brother." Thereby, he introduces a truly revolutionary change in human relationships. Paul is able to say: "There is neither slave nor free . . . for you are all one in Christ Jesus" (Gal. 3:28).

This does not mean that Paul neglected all action at the level of structures. For instance, he strongly reacted against the segregation of Jewish and Gentile Christians (Gal. 2:11). He led a vigorous campaign against the Judaizing tendency in the infant Church.

The Christian should recognize the primacy of *metanoia* (change of heart) in contributing to human welfare. At the same time, he should realize the importance of changing unjust structures and actively strive to do so with spiritual discernment and evangelical freedom.

Notes to Chapter IV

1. Cf. Rudolf Schnackenburg, *The Moral Teaching of the New Testament,* London, Burns & Oates, 1965; Nicholas Crotty, "Biblical Perspectives in Moral Theology," *Theological Studies,* 26 (1965), 579–595; Thomas W. Manson, *Ethics and the Gospel,* New York, Sribner's, 1960; Charles H. Dodd, *Gospel and Law,* Cambridge, University Press, 1957; John L. McKenzie, "Law in the New Testament," *Jurist,* 26 (1966), 166–80.

2. Charles H. Dodd, *op. cit.,* p. 8.

3. Cf. A. M. Hunter, *Design for Life. An Exposition of the Sermon on the Mount,* London, SCM Press, 1965; W. D. Davies, *The Setting of the Sermon on the Mount,* Cambridge University Press, 1964.

4. Enda McDonagh, *Gift and Call,* Dublin, Gill and Macmillan, p. 94.

5. *Op. cit.* pp. 60–61.

6. John A. T. Robinson, *Honest to God,* London, SCM Press, 1963, p. 111.

7. Cf. Jacques Dupont, *Les Béatitudes,* Bruges, Saint-André, 2nd ed., 1958.

8. Cf. Ceslaus Spicq, *Agape in the New Testament,* St. Louis, Mo., Herder, 1963, Vol. I.

9. Rudolf Schnackenburg, *op. cit.,* p. 103.

10. *Ibid.,* p. 173.

11. Paul Z. Lehman, *Ethics in a Christian Context,* New York, Harper & Row, 1963, p. 80.

12. Rudolf Schnackenburg, *op. cit.,* p. 195.

13. Cf. Ceslaus Spicq, *Agape in the New Testament,* Vol. II and III, 1965, 1966; Gerard Gilleman, "Biblical Revelation of the Primacy of Charity," *Lumen Vitae,* 16 (1961), 17–26.

14. Ceslaus Spicq, *op. cit.,* Vol. II, p. 58.

15. Ceslaus Spicq, *op. cit.,* Vol. III, p. 124.

16. Cf. Stanislaus Lyonnet, "Liberté chrétienne et la loi d'esprit selon saint Paul," *Christus* (1954), no. 4, 6–27; trans. in *The Bridge,* IV, 1961/52, 229–51; summary

in *Theology Digest,* 11 (1963), 13–15; Joseph A. Fitzmeyer, "Saint Paul and the Law," *Jurist,* 27 (1967), 18–36; John L. McKenzie, "Law in the New Testament," *Ibid.,* 15 (1966), 167–180; Michael McNamara, "Christ, Freedom and the Law," *Doctrine and Life,* 10 (1966), 530–36; P. J. Calachor, "A Plea for Liberty," *Bible Today,* 87 (1976), 1027–31.

17.   Cf. Stanislaus Lyonnet, *art. cit.,* pp. 232–33.

18.   For the Greeks, the "pedagogue" or "tutor" was a slave charged to lead a pupil to and from school and watch over his conduct while still a minor. The law fulfilled this role for the Jews till Christ came. One is freed from the discipline of the pedagogue when one has acquired the spirit of the Master.

19.   Cf. Stanislaus Lyonnet, *art. cit.,* pp. 231ff.

20.   Cf. "Live as free men, yet without using your freedom as a pretext for evil" (1 Pet. 2:16).

21.   Stanislaus Lyonnet, *art. cit.,* p. 246.

22.   Nicholas Crotty, *art. cit.,* pp. 583–84.

23.   Cf. S. G. F. Brandon, *Jesus and the Zealots,* 1967.

CHAPTER V

The Problem of Christian Ethics

1. CHRISTIAN AND NON-CHRISTIAN ETHICS

Is there a difference between the morality of a Christian, of a Hindu and of an atheist? Is there such a thing as a specifically Christian ethic? Can one be truly moral without faith? These are serious questions to which very diverse answers have been given.

Jean-Paul Sartre in *Les Mouches* has one of his characters say that justice is a human affair and that he has no need for a God to instruct him about it.

At the opposite extreme, some Protestant theologians have so interpreted Luther's *sola gratia* and *sola Scriptura* axioms as to deny the possibility of any ethical wisdom being derived from a non-Scriptural source.[1]

For instance, Karl Barth finds human ethics a sinful attempt of man to know by himself what is good and evil. It is a prolongation of the fall.[2] The whole enquiry of general ethics must be set aside by theology as a presumptuous intruder.[3] One cannot go from man to God, but rather one must begin with God's Word to us. With his single-mindedness in acknowledging the sovereignty of divine grace, Barth insists on the need for a radical reorientation of the will.

Similarly for Emil Brunner, ethical enquiry is a sinful effort of man to secure his independence over against God.[4] Real Christian life is essentially one of total obedience, while general ethics is dominated by the search for a human rational standard in opposition to God's standard.

However, all men are radically capable of coming to know God through visible creation and of discovering His will. The *imago Dei* in man has not been wholly destroyed, however much it may have been obscured. As N. H. G. Robinson points out, "Men are moral beings apart from Church and Scripture, and when Christian thought takes the form of ethics, it does not lead men into an entirely new country where a quite different language has to be learned, it does not land them on the moon but enters a field already occupied. The Christian is certainly in some sense a new creature, but that clearly means, not another species altogether, but a creature, a man transformed or renewed, whose transformation and renewal cannot be articulated apart from some understanding of his existence as a creature independently of that renewal."[5]

Without a natural or human morality, no ethical—or, for that matter, religious—dialogue would be possible with non-Christians. Without such a bridge, evangelization would seem to be a wholly extrinsic process. In fact, as Vatican II declares: "In fidelity to conscience, Christians are joined with the rest of men in the search for truth."[6]

However, Christians would be impoverishing their lives if they were satisfied with a certain philosophical ethic derived only from human wisdom. They would also deprive the non-Christian of the rich insights concerning man and his vocation which their faith offers them.

Although, even without religious faith, an ethical attitude toward life is possible, nevertheless, this can be deepened by the recognition of man's dependence on God as a creature and the acceptance of God's grace in faith. While the immediate foundation of the moral order is the value of the human person, this value is seen in its full depth when man is acknowledged as the image and child of God.

In other words, although there is in man a natural domain with its own inner consistency, actual man is not complete in himself, since he is willed by God through the gift of grace to have a transcendent fulfillment. Hence, a purely human reflection on natural morality will necessarily be incomplete. It must be open to being perfected by the light of revelation. For example, the absolute indissolubility of marriage can be understood only in its link with the Christian mystery. Further, the value of marriage, although enhanced by revelation, is also relativized, so that virginity becomes a special value ''for the sake of the Kingdom.'' This in turn tells us about the ultimate meaning of marriage itself.

2.   WHAT IS SPECIFIC TO CHRISTIAN ETHICS?

The prophets of the Old Testament had already purified the moral heritage of Israel and, through it, of humanity in general. But the Christ-event brought totally new elements into human experience, especially the revelation of the Trinity. Personalism and the communitarian destination of man received a new dimension. The person of Christ became a dynamic exemplar of the perfect moral life. The intelligence of man was opened to a new vision of moral and religious values. Love received its central place as the wellspring of all virtues.

The Christian experience facilitates a deeper understanding of natural morality, since the theological virtues of the faith commitment, of eschatological hope and Christ-like love reveal the full dimensions of the moral vocation of man. Human reason can now be tested by the unfailing light of the Gospel. As N. H. G. Robinson puts it, Christian ethics ''regards the [*summun bonum*] as fellowship, it sees love as the fulfillment of the law, and the good life as essentially something like a partnership in which we human beings are caught up into purposes in relation to which we can certainly have a sympathetic insight, namely, conscience, but which all the time immensely transcend our highest comprehension of them.''[7]

Love of neighbor, care of the needy and the like are, as such, not specifically Christian. Even the intentionality of implicit reference to an Absolute in doing good is common to everyone. Still, the Christian relates himself to God in the Spirit of Christ. This gives a new intensity and universality to love of neighbor. The presence of the Holy Spirit in the Church contributes in a special way to arriving at certain moral knowledge, though its content may be human. The sacramental and ecclesial communion are powerful means in achieving perfection. The element of renunciation finds a profound meaning in the Christian perspective.

What is specific to Christian ethics is the scripturally inspired understanding of man and the world that the Christian brings to concrete issues and that affect his solution to these problems. But it is an exaggeration to say simply with the editors of the *Civiltà Cattolica* that Christian faith and grace, which characterize Christian morality, will *necessarily* "translate themselves into new moral conduct and new commands."[8] They give as examples love of enemies, non-resistance to the wicked, renunciation of wealth, love of the cross and embracing virginity. Christians may not always be more noted for these than non-Christians.

It is *not so much the content* of moral knowledge that is derived from specifically Christian sources. The teaching and example of Christ provide, rather, a *stimulus,* a *context* and a *motivation.*[9] These, however, will have to be personalized.

The distinction between Christian morality and non-Christian morality is, in a sense, of limited validity. The phenomenology of religions has discovered that the common conception of religion is the Holy advancing toward man and of man turning toward the Holy. It is true that only the Christian revelation manifests the truest nature of this Holy and the manner of its advance toward man. But the call to perfection in Christ is addressed to all mankind without distinction since man, according to God's salvific plan, is simply man called in Christ. Mankind knows and accepts the divine call in different degrees of explicitation and intensity. Still, non-Christians concretely share more than the "natural" elements of the Christian vocation, since Christ died for all and His Spirit is working in all. Even professed atheists who in all sincerity seek the truth may encounter God, the Father of our Lord

Jesus Christ, in their inmost consciousness moved by the hidden workings of the Holy Spirit.

Hence, ethics is Christian in a universally applicable sense inasmuch as all things have been created and redeemed in Christ. Besides, for the Christian, ethics must be wholly Christian because he is called to absolute obedience to Jesus as Lord.[10]

Karl Rahner's theories of the "supernatural existential" and "anonymous Christianity" cast light on this matter.[11] Since God's universally salvific will in Christ is a universally experienced orientation toward God, this objectification of this subjectivity might not necessarily add much to the ethical self-understanding that is new or foreign to man in the concrete order. Still, the ethical implications of the sacramental life and explicit adherence to Christ in the ecclesial community should not be minimized. On the other hand, Christians should not hesitate to accept the possibility that some non-Christians might have developed some deeper moral insights. If natural morality is knowable through human reason, there is no reason why non-Christians may not at times have a clear vision in some areas, the strengthening grace of the Holy Spirit being available also to them. Besides, today, if the precept of universal brotherhood is accepted, at least in principle, by all, the Christian must see in it the fulfillment of the aspirations of every man as well as a victory of the Gospel that has acted as leaven all these centuries.

St. Thomas explicitly declares that Jesus Christ has not given any new specific moral norms in specific areas beyond those dictated by human reason.[12] So, basically, there is the same epistemological problem for the Christian and the non-Christian in discerning what is or is not a human value. The Christian must also be careful not to attribute to his faith—and thus absolutize—what may only be a passing and imperfect formulation of human morality.

In studying the relationship between human and Christian morality, we can start with that which is human and hence not inaccessible to human reason, and then reflect on the specifically *Christian intention-*

ality which determines the life of a Christian. This is a valid approach, although some Christians may find such an analysis too abstract and wish to concentrate on their faith experience and live a life of total self-surrender to God in Christ. Whatever is truly human will supposedly be included in this self-surrender.

However, such Christians must recognize that human life has its concrete demands, especially in the complex world of today. If they fail to use the God-given gift of human reason to make a proper analysis of the existential situation and to reflect on the demands made by their very humanity, they may easily be misled by the subtly corrupting atmosphere of racism, militarism and a conservative oppressive society, all of which do not fail to exploit the religious sentiment of the unwary pious man. Crusades of the past and events in South Africa and Latin America today are sufficient evidence of this danger. Besides, the problem of dialogue with non-Christians regarding the promotion of human values and human rights will remain.

Dietrich Bonhoeffer, while insisting that the point of departure for Christian ethics is the reality of God as He reveals Himself in Jesus Christ, also points out that "the reality of God discloses itself only by setting me entirely in the reality of the world, and when I encounter the reality of the world it is always already sustained, accepted and reconciled in the reality of God."[13] Hence, "the will of God is nothing other than the becoming real of the reality of Christ with us and in our world."[14]

Joseph Fuchs affirms the human aspect of Christian morality more positively: "The first thing that should be said about Christian morality is this, that it is human morality, in the best sense of the word; that the moral conduct of the Christian must essentially be human."[15] Did not Paul himself warn Christians to live honorably, since everyone will be judged by the law "written on their hearts"? (Rom. 2:15).

While religion is man's worshipping response to God who speaks his word of love, true religious morality is man's response to God's word *mediated through the created world,* which is created and recreated in the Word of God, Jesus Christ. So Bernard Häring can rightly conclude: "The moral order is concerned with the fulfillment of the order of creation. It is response to God, the correct response precisely to the extent that man takes his terrestrial tasks seriously, and earnestly accepts created values."[16]

Vatican II, therefore, exhorts Christians "to strive to discharge their earthly duties conscientiously and in response to the Gospel spirit. They are mistaken who, knowing that we have here no abiding city but seek one which is to come, think that they may therefore shirk their earthly responsibilities. For they are forgetting that by the faith itself they are more than ever obliged to measure up to these duties."[17]

Again the Council points out that "men are not deterred by the Christian message from building up the world, or impelled to neglect the welfare of their fellows. They are, rather, more stringently bound to these things."[18]

Hence, there is no room for evasion from earthly commitments under the pretext of practising Christian "spirituality." The Christian faith must motivate the disciple of Christ to strive wholeheartedly for social justice.

3. THE MORALITY OF THE ATHEIST

The religious orientation of openness to the Absolute is an essential dimension of human nature. Hence, even though an atheist may call himself a "humanist," an important element would be lacking in his moral conception, at least at the conscious level.

Still, what is human in Christian morality is not closed to him. He could discover it to the extent that he has basic openness to truth. Absence of any religious bigotry or of Pharisaical self-justification may perhaps lead to clearer moral insights in certain areas, unless his atheism itself makes him fanatical.

Transcendental intentionality toward God the Father may not be absent in the depths of the conscience. This follows from the universal (and concrete) call to salvation in Christ. At the same time, we must note that the unbelieving sinner objectively offends not only against the order of human morality, but also against the love of the Father—this again in the innermost heart, where he is conscious of himself and not only of his act, though he may not attain to a reflex consciousness of God's personal call in Christ.[19]

Because the so-called humanist does not realize or admit the significance of Christ for salvation, the sacraments and ecclesial communion, as well as the realities of the cross and the resurrection, do not have an explicit relevance in his moral life, and to that extent his moral life will be impoverished. Ignoring the situation created by the fall, the unbeliever may not be sufficiently aware of the influence of egoism upon the grasp of moral values.

Whatever the divergence in explicit position, a dialogue is possible between the believer and the unbeliever for mutual benefit. Today there is need for establishing cooperation in the search for human values. The believer must admit that, inasmuch as the humanist conceives and practices fraternal love as a non-egoistic gift of self to the neighbor for whose personal dignity and freedom he has a genuine respect, he may experience in interpersonal relationships a genuine sense of the Absolute. As Joseph Fuchs remarks: "It is still interesting and highly significant to discover that the best among today's humanists regard precisely this, the proper relationship to one's neighbor, love as in a real sense an *absolute* duty, and even indeed the *sole* absolute moral value. . . . For this very reason they discover more easily and fully in the experience of their neighbor, of the human person, the idea of an Absolute and of absolute obligation."[20]

There is also here the whole question of *secularization,* which we do not intend to treat of fully. Suffice it to cite a few witnesses to the significance of this process. As Harvey Cox puts it: "Our struggle for the shaping of the secular city represents the one way we respond faithfully to this reality [of the Kingdom of God] in our times."[21] Cox speaks of the Bible authenticating the process of "disenchantment of nature" enshrined in the story of creation, "desacralizing of politics" taught by the Exodus narrative, and "deconsecration of values" inherent in the record of the Sinai covenant.

A Christian psychologist has this to say: "It is my contention that the greater our understanding of loving, the nearer we are to the mystery we call God and that the psychological sciences have made fundamental contributions to this knowledge which Christianity has yet to grasp, let alone assimilate."[22]

So, while Dostoyevsky is right in saying that "if there is no God, there is neither good nor evil and everything is permitted," still, there can be morality without an *explicit* belief in God. It is also true that the Christian faith throws a new light on man's total vocation and thus helps in finding solutions to life problems that are fully human.[23]

Here we should note that atheism does not always arise out of the perversity of the persons concerned. Vatican II clearly points this out: "Believers themselves bear some responsibility for this situation. . . To the extent that they neglect their own training in the faith, or teach erroneous doctrine, or are deficient in their religious, moral, or social doctrine, they must be said to conceal rather than reveal the authentic face of God and religion."[24] So there is less question of "fighting atheism" than of helping our brothers see the value of religion by ourselves making it relevant in our lives. Atheism is often a reaction against the abuse of religion on the part of the pious to further their selfish interests. This can be remedied only by believers being more attuned to social justice.

4.   NOTE ON MORAL INSTRUCTION OF NON-CHRISTIANS

Morality is the perfection of *man as man,* the development of the most specific qualities of man. Man is moral, or fully human, when he lives according to the deepest exigencies of his being. This implies an integrated personality, proper adjustment to society and constant striving for the betterment of humanity. To achieve this, it might seem sufficient to cultivate discipline, honesty, loyalty, diligence, creativity, kindness and generosity.

But attempts to live according to a merely humanistic ideal, will be a failure in the long run, as is proved by wars, social upheavals and the decline in public morality in recent times throughout the world. The horizontal dimension of human life cannot stand long without its vertical reference to God. Hence there is need for a morality centered on God, the ground of all being.

We have seen that, objectively, all men are in the order of salvation accomplished in Christ. He died for all and now His salvific influence extends to all, even to those who do not know Him or who have not yet made their commitment to Him by explicit faith, baptism and membership in the Church. Hence it would be wrong to speak of a natural morality for non-Christians and a supernatural morality for Christians. All, in varying degrees, are in the order of grace and are called to live the sonship of the Father and brotherhood among men.

But, pedagogically, it will generally not be possible to provide a too explicitly Christian basis for moral instruction to non-Christians. To talk, for example, of "life in Christ" may be objectionable and even meaningless to them. However, this does not mean that we should take refuge in merely rational ethics. We could endeavor to convey, as far as possible, a Christian view of man and his relationship with God.

The concept of God presented to our students should not represent an abstract and ethereal being bereft of any vital consequences for life. Neither should He be conceived in the image of man, as a sort of mechanical distributor of rewards and punishments, or as one who is at the beck and call of man for his selfish purposes. We should present Him as the living God whose cares for man and invites him to communion with Him.

There are many elements in non-Christian religions that provide true glimpses of God: e.g., absolute transcendence in *advaita,* love and mercy among the Bhaktas. These should be utilized without yielding to cheap syncretism. The point is to discern the action of God in the lives and traditions of our non-Christian students, to help them in clarifying their insights, and to guide them to order their lives in accordance with these insights.

Fortunately, the idea of the fatherhood of God is now attractive to most people, though it is not often grasped in its true depth. The fatherhood of God implies that we act as befits His children and live in a spirit of brotherhood.

The doctrine of grace as a sharing in the life of God is very important. There is every reason to think that non-Christians are not bereft of this divine gift. It seems to be a well-founded view that a non-Christian, when he turns to God in a basic option, is "justified" and receives the indwelling presence of the Holy Spirit. St. Thomas expressed this by saying: "The first thing that occurs to a man to think about then [at the age of discretion] is to deliberate about himself. And if he then directs himself to the due end, he will, by means of grace, receive the remission of original sin."[25] This view does not take away anything from the uniqueness of Christianity and the special significance of baptism and membership in the Church. So when we are dealing with non-Christians, we should be aware that they share in a hidden way in the gift of grace and the presence of the Spirit.

Moral instruction, then, will not become a mere imparting of notions concerning God and right conduct. It will rather be a *formation,* helping the students to dispose themselves to receive and answer the call of God. Morality is not merely striving for self-perfection, which often leads to frustration or self-righteousness, but cooperating with the inspirations of grace.

In these days, when everyone aspires to freedom, our students should be made to realize that true freedom is not license to act according to one's selfish inclinations but the ability to perform what is right spontaneously and without constraint from external sanctions. Such a gift comes from grace, which is an inner dynamism or source of spiritual energy. Hindus often speak of this as a "soul-force."

The doctrine of grace also leads to that of divine love which is communicated to us. Love, which is the soul of all other virtues, is primarily directed toward God but is to be expressed in love of neighbor.

While we should inculcate a God-centered morality, we should start from the concrete problems of youth and the signs of the times. It would be uninspiring to dish out canned doctrine on God and morality. Students should be made to feel that the subject is relevant to their situation. The great political, social and technological movements of our time should be analyzed. The significance of the passionate strivings after human freedom and justice should be scrutinized in depth. Thus the basic value of human dignity will be uncovered behind the obscure gropings and struggles of the younger generation today. Then the question of the true basis of human dignity will inevitably be posed, leading to the idea of God and of our relationships to Him.

Effective moral instruction presupposes an understanding of the background and psychology of the students. Their beliefs, aspirations and attitudes, and the family and social influences on their behavior should be taken into account. To a large extent, the course on moral instruction could usefully be conducted in the form of personality development sessions.

Formal moral instruction should be conceived as only an aspect of the total religious and moral formation in school or college. Students should be initiated to prayer and trained in responsibility and service. The school atmosphere itself should be such as to promote a spirit of community.

Notes to Chapter V

1. Cf. Ernst Troeltsch, *The Social Teaching of the Christian Churches*, New York, Harper, 1960, Vol. II, pp. 528–44; 602–16.
2. Cf. *Church Dogmatics*, Edinburgh, Clark, 1957, Vol. II, 2, pp. 513–15.
3. *Ibid.*, p. 517
4. Cf. *The Divine Imperative*, London, Lutterworth, 1937.
5. *Groundwork of Christian Ethics*, London, Collins, 1971, p. 16.
6. *GS*, art. 16.
7. *Op. cit.*, p. 119.
8. "*Esiste una morale 'cristiana'?*", 123 (1972), 449–55.
9. Cf. Gerard J. Huyghes, "A Christian Basis for Ethics," *Heythrop Journal*, 13 (1972), 27–47.
10. James M. Gustafson, *Can Ethics Be Christian?* Chicago and London, University of Chicago Press, 1975, pp. 170.
11. Cf. Karl Rahner, "The Order of Redemption within the Order of Creation," *The Christian Commitment*, New York, Sheed and Ward, 1963, pp. 47–52; "Anonymous Christians," in *Theological Investigations*, Baltimore, Helicon, 1969, Vol. VI, pp. 390–98. To be called "anonymous Christians" might not be quite acceptable to non-Christians, but this is a way a Christian might see the situation of the non-Christian within his faith commitment.
12. *Summa Theologica*, Ia-IIae, 108, 2.
13. *Ethics*, New York, Macmillan, 1964, p. 61.
14. *Ibid.*, p. 77.
15. Cf. *Human Values and Christian Morality*, p. 133.
16. *The Law of Christ*, Westminster, Md., Newman Press, Vol. I, 1961, p. 47.
17. *GS*, art. 43.
18. *Ibid.*, art. 34.
19. Josef Fuchs, *Human Values and Christian Morality*, p. 120.
20. *Ibid.*, p. 135.
21. *The Secular City*, New York, Macmillan, 1965, p. 112.
22. Jack Dominian and A. R. Peacocke, *From Cosmos to Love*, London, Darton, Longman and Todd, 1976, p. 43.
23. *GS*, art. 11.
24. *Ibid.*, art. 19.
25. *Summa Theologica*, Ia-IIae, 89, 6.

CHAPTER VI

Christian Anthropology

Christian ethics is based on particular presuppositions about man, on a definite anthropology. It is not possible to speak of human activity without such a foundation. But it should also be noted that the anthropological presuppositions cannot be absolutely defined in every detail once for all, since ethical discourse is not the drawing of neat conclusions from predetermined principles, but a constant reflection on and refinement of preliminary data.

To understand the God-man relationship on which morality is based, it is necessary to understand man, not merely in the abstract, but also man of a particular time and place. As the Word was made flesh, so theology must take on an incarnational aspect. Hence, contemporary findings of psychology and sociology should play an important role in moral reflection.

In the Christian view, man is a *creature,* made to the *image of God,* fallen, but *recreated to the likeness of Christ* as an active agent in the history of salvation.

1.   MAN A CREATURE

In the pantheistic world-view of the Stoics, there was no room for a truly human ethic. The world was, as such, something sacral, something divine. Hence one could not interfere with the natural causes of things. This view was pushed to the limit by Epictetus, who considered cutting off one's hair as such an unjustifiable interference.[1] In the opposite view of latter day secularists, the world is so autonomous as to have no relationship with anything divine. Here, the world—and especially the human person—loses its significance and intrinsic value.

The Christian doctrine of creation has contributed to genuine secularization by freeing the world from a sacralization which really amounts to an alienation. It attributes an autonomous value to earthly reality, distinct from the divine but depending on it. Vatican II has made this very clear: "If by the autonomy of earthly affairs we mean that created things and societies themselves enjoy their own laws and values which must be gradually deciphered, put to use, and regulated by men, then it is entirely right to demand such autonomy. Such is not merely required by modern man, but harmonizes also with the will of the Creator. For by the very circumstance of their being created, all things are endowed with their own stability, truth, goodness, proper laws and order."[2]

God is immanent to His creatures just as He is transcendent. In this perspective, a truly human morality, or morality of man-as-man, is possible, though it finds its basis in God the Creator, and its fulfillment in salvation in Christ. To affirm God as Creator is not necessarily to assert something that happened in datable or historical time but something that concerns man's perennial relationship with God. To believe in God as Creator is to look upon cosmic evolution as God's continuing action. This vision should transform our attitude toward our environment and make us responsible, loving and caring. This perspective will also give a religious meaning to man's secular activity. Hence, all human activities in which men are truly and fully human and which are in accord with the divine will are to be seen as expressions of the creative, immanent, personal action of God—and not just those activities we have restrictedly labelled "religious." This is the basis for Christian humanism.

2. THE IMAGE OF GOD

Man appears as the first organism that is conscious of where he has come from and of the potentialities open to him. He is a spiritual being made to the image of God (Gen. 1:26). Because God has breathed His own Spirit into man (cf. Gen. 6:3), he transcends the rest of creation.

"Thou hast made him little less than God and dost crown him with glory and honor" (Ps. 8:5).

Man's likeness to God is not only in his reason, but also in his responsible conduct. He has the capacity to respond freely to the call of God. He can commit or entrust himself by entering into relationships. He is a relational being. He can be loved and can love in return.

All earthly reality is committed to the care of man as God's image. "Thou hast given him dominion over the work of thy hands; thou hast put all things under his feet" (Ps. 8:6; cf. Gen. 1:28–30). This is the meaning of personhood. To be a person is to be free from subjection to non-personal realities and to have dominion over them, to take up responsibilities, to give one's imprint to nature, to shape the world according to one's rationality. Man has not only to form the material reality distinct from himself, but also to develop his own reality, to bring his biological and instinctual determinisms within the domain of reason.

Today we are awed at the tremendous possibilites open to man to transform reality: e.g., in the atomic sphere, in the biological sphere through genetic engineering, and in the psychological sphere through behavioral conditioning. They must be accepted as opportunities for realizing the original mandate to "subdue the earth." But we must be careful that there be no manipulation that makes man less human, that violates the dignity of his personality made to the image of God.

3. FALLEN AND REDEEMED

Man is also tragically aware of his limitations and his inability to become what he ought and desires to become. Man's reason has been clouded and his will weakened by sin, and thus the image of God has been distorted.

Because man from the dawn of history abused his liberty, set himself against God and sought to find fulfillment apart from God, "he became out of harmony with himself, with others, and with all created things. Therefore man is split within himself. As a result, all human life, whether individual or collective, shows itself to be a dramatic struggle between good and evil, between light and darkness. Indeed, man finds that by himself he is incapable of battling the assaults of evil successfully, so that everyone feels as though he is bound by chains."[3]

Christ saves man from this tragic predicament. "On account of His great love, He became what we are, that He might make us what He is," says Irenaeus.[4]

Protestant theology stresses the sinful condition of man even after he responds in faith to God's loving gift in Christ: the Christian is supposed to be *simul justus et peccator*, incapable of good works on his own.[5]

Catholic theology, on the other hand, lays emphasis on the basic goodness of man even after the fall and on the inner transformation of man through grace, so that he now becomes a new creature capable of good works. Recently, however, there has been an effort to understand the element of truth in the Protestant position.[6]

Catholics are prone to present too optimistic a blueprint for the renewal of the world. The manuals of moral theology did not sufficiently come to grips with the mystery of sin in human life, though they elaborated all the ways in which man could commit actual sin and the factors that reduce the imputability of human actions.

Vatican II has restored the balance, especially in the passage we have just cited. There was a temporary romantic afterglow in the Church immediately following the Council. But the disillusionment that soon ensued and the present polarization of thought between opposite extremes should make us go back to the documents with an open mind and see the delicate balance the Council struck between a naive optimism and a gloomy pessimism concerning the capacities of human nature.

There is need for recognizing the basic goodness of man. Sin has deeply affected human nature, but the image of God has not been destroyed. Christ has radically conquered sin and its effects. By our participation in the Paschal mystery of Christ, we are called upon to combat sin's insidious presence in the world. The fullness of redemption will come only beyond history, but the power of the redemption is already at work.

Through the incarnation, God has entered human history and given a new value to all that is material and human. As the Son of God has assumed our humanity, we should not yield to any depreciation of what is corporeal and earthly. In the sacramental economy, the ordinary elements of human existence—bread, wine, oil and water—enter the celebration of the sacred mysteries and thus acquire a new significance.

Christ's resurrection also brings into existence new interrelatedness between His disciples, and this is the summit of the evolutionary process which the material of the cosmos has undergone. The Christian hopes in the final consummation in which God's creative purpose will be fully realized, and he is called upon to cooperate with it actively. This gives Christian ethics a wide social, even a cosmic, perspective.

In Christian thought, there is a tension between the incarnational and the eschatological aspects of life. The first emphasizes the responsibility of the Christian to transform the world through active involvement in its affairs. The second tends to look to the future life for fulfillment and to regard with suspicion earthly realities. An either–or approach cannot be justified in the light of the basic goodness of creation and the mystery of the incarnation on the one hand, and the reality of sin on the other.

The eschatological destiny of man should be a warning against absolutizing any present structures, institutions or ideologies. It should serve as a constant critique of anything other than the demands of the Kingdom. This critical stance should point to the need of constant renewal, while at the same time putting up with the inevitable imperfections and limitations of life.

Our moral thinking should be revised according to new insights gained from human growth and experience. But all that is new should not be accepted with an uncritical mind. While cooperating with various movements that seek to better the world, the Christian should not be blind to their limitations. The Church as such cannot identify herself with any one of them. She cannot be enamored of any one ideology, party or form of government so as to render unconditional support to it. There is need for caution when a group claims to represent the Christian religion or to fight against a godless movement. A false social conservatism or "law and order" mentality that condones manifest tyranny and oppression should be avoided. The Christian outlook guards against a naive expectation that change will be rapid and without struggle, a pessimism that sees no bright future, and a smugness that is satisfied with the *status quo*.

Man's response to the Father's self-giving must involve entrusting oneself completely to the Lord of the future. Each moral choice is a trusting step into the future, which prepares for the next step into the unknown destiny which God has prepared for those who love Him.

The Christian's response to God's call must not be interpreted as a purely human task or achievement. But he may not evade his earthly task on the plea of surrendering himself to God's plan. He may not retreat into passivity and refuse to participate in the transformation of the world.

4. NATURE AND GRACE

From the start, man was oriented to the supernatural goal of sharing in the life of God. He is called to divine sonship according to the image of the only-begotten Son of God. Since God became man in order to draw man to Himself, human life must be patterned after Christ, the perfect image of the Father (cf. Rom. 8:29). By our assimilation into Christ, we become a new being. "Put on the new nature, created after the likeness of God in true righteousness and holiness" (Eph. 4:23; cf. Col. 3:10; 2 Cor. 5:17). John characterizes this as a new birth (Jn. 3:3, 8) or as birth from God (1 Jn. 2:29; 3:9).

The new supernatural image is rooted in the possession of the Spirit. "But you are not in the flesh, you are in the Spirit, if the Spirit of God dwells in you'' (Rom. 8:9). Christian life consists in corresponding to the workings of the Holy Spirit in the depths of man's heart. This is a destiny going beyond the capacities of man as such, and hence it is called *"super*natural.''

But this is not to be understood as a two-tier system, the supernatural being added as a superstructure or top layer to the natural or bottom layer and giving rise to two separate ethics—a purely natural one and a supernatural one.[7] Though there has been a tendency to think along these lines, Vatican II has clearly rejected the approach. The Council describes man in terms of salvation history, which admits of a certain continuity between nature and grace, between creation and redemption.

The only way the divine can enter man's life is through the human, just as the only way man can now become truly human is as bearer of the divine. Elements of the natural order are now, in fact, elements of the concrete supernatural order, although they may not be inherently supernatural. The order of grace has assumed within itself the natural order. This is important in order to understand how the requirements of the natural order can be performed in a supernatural way and how grace pervades and inspires their fulfillment.

We cannot neatly divide human actions into natural and supernatural ones.[8] Divine grace is present and effective, not only in the specifically religious aspects of human life, but also in the entire process by which man realizes himself and builds up the world.

To give a concrete example, it is not true to say that a man can be an equally good teacher whether he is in the state of grace or not. Teaching is not a purely natural action. On the other hand, a supernatural spirit does not make up for technical incompetence nor for lack of politeness in dealing with others.

The need for the healing power of divine grace is evident from the sinful condition of man. Human existence is so deeply affected by sin that the passage from ignorance to wisdom, from passivity to creativity,

from self-centeredness to concern for others, can never be purely natural.
It has to be moved by divine grace, even though it be in a hidden
manner.

5. BODY AND SPIRIT

Platonists considered the body as the prison of the soul. Many of
the Fathers of the Church, affected by this dualism, have influenced
the popular preoccupation with "saving one's soul." But true Christianity does not reject or despise the body with its functions and passions,
but purifies them through divine love. Christ did not come to free souls
from bodies. Through His sacrifice, His body is glorified and becomes
the means of the sanctification of our persons, body and soul.

Biblical thought recognizes no division of body and soul. Man is
not a body and, in addition, a soul.[9] The whole man is body, and the
whole man spirit. He is a totality, a living soul. "Flesh" (*basar*) simply
means the concrete man as the source of bodily and non-bodily phenomena. The "soul" or "spirit" (*nephesh*) is the distinctively human
mode of bodily existence.

The totality applies also to the different parts of the body. The
face, for instance, is the person who has turned to someone, and so
"seeing face to face" means encountering him directly as a person. All
the parts of the body have both a physical and a spiritual meaning, not
in any dualistic sense, but in the sense that a spiritual activity takes
place through the bodily activity. Thus, increased beating of the heart
means increase in love.

So in the New Testament also, "body" (*soma*), "flesh" (*sarx*),
"soul" (*psyche*) and "spirit" (*pneuma*) refer to the whole man. The
opposition between "flesh" and "spirit" refers to the unredeemed and
the redeemed state of man. When "spirit" is distinguished from "body,"
it means that man transcends the material order. In no way does it mean
that there are two parts in man, soul and body.

Paul, especially, presents a clear vision of the whole person, body and spirit, dedicated to God's service. He appeals to the brethren "to present your bodies as a living sacrifice, holy and acceptable to God" (Rom. 12:1). "Do you not know," he asks, "that you are God's temple and that God's Spirit dwells in you?" (1 Cor. 3:16; cf. 6:19). In opposition to the Gnostic belief, Paul proposes an integral view of the human person. For Paul, the "flesh" that is to be crucified (Gal. 5:24) is not the body apart from the soul, but nature apart from God or against God. There is no trace in him of the false idea that physical sex is something dirty or bad. On the contrary, among the "sins of the flesh," he includes such things as jealousy, anger, dissension and party spirit (Gal. 5:20–21).

After centuries of misunderstanding, Vatican II has called for a return to this holistic view of the Bible: "Though made of body and soul, man is one. Through his bodily composition he gathers to himself the elements of the material world. Thus they reach their crown through him, and through him raise their voice in free praise. For this reason man is not allowed to despise his bodily life. Rather, he is obliged to regard his body as good and honorable, since God has created it and will raise it up on the last day. Nevertheless, wounded by sin, man experiences rebellious stirrings in his body. But the very dignity of man postulates that man glorify God in his body and forbid it to serve the evil inclinations of his heart."[10]

One of the reasons why Protestants do not comprehend the doctrine of the Assumption of the Blessed Virgin and why Catholics do not find much significance in its seems to be the neglect of the perspective of bodily resurrection. A lively hope in the resurrection would give a positive outlook toward bodily life on earth and would be of great importance in moral reflection regarding human life and sexuality.

Thus, moral good is to be achieved by the whole man. Spontaneous desires and emotions (which St. Thomas calls *"passions"*) should not be seen only as hindrances and dangers to moral life. In themselves, they are good and are of indispensable service in man's striving after moral perfection. According to St. Thomas, "Man seeks what is good not only with his spiritual will but also with the desire of his sense appetites (*appetitus sensitivi*)."[11]

The Stoic ideal of *ataraxia* (emotionlessness), or being unmoved by feelings of joy or affection, is quite foreign to Christianity. Unfortunately, it has influenced a certain asceticism that would condemn loud laughter at least as a venial fault! Even today, in some religious institutes, human love with its affective component is looked upon with suspicion, and attempts are made to promote a disembodied from of "charity."

It is very important to realize that man is a single, unified being, part of the physical world, subject to its laws, yet emerging from it and making it subject to himself. The physical aspect affects him even in the core of his personality. It is only through media that are physical, signs and words, that he can receive an invitation and respond to it in human freedom. Through the body, a man becomes present and available to his fellowmen. A smile, a handshake is a bodily expression of one's inner attitude.

The *universe* is the extension of the human body. The transformation of earthly reality is the common task of the human family. We should not have a merely utilitarian attitude toward the visible creation, but see in it the glory of God, as Teilhard de Chardin did. This perspective opens the way to a sane appreciation of art and all scientific achievements, which, instead of alienating man from his ultimate goal, become steps in his journeying toward God.

Again, because of his corporeal nature, man is a *historical phenomenon*. He exists in time and is subject to change and development. Man is the image of God, not only by his static givenness, but also by his continued *becoming*. It is only gradually that he develops a capacity to understand and respond in love. This development passes through critical stages in life. Consequently, the individual human act must be situated in the context of the person's development in the particular atmosphere in which that development takes place.

The individual person is immersed in the whole process of cosmic development. In the present hour of decision (*kairos,* or God-given time of grace), he must assume the potentialities of his environment and develop the heritage of his past in the context of the whole history of salvation. At the beginning and end of history, there is not fate, but God, who calls man at each moment.

The capacity to know and to choose is given only as potentiality at birth. It must be gradually, and at times painfully, acquired in the teeth of inherent limitations, physical handicaps and the obstacles placed by the ambience.[12] The classical factors impeding knowledge and freedom must be seen in the light of the new findings of modern psychology and sociology.

————o————

Notes to Chapter VI

1. "The Golden Sayings," I. 16, *Harvard Classics,* ed. by C. E. Eliot, New York, Collier, 1910, Vol. 2, p. 152.
2. *GS,* art. 36.
3. *Ibid.,* art. 13.
4. *Treatise Against Heresies,* 5, pref., *Early Church Classics,* ed. by H. R. M. Hitchcock, London, S. P. C. K., 1916, Vol. 2, p. 89.
5. Cf. J. Dillenburger and C. Welde, *Protestant Christianity,* New York, Scribner's, 1954, pp. 255–283. There was the opposite trend in liberal Protestantism at the turn of the century, and the secularizing trend in the 1960s largely ignored the reality of sin.
6. Cf. Karl Rahner, "Justified and Sinner at the Same Time," *Theological Investigations,* London, Darton, Longman & Todd, 1969, Vol. VI, pp. 218–30.
7. For the dangers of such "extrinsecism," cf. Karl Rahner, *Theological Investigations,* Vol. I, pp. 297–317.
8. See Henri de Lubac, *Mystery of the Supernatural,* London, Chapman, 1967.
9. Cf. Edward Schillebeeckx, *World and the Church,* London, Sheed & Ward, pp. 231ff.
10. *GS,* art. 14.
11. *Summa Theologica,* Ia-IIae, 24, 3.
12. Cf. Edward Schillebeeckx, *op. cit.,* p. 239.

CHAPTER VII

Personalism and Call to Community

1. THE TRINITY IN THE CHRISTIAN LIFE[1]

Christian morality is not an abstract, lifeless system of imperatives, a maze of laws and principles. What is distinctive about Christian ethics is the basic structure of *God's self-gift* to man and *man's response* to that gift in Jesus Christ. It is the way of life that is derived from the covenant relationship into which God has entered with man through the Christ-event.

The salvific dialogue with God always begins with His initiative. The Gospel denounces the wilful man, the man who, by his own will power, seeks to bring himself into conformity with a set of rules or with the image which he has chosen for himself. Such a man thinks that he can justify himself by his own efforts, while salvation, in fact, comes from the surrender of faith. It is a *response to the gift* which God gratuitously offers.

True morality, then, is a redemptive process by which man's life is transformed by the divine gift of salvation. This is not opposed to genuine self-realization. For the call of God is not an obligation thrust on us, but a grace that enables us to develop our human potentialities. When a man opens himself to the gift of God, he is on the road to true development of his personality.

While the Old Testament revealed God's immense love for mankind, the New Testament comes to reveal that "God *is* love" (1 Jn 4:8). The chief message which Christ came to bring, the most sublime secret He came to share, is that God is communion and that we are called to share in that communion. Jesus calls His disciples to such an intimacy that He reveals His intimacy with the Father: "No longer do I call you servants, for the servant does not know what his master is doing; but I have called you friends, for all that I have heard from my Father I have made known to you" (Jn 15:15).

God is not a solitary being without relationships. God is community of three divine Persons. God is Father in relationship to another Person, who is His Son. The Father knows Himself so perfectly that His thought is the Eternal Wisdom that is a distinct Person. The Father gives all that He has to the Son, communicates Himself wholly to the Son in all that He is, so that the Son is His *perfect image* (Col. 1:15). The Son is *wholly open,* accepts that total communication of being from the Father. While the Father manifests the graciousness of giving, the Son manifests the graciousness of receiving.

The mutual love of the Father and the Son is itself a personal reality which we call the Holy Spirit, who is the spirit of mutuality and communication.

So, according to Christian belief, what is at the heart of reality is not merely a "prime mover," "uncaused cause" or "prime matter"; nor is it some abstract unity. It is a communion, the mutual love of the three members of the Trinitarian community.

The sum and substance of the New Testament is contained in the prayer of Jesus for His disciples at the Last Supper: "That they may all be one; even as thou, Father, art in me, and I in thee, that they also may be in us, so that the world may believe that thou hast sent me. The glory which thou hast given me I have given to them, *that they may be one even as we* are *one*" (17:21–22).

There is a *we* in the Godhead. As we confess in the Creed attributed to St. Athanasisus: "We worship one God in the Trinity in unity, without either confusing the persons or dividing the substance; for the Father's person is one, the Son's is another, the Holy Spirit's another; but the Godhead of the Father, the Son and the Holy Spirit is one, their glory is equal, their majesty coequal.''[2] Here we have the fulfillment of the impossible dream of total distinction and total union. We have a closer union than lovers ever dreamt of, with one substance, one existence; and yet there is distinction sharper than between two human individuals. What distinguishes also communicates the divine nature which unites.

To the extent that we can penetrate the divine mystery, the seeming contradiction is resolved by the fact that the perfect *self-identity* of each Person permits the *total sharing*. According to the scripturally founded explanation of St. Augustine, this sharing consists in knowing and loving. The life of the Blessed Trinity consists in perfect and everlasting *knowing and being known, loving and being loved*. The three divine Persons are completely transparent to each other. The Father is person by expressing His being, love, glory and wisdom in His Word, the Son, who is the true image and radiance of His glory. When He manifests Himself, He glorifies His Son. "This is my beloved Son with whom I am well pleased" (Mt. 3:17). The Son is the total response to the Father's pouring out in love. He does nothing by Himself, says nothing by Himself. "I do always the things that please him" (Jn. 8:29). He manifests the Father, constantly announces the glory of the Father. "Now they know that everything that thou hast given me is from thee; for I have given them the words which thou gavest me" (Jn. 17:7–8).

The Holy Spirit is the unifying bond, the "being with" of the Father and the Son in mutual self-giving. The Spirit "will not speak on his own authority, but whatever he hears he will speak. . . . He will glorify me, for he will take what is mine and declare it to you" (Jn. 16:13–14).

When God created the world, it was to freely communicate His goodness, reach out to share something of Himself, to share His infinite love. God loves, not out of need, but out of infinite abundance.

When God made man, He fashioned him in His own image (Gen. 1:27). He made him male and female, as complementary beings needing one another for fulfillment of self. God wanted man and woman to share in the life and love of the Trinitarian community in the family, the primary form of interpersonal communion, the basic cell of the human community.

Through Christ's coming forth from the Father and returning to Him, there is opened up the divine plan of mankind being called to be sharers, "concelebrants" of the love of the Triune God.

The Church has used the terms *person* and *nature* to express the ineffable mystery of the Blessed Trinity. While the everyday experience of a person as a center of knowledge, love and free activity helps in catching a glimpse of the inner mystery of God, the revelation of the Trinity in turn casts light on human personality and its manner of fulfillment. In the Persons of the Trinity the reality of self-possession and self-communication are verified in an eminent degree. Total distinction and mutual immanence go together. Thus we have an assurance that the greater the genuine self-identity, the greater is also the possibility of communion, and that loving self-giving is the way of achieving personality fulfillment. True love unites without devouring, burns without consuming. The Trinity suggests a middle course between selfish individualism and stifling possessiveness. Thus we see the relevance of the Trinitarian doctrine in actual life.[3]

2. CHRISTIAN PERSONALISM[4]

Modern philosophy has brought out the importance of the concept of personality.

a) It implies *autonomy,* "to be in-itself and for-itself." It is individualization not only "from below" (described by material qualities), but also "from above" (by the unique call to existence). Hence the ethical life of man must be viewed not only in its general aspects but also in the light of the unique vocation of each person.

b) Human personality also implies *self-realization* through free activity. Not only is the person the subject of moral activity, but this latter contributes to the development of the personality, which is only radically given at birth. Because of this developmental aspect, human action cannot be judged in abstraction from the concrete state of the acting person.

c) Thirdly, human personality implies *responsibility*. Inner activity does not indicate isolation from exterior involvement. Man develops his personality only through intersubjectivity. He is not passive before God. He is called upon to respond to the call of God to build up the human community and the whole world.

Christian revelation confirms this vision. The infinite transcendent God addresses man as gift and call to a shared partnership in His own reality and life. God enters into an I-thou relationship with man. He Himself assumes human nature and lays down His life for man's salvation. Thereby, finite man achieves absolute value and significance. Each man becomes more than an individual representative of an abstract species. His individuality cannot be dissolved in a greater whole or collectivity. He may never be treated as an object or as a means to an end. Not even God Himself ever disregards his freedom.

Hence the Christian religious experience, based on salvation history, suggests the concept of person as that of "the corporeal-spiritual being who freely disposes of himself and who is of absolute significance." In this perspective, in the classical definition of Boethius: *"rationalis naturae individua substantia,"* *individua* is to be understood as "of unique value" or "with self-identity," and *substantia* as "insistence" or "subsistence in self" calling for "ek-sistence" or openness to others and the world.[5]

The finite human person is a spiritual being localized in space and time in his bodily reality. Though called to freedom, he cannot completely possess or dispose of himself. The material element in him, the biological and psychic determinisms as well as external influences limit the scope of his freedom. He cannot fully catch up with himself. He can try to fulfill his nature only by successive historical acts. But this should not lead to pessimistic conclusions. Man is called by God's grace to transcend his limitations, to realize his potentialities more and more, and to humanize the world. His activity goes beyond mere survival and propagation. It is directed to communication (language), beauty (art), worship (liturgy), discovery of truth (science), mastery over nature (technology) and social organization (politics). All these activities should be inspired by mutual love and respect.

Here we may briefly present some modern concepts of personalism and evaluate them according to the Christian view:

a) *Existentialism* is a revolt against traditionalism with its rigid structures as well as against the stifling anonymity of modern industrial society. It brings out well the tension between the impersonal forces that tend to submerge man and the unique worth of the human person. It accords primacy to the demands of the unique situation over fixed norms. But there is a tendency to individualism and atomization of society which could be overcome by introducing the spirit of community and stressing the basic values of man.

b) *Marxism* seeks to bridge the gulf between thought and reality. It identifies the various forms of alienation in human society and attributes them to feudal or capitalist forms of production with their class exploitation. According to Marx himself, the inherent contradictions within capitalism will bring about the downfall of the system and usher in an era of equality and universal prosperity. An enlightened group is called upon to be the vanguard of such a revolution. While there is a latent respect for the human person manifested by the ardent desire for equality and for overcoming alienations, the system is unable to provide adequately for the true welfare of the human person because of its materialistic and deterministic presuppositions, which would lead to collectivism of the masses rather than community of free persons.

c) *Liberalism* is apparently the opposite of Marxism. It strongly emphasizes individual liberties; but it is based on exploitative capitalism, so that the fundamental freedoms of which it makes much are, in practice, restricted to the privileged classes, who prosper at the expense of the dispossessed "proletariat." It, too, is based on a materialistic concept of man and society, with the emphasis on production and the unbridled profit motive at the cost of personhood. It is revealing that capitalist elements like class-structured society, private ownership and competition are validated by the fact that these have their roots in primitive animal instincts.[6]

Today, in an age of unparalleled organization and socialization, the promotion of the dignity and freedom of the human person is of extreme importance. There is need to respect absolutely every person for himself, regardless of sex, age, race, social status, wealth and usefulness. The worth of a human person cannot be gauged merely by his economic contribution or social usefulness. Vatican II has warned: "Everyone must consider his every neighbor without exception *as another self,* taking into account first of all his life and the means necessary to living it with dignity."[7]

One who does not respect the image of God in another does not respect his own person. Racial discrimination, castism, economic exploitation, cultural imperialism, subhuman living conditions, torture, disgraceful working conditions and bonded labor are some of the many evils which have been too much neglected by moral theologians. There is no doubt that prostitution, murder, mutilation and abortion strike at the root of reverence for the human person.

3.   COMMUNITARIAN VOCATION[8]

Intersubjectivity, or communication, is basic to human personality. Not only is it "not good for man to be alone," but man in his very essence cannot be an isolated individual; the whole of his nature directs him to community living. If corporeity indicates man's solidarity with material creation, intersubjectivity marks him out as a specific being.

Man exists in a web, as it were, of innumerable contacts that bind him to other people. The web forms a kind of field in which every movement causes change, new tensions and releases. At the very heart of man, therefore, there is intersubjectivity. It is not something he can choose to avoid or escape. The self is not a packaged object that can be kept wrapped up. "The self I give to another is one that I acquire in giving."[9]

Biologically, man, from the first moment of union of sperm and ovum, is the fruit of mutual interaction; but precisely as man, he is the fruit of love. Man is born into a basic community or family. He grows and develops through sharing life in the community, without which he would not develop as a human being. Today, this concept of person-in-community needs to be emphasized in the face of extreme individualism on the one hand, and excessive collectivism on the other.

Man, as member of a historical community, is a cultural being. He is influenced, though not wholly determined, by the prevailing modes of thought, economic conditions, social structures and all other factors that make up the concrete life of the particular society in which he lives. His openness to the divine invitation and his response will, to a certain extent, be culturally conditioned.

The life of the individual is also conditioned as a sexual being, male or female. The implications of this fact should be kept in mind while discussing moral education. It should be noted, however, that the respective roles of male and female and their opportunities for human development have been culturally determined to a large extent. There is need for reevaluating their roles in the light of experience and the Gospel vision of the equality of man and woman.

The communitarian vocation of man as well as the needs of the times demand that we go beyond a narrowly individualistic ethic. Vatican II declares: "It grows increasingly true that the obligations of justice and love are fulfilled only if each person, contributing to the common good, according to his abilities and the needs of others, also promotes and assists the public and private institutions dedicated to bettering the conditions of human life."[10] The Council censures those who neglect the needs of society, resort to various frauds and deceptions in avoiding just taxes, and ignore laws designed to protect public health and safety.

The full communitarian range of the Christian vocation can be understood in the context of God's self-giving to mankind. God's revelation has always been directed to a people or community. Vatican II has brought out this idea in one of its key texts: "It has pleased God to make men holy and save them not merely as individuals without any mutual bonds, but by making them into a single people, a people which acknowledges Him in truth and serves Him in holiness."[11] God wants to save men through community. He wants one organism, one medium of His saving presence in the world. This is the Church, the Spirit-filled community, the Body of Christ. "For all of us, who are sons of God and constitute one family in Christ, as long as we remain in communion with one another in mutual charity and in one praise of the Trinity, we are responding to the deepest vocation of the Chruch and partaking in a foretaste of the liturgy of consummate glory."[12]

This does not contradict the communitarian vocation of the whole of mankind, since, according to the Council, "by her relationship with Christ, the Church is a kind of sacrament or sign of intimate union with God, and of the unity of all mankind. She is also the instrument of such union and unity."[13] She does not exist for herself, but for the sake of mankind in order to be a leaven of communion for all men, since she catches up all men's natural aspirations for unity and gives them hope of perfect realization in the communion of saints. In Scripture we see that, beyond the historic covenant with Abraham and Moses which founded the Israelite People of God, Yahweh makes a covenant through Noah with the whole of mankind (Gen. 5:8). We could go even further back to the very origins of man. The creation narratives describe the original love-relationship of God with mankind. The immediate consequence of the rebellion of man against God was disruption in human relationships.

The covenant with Abraham was itself clearly meant to affect all men: "By you all the families of the earth will bless themselves" (Gen. 12:3; 26:4; 28:14). Despite the infidelity of the poeple, Yahweh remains faithful and promises through the prophets a new and everlasting covenant (Jer. 31:31ff; Ez. 16:60). This was to be realized in the new poeple that Christ called to Himself, in which there was to be no difference between Jew or Greek, slave or free, male or female (cf. Gal. 3:28).

Paul takes up the famous parable of classical writers concerning the body and its members and gives it a new depth, since now it is the Spirit of Christ that unites the members of the Church with each other by uniting them with the Lord (cf. Rom. 12:4; 1 Cor. 12:12–14). The Christian is called to responsible service that builds up the Church. He must have a special concern for the weaker brethren. "If food is the cause of my brother's falling, I will never eat meat, lest I cause my brother to fall" (1 Cor. 8:13; cf. Rom. 14:13–21).

The nature of the Church as communion comes out clearly in the long Eucharistic passage in 1 Cor. 10–13. Paul makes the strong affirmation: "Because there is one bread, we who are many are one body" (10:16). When the Christians gather for the Eucharistic love feast, they must learn to "discern the body" (11:28–29): namely, recognize that the Church is the Body of Christ. The Ephesians are asked to be "eager to maintain the unity of the Spirit in the bond of peace" (4:3). Paul's most sublime passage on the mystery of Christ is meant to foster the same kind of humility, sacrifice and love that Christ Himself manifested (Phil. 2:1–11).

The gift of the Spirit, in fact, binds the first Christians into a dynamic community of love. The Acts of the Apostles give us a graphic picture of this life. "And all who believed were together and had all things in common" (2:44). "Now the company of those who believed were of one heart and soul, and no one said that any of the things which he possessed was his own, but they had everything in common" (4:32).

This corresponds to the deepest aspirations of man. To be human is to enter into a network of human relationships. The very process of human understanding depends on learning a language, a vehicle of communication, and on receiving ideas and ideals from one's familial, local and wider community. It is through interchange that one acquires knowledge, becomes aware of his human vocation, and is able to respond to it.

From the communitarian nature and vocation of man, Enda McDonagh deduces an important moral criterion: "The true response of man to God's gift is the promotion of the community of mankind, the development of mankind as God's people. Whatever human activity then promotes this community is a correct response to God, a morally good activity; whatever hinders or disrupts the community is a failure in response, a morally bad activity. Community building becomes the criterion or norm of morality. It is for this reason above all that one speaks of the Christian ethic as community ethic.''[14]

We should note that it is not only individuals who have obligations toward society. The subject of moral obligation may be a group or society. One has only to think of the concern which a society feels for the victims of natural calamities. Today, privileged groups are beginning to feel their obligations toward those who are suffering from injustice, exploitation, war, racial or class discrimination. Still, only a small segment of the privileged classes has been moved to do something to right these wrongs. The response is still meagre and often diversionary, not much different from the way affluent individuals in the past salved their conscience by giving out doles to the poor. It is still too much like supererogatory generosity in the spirit of patronage rather than inspired by basic justice. Nevertheless, the growing awareness of group responsibility is a welcome feature.

Christian personalism would endorse the distinction introduced by Ferdinand Tonnies (1887) between *Gemeinsehaft* (community with interpersonal relationships) and *Gesellschaft* (social organization).[15] But the two need not be opposed. They are complementary. Personalism with the corresponding community dimension stresses the dignity of each human person, his basic rights and the importance of mutual relationships. But it should take into account the social context in which these develop. Social structures do not evolve through blind fate but are largely brought about through conscious decisions of individuals, especially of the enlightened elite, who have greater opportunities and capacities to influence society. We should admire the courage of those who dare to withstand the pressure of environmental forces.

Besides, I-thou-we relationships should not be confined to basic groups, like the family or small friendly communities, but extended to wider spheres of life, lest these relationships be stifled by massive forms of impersonal structures or the members of the smaller groups be alienated from the real world. While basic communities can provide personal fulfillment to the members and be a ferment of community in the world if they are rightly oriented, they must constantly beware of being shut in on themselves and forming little ghettos which, in the long run, will only disintegrate and bring on frustration.

Vatican II has restored a communitarian vision to religious life, which is an intensified form of baptismal life.[16] It is the concentrated presence of the ecclesial community in the world. Every religious community should be a living embodiment of the first Christian community in Jerusalem. The three vows must be understood and practiced as three expressions of love, of total sharing, of participation in community building. Rules and regulations have meaning only inasmuch as they foster this community spirit. The relationship between superior and confreres must be inspired by the same spirit.

Just as the Trinity is the unity of three distinct Persons, the community should also maintain *unity in diversity*. Each person must develop his personality, cultivate his talents to the maximum extent possible. The community itself should foster the distinctive characteristics of each member. There should be no attempt at forcing a colorless uniformity or rigid conformity. All should realize that each member has a unique personality and, hence, a unique contribution to make to the community, without which the community would be that much poorer.

There must be greater and greater interpersonal communication. For this, there is need for initial acceptance and an atmosphere of openness and trust. Mutual dialogue should bring about genuine encounter of personalities leading to greater acceptance. The differences in temperament and ideas are not suppressed but harmonized in order to achieve a more perfect unity. The talents of each are made to serve the common good while enriching the personality of each. In the Trinity, the fullness of personal existence coincides wtih the fullness of mutual exchange. This shows that there is no opposition between the gift of self and self-fulfillment. Between the one and the other, there is a constant interplay which makes both advance.

From this it follows that the relation between the different members should not be based on the principle of "peaceful coexistence" or on domination or paternalism. It should not be characterized merely by social roles but by increased sharing of life.

4.   PERSON-CENTERED MORALITY[17]

The dichotomy between body and soul produced individualism, a one-sided preoccupation with "saving one's soul." The *devotio moderna* of the fifteenth and sixteenth centuries, which left a deep imprint on popular piety during the succeeding generations, was strongly affected by this trend. Even as beautiful a book as the classical *Imitation of Christ* betrays an undue tendency toward individualism. The author quotes with approval the words of Seneca: "As often as I have been amongst men, I have returned less a man."[18] There is no concern for the transformation of structures or for the welfare of the human community. It is not surprising, then, that lesser devotional works tend to foster a piety divorced from the day-to-day cares of life. One is supposed to forget everything about real life when one enters a church to pray, and concentrate on how to make "progress in the spiritual life," on how to "gain merit." The world is looked upon as a prison from which one has to escape in order to be holy.

However, Christian life does not consist merely in the faithful observance of a set of rules (*law-centered* approach) or the performance of a series of good acts (*act-centered* approach), but is a personal response to the call of a personal God within the community (*person-centered* approach).

When one experiences the moral call to response as emanating from the medium, for instance, of the bodily need of one's neighbor, with its implicit call for recognition and respect, the moral response must be in the direction of the other. Turning back on the self by refusing to answer the call or responding to it only as a means of promoting one's own spiritual interests is a failure to respect the other as other and, hence, is a moral failure. One is called to break out of the self, to reach out to the other by recognizing, respecting and meeting his need.

Interpersonal relationship means recognizing the other primarily as *gift,* a free and enriching offer. The first reaction called for is one of thanksgiving for the gift. Otherwise, the moral call to respect the rights of others will be experienced as a burden. The presence of the other with his irreducible difference will constitute a threat. There may be the fear that the other might destroy me, absorb me into his world, or at least not recognize my independent existence. But the fear is largely due to my not wanting to recognize the other's autonomy and uniqueness. There is need for transforming the threat-fear reaction into a gift-call relationship.

Non-personal realities must be seen as means of personal relationships. If there is a preoccupation with things rather than personal expression, there is danger of depersonalization and dehumanization. One of the major moral tasks in an increasingly technological world is to awaken and develop sensitivity to this personal dimension. Production figures and the profit motive should not be allowed to smother the human personality.

Without recognition and respect for persons, there will be blind swings in sexual mores from Puritanism to permissiveness. While Puritanism, which tries to repress sex as dirty, degrades persons, permissiveness trivializes sexual communication and inevitably diminishes respect for the other as well as for oneself.

The dignity of the human person demands that we never treat another as a *thing,* as a *means,* even for a supposedly good purpose. The personal dignity of a man may never be violated even to accomplish the greatest good. Consequently, nothing can justify torture.

To relate to another personality, I must know him as a person, as a *subject,* not as an *it.* When I objectify another, I make him impersonal;

I view him as an object, outside of and away from me. I tend to compute his value or usefulness for me. When I treat another as an *it,* I threaten his reality as a person; I cut myself off from the rich reality of this other person and so impoverish myself.[19]

It would be wrong to consider another merely as an occasion for practicing virtue, to the neglect of his unique worth and basic rights. It is deplorable that some pious rich often treat poor people as the "object" of commiseration and condescension or as opportunities of practicing charity or gaining merit.

It is not right to try to achieve results at the expense of persons. Even from the point of view of efficiency, it does not pay in the long run to disregard the feelings and interests of others. It is only by drawing out what is best in each one that we can achieve truly great works.

Concentrating on respect for persons would go a long way in promoting good moral behavior. For instance, the primary norm for the boy-girl relationship is mutual respect. The boy must respect the personal dignity of the girl and not look upon her merely as an attractive body or as an object of pleasure. The girl must respect herself and learn to draw respect from the boy, insist on being respected, and avoid subtle ways of tantalizing him. Thoughtless reactions like infatuation or rapid "falling in love" followed by equally rapid "falling out of love" are signs of personal immaturity.

Similarly, workers should be treated as persons and not as cogs in the wheel of industry or as a mere factor in the process of production.

Such a personal approach does not exclude the need for concrete moral norms. But these again should be understood, not as lifeless, impersonal demands, but as modes of promoting personal dignity.

A person-centered approach will suggest a program of conscience-formation based, not on mechanical conditioning or imposed patterns of behavior, but on the development of a free and loving response to the call of God. Personalism admits a sane flexibility and dynamism amidst continuity, according to the very law of life. The law of growth will be accepted as an essential dimension of moral life. As Bernard Häring puts it: "Man's dynamism and creativity, granted by God to his image, is a mirror of God's design for mankind and for each individual person, and is an essential part of the Christian vocation. By responding to it, man renders thanks to his Creator and gives witness to his faith that God is the fullness of life."[20]

————○————

Notes to Chapter VII

1. Cf. Ceslaus Spicq. *The Trinity in our Moral Life According to St. Paul,* Westminster, Md., Newman, 1963; John J. Greehy, "The Blessed Trinity and the Christian Life," in *Moral Theology Renewed,* ed. by Enda McDonagh, Dublin, Gill, 1965, pp. 70–84; J. B. Mackey, "Preaching on the Blessed Trinity," *Furrow,* 21 (1970), 6–18; G. F. Macknell, "The Trinity and Human Love," *New Blackfriars,* 53 (1972), 270–75; Joseph Mattam, "The Mystery of the Trinity in Christian Life," *Vidya Jyoti,* 40 (1976), 338–48.

2. See text in J. N. D. Kelly, *The Athanasian Creed,* London, Adam & Charles Black, 1964, pp. 17–18.

3. Though with some exaggeration. Karl Rahner remarks: "One might almost dare to affirm that if the doctrine of the Trinity were to be erased as false, most religious literature could be preserved almost unchanged throughout the process." *Theological Investigations.* London, Darton, Longman & Todd, 1966, Vol. IV, p. 78.

4. Cf. Jean Mouroux, *The Meaning of Man,* New York, Sheed and Ward, 1948, pp. 115ff; Martin Buber, *I and Thou.* New York, Scribner's, 2nd ed., 1958; Rosemary Haughton. *The Transformation of Man,* London, Collins, 1967.

5. Cf. Max Muller and Alois Halder, "Person," in *Sacramentum Mundi.* New York, Herder & Herder, 1968, Vol. IV, p. 405.

6. See R. Ardrey, *The Territorial Imperative,* London, 1967.

7. *GS,* art. 27.

8. Cf. Helen M. Beha, *Living Community,* Patna Sanjivan, Milwaukee. Bruce, 1973; Helen M. Mencel, "The Church as Community," *Bible Today,* 1970, no. 49, 39–46.

9. K. Gallagher, *Philosophy of Gabriel Marcel,* New York, Fordham University Press, 1962, p. 69.

10. *GS,* art. 30.

11. *LG*, art. 9.

12. *Ibid.*, art. 52

13. *Ibid.*, art. 1.

14. *Invitation and Response*, Dublin, Gill and Macmilan, 1972, p. 53.

15. Cf. translation, *Community and Society*, New York, Harper and Row, 1963.

16. Cf. *Perfectae Caritatis*, art, 15.

17. Bernard Häring, *Morality Is for Persons*, New York, Farrar, Straus & Giroux, 1971;
     Louis Janssens, "Personalist Morals," *Louvain Studies* 3 (1970), 5–16.

18. Book I, Ch. 20.

19. Cf. Helen M. Beha, *op. cit.*, p. 25–26.

20. *Morality Is for Persons*, p. 30.

CHAPTER VIII

Christocentric Morality

1. THE PLEROMA OF CHRIST

Christianity is not an adherence to a doctrine nor an observance of an ethical code, but the *personal following* of Christ, the God-man. Jesus Himself prayed for His disciples: "And this is eternal life: that they may know thee, the only true God, and Jesus Christ whom thou hast sent" (Jn. 17:3). With the Christ-event, the self-revealing and self-giving of God to man attained its fullest depth and widest range. In Him also the human response reached its highest degree. He is "the Way, the Truth and the Life" (Jn. 14:16), since in Him God comes close to man and man can effectively come to God.

Christ is the *prototype* according to which we are all created and to which we must all conform. "He is the image of the invisible God, the firstborn of all creation. . . In him all the fullness (*pleroma*) of God was pleased to dwell" (Col. 1:15, 19). The Father willed Christ, the God-man, to be "the firstborn among many believers" (Rom. 8:29). Hence, all of us together must regard ourselves as forming a brotherly community.

Paul expresses Christocentric morality thus: "He is the source of your life in Christ Jesus, whom God made our wisdom, our righteousness and sanctification and redemption" (1 Cor. 1:30). By speaking of the "law of Christ" (Gal. 6:2), he expresses the centrality of Christ in moral life.

When Paul says that "in him all things were created through him and for him" (Col. 1:16), he refers, not simply to the eternal Word of

God, but to the God-man, the eternal Word made flesh. Jesus Christ, the incarnate Word of God, is the original pattern in whom and toward whom all creation, particularly man, was created. He is the archetype of all human and Christian existence. He contains in Himself all those natural and supernatural potentialities that every man is called upon to realize. He is thus the source and measure of the life and grace that comes to every man from God. He is the Creator and Head of all creation. The entire cosmos awaits the new order, in which the Son will manifest Himself as the Lord of the universe, gathering the redeemed to Himself in one Body and offering them to the Father.

Pierre Teilhard de Chardin in his evolutionary perspective shows very well that everything in the cosmos has a Christic sense; that, because of the incarnation, the Son of God is organically linked to the universe; that every advance in being is at the same time a march toward the fullness of Christ, who is "the structural axis of the world" and "the center of the great cosmic sphere."

According to Teilhard, love energy, the only force capable of moving free man toward unity, must have something to draw it. So the whole process of hominization postulates a real and present Center, an *Omega-point*. Christian revelation, he believes, can bridge the gap between the philosophical hypothesis of such a Center and the historical fact. He identifies the Christ of revelation with the Omega-point postulated by evolution. "In place of the vague forces of convergence, demanded as a terminus for evolution, we now have the well-defined personal reality of the Incarnate Word, in whom all things hold together."[1] The success of evolution depends on the existence and discovery of a centralized star which is not some*thing*, but some*one*.

Christ is, therefore, the author of evolution as well as the focal point which polarizes the whole evolutionary process. He is the point of encounter between God and the world, the place where the two realities are joined in embrace. In the person of Jesus of Nazareth, the real Omega took flesh and became part of that evolutionary current for which He Himself is responsible.

Teilhard has developed the Pauline doctrine that Christian spirituality is the formation of the pleroma, the future of the whole Christ in His Mystical Body. He has shown that Christian perfection is a sharing in the cosmogenesis, since Christ forms, as it were, a physical center for mankind and the whole material universe in its evolutionary movement. "Through his Incarnation he entered not only into manhood but also into the universe that bears mankind, and this he did, not simply in the capacity of an element associated with it, but with the dignity and function of a directive principle, or center, upon which every form of love and every affinity converge."[2]

Thus, because of the Divine Milieu of the personal omnipresence of Christ, "all the good that I can do, *opus et operatio,* is physically gathered in by something of itself, into the reality of the consummated Christ."[3]

Teilhard felt strongly that "the great schism which is threatening the Church" is the fact that "Christian" and "human" no longer tend to coincide. Hence he wants the Christian to be awakened to the realization that the whole of his human effort can be Christified if it is seen as a participation in the process by which God builds the pleroma of Christ.

2. CHRIST IS THE NORM OF MORALITY

As we shall see later, since there is a natural order of creation, there is also a natural moral law, but it does not stand by itself. It is subsumed into the single concrete "law" for all men: the "law of Christ." This is not simply superadded to the natural order. The overlordship of Christ produces an integral attitude by which the natural duties are colored and transfigured.

Although we cannot reproduce the historical existence of Jesus, we can imitate or relive, each in his own way, the pattern of His life in our life situation today. We are called to love our neighbor as He loved us (Jn. 13:34). We must abide in His love (Jn. 15:10). "He who says that he abides in him ought to walk in the same way in which he walked" (1 Jn. 2:16).

Paul asks the Philippians: "Have this mind among yourselves, which you have in Christ Jesus" (2:5). For the Christian, to live is to "put on Christ" (Rom. 13:14). The man Jesus is not only the manifestation of the ineffable holiness of God, He is also the total adequate response to God's absolute summons to holiness, the mirror of every religious and moral perfection.

The disciple of Christ is called not just to learn from Him as from other rabbis. He must acquire His attitudes and share His life and destiny, not only by an external association, but by an internal, transforming participation as of branches of the same vine or members of the same body. Sonship to the Father is, at the same time, brotherhood with each other. Sharing the life of Christ, the Son of God, His disciples become "sons in the Son." In every moral situation, they are faced with an invitation to respond to the Father as sons.

The events of Christ's earthly life, like washing the disciples' feet, are examples for our *imitation*. "For I have given you an example, that you should do as I have done to you" (Jn. 13:15). Yet imitation does not mean mere repetition of the external gesture. The Christian must realize his self-identity and, hence, try to pattern his life after the model of Christ according to the particular circumstances of his own life. Consequently, we have not so much to copy Him externally as to *follow Him personally*, to enter into personal communion with Him (cf. Mk. 1:16–20; 12:14; 3:13).

Christ is not merely a moral authority or a "Teacher of Righteousness," as in the Qumran sect. We do not stand near Him looking over His shoulders, as it were, and perhaps following the movements of His pointing finger, but we enter into an intimate relationship with Him. We must share in the living reality that is Christ, be united with Him as branches on a vine (Jn. 15:1–5). We are called to *self-surrender* of the whole person to Christ, leading to a mystical identity with Him, so that we could say with Paul: "It is no longer I who live, but *Christ lives in me*" (Gal. 2:20).

Hence, the most basic source of Christian morality is, not the explicit moral teaching of the prophets or even the sayings of Jesus, but the very Person of Jesus Himself, who is the center-point as well as the end-point of the relationship between God and man. Jesus' attention to the needs of the people, His particular concerns for the poor and the sick, the spontaneity and warmth of His response to people are a tremendous inspiration to His followers. Jesus has also shown how satisfaction of external needs is subordinate to the ultimate needs of salvation and to bringing about the Kingdom of the Father. The moral teaching of Jesus is better illuminated when it is understood as the articulation of His own life-style.

Thus Christ becomes our *supreme "law,"* not so much because He sets external norms of action for us, as because He gives the *inner capacity* of being conformed to Him. "God's love has been poured out into our hearts through the Holy Spirit which has been given to us" (Rom. 5:5).

Vatican II does not favor a moral theology that is primarily a code of principles and obligations imposed upon the Christian, nor a view of Christ principally as a sublime ethical teacher. Christian moral theology should expose how man is personally called in Christ by a personal God to salvation and to a daily life in accordance with this call. Christocentric morality will not be mere conformity to a hidebound collection of rules. As Josef Fuchs puts it, "A moral theology that takes serious account of the meaning of 'vocation in Christ' must certainly display some of the dynamism that belongs to the existence of God's call to us, to the grace of the ever-active Holy Spirit within us, to the unending pursuit of a perfection we never fully achieve, and to the love that can never be adequately expressed and never sufficiently satisfied."[4]

According to Vatican II, the following of Christ as proposed by the Gospel is to be regarded by all religious communities as their supreme law.[5] However, the Council declares that "all the members [of the Church] ought to be molded into Christ's image until He is formed in them."[6] All Christians are made "sharers in the priestly, prophetic and kingly functions of Christ."[7] "As members, they share in a common dignity from their rebirth in Christ. They have the same filial grace and the same vocation to perfection."[8]

The Council further points out that not only Christians but all men are called to salvation in Christ, not only as a general destination but as a common vocation.[9]

3.   THE RESPONSIVE CHARACTER OF MORALITY

God's initiative in calling man to salvation and perfection in and through Christ, brings out the dialogical and responsive character of Christian morality. The coming of the Son of God in our flesh in order to share our life should enable us to appreciate the personal love of the Father calling for a personal response even when we obey the universal norms of morality.

This relational character of Christian morality must not be understood in narrow, individualistic terms. The I-thou relationship should be open to the we of the whole human family. The community range of Christian morality can be understood in the context of God's self-giving to mankind. God's revelation, we have seen, has always been directed to a people. It has been invitation to a convenant relationship. In the New Testament this emerges as the community of all mankind without distinction of Jew or Greek, bond or free, friend or foe. As a son of the Father in Christ, the Christian becomes a brother of every one of his fellowmen. Consequently, the Christian life can be summed up in love of God and love of neighbor, not excluding one's enemies. The new commandment of love is the primary and all-embracing expression of the new fellowship with God and neighbor in Christ. All other moral demands are only particular determinations of the love of sonship and brotherhood.

The communitarian character of the Christian vocation also reveals its historical dimension. Just as God's self-giving to mankind has a history, so necessarily has man's response. At the center of this development stands Jesus Christ. As the expected Messiah, the Redeemer and Lord who is to come, He directs every stage of God's relationship to man. So also He is for all, in varying degrees of realization, the unique way to the Father, whatever their conscious beliefs might be. Although we should not minimize the importance of explicit relationship to Him in His Church, neither should we neglect the role of Christ as the focal point of all history, as the invisible source of all grace and the term of all perfection.

The historical dimension also points to the need for growth in moral understanding and responsibility, through which each person and group has to pass amidst the vicissitudes of life.

In the perspective of Paul, the relational character of Christian morality embraces the whole universe. Albert R. Jonsen expresses this very well: "Christ is the norm of morality insofar as he is the expression of the relationship in which man exists with God. He is the norm insofar as his life, word and example manifest the values of fellowship and communion with God. This is more than external manifestation. It reveals that the Father's will and fellowship is expressed not only in the life, word and example of Jesus Christ, but also in all the personal and objective values of creation recapitulated in him. Thus the created order itself expresses the divine will for fellowship.[10]

We have already seen how Teilhard develops the cosmic dimension of man's relationship with God. This is very important in order to overcome the constant temptation to individualism, which is satisfied with an individual or narrow group relationship with God. In such a closed perspective, one could reach, not the real God, but a creation of one's own petty imagination.

Bonhoeffer expresses the universal dimension of Christ's life by saying that He was "a man for others." He was the responsible man *par excellence,* in that His whole life was given over to the service of others. What He is and means defines the reality to which all men are to conform in their response to each other and to the world, since He Himself has experienced the essence of the real in His own body as no one else has, having borne within Himself and fulfilled the essence of reality. "In Jesus Christ, the real man, the whole of reality is taken up and compressed together; in Him it has its origins and its essence and its goal. For that reason, it is only in Him and with Him as the point of departure, that there can be an action which is in accordance with reality."[11]

The Christian vocation in Christ is a gracious call. However, its *threat* aspect should not be neglected. As the gift of God reaches its climax in Jesus Christ, so also does the challenge to respond. "Everyone to whom much is given, of him will much be required" (Lk. 12:48). The proclamation of Simeon is a warning: "Behold, this child is set for the fall and rising of many in Israel . . . that thoughts out of many hearts may be revealed" (Lk. 2:34–35). Tyre and Sidon will be judged more tolerantly than the notorious Chorazin and Bethsaida, where Jesus performed His mighty works (Lk. 10:13f). Jesus challenges the self-complacency of people by declaring: "Do not think I have come to bring peace on earth; I have not come to bring peace, but a sword" (Mt. 10:34).

Still, in the context of man's sinful condition, the message of Jesus is above all a *reconciling* gift. Hence the whole call to respond has an aspect of repentance or return (*shub*), a radical change of heart (*metanoia*). It involves a constant liberation from selfish entanglements. There is need for *mortification* of egoistic desires. The total gift of self in return for the self-gift of God can be achieved only if there is willingness to take up the cross and follow Jesus.

4.   THE PASCHAL DIMENSION OF LIFE IN CHRIST[12]

The Exodus is the figure of redemption, of the victory of God over evil powers. For the Israelites, it meant the end of servitude and entry into the new life of free service of God. It was commemorated at the feast of the Passover, when unleavened bread was used. The prophets foretold the messianic times as a new Exodus (cf. Is. 43:19).

In the New Testament, the paschal mystery of the death and resurrection of Christ is the core of the apostolic preaching, as it is the center of the economy of salvation (cf. 1 Cor. 15:3–4; Phil. 2:6–11). The fundamental principle of Pauline morality is that we must be *conformed to the death and resurrection of Christ.* "We know that our old self was crucified with him so that the sinful body might be destroyed. . . . So you also must consider yourselves dead to sin and alive to God in Christ Jesus" (Rom. 6:5–11).

The whole of Christ's life leads up to the paschal mystery and, hence, the imitation and following of Christ must also be in the light of the same mystery. The program of Christian life is a *paschal program,* a "passage" of humanity with Christ to the Father. As we have risen with Christ, we must also have a new life in Christ. "If anyone is in Christ, he is a new creation; the old has passed away; behold, the new has come" (2 Cor. 5:17; cf. Rom. 8:13; Eph. 4:24; Col. 2:20; 3:3, 10).

Referring to the need for guarding against moral corruption, Paul says: "Cleanse out the old leaven, that you may be a new lump, as you are really unleavened. For Christ, our paschal Lamb, has been sacrificed. Let us, therefore, celebrate the festival, not with the old leaven, the leaven of malice and evil, but with the unleavened bread of sincerity and truth" (1 Cor. 5:7–8).

The rabbis made use of the image of leaven to designate the evil inclinations of the heart, which impede the accomplishment of God's will. Abstention from leavened bread, on the occasion of the Passover, which opened the new year (cf. Ex. 12:12), symbolized the desire to detach oneself from any impure element which might have infected the year that was ending. Christians have been "washed, sanctified and justified" in baptism (1 Cor. 6:11). They should "become what they are" and live a holy life in the sight of God. The disciple of Christ already shares in the Passover of Christ; so he should no longer be in possession of the "old leaven." It would be a contradiction. He has to renounce all sinful ways (Rom. 6:12–14).

In this perspective, the fight against sin, which is an essential component of the Christian life, loses the negative character that seems to paralyze so many. It is not a question of fleeing from a taboo, but of conforming oneself to the mystery of Christ. The Christian is a "new lump." He is called to "a newness of life" (Rom. 6:4). "If then you have been raised with Christ, seek the things that are above, where Christ is seated at the right hand of God" (Col. 3:1).

The once-for-all event of Christ's sacrifice inaugurates and renders possible a new era for humanity. The history of the redeemed sons of God becomes, as it were, the extension of the "hour" of Jesus (Jn. 13:1). Sharing in the resurrection and ascension of Christ leads the Christian to live in union with the heavenly Christ, to tend toward "the things that are above."

Christians are called to be "light" in the world. They should "walk as children of light" (Eph. 5:8). In 1 Pet.1–2, where many exegetes see a paschal and baptismal catechesis, the paschal typology is exploited to the full in the course of an exhortation to complete purification and renewal of life. The blood of the Lamb without stain has freed Christians from the "futile ways inherited from your fathers" (1:18) in order that they may be "holy in all their conduct" (1:14) and realize the true spiritual exodus from darkness of former times "to the marvelous light of God" (2:9). They are "to put away all malice and all guile and insincerity and envy and all slander" (2:1).

Paul exclaims: "Let us, therefore, celebrate the festival" (1 Cor. 5:8). The entire Christian existence should have the joyful character of a feast, since we are already participating in the resurrection of Christ. "Rejoice in the Lord always; again I will say, Rejoice" (Phil. 4:4). The joy of deliverance from evil should radiate from the heart of every Christian. That nostalgia for a feast without decline, underlying many Old Testament texts, will find its fulfillment in the heavenly liturgy, where the multitude of the redeemed singing the song of the Lamb will "follow the Lamb wherever he goes" (Rev. 14:8). But already now we enjoy a foretaste of that heavenly joy. There is no place in the Christian life for pessimism or anxious scrupulosity.

However, the experience of Christian joy in the present state does not eliminate sharing in the cross of Christ. It implies a constant *self-denial*. Jesus has said: "If any man comes after me, let him deny himself and take up his cross daily and follow me. For whosoever saves his life will lose it, and whosoever loses his life for my name's sake will save it" (Lk. 9:23–24). By our conformation with the self-emptying (*kenosis*) of Christ we participate in His glory (*doxa*) (cf. Phil. 2:7–9).

We have been "baptized into his death" (Rom. 6:3). "As often as you eat this bread and drink this cup, you proclaim the Lord's death until he comes" (1 Cor. 11:26). We do this, not only in word or sign, but in the actual experience of painful suffering in our daily life. We are "always carrying in our body the death of Jesus, so that the life of Jesus may be manifested in our mortal bodies" (2 Cor. 4:10). In other words, through participation in the paschal mystery of Christ, our sufferings become eminently fruitful.

Here is the ultimate solution of the problem of evil in the world. Try as we may, we can never entirely banish suffering in this earthly life. The broken body of Christ and the blood spurting from His wounds are definite proof that the Father loves us in spite of everything and that what often appears as meaningless suffering can become a means of personal fulfillment and growth of the community through union with the passion of Christ mediated by the Eucharist. During Diocletian's persecution (ca. 300), the martyrs of Abitana cried: "Without the Sunday Supper we cannot live." Union with the passion of Christ transforms and ennobles all the toil, pain and anxiety of man and gives him the courage and strength to rejoice even in the midst of the sufferings of this life because of the fruit that can be derived from them.

The new Passover accomplished by Jesus is shared with all men, but it attains its fullness in them only at the end of time. Life on earth assumes, then, the form of a *pilgrimage* toward the final fulfillment.

It is a launching out into the unknown, but with the assurance of the Lord's presence and protection. This has tremendous consequences for Christian morality. While prudence has to be used in carefully weighing the values involved in arriving at a decision, there is always an element of risk, which is actually an aspect of trust in God.

5. FULFILLMENT AND RENOUNCEMENT

Jesus said: "I came that they may have life, and have it abundantly" (Jn. 10:10). As Teilhard de Chardin points out: "It is a truly Christian duty to grow, even in the eyes of men, and to make one's talents bear fruit, even though they be natural. It is part of the essential Catholic vision to look upon the world as making . . . a specific power of knowing and loving, whose transfigured term is charity, but whose roots and elemental sap lie in the discovery and delectation of everything that is true and beautiful in creation."[13]

Authentic Christianity does not approve of hedonism or the unbridled indulgence of the lower passions, which would oppress the spirit and debase the passions themselves. But it promotes true fulfillment at all levels. St. Paul has no hesitation in saying: "Whatever is true, whatever is honorable, whatever is just, whatever is pure, whatever is lovely, whatever is gracious, if there is any excellence, if there is anything worthy of praise, think about these things" (Phil. 4:8).

The evangelical counsels themselves have nothing to do with a negative attitude toward human life and its values. Teilhard has expressed this beautifully: "I want, by practicing the counsels of perfection, to salvage through self-denial all the heavenly fire imprisoned within the threefold concupiscence of the flesh, of avarice, of pride; in other words, to hallow, through chastity, poverty and obedience, the power enclosed in love, in gold, in independence.[14]

A certain detachment conduces to a better appreciation of God's creation. St. Francis of Assisi, when he had renounced his patrimony, could experience the whole creation as belonging to him. It became for him an object of contemplation through which he could reach God.

Some detachment from earthly reality helps in appreciating its reference to the Absolute which is the final end of all things. It also brings out a certain inner liberation.

Early Christian ascetics reacted against a frivolous society that misused earthly pleasures. Unfortunately, some of them came to distrust any spontaneous impulse and condemned all enjoyment of sensible pleasures, even the most innocent ones. Some of them even tortured themselves. There is need for avoiding these excesses by adopting a positive attitude toward all creation without, however, ignoring the value of a right kind of detachment.

The mysteries of the incarnation and resurrection show that the whole of Christian life is a joyous and gracious acceptance of God's salvation, which penetrates the whole of creation. Christian *renouncement* must be understood in this context. "Christian asceticism must above all correspond to life. This means that self-denial must be integrated into a life of worshipful love of God and loving service of one's neighbor, looking toward the blessed liberty of the children of God."[15]

The Gospel emphatically calls for *self-denial*. Still, it is not the authentic self that is to be denied, but all that prevents genuine growth, especially the egoistic tendency of fallen man. St. Paul is quite radical in speaking about *mortification:* "Put to death [mortify] therefore what is earthly in you" (Col. 3:5). But he is referring to all that is disorderly in man.

As a result, it is not life that is to be destroyed, but what hinders the fullness of life. It is not a fight against the ego, but against an egocentric way of life. Mortification is a breaking through the crust of the ego so that the deeper personality may be revealed.

Besides, mortification concerns not so much the body as the inordinate tendencies in the whole self. "Mortification does not attack the body, but especially spiritual pride, self-glorification and self-righteousness. It is, however, also an effort to subject the body and its passions to the spirit that is turned toward Christ."[16]

All Christian mortification must be based on a positive acceptance of and respect for the created order, and a sense of responsibility for the development of the world and fidelity to one's temporal task. The body as the expression of the human spirit must be respected. There should be no element of masochism or self-hatred or depreciation of the body and material things. No opposition should be set up between the body and the soul. The Gospel call to renouncement is an invitation, not to suppress our emotions or potentialities, but to wrestle with the forces that block development of human life. Though self-denial for its own sake is unchristian, still there is need for discipline and sacrifice in order to achieve genuine fulfillment.

Mortification of the body should be understood as the process of harmonizing the senses with the movement of the spirit toward God. Dominating the disorder of the senses has a painful aspect, but the process should lead to serenity and joy.

Basically, Christian asceticism is an exercise of faith or total self-surrender to God. Thereby, man renounces any isolated attempt of his own to find the meaning of his own existence, of the world in general, and of its history. "He trusts him who has promised eternal life, without having any other guarantee than God himself."[17]

The eschatological perspective relativizes all earthly reality. In our pilgrim state, there should be no inordinate clinging to opinions, plans and structures. The greater glory of God (*A.M.D.G.*) should be the norm for using or renouncing any temporal reality.

Asceticism calls for accepting one's limitations and weakness. One may want to achieve all possible values and realize fulfillment in every line. But, in practice, one has to make painful choices. This may often lead to frustration. Everything does not proceed according to our predetermined plans. We must then be ready to adjust to the realities of life.

What is known as *Ignatian indifference* is a willingness to be called, implying painful renouncement and loving readiness to serve, just as Christ placed Himself entirely at the Father's disposal for the sake of the Kingdom and was ready to expose Himself to the hatred and malice of human selfishness. Christ undertook great hardships in the proclamation of the Gospel, readily suffered insults, and freely embraced the most cruel passion and death.

There is no doubt about the intrinsic sufficiency of Christ's passion for the redemption of the world inasmuch as it is a total response to the Father's will in the name of all humanity. Still, the disciple of Christ is called upon to share the redemptive process by accepting his share of pain and suffering. That is why Paul speaks of "always carrying in our body the death of Jesus" (2 Cor. 4:10). He says: "I bear the marks of the Lord Jesus in my body" (Gal. 6:17). "What is lacking of the sufferings of Christ I fill up in my flesh for His body, which is the Church" (1 Cor. 1:24). "I chastise my body and bring it under subjection" (1 Cor. 9:17).

The cross should be a symbol, not of sadness, but of a spirit of loving and joyful sacrifice. It must appear, not inhuman, but superhuman.

We have seen that the basic mortification is interior—the overcoming of the tendency to selfishness and pride. This abnegation of spirit needs to be expressed by external mortification. Even self-imposed practices of penance have their value, provided they are motivated by the desire to acquire greater self-integration and, thereby, the submission of the whole personality to God. Each age and culture has its own specific variations of bodily mortification which are good to the extent that they contribute to the wholeness of the personality.

Ascetic practices should not lead to Pharisaic self-righteousness. Besides, multiplicity of practices should not become an end in itself or a flight from life and its demands. Each person must learn to discern what is actually helpful to him in order to gain self-mastery and a spirit of generosity.

Bernard Häring calls exceeding the boundary of moderation "sinful mortification."[18] It can lead to grave danger to health or even moral disaster. Häring quotes the words attributed to St. Jerome: "There is no difference between bringing about death slowly over a long period of time or in a brief interval."[19]

The insights of depth psychology have shown that certain excesses are due to a hidden self-hatred. What is wrong with man is, not that he loves himself much, but that he often dislikes himself and unconsciously desires to inflict pain upon himself. At times he may unconsciously turn unresolved hostility toward others against himself. This is quite evident in a child who refuses to eat because he is angry with his mother. Unresolved guilt feelings may also lead to self-punishment. Hence it is necessary to have a positive outlook on life and to handle one's feelings of anger and guilt rightly.

A special word needs to be said about *fasting*, which is clearly encouraged in the Bible. It is not a way of despising the body nor an attempt to break it down. It is a means of achieving self-control and of counteracting the tendency to abuse food and drink. It is also a way of manifesting the primacy of spiritual realities. The Eucharistic fast especially has this significance. Relaxation in the regulations regarding fasting is meant to make this exercise more personal, so that each one can do what brings him the maximum spiritual profit. Fasting also has a strong communitarian dimension. The Fathers of the Church explained it as a means of depriving oneself of something in order to share it with the poor. Today this has a special significance. Fasting provides some little experience of the hunger pangs of the poor and enables one to relieve their distress at least in a small way. Hence there should be no formalism in fasting. It should be a sincere gesture of solidarity with the poor and the needy. It should always be undertaken with a humble and cheerful heart (cf. Mt. 6:16–18).

Abstinence is a milder form of fasting. It has nothing to do with the distinction between clean and unclean foods. "For every creature of God is good and nothing is to be rejected that is accepted with thanksgiving" (1 Tim. 4:2; cf. Rom. 14:14). Different foods may have different effects on the passions. Personal dispositions and moderation are most important.

Today we are emphasizing the Christian call to build up the community. This requires openness, sensitivity to the needs of others, and readiness to adjust and cooperate. All this implies great self-sacrifice, which at times can be most crucifying. A certain saint is reported to have said: "Community life is my greatest penance." This could be wrongly understood as a lament from one who found life together almost unbearable. It could also be understood in terms of the challenges which community life poses. It has been rightly said that the hair shirts of modern life are primarily all the pinpricks which one must be ready to bear cheerfully if one is to contribute to community building. We must recall here that all Christians are called to build up the ecclesial community, beginning with the family, or the "domestic church."

We may end this section on the living out of the paschal mystery by quoting the words of Teilhard: "In the general rhythm of life, development and renunciation, attachment and detachment, are not mutually exclusive. On the contrary, they harmonize, like breathing in and out in the movement of our lungs. They are two phases of the soul's breath, or two components of the impulse by which the Christian life uses things as a springboard from which to mount beyond them."[20]

———o———

Notes to Chapter VIII

1. *The Future of Man,* London, Collins, 1964, p. 34.
2. *Le Milieu Divin,* London, Collins, 1960, p. 112. "Physical" here is opposed to juridic, abstract, extrinsic. It is not to be understood in a material sense.
3. "Cosmic Life," *Writings in Time of War,* London, Collins, 1968, p. 58.
4. *Human Values and Christian Morality,* p. 11. Cf. Norbert Rigali, "Christ and Morality," *Concilium,* 1978, 12–20.
5. *PC,* art. 2.
6. *LG,* art. 7.
7. *Ibid.,* art. 32.
8. *Ibid.*
9. *Ibid.,* art. 13; *AG,* art. 5.
10. *Responsibility in Modern Religious Ethics,* Washington, Corpus Books, p. 97.

11. *Ethics,* p. 198.

12. Cf. Roger Le Deaut, "Paschal Mystery and Morality," *Doctrine and Life,* 18 (1968), 262–69.

13. *Le Milieu Divin,* p. 79.

14. "The Priest," *Writings in Time of War,* p. 222.

15. *Road to Relevance,* Staten Island, N.Y., Alba House, 1970, p. 108.

16. Bernard Häring, *ibid.,* p. 116.

17. Friedrick Wulf, "Asceticism," *Sacramentum Mundi,* ed. by Karl Rahner et alii, Montreal, Herder, 1969, Vol. I, p. 112.

18. *The Law of Christ,* Vol. I, p. 54.

19. *Ibid.*

20. *Le Milieu Divin,* p. 82.

CHAPTER IX

Worship and Life

1. THE CELEBRATION OF DAILY LIFE[1]

In the early Church, the bond between worship and daily life was perfectly realized. The fruits of holiness were nourished by the liturgy. The ardent love of Christ which imparted strength and joy to the martyrs, the ideal of perfect chastity which moved the virgins, the delicacy and depth of fraternal love which made the brethren "one heart and one soul" (Acts 4:32), were all inspired by the sacred rites of the liturgy. The acts of the martyrs offer eloquent testimony to the liturgical spirit which animated the confessors of the faith. The words that came spontaneously from their lips at the supreme moment of their trial were often the same expressions that they were accustomed to use in liturgical celebrations. The gestures with which they bade farewell to their brethren were the same as those of liturgical gatherings. It was the same mystery of Christ that was celebrated in the liturgy and lived out in the ordinary events of life or manifested in extraordinary events like martyrdom.

The ancient liturgy was known for its depth and sobriety. Gradually, however, there was increasing solemnity, which, while at first satisfying the emotions of the participants, became increasingly formalistic and devoid of spirit. People who were desirous of spiritual perfection fostered ascetical practices and private devotions insufficiently related to the celebration of the central mysteries. The rites of the Church themselves were appreciated only insofar as they were matters of duty, or offered a means of purification which was often understood in too individualistic and mechanistic a sense.

In the recent past there was an excessive preoccupation with the validity of the sacraments, as if nothing else mattered. Concentration on the correct pronouncing of the formulas and the exact observance of the rubrics at times bordered on the magical.

Many efforts were made, even during the Council of Trent, to counteract the divorce between liturgy and Christian life. But it is only of late that the revival of liturgical spirituality seems to be making considerable headway.

Vatican II has declared that "the liturgy is the *summit* toward which the activity of the Church is directed; and at the same time it is the *fountain* from which all her power flows. . . . The renewal in the Eucharist of the covenant between the Lord and man draws the faithful into compelling love of Christ and sets them afire. From the liturgy, therefore, and especially from the Eucharist as from a fountain, grace is chaneled into us, and the sanctification of men in Christ and the glorification of God, to which all other activities of the Church are directed as toward their goal, are most powerfully achieved."[2]

Therefore, people must be awakened to a sense of their personal involvement in the liturgical celebration. Some still need to be drawn out of their preoccupation with their own private devotions. "This demands that they be shown how the Mass is the wonderful encounter of the Christian community with God through the glorified humanity of Christ our Brother, how each one is involved in it and how it must be considered the most relevant act for one's personal life as well as for one's service of mankind."[3]

The difficulty of creating a sense of community in vast urban complexes, where people are largely strangers to each other or separated by wide diversity of class, culture, language or social status, must be faced. There should be a realistic understanding of the parish as a Eucharistic community. This is in many cases an ideal rather than a reality that can be immediately achieved. Initially at least, it would be advisable at times to work with smaller, homogeneous groups without, however, leaving them in their isolation.

Loss of a sense of symbolism in industrial civilization may seem to pose an additional problem. But psychologists like Carl G. Jung have shown that, in the depths of his subconscious, man is deeply in need of certain "proto-symbols." There is need of inventiveness to adapt the secondary symbols of the liturgy to the condition of different groups.

Without yielding to arbitrariness, which would be disrespectful of the communal and sacred nature of Christian worship, maximum advantage should be taken of the wide degree of flexibility now allowed and even fostered by the new rituals. The active participation of the assembly should be promoted through effective means of communication. Vatican II clearly asks that every effort be made to make the celebration meaningful and relevant to the particular situation of the particular assembly. "The age and condition of their people, their way of life, and their degree of religious culture should be taken into account."[4]

It would be most unfortunate if the current liturgical reform were to be understood as merely a change of rites and rubrics. This would lead only to the substitution of new ritualism for the old one. We should draw inspiration from the creative periods of the ancient liturgy, especially in mission areas where Christianity confronts new cultures.

2. THE SACREDNESS OF THE BODY AND TEMPORAL REALITIES

Worship is recognition and acceptance of reality, of man's essential relationship with God, which gives the deepest meaning to human life. It frees him from slavery to false gods that claim his attention.

Liturgy fosters the spirit of *thanksgiving,* the recognition of God's self-gift and other gifts. Thereby, man is called to respond to that gift by being faithful to God's call. It gives him an appreciation of human existence and of all creation. Thus it gives a positive and optimistic note to life.

Man, we have seen, not only *has* a body, but *is* a body vivified by a spiritual soul. If the body is conditioned by the soul, it influences and conditions the soul in turn. The body is the soul's instrument for attaining the welfare of the whole person. It is the means of communication between men and, hence, the basis of human society.

Once God has willed to divinize man, respecting his manner of being and activity, we can expect Him to use the body and sensory experience to bring this about. Through this means, the divine is present to the human and operates through the human, including sensory activity, in order to communicate to man a sharing in the divinity. This is the fundamental law of *sacramentality*.

Again, if the communication of divine life is to be made in the context of man's social nature, it can only be in an incarnate and sacramental manner. And since man through the body is bound to material creation, his divinization as regards the body involves in some way the whole of creation.

The eternal Word of the Father wished to become personally visible and audible to man. The physical body of the incarnate Son of God is the source and pivotal point of every divine communication to man and, consequently, of cosmic unity as well. Hence, the transmission of divine life is linked with material things and sensory acts. Faith and sacraments put man in saving contact with Christ's flesh and with what He did and suffered in His flesh. Man also begins to share in the triumph of Christ's body in the resurrection.

Liturgy, then, fosters a deep appreciation of the body and all bodily activities. It constantly reminds us that the body, far from being evil, is the expression of the spirit and an instrument of sanctification. It helps us to transcend the dichotomy between body and soul from which Christians in the West and in the East suffer because of imperfect and even erroneous philosophical conceptions.

It is easy to see the importance of this point of view for sexual morality. It should also help to renew our understanding and practice of Christian mortification. This does not consist in despising or torturing the body so that the soul might thrive, but in subduing or putting to death whatever is disordered in our lives (cf. Col. 3:5; Rom. 8:13).

Because of the Christian mystery that is celebrated in the liturgy, the world acquires an entirely new significance. Now, the things of the world, which are an extension of the human body, have a new value beyond their own natural value. They appear as symbols or effective signs of the personal activity of God wishing to share His own life with men. Thus, the water of baptism, the bread of the Eucharist, and so on with each sacrament, become signs and means by which man is taken up into the sphere of the divine.

Teilhard de Chardin expresses this beautifully. He points out that "the sacramental action of Christ, *precisely because it sanctifies matter,* extends its influence beyond the pure supernatural, over all that makes up the internal and external ambience of the faithful."[5] The Eucharistic host reminds him of the orb of the whole visible universe. "Since today, Lord, I your priest have neither bread nor wine nor altar, I shall spread my hands over the whole universe and take its immensity as the matter of my sacrifice. Is not the infinite circle of things the one final Host that it is your will to transmute? The seething cauldron in which the activities of all living and cosmic substance are brewed together—is not that the bitter cup that you seek to sanctify?"[6]

The transubstantiation of the Eucharistic bread, in a way, affects the whole of matter. "When Christ, carrying further the process of his Incarnation, comes down into the bread in order to dwell there in its place, his action is not confined to the particle of matter that his Presence is at hand, for a moment, to etherealize. The transubstantiation is enriched by a halo of divinization—real, even though less intense—that extends to the whole universe."[7]

Thus the Eucharistic celebration gives Teilhard an impetus to co-operate in transforming the whole universe. "I shall look beyond the white host, accepting its domination, and with all the strength of my desire and my prayer, with all my power, over every substance and every development, I shall pronounce the words: *Hoc est corpus meum.*"[8]

From this perspective we see that man need not abandon earthly reality in order to realize union with God. On the contrary, it is through the body and the things of this world that he expresses his religious attitudes and reaches God.

Christ has bridged the gulf between the profane and the sacred. In Christ everything is redeemed and sanctified. It is significant that the act of redemption itself was accomplished, not with solemn liturgical solemnity, but through a supreme act of fidelity to God in a human conflict situation in history. Thus, in the "new creation" brought about by Christ, the secular reality itself can be realized as worship.

Jesus told the Samaritan woman: "The hour is coming, and now is, when the true worshippers will worship the Father in spirit and truth" (Jn. 4:23). So St. Paul exhorts the Romans that they should present their bodies "as a living sacrifice, holy and acceptable to God, which is your spiritual worship" (Rom. 12:1). "Body" in Semitic usage, we have seen, means all that belongs to man: the human personality with all its secular implications. Since Christian life in the world is concerned with the world and its problems, these must be, for the Christian, aspects of worship of God. Life in the world shared with one's fellowmen must be a "spiritual sacrifice." Profane or secular activity, especially commitment to the just ordering of human society, should become the expression of mankind's striving toward God. Here we may recall the famous saying of St. Irenaeus: "God's glory is man fully alive."

However, this "Christian secularization," rightly understood, does not exclude special acts of worship. The worship of God expressed in and through secular activity for the good of mankind calls for grateful celebration in the liturgy if it is to find its full depth and value. Human life is not fully meaningful without "Eucharistic" (thanksgiving) celebration. Intensive commitment to the service of one's fellowmen should flow out of the "festal gathering" (Heb. 12:22), in which the source of fraternity is experienced in explicit praise of the common Father of all mankind.

On the other hand, the explicit worship of God in the liturgy is without any value if the reality of "secular worship" that underlies it— dedication to the service of mankind—is not present. This is clear from the denunciation by the prophets of empty ritual devoid of justice. St. Thomas remarks that "visiting widows and orphans" (a typical medieval form of social service) is itself religious, but that religion is expressed more directly by acts of adoration and sacrifice.[9]

Hence secular activity and the liturgy are not alternatives, as some unfortunately seem to think. It is a pity that many people moved by ardent longing for righting wrongs in society find worship irrelevant to their concerns, and that some get so involved with the fine points of the liturgy that they seem oblivious of the tremendous problems confronting contemporary society. The liturgical celebration must be seen as a call to Christian commitment to the service of mankind according to the concrete situation of the historical moment. It may be noted that John, who does not recount the institution of the Eucharist, relates the washing of the disciples' feet, which brings out the "reality" signified by the celebration—namely, fraternal service. Paul, after narrating the institution of the Eucharist in 1 Cor. 11, immediately goes on to explain its fruit, which is effective charity in Christ.

3.   CALL TO COMMITMENT

The sacraments are not isolated events in the Christian life. They are the high points of the important aspects of daily life. Hence the relevance of the sacramental celebration to daily life must be clearly perceived.

The liturgical movement closely resembles salvation history in that we see throughout a pattern of revelation and response: God revealing Himself as a loving Father and seeking to evoke a response of faith in man. In Scripture we read of the wonderful events of God's saving intervention on behalf of man. This God-man relationship was formalized in the covenant. Israelite worship was, in fact, a constant renewal of the covenant. The celebration of Yahweh's saving deeds was a way of experiencing anew His protection and pledging the people afresh to live according to the exigencies of the covenant. This is no less true of the "New Israel" and the new covenant in Christ.

Thus God's saving activity continues to be present today through the liturgy. As man was called to commitment to God through these saving events, he is likewise called today through the same acts sacramentally made effective. God's love for man manifests itself most eminently in the gift of His Son. Man's basic response to God's self-revelation and self-communication is faith, a total surrender of self. This implies a movement of love of God and love of neighbor. "In the celebration of the sacraments and in a life proceeding from their grace and their mandate, God's love and the response of the redeemed should be visible, experienceable."[10]

In the liturgical celebration, the Christian makes a commitment to the whole Christ, to participate in building up the Body of Christ through a life of dedicated service. In his moral life, he lives out the implications of this commitment. In the liturgy, the Christian accepts in a general but unconditional way the demands of service to his neighbor: in his daily life he responds to these demands in the concrete. The commitment to service made in the liturgy needs to be localized, particularized and concretized. "As the one eternal covenant is renewed day after day through changing times and circumstances, every specification of the basic act of commitment becomes a mediation of fundamental response to the covenant of love. The liturgy actuates the covenant in such a way that Christian morality becomes a mediation of the covenant union with God."[11]

The sacraments give man a share in the divine sonship of Christ and His sacerdotal mission. Christian holiness is the reflection of the divine *doxa* (glory), proceeding from God through Christ and drawing man to God. We do not begin to sanctify ourselves, but it is God who sanctifies us through the sacraments. This ontological sanctification calls for moral holiness, or the living out of the call to service of God and neighbor.

Through the sacraments we enter into the divine plan, the mystery of salvation. Sacramental grace is an earnest of the glory of God that is to be manifested in the Parousia. While we are drawn toward the final consummation, and in some real sense are already "raised up in

Christ'' (Eph. 2:6; Col. 3:2), we are also entrusted with the task of sanctifying the world. The sacraments ''make this miserable existence of ours the great interlude in the history of salvation between the decisive victory through the cross and the resurrection and the glorious triumph of the Second Coming.''[12]

The sacraments are effective signs of the new covenant of love and, hence, a call to unity and fellowship. They are a social ferment and a force that is effective even in the details of our material existence.

Christian morality is not the performance of isolated good acts, or mere conformity to laws in a more or less mechanical style. Every human act is the expression of the basic option made in the core of one's personality. Baptism is the first call to this fundamental option, which has to be personally ratified when one reaches maturity. It would be fruitful to regard confirmation as the sacrament of Christian maturity, when the young Christian personally assumes responsibility in the Christian community. This can be brought out more clearly if the sacrament is received at a time when the person is likely to make his fundamental option (although there are valid reasons for the oriental custom of giving the sacrament together with baptism in infancy).

4. PERSONALISM AND CALL TO COMMUNITY

Christian morality is a *personal response* to the call of God to commit oneself in love. The personal dimension may be said to be the most characteristic feature of Christian morality. Proper celebration of the sacraments fosters a deep awareness of personal relationships.

The sacraments are *not things* to be used for one's spiritual profit, but *sacred actions* in which there is a *personal encounter* between the Christian and Christ in the community.

The liturgy is structured as a *dialogue* in which there is an interchange of revelation and response. It begins with attentive listening to the Word of God making a personal call here and now. Then there is the response of faith or total self-surrender to God, which is to be expressed in commitment to service. Liturgical dialogue demands *openness,* which is an essential requirement for any genuine interpersonal exchange. The attitude of openness is to be carried over into one's daily dealings with other people, so that every action becomes a personal encounter, an element of the I-thou relationship that should be cultivated between the members of Christ's Body. It should be noted that if there is formalism in liturgical celebration, it will also lead to formalism or legalism in daily life.

Other persons are not objects to be exploited even for one's "spiritual good," but subjects of freedom to be respected and served. The moral response of the Christian is fundamentally a mutual presence of service, which is the fulfillment of the commitment made in the liturgical celebration. The concrete forms of service are determined by the objective demands of the situation. Hence, again, the authenticity of worship must be judged by incarnational forms of service according to the real needs of one's neighbor. Otherwise, one would be serving oneself under the guise of serving others, using them as a means of self-fulfillment.

The Church is both the Eucharistic community, or the assembly of the People of God for the celebration of the paschal mystery, and the *sacramentum mundi,* the "sign of the world," or the whole of mankind united and brought into intimate union with God. We celebrate in the liturgy of the Church what is being accomplished in human history, so that the latter becomes in some way "salvation history," and in this way humanity is drawn into the mystery of Christ and thus finds its deepest fulfillment.

Christ came to gather together the scattered children of God. It is mainly through the sacramental activity of the Church that this is now coming to pass. When man is reestablished in a right relationship with God, a community is being formed. "The cup of blessing which we bless, is it not a participation in the body of Christ? The bread which we break, is it not a participation in the body of Christ? Because there is one bread, we who are many are one body, for we all partake of the one bread" (1 Cor. 10:16–17). The individual participates in the death and resurrection of Christ through the act of self-transcendence by which he goes out of himself in love toward his fellowmen. He dies to himself and rises to a new life in Christ insofar as he enters into a new relationship with them. The liturgy provides the basic experience of encountering other persons as brethren in Christ.

Genuine cult, in its very essence, is an expression of the community of men standing before God. Each one becomes gratefully aware how much his personal faith is also supported by the power of the faith of the whole community. Nothing, in fact, does more to form community than communal worship. Through the celebration of the sacraments, the all-unifying and saving solidarity of mankind with its Redeemer becomes effective.

On the other hand, since a genuine community is made up of real persons who have their own spiritual depth, a liturgical community presupposes that each person cultivates his personal spirituality in order that he may have something to contribute to the assembly even while he is enriched by it. Whenever possible, the personal contribution should be fostered through spontaneous prayer and the adaptation of rites and prayers to the needs of those assembled.

The personal and communitarian character of the liturgy should help in overcoming the false opposition between private prayer and community worship. In recognizing their sonship to the Father, men at the same time recognize their brotherhood with one another. The personal deepening which private prayer can develop can, in turn, enrich the public expression of this same communal reality in the liturgy.

The sacraments are not individual favors from God. They are effective signs of the new covenant and, hence, invitations to unity and fellowship. They are a social ferment that is effective in binding men together in the everyday events of life.

The importance of baptism, confirmation and the Eucharist for the realization of community is well recognized. The sacrament of penance or reconciliation also has a significant role in building up the Christian community; it is reintegration, not only with God, but also with the community. In ancient times, absolution was called "receiving the peace of the Church." It was believed that the sinner who had offended God by harming the community had to return to God through reconciliation with the community. This aspect of sacramental confession needs to be emphasized again.[13] Man suffers from alienation from God and from other men; he also suffers from disharmony within himself. The sacrament of reconciliation heals this alienation and disharmony. It brings about a profound peace, not always sensibly felt, in the depths of the heart.

The anointing of the sick sanctifies the whole process of healing, so that not only the illness of a particular man is healed but his relationships with others are restored. Holy orders consecrate the priest for ministerial service and mediation. Matrimony dedicates a Christian couple to found a "domestic church," a new cell of Christ's Mystical Body. By receiving each other as God's gift, man and wife are to be signs of God's love in the world.

The genuineness of liturgical worship may be gauged from its effect in overcoming caste and other social barriers. Unless the spirit of unity is fostered, the liturgical rites become countersigns. Paul refers to those who fail in fraternal charity as not "discerning the body" of the Lord.[14]

The active participation of all the people in the liturgy should restore to the laity their rightful place in all the activities of the Church. If the laity are only passive spectators during liturgical services, they are likely to feel alienated from other Church activities. But a more active role in worship would be a sign of and a stimulus to involvement in the proclamation of the Gospel and Christian service in daily life.

When we want to find out the actual relevance of liturgical celebrations in the life of a particular Christian community, we should not be satisfied with spontaneous impressions or vague conjectures. The resources of pastoral sociology should be utilized to uncover to what extent the social implications of the liturgy are realized, and to ascertain how far participation is understood as mere fulfillment of individual obligation or as a means of awakening the spirit of community and solidarity.

5. LIFE IN CHRIST

The classical presentation of Christian doctrine was as follows: (1) the articles of the Creed; (2) the sacraments; (3) the commandments. The idea was that the sacraments were to be seen as entries into vital contact with the saving mysteries of Christ, and the commandments as ways of living according to the demands of this encounter. However, in the eighteenth century, the treatment of the sacraments in catechisms and moral treatises was placed after the commandments, which came to occupy the central position in the scheme of instruction. With this displacement, the connection of the sacraments with the mysteries of Christ was obscured. They became, above all, aids in keeping the commandments. Gradually, their treatment grew casuistic and juridical. The mysteries of Christ were seen as mere historical events or mere examples for imitation, without vital significance or effective dynamism for the Christian life, which was largely reduced to the exact keeping of the commandments, although leaving room for a "higher spirituality" for some chosen souls.

We are now again experiencing the need for returning, not so much to the classical presentation, but to something like the *mystagogic* (sacramental) *catechesis* of St. Cyril of Jerusalem, in which Christian doctrine, worship and life are seen as different aspects of the Christian mystery. Recent moral theology emphasizes that Christian morality is a participation in the life of Christ, who is the archetype and source of all human and Christian existence. The program of Christian life, we have seen, is a paschal program, which implies for each Christian a progressive incorporation in Christ and a gradual adoption of His sentiments and attitudes. The commandments must be seen only as minimal expressions of our fidelity to Christ. The celebration of the Christian mysteries in the liturgy is a constant call to go beyond the minimum and strive daily to be more and more like Christ.

The mystery of Pentecost appears in Christian tradition as the gift of the new law to the People of God. The coming of the Spirit is compared to the theophany on Sinai. Just as Moses ascended the holy mountain and brought down the two tablets of the law, so Christ, the new Moses, ascends into heaven and sends down the Holy Spirit, who is Himself now our new law. This is in fulfillment of what the prophets foretold regarding the law which the Lord would imprint in the hearts of men in the new covenant (cf. Jer. 31:31–33; Ez. 36:26–27). In the Eucharistic celebration, the Church again offers up the Lord, who once for all died, rose and ascended for us to the throne of the Most High, whence we receive in holy communion the most precious gifts of the body and blood of the Lord as sustenance for our spiritual life.

Henceforth, the basic norm of the Christian life is not any external imperative, but an internal principle derived from our "being in Christ." The Spirit of Christ Himself works in us, so that we can be said to be "led by the Spirit" (Rom. 8:14). The Holy Spirit Himself becomes our "law" by illuminating our minds and moving our wills to that which will bring about the full realization of our human and Christian potentialities.

The gift of the Spirit comes to us mainly through the sacraments, which give us a new spiritual dynamism. The progressive divinization that results from a sharing in the mysteries of Christ in the liturgy is the basis of all genuine Christian mysticism. There may be degrees in mystical union with God, and there may be special manifestations of them that are rare and extraordinary. But every Christian is called to the essence of mystical union, which consists in immediate union with God through sharing in the life of Christ. This takes place "in mystery" in the liturgy, and "effectively" by the reproduction of the pattern of Christ's life in our daily life.

Hence, although there may be some justification for distinguishing between morality, spirituality and mysticism according to the intensity of union with God, the distinction should not be overdrawn. One should especially beware of reserving the higher reaches of Christian perfection, by whatever name they are called, for some special categories of people, leaving the "practice of the commandments" to "ordinary" Christians.

The action of the Holy Spirit is expressed by the virtue of charity. This divine gift springs from God's love for man (cf. 1 Jn. 4:10) and is communicated by the sanctifying action of Christ in the sacraments. We have seen that charity is the form of all virtues. However, love can be fully genuine only if it is *worshipful love*. The profound and tragic alienations of the modern world can be overcome only by a deep spirit of adoration.

One who is thoroughly permeated by the divine *agape* spontaneously fulfills the requirements of the law, which has only a pedagogical function in guiding our imperfect minds and supporting our weakness until we have achieved full spiritual maturity. The liturgy of the Word calls us to the self-surrender of *faith,* constantly reminds us of the primacy of love in Christian life, and proposes concrete guidelines for expressing this love, lest self-love be mistaken for genuine Christian love. The liturgy of the sacraments communicates to us the divine gift of love; it invites and enables us to share in the sacrificial love of Christ.

The sacraments are anticipations of the final fulfillment. Hence they are signs of *hope*. They are all "pledges of future glory," as St. Thomas says of the Eucharist. Through the sacraments the Christian effectively enjoys a foretaste of heaven amidst the trials of this life. This aspect of hope is very important in the present situation with all its doubt and disillusionment.

The gift of the Spirit and of His love gives us a sense of *liberation*. This does not consist in doing just what we like or in providing "an opportunity for the flesh" (Gal. 5:13), but in the ability to control one's disordered tendencies and to put oneself at the disposal of others. It implies, therefore, the atmosphere in which a person is open to others, gives himself to others and receives gratefully from them. The liturgy celebrates the freedom which the Lamb of God has earned for us by His Passover and which makes us the sons of God, instead of slaves of sin and of the devil.

Love and freedom, which are the chief signs of maturity, are not realized all at once. The sacraments do not produce them automatically. They are *calls to maturity*, to perfect openness and total response. Current spirituality is much preoccupied with the question of Christian maturity. A right understanding of the personal nature of the sacraments should help us to grow in maturity.

Thus the renewal of the liturgy and of morality go together. "Sacramental celebration must not be seen as separate from the moral life; it is a part of moral life and the proclamation of its deepest meaning. The sacraments themselves are moral acts, basic acts of building a loving community. They represent and focus all such acts and proclaim that their true meaning is to be found ultimately in the paschal mystery and is expressed in the Church's inner nature. They proclaim the hope that human brotherhood survives in Christ transformed and glorified."[15]

———o———

Notes to Chapter IX

1. Cf. Donald P. Gray, "Liturgy and Morality," *Worship*, 39 (1965), 28–35; Clement Dillenschneider, *The Dynamic Power of the Sacraments*, St. Louis, Mo., Herder, 1966; Bernard J. Cooke, *Christian Sacraments and Christian Personality*, New York, Holt, Rinehart and Winston, 1965; Bernard Häring, *The New Covenant*, London, Burns and Oates, 1965.
2. *SC*, art. 10.
3. Joseph Putz, "Priests and the New Liturgy," *Clergy Monthly*, 34 (1970), 442.
4. *SC*, art. 19.
5. *MD*, art. 115.
6. "The Priest," *Writings in Time of War*, London, Collins, 1968, p. 205.
7. *Ibid.*, p. 207.
8. *Ibid.*, p. 208.
9. *Summa Theologica*, IIa-IIae, 81, 1, 1.
10. Bernard Häring, *This Time of Salvation*, New York, Herder and Herder, 1966, p. 149.
11. Eugene A. La Verdière, "Convenant Morality," *Worship*, 38 (1964), 243.

12. Bernard Häring, *The Law of Christ,* Vol. II, 1963, p. 151.

13. Cf. George V. Lobo, *Renewal of the Sacrament of Reconciliation,* Allahabad, St. Paul Publications, 1976, pp. 11–14.

14. Cf. J. Murphy-O'Connor, "Eucharist and Community in First Corinthians," *Worship,* 51 (1977), 56–69.

15. Donald Murray, "Sacramental Spirituality," *Doctrine and Life,* 29 (1978), 220.

CHAPTER X

The Role of the Spirit
in the Christian Life

1. THE GIFT OF THE SPIRIT

Authentic Christian life is not so much the exercise of virtues as cooperation with the action of the Spirit. By condemning Pelagianism, the early Church had affirmed the primacy of the grace of the indwelling Spirit in the process of sanctification. However, till recently, especially in the Western Church, the place of the Holy Spirit was not given due importance. This may be the main reason for the aberrations of legalism.

We see the Spirit active at the dawn of creation as He hovers over the primeval waters (cf. Gen. 1:2). Whenever Yahweh acts or speaks, His Spirit is at work. Whenever something marvelous and new is to be done, God's Spirit is at hand.

The Spirit is active in the revelation of the Word of God. We see a Samson working mighty deeds whenever the Spirit comes upon him (Judg. 14:6). Likewise, Samuel prophesied when the Spirit of God came upon him (1 Sam. 10:10). As 2 Peter says: "No prophecy ever came by the impulse of man, but men moved by the Holy Spirit spoke from God" (1:21). Indeed, when the prophet speaks for God, he receives God's Spirit, which endows him with the gifts of wisdom and understanding.

The Psalmist prays that the holy Spirit be not taken away from him (51:11). Ezechiel prophesies: "A new heart I will give you, and a new Spirit I will put within you; I will take out of you a heart of stone and give you a heart of flesh. And I will put my spirit within you" (36:26–27).

The Spirit began the new creation by "overshadowing" the humble maiden of Nazareth (Lk. 1:35). At the beginning of Jesus' public life, the Spirit descended on Him and consecrated Him for His mission. We see the Spirit at work in Jesus, filling Him with power and directing Him to Jerusalem for the fulfillment of His mission by dying and rising.

When the mortal frame of Jesus is shattered by death, His Spirit is poured out over all the earth. When the Spirit comes upon the Apostles at Pentecost, they are completely transformed. They lived with Christ and drank in His words of wisdom. Still, until they had received the outpouring of the Spirit, they were timid and slow of understanding. But with the hurricane of Pentecost, they were radically changed. The Spirit of Christ filled them with joy, courage and spiritual energy.

The announcement of Jesus: "He who believes in me . . . out of his heart shall flow rivers of living water" (Jn. 7:38–39) is explicitly related to the receiving of the Spirit. The symbolism of the tongues of fire in the Pentecost narrative shows that the Spirit is no longer remote and inaccessible. The Apostles can now proclaim the message of Christ with power—that is, with authority and effectiveness. The Spirit comes as comforter and enlightener, as Jesus foretold (Jn. 14:16–26).

The Spirit is received by the believer in baptism, which is a rebirth (birth from above, or birth anew) (cf. Jn. 3:3). It is a birth, "not of blood nor of the will of the flesh nor of the will of man, but of God" (Jn. 1:13). The gift of the Spirit makes us truly the children of God. "See what love the Father has given us, that we should be called the children of God; and so we are" (1 Jn. 3:1).

To receive and possess the Spirit means, first of all, the ability and readiness to bear witness to Christ when called upon to do so. Though the *Pneuma* is not the *Logos,* John ascribes to the Paraclete the functions of teaching, recalling, testifying, proclaiming.

The Holy Spirit is the mainspring of Christian life, not only in its beginning, but throughout its development. It is the Spirit that prays within us. "When we cry, 'Abba, Father,' it is the Spirit Himself bearing witness with our spirit that we are children of God" (Rom. 8:16). "Likewise the Spirit helps us in our weakness; for we do not know how to pray as we ought, but the Spirit himself intercedes for us with sighs too deep for words" (v. 26).

Although there can be no duality of baptism and the first sacramental baptism in water is also baptism in the Holy Spirit, the charismatic movement cannot be faulted for speaking of the "baptism in the Spirit." Alas, it too frequently happens that Christians do not live in sufficient awareness of the Spirit and do not manifest the fruits of the Spirit in their life. So, if they are effectively converted to the Lord Jesus, they can experience a new spiritual rebirth. Sometimes the new awareness of the presence and activity of the Spirit in their life can be an overpowering experience and can manifest itself in a new life of fervor. This experience can be called, in the words of Louis Cardinal Suenens, "a revitalizing of the sacramental graces"[1] received in baptism and in other sacraments.

Even in our times the Spirit imparts various *charisms* (gifts), like that of prophesying, healing and tongues. All these are directed to the upbuilding of the Church (cf. Eph. 4:12). However, it is hunble, selfless and devoted love that is the supreme charism of the Spirit (cf. 1 Cor. 13). It is good to recall here that the possession of the Spirit must also bear the fruits of "joy, peace, patience, kindness, gentleness and self-control" (cf. Gal. 5:22–23).

Baptism is essentially an incorporation into the Church, the Body of Christ. "For by one Spirit we are all baptized into one body" (1 Cor. 12:13). The Spirit, the bond of love between the Father and the Son, energizes the Body of Christ and gives it form, vitality, unity and organic diversity. The Spirit binds the Church into a single fellowship of faith, love and devotion.

The Church began with the Pentecostal experience. In the beginning, the interventions of the Spirit were most numerous, and not seldom quite dramatic. It is the Spirit that clearly directed the course of events and moved the leaders as well as the whole community of the faithful. Later the manifestations of the Spirit became more subdued, but the paramount importance of the Spirit and His gifts was recognized. Christian life was called the "spiritual life" by the Fathers. Those who directed the faithful along the path of Christian perfection were called "spiritual fathers." They were supposed to have had a special experience of the power and action of the Spirit in their own lives.

Even when devotion to the Holy Spirit became less conspicuous in the Church, the importance of spiritual discernment was recognized by such guides as St. Teresa and St. Ignatius, among others. The gifts of the Spirit are clearly manifested in the lives of saints like the Curé of Ars or Don Bosco.

Pope John XXIII called the Second Vatican Council "a new Pentecost." It stressed the role of the Spirit in the life of the Church, and declared that for the exercise of the apostolate, "the Holy Spirit, who sanctifies the People of God through the ministry and the sacraments, gives to the faithful special gifts as well."[2]

The Council brings out the role of the Spirit in the sacraments and scriptures as well as in daily life. "Christ is now at work in the hearts of men through the energy of His Spirit."[3] "Christians are led by the Holy Spirit in their journey to the kingdom of their Father."[4]

The Council asks that "lay persons should learn to advance the mission of Christ and the Church . . . by being sensitive to the movements of the Holy Spirit, who gives life to the people of God and would impel all men to love God the Father, as well as the world and mankind in Him."[5]

One of the main insights of Vatican II is the self-understanding of the Church as a *Spirit-filled community*. "In order that we may be increasingly renewed in Him (cf. Eph. 4:23), He has shared with us His Spirit, who, existing as one and the same being in the head and in the members, vivifies and moves the whole body."[6] We can at once see the importance of such a conception for the renewal of Church law. The Church could not dispense with all legislation, but it must be careful to steer clear of legalism. The laws of the Church must be imbued with the spirit of love.

Today it is apparent that young people will not come to the faith except through a spiritual experience. It is at the same time remarkable what wonders the Spirit can accomplish in the hearts of so many people, young and old. There may be a tendency in certain circles to stress the more emotional aspects of the spiritual life. But every great spiritual renewal had its emotional dimension. Some excesses here and there, while recalling the need for prudence, cannot justify a negative stand toward charismatic movements. The Spirit blows where He will and how He will.

2. THE LAW OF GRACE

Creation itself is a gift of God. Throughout the Old Testament, there is one constantly running theme which expresses the special favor and promise of God: the theme of the covenant. This denotes God's progressive self-communication to man, the privileged intimacy of a special relationship. While many images are used to express it—for instance, a mother's love (Is. 49:15; Deut. 32:10–11) and a shepherd's care (Ez. 34:11–13)—the most poignant is that of the fidelity of a spouse (Is. 54:5–6; the whole of Hosea).

God's self-communication comes to a climax in the Christ-event, from His incarnation to the outpouring of His Spirit at Pentecost. The gift or grace of the Spirit implies a share in the divine life and an indwelling of the Triune God in the hearts of men and in the community of the faithful. "We will come to him and make our home with him" (Jn. 14:23). The Christian is spoken of as "temple of the Holy Spirit" (1 Cor. 3:16; cf. 6:19).

Thus Christ, who is the universal exemplar and norm, communicates His life through the grace of the Holy Spirit. "If the Spirit of him who raised Jesus from the dead dwells in you, he who raised Jesus from the dead will give life to your mortal bodies [i.e., vivify your earthly existence] also through his Spirit which dwells in you'' (Rom. 8:11). The Spirit of Christ Himself acts in us, so that we are "led by the spirit" (Rom. 8:14). He Himself becomes our primary "law" by *illuminating our minds* so that we can understand the call of Christ, and by *moving our wills* to perform the works of love.

The Spirit moves each individual in an unique way. *His grace is the ultimate "form" of man* in his present condition and, hence, is the concrete norm of the Christian life.

The life of Christ that comes to us from the grace of His Spirit is not an extrinsic gift, but an internal elevation and transformation. As Josef Fuchs puts it: "We must view grace as giving the highest and final determination to man's being, and also his activity. . . . It must be viewed as grace forming the individual man, or rather this particular man who comes to the highest fulfillment for which he exists through this precise grace of Christ.''[7]

Hence, the supreme norm of morality is, *not an external imperative,* but an *internal principle* derived from our spiritual being in Christ. This movement of grace, to those who cooperate with it, will not be experienced as a law constraining from without, but as an inner dynamism through which one realizes the deepest aspirations of his being. "If one is carried by the grace of the Spirit of Christ, the imperative of being man-in-Christ will be one's own willing and loving. The more one allows oneself to be caught up by the grace of Christ, the more will this imperative, which is based on both the natural law and the supernatural order, become one's own innermost concern, one's inner law.''[8]

The law of grace and our incorporation into Christ do have experiential effects. Our whole understanding of the moral life is changed; our perception of moral values is deepened and sharpened; we see the importance of persons and what contributes to their good. Our motivation is purified and enlivened. The presence of the Spirit sensitizes the conscience to the direction of God's saving action in the world, and empowers hesitant man to move forward to build up the world in communion with his fellowmen.

It should be noted that the grace of Christ impels us to observe, not only the general principles of rectitude, but also the concrete demands that flow from our individual existence or the particular call for each to attain fullness in Christ.

Further, as divine grace is not a thing, but God's personal self-gift to man or a sharing in the interpersonal relationships in the Blessed Trinity, the movements of grace must not be understood in an impersonal way. They are personal calls asking for personal response.

The law of grace is never static. It is a dynamic orientation toward an ever-fuller life through love of God and neighbor. To the extent one is led by grace, he is not motivated by the fear of punishment for transgression and is not limited by the negative and minimalistic sphere of prohibitions. He goes far beyond the dangerous boundary of serious sin and strives toward positive perfection. He has outgrown the stage for which the prohibitive law is made. On the other hand, the more one accepts the invitation of grace unwillingly, the more burdensome morality becomes to him. Obligation assumes the character of imposition. One experiences an internal feeling of resistance to the will of God.

As Paul points out, the Christian life implies a continuous tension between the egoistic demands of the flesh and fidelity to the Spirit, between slavery to sin and filial love. "For those who live according to the flesh set their minds on the things of the flesh, but those who live according to the Spirit set their minds on the things of the Spirit. To set the mind on the Spirit is life and peace. . . . For you did not receive the spirit of slavery to fall back into fear, but you have received the spirit of sonship" (Rom. 8:5, 6, 15).

In the words of St. Thomas, "Since the grace of the Holy Spirit is like an interior habit bestowed on us and inclining us to act aright, it makes us do freely those things that befit grace, and shun what is opposed to it."[9]

By receiving the spirit of sonship, we are effectively liberated from the flesh, the slavery of the law, sin and the devil. The grace of the Spirit becomes a principle of true interior freedom.

Thus the grace of Christ becomes the driving force pressing us from within to the full realization of our human and Christian existence. The more we allow ourselves to be caught up by this inner dynamism, the more spontaneously we will tend to the perfection of life in Christ. "The spirit of the man who has been regenerated is the Holy Spirit: the place of dwelling and the organ by which he perceives and accepts the Holy Spirit's movements."[10]

St. Thomas has presented a clear synthesis of the elements of the Christian life. According to him, the *principal element* of the new law is *grace:* "That which is preponderant in the law of the New Testament, and wherein all its efficacy is based, is the grace of the Holy Spirit, which is given through faith in Christ. Consequently, the new law is chiefly the very grace of the Holy Spirit."[11] The "new law" is evidently not a law in the ordinary sense. It is the direction of the indwelling Spirit.[12] It is the very gift of our sonship from God as it calls for expression in our daily life.

The *secondary element* is the *various precepts.* "Nevertheless, the new law contains certain things that *dispose us* to receive the grace of the Holy Spirit, and pertain to the use of that grace; such things are of *secondary importance,* so to speak, in the new law."[13]

St. Thomas makes it clear that it is only the chief element, the grace of the Holy Spirit, that "justifies." "The other element of the evangelical law is secondary, viz., the teachings of faith [external formulations] and those commandments which direct human affection and actions. And as to this, the new law does not justify."[14] The secondary elements, or outwardly formulated commands, help to guard against the danger that carnal man may falsely and egoistically interpret the movements of the Spirit. "The commandments will help not to misunderstand the driving power of grace and love, not to interpret it in the manner of a 'man of flesh' and try to realize it in this manner. In this way the outward law is a help and a salutary constraint, serving the primary element of the law of Christ."[15]

The secondary elements must be seen as *mediations,* more or less perfect, of inner grace. It is possible, and up to a point necessary, to derive formulated demands from the primary law of love, e.g., the prohibition against lying. However, they should be kept to the minimum and clearly seen as secondary. The creative character of the primary relationship between God and man should never be obscured.

As Paul repeatedly declares, the Christian is no longer under the law. If he chooses to remain under it, it is because he is still "flesh," because he does not wish to assume the maturity of his new creative relationship with God. The Galatians fell into a state in which the works of the law tended to replace the personal, filial and grateful ties with God (Gal. 3:1–3). The Corinthians tried to turn the structures of the Church into realities with which they proposed to lay hold of the power of God. They substituted pride and vainglory for a thankful attitude to God, who had given them everything (1 Cor. 3–4). In a way, both these attitudes were idolatrous.

In this connection, St. Thomas refers to the explanation of St. Augustine concerning the saying of Paul, "The letter kills, but the Spirit gives life" (2 Cor. 3:6): "Augustine explains this (*De Spirit. et Lit.,* c. 17) by saying that the letter denotes any writing that is external to man, even that of moral precepts such as are contained in the Gospel. Wherefore, the letter—even of the Gospel—would kill unless there were the inward presence of the healing grace of faith."[16]

St. Thomas is careful to point out that Christians are not necessarily more perfect than others. Comparing Christians to the Hebrews, he says: "There are some in the state of the Old Testament who, having charity and the grace of the Holy Spirit, looked chiefly to spiritual and eternal promises, and in this respect they belonged to the new law. In like manner, in the New Testament there are some men who have not yet attained to the perfection of the new law."[17] This could very well be applied to the relative merits of individual Christians and non-Christians today.

3. THE PRIMACY OF LOVE

The double commandment of love (Mt. 22:34–40; Mk. 12:28–34; Lk. 10:25–28), which sums up the whole law and the prophets, is explicitly taken from the Old Testament (Deut. 6:5; Lev. 19:18). But in Christ's teaching, the two elements or aspects are so joined together as to give a new extension and depth, so that the Lord can speak of it as His "new" commandment (Jn. 13:34). Christ reveals the scope and demand of charity in His very person and life.

In his first epistle, John insists on love of neighbor as the criterion of genuine love of God (3:17, 20–21). For Paul, love is the more excellent way that gives meaning to everything else in a man's life (1 Cor. 12:31; cf. 13:1ff). It is the bond of perfection (Col. 3:14), through which all other moral demands are fulfilled (Rom. 13:8–10; Gal. 5:14).

Man is already created in the image of God (Gen. 1:26) with the capacity to know and love. Yet the divine gift of *agape* in Christ transcends the purely human, not in the sense of being superadded to it, but marvellously transforming it, drawing it into the sphere of the divine. "In this is love, not that we loved God, but that he loved us" (1 Jn. 4:10). "See what love the Father has given us, that we should be called children of God; and so we are" (1 Jn. 3:1).

Through the divine gift of *agape*, man not only receives a new glimpse of God's lovableness but is caught up into the sphere of God's own love, into loving as God does, since God, who is love (1 Jn. 4:8), communicates Himself to man through Christ, who is the supreme manifestation of the Father's love (Jn. 15:9–12), and through the power of the Spirit, who is the bond of love between the Father and the Son. Indeed, "God's love has been poured into our hearts through the Holy Spirit which has been given to us" (Rom. 5:5). It is not enough to offer God our works (practices of virtue); we must offer our very person, too: we must love God with all our heart. All our works must be expressions and tokens of our personal surrender to Him. Similarly, we must recognize in our fellowmen children of God and, hence, true brothers and sisters in Christ. All our relations with them must be characterized by this realization. Vatican II points out that Christ has "taught us that the new commandment of love was the basic law of human perfection and hence of the world's transformation."[18]

Teilhard de Chardin has shown the importance of love in the evolutionary perspective. The future of the *noosphere* (realm of the mind), for Teilhard, hinges upon the growth of *"amorization,"* or free circulation of love energy over the surface of the earth, since love is the highest form of that radial energy upon which the evolutionary progress depends. "To what force is it given," he asks, "to merge and exalt our partial rays into the principal radiance of Christ, the beginning and end of all spiritual relationship?"[19]

In an analogous sense, Teilhard does not hesitate to call love a property of matter, life and man. Love is the basic energy of life, the only natural means by which the ascending movement of evolution can continue. Without love we are faced with the prospect of standardization and slavery, the fate of the termite and the ant. Love, he says, "links those who love in bonds that unite but do not confound, causing them to discover in their mutual contact an exaltation capable, incomparably more than the arrogance of solitude, of arousing in the heart of their being all that they possess of uniqueness and creative power."[20] He insists that "love alone is capable of uniting living beings in such a way as to complete and fulfill them, for it alone takes them and joins them by what is deepest in themselves."[21]

Hence all genuine moral effort is, in fact, working with Christ to amorize the cosmos, to bring love into it. Love is the key to the whole moral order. It is that "psycho-moral energy" which "physically builds up the universe."[22] Its deliberate rejection, therefore, would be a true injury to one's person as well as to humanity as a whole.

Moral virtues or actions are incapable of making a man morally good unless they are *expressions* or *mediations* of a love which is self-giving after the manner of Christ's love for the Father and His brethren, and a *participation* in that selfsame love. This is what is meant by *the primacy of love* in moral life.

St. Thomas has expressed this by saying that charity is the *form* of all other virtues. "It is charity which directs the acts of all these virtues to the last end, and which, consequently, *gives the form* to all other acts of virtue."[23]

"Form" here does not refer to the formal cause, but to the voluntary ordaining of the moral reality to the ultimate end. Each virtue has a special form of its own, which accounts for its particular nature, as well as a general form, which properly makes it a virtue by communicating to it its own perfection. This latter is no other than charity or intrinsic ordering of the act to the final end. As St. Thomas writes, "Since true virtue is that which is directed to man's principal good . . . no other virtue is possible without charity."[24]

Already on the natural plane, the moral act is informed by natural love, which is the form of natural virtues, since love is the fundamental movement of our being by which we seek union with God and others. On the supernatural plane, charity is the intrinsic elevation of our principle of action inasmuch as it is divinized by grace. However, since man in the concrete is in the supernatural order, this distinction is of limited significance.

Charity not only informs a virtue when it passes into act, but is already present in the very essence of the particular virtue, which, nevertheless, possesses its proper nature.[25] Thus, for St. Thomas, charity is the very *soul of moral life,* penetrating it through and through.

It must be carefully noted that the primacy of charity should not be understood to mean that love is the greatest of virtues, with love being put alongside other virtues. The following discussion, we hope, will help discard the common habit of considering love as one among the moral virtues, although calling it the most important. Love is not so much a virtue as *virtue of virtues.* It is found in every virtue and hence in every area of life.

The old manualists considered only the material aspect of human acts while neglecting the soul of morality. Moral theology thereby lost its inspiration and was atomized into unconnected chapters dealing with various duties. These, divorced from the dynamism of love, lack the driving power that would lead man to God. Nowhere is this clearer than in the separation of love from justice. The virtue of justice is made to deal with minimal obligations, while "charity" is limited to acts of "supererogation."

It is of the utmost importance to realize the true relationship between love and justice. Certain pious people are prone to think that it is enough to concentrate on love, to feel love, pity or mercy for the poor and now and then dole out "charity" out of supposed generosity. They may not directly steal or injure others; but they do not feel any qualms of conscience in supporting an unjust social structure, provided what is called "law and order" is maintained, even though it may be promoting supreme lawlessness that oppresses the poor. On the other hand, certain anarchical revolutionaries are so obsessed with bringing about immediate justice and equality that they seem to forget the need of love and reconciliation. As a result, many revolutions result only in graver injustice than the previous system, apart from the disproportionate cost in terms of human suffering.

As an example of a poignant rejection of love that neglects justice, we may cite the remark of Sammy Davis, a popular black American entertainer who repudiated Christianity and became a Jew: "As I see it, the difference is that the Christian religion preaches 'Love thy neighbor' and the Jewish religion preaches justice, and I think justice is the big thing we need."[26] Davis may have been wrong in making a sweeping generalization or in misunderstanding the true character of Christianity; but his bitter words apply to anyone, of any religion, who thinks that it is enough to preach or feel love without practicing justice. It is tragic that some pious people try to practice love without justice, while others, who are less pious, strive for justice without the attitude of love. There should be no such specialization.

As Bernard Häring teaches, "In a sense, it can be said that love is the only absolute value or law. But then we must know what we mean by 'apart from.' We cannot mean that sincerity, gentleness, temperance, justice, the courage to sacrifice, or respect for self and others are something apart from love. They are the very features of the countenance of love, the elements of its composition. In them and through them, love shows its face. Love is all morality, not in the sense of excluding the other virtues, but in the sense of including them all and giving them their real meaning and value."[27]

A one-sided emphasis on love that neglects justice can lead to paternalism, which degrades the objects of its supposed compassion. As Edward Schillebeeckx remarks: "However well it may be intended, this paternalism which condescends in mercy may well contain a fundamental failure to appreciate the primary condition for true love-justice. . . . The minimum demand for love is justice, which is the presupposition of love and indeed to some extent enters into the very essence of love itself. Before a human person can be received into a loving I-thou relationship so as to give form to a truly human community of persons, this love demands the recognition of the other person in his inalienable personality and independence."[28]

Here we may refer to what is known as *bourgeois ethic,* which is a caricature of a genuine morality of love. It has three main features:

1) An inbuilt inhibition against hurting others at close quarters, but little against causing terrible misery like starvation or death to thousands through speculation on the stock exchange, manipulating prices, etc. Its practitioners are shocked at a murder committed in the neighborhood but callous at the mass killing of thousands of people by a bomb dropped from a great height or in remote areas.

2) Being concerned about the rights of a few to the utter neglect of the rights of innumerable others, who are thought to be of little significance. Thus the bourgeois press will publish sensational accounts of the kidnapping of one individual, but will report as a matter of fact the death or imprisonment of thousands of others.

3) "Little morality of little things" as opposed to the wider morality that gravely affects the destiny of mankind over long stretches of

time. Together with this, there is the danger of mistaking "personal" for what is immediate, superficial and temporary.

The extent to which love divorced from justice can go was manifested in some well-meaning people who objected to social reforms in the nineteenth century on the grounds that if there were no more poverty, there would be no more occasions for practicing the supernatural virtue of charity.

Today, fortunately, the poor have realized that nothing is more inimical to their interests than the patronizing attitude of "liberals" who would want to relieve their distress without destroying institutional injustice and, in the process, assuage their own guilt for belonging to the exploiting class.

There is urgent need for going beyond empty love and practicing *effective love through striving after justice,* whatever it might cost. Referring to social services, Edward Schillebeeckx rightly says: "The fact that what was previously mercy has now become justice is a clear indication that man's awareness is becoming increasingly interior, profound and spiritual. At the same time, it also means that *caritas* itself continues to call forth an increasingly deep sense of justice, to regard charitable elements as pertaining to justice and thus, as disinterested, overabundant and brotherly love, to grow towards the full human form of love."[29]

Similarly, in the matter of sexuality, while there can be no true chastity without love or respect for persons, there cannot, on the other hand, be true love without respecting the order of chastity. "It's all a matter of loving" may be no more than an excuse for avoiding the difficult task of making difficult choices. Rationalizing extramarital intercourse may well be a form of self-deception.

From the examples of justice and chastity, we can see the merits and the limitations of a "love ethic," an ethic that would make love the sole criterion for morality. Its good points derive from these two facts: 1) that moral life requires a flexibility which love alone can provide, since the primary object of morality seems to be meeting the needs of others with understanding and concern; 2) and that rule morality tends to be minimalistic and to foster self-righteousness at the expense of generosity and compassion.

But Stanley Hauerwas cautions: "Most of our loving is more an assertion of self than a recognition of the other. We seldom love the other as he is; rather we love the other by imposing upon him our preconceived image of who he is. For we cannot stand to love the other in his particularity. . . . We, therefore, love the other only as we make him an aspect of our plan. . . . We do not fall in love with a real person, but with the person we have created through our fantasy."[30]

Even as progressive a theologian as Charles E. Curran has difficulty with making love the "stance" of moral theology. He finds it too simplistic to reduce all morality to love.[31] If love is to have an all-encompassing and exclusive role in developing moral theology, it should be capable of a clear definition. But it is a most complex reality which includes many aspects: *agape* (love of self-giving), *philia* (love of friendship), *eros* (love of desire), etc.

Jesus does not so much tell us to love as to establish the conditions that make love possible. He accompanies His great commandment with the parable of the good samaritan. This is not only an illustration of the principle of love, but is the moral meaning of the principle.

It must not be imagined that Jesus came to teach the mere platitude that we ought to love everyone. He came as the very embodiment of true love, which implies truth, justice and sacrifice. "Christian ethic is ultimately an ethic of truth or it is neither Christian nor an ethic substantive enough to deal with the human condition. Love can only be authentic when it faces the conditions under which we must love in this existence."[32]

Nowadays, there is a tendency to desire a morality that needs no discipline or training. "Love" seems to foot the bill, as it appears to require no more than immediacy of response. Such trivialization of the ethic of the Gospel would trivialize our own lives.

Many married couples live in a superficial relationship because they dare not face the truth about themselves. Likewise, we often find it easier to be honest with strangers than with those closest to us, since with strangers we have nothing to lose by revealing the truth about ourselves.

A love ethic, then, must not be such an ethic of ease as to assume that we can reach no higher than our immediate desires. Man is prone to illusions, and no illusion is more resistant than the assumption that we must always be right because we seem to act from love. A superficial love seeks to escape all pain and effort. "Being unwilling to make others and ourselves suffer for our principles is but to admit that nothing in this life is worth ourselves or others making a sacrifice for."[33] While saying this, it is presumed that the "principles" in question are not arbitrary.

We should again note that the biblical message provides the criteria to distinguish between true love and its counterfeits, between the works of the Spirit and works of the "flesh" (cf. Gal. 5:22–23). St. Paul also spells out in detail what true love in daily life means. It should be patient and kind; not jealous or boastful; not arrogant or rude; not insisting on its own way; not irritable or resentful; not rejoicing at wrong, but in the right; bearing all things, believing all things, enduring all things (1 Cor. 13:4–7).

Love does not destroy the law; it fulfills it. But in fulfilling the law, love does destroy its form *as law* and makes it a creative and liberating factor in human affairs. Law by itself is inhuman; but love by itself may be blind. Therefore, while the law requires the dynamism of love, love in return calls for the pedagogy of the law.

One who is thoroughly penetrated by the divine *agape* may not need the external guidance of the law, since he would spontaneously fulfill the demands of the law and seek the values that the law strives to embody. This is the meaning of St. Augustine's profound saying, *"Dilige et quod vis, fac"* ("Love and then, what you will, do," not "Love and do what you please"). One who has a sincere and mature love will naturally will or intend what is truly in accordance with human perfection and God's will. This calls for great spiritual maturity and discernment. To the extent that one has attained mature love, one no longer needs the law. However, in this mortal pilgrimage, a humble man will admit his imperfection and accept the pedagogy of the law.

The Christian, then, must above all seek to cultivate a loving heart. He will cultivate a sacrificial love after the example of Christ. But he will give due (although secondary) place to law, which he will understand, not as an end in itself, but as a mediation of love.

4. THE UNITY OF LOVE OF GOD AND LOVE OF NEIGHBOR

There is a certain tension between the service of God through religious observance and the service of man through socio-economic activity. Often religion is looked upon as an escape from the real problems of life. On the other hand, some feel that complete involvement in social activities leads to neglect of spiritual realities and responsibilities. In order to remove such misunderstandings, it is necessary to comprehend the real nature and internal unity of the love of God and love of man.

Let us go back to the New Testament. Jesus declares that the two commandments upon which the law and the prophets hang are equal (cf. Mt. 22:39–40). At the final coming of Christ, His criterion for judgment will be love of neighbor: "Come, O blessed of my Father, inherit the kingdom prepared for you from the foundation of the world; for I was hungry and you gave me food. . . . Truly, I say to you, as you did it to one of the least of these my brethren, you did it to me" (Mt. 25:34–35, 40). Neglect of this love is anarchy and it will be the first of the sufferings in the last days (cf. Mt. 24:12). On the other hand, Christ as the incarnate Son of God will consider anything that is done to the "least of His brethren" as done to Himself.

According to St. Paul, love of neighbor is *the* fulfillment of the law (Rom. 13:8,10: Gal. 5:14). It binds everything together in harmony (Col. 3:14). It is the "better way" (1 Cor. 12:31). Since "God is love," says John, "he who abides in love abides in God" (1 Jn. 4:16). In fact, the love of God, who is transcendent, is possible only through the mediation of the love of neighbor. Therefore, John writes, "If anyone says 'I love God' and hates his brother, he is a liar; for he who does not love his brother whom he sees, cannot love God whom he has not seen" (1 Jn. 4:20).

As Karl Rahner points out, since we cannot reach God in gnostic-mystic interiority alone, we can attain the God in us in *mutual brotherly love*.[34] "The love of God unreflectedly but really and always intends God in supernatural transcendentality in the love of neighbor as such, and even the explicit love of God is still borne by that opening in trusting love to the whole of reality which takes place in the love of neighbor."[35]

Fraternal love is the participation in God's love for us in Christ. We express this love in our relationships with others. Those who are blessed with the living presence of the Father and the Son through the Holy Spirit love others with the same divine love. They, too, will be one even as the divine Persons are one (Jn. 17:21–23).

The gift of divine sonship in Christ necessarily calls for mutual love among men. If one claims to live the life of Christ, one must also love as He loved (Jn. 15:10; 13:34).

Human relations provide man with the direction which presents the desired vista of an intersubjectivity with God, since man gains mature possession of himself in giving himself to others. "As the absolute ground of being, God is the transcendent Third in all human experiences and, above all, in our interpersonal relationships. . . . Under this aspect, God is experienced in and through our love toward our fellowmen and the world, realizing fully that we ourselves are not the ultimate source of this human love and the secular involvement."[36]

Brotherly love, therefore, cannot be considered merely as a preparation for the love of God, nor its consequence, nor even its touchstone. Instead, it is love of God itself manifested in action. If God is seen in all His creation, He is seen most clearly and most strikingly in the experience of brotherly love. That is why St. Thomas says that we love God and man in the very same act. We need not hesitate to affirm that human love, if it is sincere, touching the very depths of existence, is truly inspired by God's saving grace, even though one may not be conscious of it.

We should not see any dichotomy between God's redemptive activity and man's dedicated work on earth. A moral act performed freely becomes a saving act. The content of this act and its inspiration may not derive explicitly from God's revealed Word, and may not appear to relate to God; even then, this act can become redemptive by God's universal salvific will. God continuously pours out His sanctifying grace on all men. He thus divinizes all activity flowing from genuine human virtue. Whenever we see total and sincere self-giving, we should perceive God's saving grace moving it. Thus, we are called upon to accept and respect, not only men of other faiths, but also those who call themselves atheists. He who does not acknowledge the work of saving grace wherever men are engaged in selfless service for the humanization of the world, is not a man of faith. At the same time, a man of faith must present religion, not as an escape from commitment to this world, but as a deepening of that commitment and as an effort to realize the most profound aspirations of man. He has to meet the challenge of Marx, who called religion "the opium of the people" when many men of religion were using the promise of a life hereafter and the consolations it offered to prevent the oppressed from revolting against unjust social structures. Religion is not genuine until it uncompromisingly stands for the perfection of what is deeply human and for the unity of all men. Religion should work like a leaven in society in order to hasten the process of hominization.

Every selfless activity directed toward the universe begins and ends in God. The deep-rooted I-thou relationship man has with God should manifest itself in his I-thou relationship with other human beings. As Teilhard de Chardin puts it: "Christian charity, which is preached so fervently in the Gospels, is nothing else than the more or less conscious cohesion of souls engendered by their communal convergence *in Christo Jesu*. It is impossible to love Christ without loving others (in proportion as these others are moving toward Christ); it is impossible to love others (in a spirit of broad human cohesion) without moving closer to Christ."[37]

This does not mean that it is meaningless to stand before God in prayer. In fact, communion between human persons is deepened by a conscious relation to and contemplation of Him "in whom we live, move and have our being" (Acts 17:28). Jesus Himself spent long hours in silent communion with the eternal Father even while He spent His whole life in the service of His brethren. In the present crucial period of the world, we should realize that only a living faith in the one true God can provide adequate motivation for a profound and persevering service, especially in caring for the underprivileged and abandoned.

The whole universe is a manifestation of the glory of God. It is also a sign of God's love for man, for whom it is created. The world is not a finished product. In the great task of perfecting the universe, God invites men to cooperate with Him in a spirit of brotherhood. Thus God's glory will be perfected, and man will share in this glory. In the words of Teilhard, "Since everything in the universe is ultimately moving toward the Christ-Omega . . . everything becomes physically and literally lovable in God. And God in turn becomes accessible and lovable in everything around us."[38]

The bond generated between us and the universe when we see the image of God in all things should sow in us the seeds of an optimism that will outweigh the moral and physical evil existing in the world. Evil throws out a challenge to keep hoping in the final triumph of God's truth. We are invited to face evil with the help of God's grace. Love is the basis of our faith in God's providence, which is able to bring good out of evil. It is again love that inspires men to become instruments in God's hand in the fight against the social evils that assail God's children.

Love is the basic force in life. According to Teilhard, it is the natural medium in the upward movement of evolution. Today, more than ever, love should be injected into every human undertaking. Totalitarian structures and various forms of slavery take root in the absence of love. Only when the whole human race becomes one in love can it become a totality that will enhance the deepest qualities of man and bring about the fulfillment of the total person. For this, it is not enough to love individuals, but our love should embrace the whole human community and even the whole universe.

5. LOVE OF SELF AND LOVE OF OTHERS

Jack Dominian rightly bemoans the odium with which the idea of loving oneself is surrounded in certain Christian circles. Man's first enemy is made out to be himself. He goes to the extent of saying: "The most basic tenet of the Judeo-Christian faith of loving our neighbour as ourselves has not only been hardly developed as yet but, in fact, there is not the remotest hope of really succeeding in loving our neighbour in a sustained manner until we first have learned to know the meaning of loving ourselves."[39]

In the otherwise excellent spiritual work *The Imitation of Christ,* there is unfortunately a strong streak of self-depreciation, too much concentration on one's miseries. In the mind of John Calvin, too, man is supposed to be essentially evil and powerless: "For I do not call it humility if you suppose that we have anything left. . . We cannot think of ourselves as we ought without utterly despising everything that may be supposed an excellence in us."[40]

Repeated warnings against love of self have often been powerful ideological tools in suppressing spontaneity and the free development of personality. One is continually invited to complete submission and sacrifice of self. Only those acts are considered to be unselfish which serve, not the individual, but only someone else or some interest outside of oneself.

Freud's theory of the *libido* seems to move in the same direction—the more I turn toward the outside, the less love is left for myself, and vice versa. On the other hand, one of the merits of Transactional Analysis is to have shown the harm caused to people by feeling "I'm not O.K.!" Psychiatry in general has uncovered *neurotic* unselfishness, which is superficially felt as a redeeming character trait on which a person can pride himself. He can boast that he does not want anything for himself. But he is puzzled to find that his self-effacement is not satisfying, but only causes depression, fatigue and inability to work. In fact, he is paralyzed in his capacity to love and is pervaded by hostility against life in general. Behind the facade of unselfishness, there is in fact an intense, though subtle, self-centeredness.

We are discovering that we cannot love unless we first experience love. There is need of affirmative acceptance of self in spite of limitations, and need of a positive appreciation of our potential. How can we love others unless we first experience a sense of value in ourselves which we can donate to others? How can we give ourselves if we are plagued with a feeling of worthlessness?

Feelings of inadequacy and inferiority in one's personality are generally countered by defense mechanisms, so that a great deal of psychic energy is expended in protecting oneself from real or imaginary evil parts of one's personality. There is that much less strength left for generosity and self-donation. A study of the psychological development of personality shows that realization of autonomy and personal affirmation are basic to genuine love. "In order to love others, we must first attain a sense of separate personal availability to ourselves and become aware that we are not a mere extension of our parents. Secondly, we need to feel that what belongs to us, our bodies and minds, feel and are good, so that what we offer others is basically good."[41]

In the past, humility was often presented as self-depreciation so that the self might be kept under control. But true humility implies acceptance of reality, the good as well as the bad in us. The good we should refer to God, and the bad we should try to overcome with His grace. The most humble Maiden of Nazareth did not hesitate to proclaim: "He who is mighty has done great things for me" (Lk. 1:49).

Hence, there is no basic contradiction between love of self and love of others. If it is a virtue to love my neighbor as a human being, it must also be a virtue to love myself, since I too am a human being. Respect for one's own integrity and uniqueness cannot be separated from respect for and love and understanding of another person. That is why Jesus bids us: "You shall love your neighbor as yourself" (Mt. 22:39). Paul finds it natural that a man loves his body person: "For no man ever hates his own flesh, but nourishes and cherishes it" (Eph. 5:29). Likewise he says: "Husbands should love their wives as their own bodies. He who loves his wife loves himself" (v. 28).

Genuine love implies care, respect, responsibility and active striving for the growth and happiness of the beloved, which are based on one's capacity to love. Since love of one person implies love of man as such, my own self, in principle, must be as much an object of my love as is that other person.

Selfishness, on the other hand, is not the same as love of self but is caused by the very lack of it. The selfish individual is interested only in himself, wants everything for himself. Since he judges everyone and everything from the point of view of "use-fulness," he is unable to experience relationship and is basically unable to love.

As Erich Fromm puts it: "The selfish person does not love himself too much but too little, in fact he hates himself. This lack of fondness and care of himself, which is one expression of his lack of productiveness, leaves him empty and frustrated. He is necessarily unhappy and anxiously concerned to snatch from life the satisfaction which he blocks himself from attaining. He seems to care too much for himself but actually he only makes an unsuccessful attempt to cover up and compensate for his failure to care for his real self. It is true that selfish persons are incapable of loving others, but they are not capable of loving themselves either."[42]

Selfishness can be compared to greedy interest in others—for instance, in a dominating mother. While she believes that she is specially fond of the child, she has actually a deeply repressed hostility toward him. She is overconcerned, not because of her love for the child, but because of the need to compensate for her inability to love him.

————o————

Notes to Chapter X

1. *A New Pentecost,* London, Darton, Longman and Todd, 1974, p. 81.
2. *AC,* art. 2.
3. *GS,* art. 38. Cf. Pierre-Thomas Camelot, "God, a Spirit who Makes One Live," 1 *Concilium,* 1978, 21–28.
4. *GS,* art. 1.
5. *AC,* art. 29.
6. *LG,* art. 22.
7. *Human Values and Christian Morality,* p. 82.
8. *Ibid.,* p. 83.
9. *Summa Theologica,* Ia-Ilae, 108, 1, 2.
10. Ceslaus Spicq, *St. Paul and Christian Living,* p. 63.
11. *Summa Theologica,* Ia-Ilae, 106, 1.
12. *Ibid.*
13. *Ibid.*
14. *Ibid.,* 106, 2.
15. Josef Fuchs, *op. cit.,* p. 86.
16. *Summa Theologica,* Ia-Ilae, 106, 2.
17. *Ibid.,* 107, 1, 2.
18. *GS,* art. 38.
19. *Le Milieu Divin,* p. 125.
20. *The Future of Man,* London, Collins, 1964, p. 58.
21. *The Phenomenon of Man,* London, Collins, 1959, p. 265.
22. Cf. *The Future of Man,* p. 54.
23. Ila-Ilae, 23, 8.
24. Ia-Ilae, 49, 1.
25. Gerard Gilleman, *The Primacy of Charity in Moral Theology,* Westminster, Md., Newman, 1959, pp. 31ff.
26. Quoted in Josef Fletcher, *Moral Responsibility,* Philadelphia, Westminster Press, 1967, p. 42.

27. *Morality Is for Persons*, p. 126.

28. *Word and Church*, London, Sheed and Ward, 1970, p. 216.

29. *Ibid.*

30. *Vision and Virtue*, Notre Dame, Ind., Fides, 1974, pp. 33–52.

31. *New Perspectives in Moral Theology*, Notre Dame, Ind., Fides, 1974, pp. 48–52.

32. Stanley Hauerwas, *op. cit.*, p. 117.

33. *Ibid.*, p. 122.

34. *Theological Investigations*, London, Darton, Longman and Todd, 1969, Vol. VI, p. 235.

35. *Ibid.*, p. 247.

36. Edward Schillebeeckx, *op. cit.*, pp. 164–65.

37. *Le Milieu Divin*, p. 125.

38. *Science and Christ*, p. 168.

39. Jack Dominian and A. R. Peacocke, *From Cosmos to Love*, London, Darton, Longman and Todd, 1976, p. 43.

40. *Institutions of the Christian Religion*, Ch. 13, Philadelphia, Presbyterian Board of Christian Education, p. 681.

41. Jack Dominian, *op. cit.*, p. 54.

42. *Man for Himself*, New York, Fawcett World Library, 1920, pp. 135–36.

CHAPTER XI

The Natural (Moral) Law

We have seen that, although the primary source of Christian morality is the interior grace of the Spirit of Christ, still the weakness of man needs the aid of law. It can save him from superficiality and arbitrariness if it is the expression of genuine moral value. In its absence, there may not be sufficient protection against the domination of some over others. The discovery of moral laws and principles is an attempt to make us alive to the basis of creative human interaction. But the objectivity of the law, which ought to be a protection against subjective arbitrariness, is always in danger of legalistic pretensions. So it must be based on the shared commitments and values of a loving community.

Law in its widest meaning is any constant of action and reaction; thus we can speak of the laws of physics, chemistry and so on. Here we are concerned not only with human activity like the arts, which have their own canons, but with the activity of *man as man*—the directing of his life to his final end. Such laws can be either *positive,* i.e., framed by human authority, or *moral,* derived immediately from the inner being of man. These latter are a reflection of the divine plan concerning man and, especially in the Catholic tradition, are said to belong to the ''natural law.''

Law has two dimensions: 1) It is an expression of an intrinsic human *value* and of the call of God. Looked at from this perspective, law is internalized. It appears as an invitation to love and as a way of attaining human perfection. Hence it is not felt as a burden. 2) It is also a *demand* and, as such, seems to come from outside and appears like a constraint provoking resistance. It is, therefore, very important in moral education to propose law in the right perspective, primarily as *an expression of a human value*. Demand there is, but the demand must be shown to flow from a value, and the emphasis should clearly be on the value. Thus, children should be helped to see that, underlying the commandment "Don't lie," is the value of openness to each other in the spirit of brotherhood.

1. HISTORY OF THE NATURAL LAW DOCTRINE

To the Greeks, the world in which they lived was a *cosmos,* an ordered and harmonious whole. The Stoics, by assuming an *immanent Logos* in nature and in man, identified the principle of reason in every individual man with the cosmic order of the universe.

The Stoics evolved a concept of the natural law that was not much different from the laws regulating the physical order of the universe. Thus, from the start the concept had a physical bias among the Greeks, although they were rather flexible in making concrete applications.[1]

Later, Roman jurists noted certain common elements amidst the wide variety of laws and customs of the peoples that came under the *Pax Romana*. This was called the *ius gentium* (law of the nations), distinguished from the *ius* proper to each nation. It roughly corresponded to what is referred to as "common law" in Anglo-Saxon countries.

The *ius gentium,* acknowledged as the work of human reason, was accepted as the common heritage of all peoples and became a unifying and integrating force in the Empire. It was practically equivalent to the natural law. However, the Romans ultimately accepted the Hellenistic view of the basis of the *ius naturale*. According to the great Roman jurist Ulpian, it is "that which teaches all animals," i.e., the law common to man and animals apart from any intervention of human reason. This posed the danger of identifying natural law with brute natural tendency.

Although the early exponents of the natural law were under the impression that they were expounding a universal concept of law applicable to all historical and cultural situations, their concept was, in fact, largely conditioned by their mechanistic world view and a horizon that was limited to a small part of the world.

Hence, the origin of the concept of natural law was not so happy. However, although early Christianity largely derived its semantic framework from the Greeks and the Romans, it certainly transformed the idea. Already Paul, who speaks about the Gentiles doing by nature (*physis*) what the Jewish Torah requires (Rom. 2:14), immediately adds that the law is written in their "heart." Hence the Christian view is more concerned with what is specifically human than with what belongs to the physical universe or the animal world.

St. Augustine links the Platonic-Stoic idea of the eternal law with the thought of the personal God creating through His eternal Word (Jn. 1). He derives this idea from the Hebrew tradition, according to which the harmony observed in nature is not a mechanical unity but one brought about by the personal will of Yahweh. Nature itself becomes dependable because of the dependable will of Yahweh.

The formulation of the natural law at the hands of the great medieval thinkers saw a considerable evolution under the influence of the Gospel and centuries of Christian tradition.

In his great synthesis on law in the *Summa Theologica,* Ia-Ilae, QQ. 90–108, St. Thomas adopts a personal perspective. While the Stoa had identified law with the cosmic order, for St. Thomas the eternal law is the same as God's wisdom and providence. Man, unlike irrational beings, participates in this eternal law through reason. "The light of natural reason which enables us to distinguish between good and evil—which belongs to the natural law—is nothing but an imprint of the divine light in us."[2] This is far from the physicist or biological mentality which many critics of the natural law concept find in it today.

Natural law, according to St. Thomas, consists in certain fundamental moral judgments acquired intuitively and not by deductive reason. These self-evident principles of the moral order can be reduced to "Good is to be done, and evil is to be avoided." Only these first principles are absolutely universal. Other general laws, derived from these, may perhaps admit of exceptions because of accidental circumstances.

After St. Thomas, there was a strong voluntaristic trend that attributed natural law to the positive will of God. Later, there was a swing back to rationalism, which, this time, was excessive and tended to neglect the human perspective of St. Thomas. During the last century, natural law theories were further influenced by the rationalism of the era and the Church's tendency to adopt fixed positions as a defensive reaction against the challenges of the modern world. The concept acquired a rigid connotation at the hands of the manualists, although those who have studied their works at first hand will notice a lot of nuances which have escaped the casual observer or the hasty critic.

St. Thomas had distinguished between *lex naturalis,* or human reason seeking to regulate total human conduct, and *ius naturale,* comprising the basic tendencies and inclinations which needed to be studied empirically and regulated by reason. Later manualists reduced natural law to the given aspects of the *ius naturale* and thereby downplayed the creative and regulative role of reason as well as the function of empirical investigation.

The renewal of Thomistic studies at the turn of the century prepared the way for an understanding of the humanistic dimensions of the natural law. They were well brought out in writings such as those of Jacques Maritain. However, as this trend was not sufficiently strong, with the current stress on freedom and the concrete existential situation, there has been considerable disaffection toward the concept of natural law. There have also been several efforts to revitalize the doctrine. We are now witnessing a strong polarization between those who react against the old rigidity and those who adopt defensive postures.

The magisterium of the Catholic Church, during the past hundred years, has been increasingly using the natural law in its exposition of social, medical and sexual ethics. Pope Pius XII frequently emphasized the validity of the natural law and the Church's right and duty to interpret it. The two great encyclicals of Pope John XIII, *Mater et Magistra* and *Pacem in Terris*, are a magnificent charter of human rights based on the natural law.

Vatican II has presented a decidely personalitic view of the natural law. It has recourse to the doctrine in several places. Regarding the question of war, "the Council wishes to recall first of all the permanent binding force of the natural law of nations and its all-embracing principles."[3] The Church is said to strengthen peace "by imparting knowledge of the divine and natural law."[4] It is the duty of the Church "to declare and confirm by her authority those principles of the moral order which have their origin in human nature itself."[5] Speaking of the methods for regulating births, though the Council does not intend to finally resolve the question then under study by a papal commission, it states that "they must be determined by objective criteria. These, based on the nature of the human person and his acts, preserve the full sense of mutual self-giving and human procreation."[6]

Pope Paul VI has largely based his teaching with regard to the development of peoples (*Populorum Progressio*) on the natural law. *Humanae Vitae* calls natural law "an expression of the divine will."[7] It asks couples to conform their activity of transmitting life "to the creative intention of God, expressed in the very nature of marriage and its acts."[8] The encyclical bids them to respect "God's design" and speaks of "laws attached by God to the very act of generation."[9]

The Reformers, on the whole, rejected the idea of the natural law because of their view that sin has so affected creation and human reason that these can no longer serve as source of ethical knowledge.[10] Helmut Thielicke sees here a basic difference between Catholicism and the Reformed tradition: "The possibility of working back to the ethical order depends upon the understanding of sin, upon the degree to which we think the being of the world is altered and impaired by the result of the fall."[11]

Protestant theology has generally stressed the immediate character of God's relationship with man, although it has had to make room for some form of mediation. Catholic theology has, on the contrary, developed the idea of the mediations of divine action in terms of the Church, the sacraments, natural law and Church law. Catholic moral theology has tended to be somewhat overoptimistic about man's power to attain moral knowledge through human reason, while Protestant moral theology has inclined in the opposite direction.

Still, the theory of the natural law has retained its hold in some Anglican circles. English tradition, especially in social ethics, adopted the idea of "created orders," "God-given or natural intentions," e.g., the family and the state. Lutherans, too, have been speaking about "orders of creation."

Ferdinand Tonnies (1887) tried to find a sociological basis for the natural law. Archbishop William Temple called a wartime conference on "The Life of the Church and Order of Society" in 1941 to discuss a coherent scheme of war and peace aims, at which several papers based on the natural law were read.

In spite of their depreciation of fallen human nature, Emil Brunner and Dietrich Bonhoeffer were constrained to make room in their ethical system for a rough counterpart of natural law morality. Brunner referred to "divine orders": marriage and family, labor, government or state, culture and Church. Bonhoeffer spoke of "mandates," since this term refers more clearly to a divinely imposed task rather than to a determination of being.

German Protestantism had tended to entrust all that was not explicitly determined in the Scriptures to the discretion of civil authority. But the incredible horrors of the Nazi regime produced a shock and, to an extent, brought home the need for human ethical reflection by whatever name it might be called. Thus, in fact, there was some revival of the natural law perspective after the war.

In recent years, especially in the United States, Protestants increasingly recognize the existence of a common ground for morality which Christians share with others. They would admit the basic goodness of creation as a source of moral wisdom, provided its imperfection and selfishness are recognized.

After a thorough study of the problem of theological ethics and the ethics of Neo-Protestantism, N. H. G. Robinson comes to the conclusion that "it is impossible to resolve the dilemmas in the current discussion of the Christian ethic unless one is prepared to affirm a doctrine of natural morality, of which the traditional doctrine of the natural law was but one possible version."[12]

So, for many Protestants, it is no longer a question of rejecting "natural" morality, but of determining the kind that is acceptable within the Christian context. Protestants, on the whole, still fight shy of the term *natural law*. However, some are now ready to use it. David Little is one of them. He refers to natural law as "a set of empirical generalizations about human nature that is constant, both spatially (cross-culturally) and temporally (historically), from which a set of moral prescriptions can be derived."[13] Although he would soften the claims of traditional natural law theory, he is moving toward the natural basis for the formulation of perduring moral norms.

2.　FOUNDATION IN THE BIBLE[14]

It is vain to look for a systematic formulation of the natural law doctrine in the Bible. Even the term is nowhere to be found. Still, there are several indications of its substance.

Most of the ethical teaching of the Old Testament is derived from the ancient wisdom of the peoples bordering Israel, although it has been assumed into the perspective of the Yahwistic faith and the bond of the covenant. This is true especially of the decalogue, which represents the principal demands of God on His covenanted people. The Wisdom literature is drawn from the instructions of the sages on life and conduct, although it is given a new religious purpose by the biblical writers.

Christ brought a radical newness to man. But this does not mean that the purpose of God for man has altered. "Is the God of our redemption the same as the God of creation? The inevitable answer is that He is the same God. Whenever He confronts mankind, from the moment when through His word man was created, God always confronts him in the charity which was finally disclosed in God's self-sacrifice."[15]

With reference to clean and unclean foods, Jesus hints at the distinction between Jewish ritual regulations, which cease to bind in the new covenant, and the permanent law written in the very heart of man and hence continuing to retain its validity (Mk. 7:14–23).

In condemning divorce Jesus appeals to the established order of creation. "For your hardness of heart Moses allowed you to divorce your wives, but from the beginning it was not so" (Mt. 19:8). The "beginning" here refers to God's original plan. The very nature of man rightly understood points to the ideal of permanent monogamy.

Paul's exposition of sin and redemption presupposes a law known from the reality of creation by virtue of human reason (Rom. 1:19ff). Though the Gentiles are without the positive guidance of the Torah, the embodiment of the positive will of God, they are guilty of acting against the dictates of their reason. Their basic fault of not acknowledging God leads them to "dishonorable passions" or "unnatural vices" (1:26). Jews and Gentiles alike are under judgment, the former because of the injunctions of the Torah, the latter because of the law imprinted in their heart. "When Gentiles who have not the law do *by nature* what the law requires, they are a law to themselves. . . . They show that what the law requires *is written on their hearts,* while their conscience also bears witness" (2:14–15).

According to Paul, therefore, the distinction between good and evil is founded in the nature of things. The decalogue does not establish the distinction between moral good and evil but declares what is already so. The law of God was imprinted in the heart of man by the very fact of creation. This imprinting in the heart does not mean that the law is ready-made and has only to be read off. It only means that man has the radical capacity to reflect on his being and thereby discern how he should act in particular areas of life and in particular situations.

The primitive Christian community soon realized that the Lord had not left definite directions in every matter. Paul himself exhorts the Romans to obey civil authorities, who are in the place of God (13:1ff). But beyond them, there is the need of referring to the very exigencies of human nature uncovered by the light of human reason. Thus Paul himself proposes catalogues of virtues and vices taken from Hellenistic Judaism which, as such, are not derived from biblical revelation. Still, the sins in the catalogues are said to exclude from the Kingdom of God (1 Cor. 6:9–10; Gal. 5:19–21; 1 Tim. 1:9–11). Paul seems to appeal to the intrinsically moral nature of the demands he makes on the believers. What is typically Christian is only the motive that should impel them in their fulfillment.

3. THE MEANING AND BASIS OF THE NATURAL LAW

Contemplating the melancholic state of humanity, Vatican II wishes to recall "the permanent binding force of universal natural law and its all-embracing principles. Man's conscience itself gives even more emphatic voice to these principles."[16] The human conscience reveals to man certain moral norms which he feels bound to obey, independent of his own will. International law, and especially the Universal Declaration of Human Rights by the United Nations, is based on this common conviction.

The axiom *agere sequitur esse* (action follows being) applies in a special way to human life. It implies that man has freely to act according to the divine plan for which he has been created. He has to discern responsibly what action conduces to the glory of God and his own true filfillment.

Now, in view of the rejection of the two-storey image of the relationship between nature and grace, we must not regard Christian morality as simply an addition of natural law (applicable to all men) and divine positive law (applicable only to Christians). Since, in fact, there is no purely natural order that is the subject of moral experience, and since the only existing order is that in which all men are called to be sons of God in Christ, no such simple *separation* and addition are possible. Still, as it is possible to *distinguish* reflectively between the human and the divine in Jesus Christ, although they are inseparable in reality, so also is it possible to distinguish in the vocation of man between what is purely human and the transforming modality that follows from his supernatural vocation.

Much of the confusion and controversy regarding the natural law arises from differing understandings of "nature." Some Catholic writers have understood by "nature" the hypothetical state of "pure nature" in which man would have been if he had not in fact been called to the supernatural order. Such a view gives an air of artificiality to the natural law doctrine. Some recent Catholics, especially in Germany, oppose "nature" to what is specifically human or personal and hence find the whole concept of the natural law too physical or biological.

Lutherans generally understand by "nature" the original situation of man before the fall. They restrict "nature" too narrowly to one stage of salvation history. As this "nature," according to them, has been radically infected by sin, they cannot accept it as a valid basis for morality.

These misconceptions point to the need of carefully defining the concept.[17] First of all, "nature" in the term *natural law* is not opposed to the "spirit." It is rather the whole *spiritual-corporeal essence of man inasmuch as it is the principle of action.* "Nature" here is considered in distinction and abstraction from the supernatural order, which is known only through revelation.

Hence, it is not the physical or biological condition of man that is considered, nor the "original state" of man before the fall; but it is primarily his "metaphysical nature," which simply means those elements which are present in every man *in every conceivable situation.* If one denies the existence of such elements or is unable to grasp their meaning—and, alas, this is true in the case of many because of an excessively phenomenological mode of thinking—then the concept of the natural law would not make much sense to him. Instead of arguing interminably about the natural law, it would be worthwhile to uncover the philosophical presuppositions in the mind of each protagonist in the debate.

The normative value of human nature for morality ultimately depends upon the fact that man is the *image of God*. By creating an image of Himself, God, through this image, calls for a particular form of response. Man's reflection on himself provides a certain picture of his relationship with God. It manifests certain personal and social values, as well as the modes of behavior in which these values are to be realized. Because his being is derived immediately from God, he is bound to live his life according to this pattern. In fact, the basic expression of the natural law begins when *homo sapiens* reaches the stage when he can adore God and love his neighbor as God's image, though he may not yet have the capacity to conceptualize this in abstract terms.

It is true that mankind is evolving and that every man has his own unique personality. But what is it which makes every individual of the human species—granting that there is such a species—a man? Is there something that properly characterizes human beings and distinguishes them from every other kind of being? This element is what is meant by "nature" in natural law.

The moral possibilities of human nature and man's capacity for moral knowledge may be realized in different ways in the course of history or in different cultures, but these can never escape certain *basic directions* without altogether denying that humanity. What these directions are may be difficult to formulate in a way that will not involve historical conditioning. Yet this does not invalidate the notion of the natural law nor rule out the value of discovering its main orientations. Indeed, at a time when mankind is coming together, when the search for what is human is being carried out with unprecedented zeal, it would be suicidal to deny the importance of determining the common exigencies of human nature. It would make documents like the Universal Declaration of Human Rights completely useless. The way would be open to arbitrariness and ever-increasing mutual exploitation.

Due to the widespread misunderstanding of the term *natural*, some would suggest that it be dropped altogether.[18] For the most part, it might be sufficient to speak of moral values and obligations. But we would have to admit, at least implicitly, that there is a moral order flowing from humanity as such, and about which it is possible to enter into dialogue with people of widely differing cultural backgrounds and religious persuasions.

Hence a right appreciation of the natural law presupposes two things: a)   a metaphysical level of thinking; b)   a proper understanding of the relationship between the natural and the supernatural orders. It should be clear that the two are not like upper and lower storeys and that the supernatural does not in any way supplant the natural, but elevates and transforms it without absorbing it.

Josef Fuchs rightly warns that "what can be directly 'read' in man's biological nature is only the manner in which nature works spontaneously if man does not intervene, or also the possible results man can achieve if he wishes to make use of nature functioning in this manner."[19] For instance, by studying reproductive processes, one can discover how pregnancy occurs and how it could be avoided. But what use of biological laws is morally justifiable cannot be immediately discerned from their workings. It would be a "naturalistic fallacy" to think that values can be immediately deduced from bare facts, or that we can tell from a mere description of a state of affairs that it ought or ought not to be brought about. "The norm of conduct of moral behavior cannot simply be found in the fact of its conformity with physical nature as such, but rather in its conformity with the human person taken in his totality—not, therefore, without regard for the peculiarity of purely physical nature."[20]

Here, there are three main trends. The more "situationist" one would not give much importance to the physical structure. The "traditionalist" view would accord it too much importance. A more balanced view would carefully use the *recta ratio* and examine to what extent a particular intervention into biological processes would amount to loss of human values or undue manipulation of the human person, so that there would be an objective moral evil even though one might not subjectively advert to it and would hence be free from personal or subjective guilt.

We have been insisting that "natural law" refers to the basic directions of human nature found in every conceivable situation of man. One should not conclude from this that the natural law is something unreal or ethereal. An adequate exposition of the natural law should also take into consideration the full actuality of nature according to man's basic physical, psychic, spiritual and social dimensions, which are to be realized in existing circumstances. As Bernard Häring writes: "Natural law means the very nature of man in his concrete, historical reality, insofar as he has the capacity to understand himself, his calling and vocation and the meaning of his person and his relationship to God, to fellowmen and to the created universe."[21]

Johannes Messner, a renowned jurist who has based his social doctrine on the natural law, calls these elements the "existential ends" of man. He sums them up as follows: "Self-preservation, including bodily integrity and social respect (personal honor); self-perfection physically and spiritually, including the development of one's faculties for the improvement of the condition of one's life and provision for one's economic welfare by securing the necessary property and income; the enlargement of experience and knowledge; marriage and the rearing of children; interest in the spiritual and material welfare of one's fellowmen as human persons equal in value; social fellowship, to promote common utility, which consists in the maintenance of peace and order and in opportunity for all members of society to attain full existence by sharing proportionally in the welfare of society; the knowledge and worship of God and the ultimate fulfillment of man's destiny through union with Him."[22] More could perhaps be added to this list. It must be acknowledged that traditional authors neglected many of these elements and so presented an impoverished picture of the natural law.

4. UNIVERSALITY AND HISTORICITY

Inasmuch as the natural law is based on the enduring nature of man, it binds every man at all times and in all places. "All are called to attain the same final goal and to respect the same existential ends in essentially the same way, even if this way presents a varied picture in the details of its realization."[23]

Hence, unlike positive human law, natural law does not admit of excuses or dispensations in the strict sense. The apparent dispensations in the Old Testament regarding some vital matters like polygamy are to be explained more by a divine pedagogy. God, through Moses and other leaders of the people, does not positively "permit" but either "tolerates" an abuse that cannot yet realistically be removed or "regulates" its evil consequences. Thus divorce is not positively permitted in the Old Testament, but rather attempts are made to mitigate its evil effects through certain safeguards, such as "the bill of divorce" that is required of a man who wants to put away his wife. Similarly, Abraham's readiness to sacrifice his son was not laudable insofar as he wanted to kill his son, but insofar as he was ready to offer a supreme sacrifice according to his lights or as he perceived God's call in the culture of his time. There is no need of postulating "dispensation" from God regarding the commandment "You shall not kill."

Slavery and torture are always evil inasmuch as they strike against the basic dignity of man. But slavery may have become such a part of the social system that no one in a particular culture saw anything wrong in it. It cannot, however, be said that it was "right" under certain circumstances. Toleration or silence by some New Testament writers should not be understood to mean approval. While it would be an anachronism to judge people of the past according to present-day lights and standards, it is certainly necessary to condemn behavior such as slave-keeping as an intrinsic violation of human rights even though the persons concerned may have been in good faith. Here we are faced with the crucial distinction between objective and subjective aspects of morality—a distinction which, if overdrawn in the past, is unduly minimized or even ignored by some today.

Closely connected with the universality of the natural law is the question of moral absolutes. According to the traditional view, there are certain norms, even with regard to specific matters, which do not allow of any exception under any circumstance. Many modern theologians deny the validity of such absolute norms. This question is of such importance and complexity that it will be treated separately in the next two chapters.

The immutable elements in human nature can be concretely realized only in changeable forms. Hence there will be a *relative element* in the natural law or, rather, an accidental change corresponding to accidental modifications in human nature itself.

The different stages in the history of salvation cannot but affect the natural law. Thus the right of coercion on the part of the state, the permissibility of material cooperation in an evil action, mental restriction, and, according to some, the right to private property are all consequent on the fall of man. However, the fall cannot be invoked to justify grave offenses against humanity. Many authors in the Middle Ages tried to excuse the institution of slavery in this way. They ought to have realized after a thousand years of Christianity that the buying and selling of fellow human beings is radically against human dignity and hence intrinsically evil. Even if they did not realize it, the justification of slavery is not valid.

Man is "being" and "becoming," which is an essential law of his "being." Hence *historicity* is part of the natural law. Bernard Häring has pointed out the twofold source of the profound dynamism of the natural law: 1) Stone Age man and modern scientific man are very different in their interests, language, horizons and ability to conceptualize life, and their worlds provoke altogether different kinds of thought and questions; 2) as man begins to shape his world, he himself changes and his basic capacity of self-understanding and self-expression grows.[24]

Vatican II itself has noted that, on account of the rapid and profound changes that have taken place in recent years, "the human race has passed from a rather static concept of reality to a more dynamic, evolutionary one. In consequence, there has been a new series of problems, a series as important as can be, calling for efforts of analysis and synthesis."[25] However, the immutable aspects of human nature do not thereby disappear.

The question of usury is frequently brought up in discussing the historicity of the natural law. There has definitely been a development in the Church's stand on the matter. Some see this as a clear change of doctrine and bring it up as a precedent for changes in other areas.

But is it really a case of change in doctrine or is it only a question of a different application of a general principle due to changed circumstances? The Second Lateran Council in 1139 condemned "rapacious usury" as detestable and repugnant to divine and human laws. Taking of interest was not justified when it implied mere exploitation of the neighbor's need. However, when money became productive, this was no longer necessarily so. The principle that one may never take undue advantage of his neighbor's need remains as valid as ever. But in modern times when one takes interest, he is legitimately compensating himself for the impossibility of investing his money in other productive ways. While not denying the undoubted merits of John T. Noonan's research into the subject of usury, one may ask whether he has given sufficient attention to this point.

Maintenance of the blanket condemnation of interest-taking down into modern capitalist society (until the nineteenth century) may not have been tenable. But critics of this slow-moving attitude of the Church do not seem to note sufficiently the evils of capitalism, in which there is unbridled competition and unscrupulous exploitation of the poor.

There is often the *need for a better formulation* of the natural law. The precise meaning of the commandment "You shall not kill" was only gradually understood. The matter is again being debated nowadays. A perfectly satisfactory understanding of the law of veracity has till now eluded ethical thinkers.

At times we fail to see sufficiently that past formulations have been bound up with the conditions of the time. "Stereotyped formulations, taken out of their historical context and merely repeated, not interpreted, do not convey any abiding truth about man and the Lord of history. How much Stoic psychology, biology and medicine of Galen and other early thinkers, vestiges of Roman and German culture, and the jurisprudence of the absolutist age in Europe, still remains in our manuals? Even the official teaching of the Church has sometimes been more handicapped than helped by this type of natural law thinking."[26]

We may also point out that certain formulations of international law regarding human rights, which are made to look like the most basic elements of the natural law, have been elaborated with the advantage of vested interests in view and are an obstacle to the promotion of vast multitudes of poor and dispossessed people.

5. KNOWLEDGE OF THE NATURAL LAW

Because of man's power of reflection, the truths of the natural law are, as such, knowable by the light of human reason. "Knowledge of the natural law basically signifies knowledge of the concrete human being and its given relationship to God, our fellowmen and the world. This is merely to assert a true knowledge of being. It means, moreover, knowledge of the inherent human demand to unfold the concrete being of man by activating one's own life and thus live it out true to reality."[27]

Natural moral knowledge was implicitly taught when Vatican I affirmed that God, as the origin and end of all, can be known from creation by the light of human reason.[28] The knowledge of God here, as shown by the acts of the Council, is not only theoretical but also practical, implying the apprehension of at least the fundamental principles of morality. Pius XII in the encyclical *Humani Generis* has declared this explicitly.[29]

It is true that the fall has weakened the power of human reason. Still, the mind's radical capacity to perceive the natural law has not been destroyed. The basic principles of the natural law are accessible to all those who have attained moral maturity.

There is no reason to doubt the capacity of simple, unlettered people to perceive the natural law. Pius XII in the encyclical *Summi Pontificatus* states that the voice of nature teaches "even the uneducated, and, what is more, those who do not enjoy the cultural values of mankind, what is just and unjust, permitted and forbidden."[30] Those who boast of a veneer of civilization do not always display a more refined sense of moral values.

The discernment of the natural law is not necessarily through logical deduction. It is often done through the application of moral insight or intuition and may be achieved in the depths of one's conscience. In this connection, St. Thomas uses the expression *appetitus rectus* (right sense). The general orientations regarding the goodness of moral conduct are arrived at through the grasp of human values. Concrete moral judgments further demand experience and understanding of the physical, psychological and social situations of man. One has to discern what manner of acting, taking every factor into consideration, fosters genuine human growth. It should be noted that systematic ethics is simply the elaboration and synthesis of everyday spontaneous moral knowledge.

The knowledge of particular moral norms is dependent on many factors. An affective disposition toward a particular virtue facilitates the perception of norms belonging to a certain area of life. Thus St. Thomas speaks of *connatural* sensitivity to moral truths.[31] On the other hand, evil habits and egoistic tendencies impede the knowledge conducive to moral formation in an individual. Still, there is need for some caution in interpreting affective dispositions, since they can generate what looks like objective insight but may in fact be subjective illusion. They should be tested by means of calm reflection and sharing of human experiences.

Psychic blocks can also hinder the moral formation of an individual. Thus a psychopath may not be able to realize his basic social obligations. Likewise, right moral knowledge presupposes a sound philosophy or mode of thinking.

As human knowledge is acquired in a social context, the proper atmosphere is needed for the moral development of the individual. A person brought up, for instance, in a milieu that takes exploitation of the poor for granted will find it difficult to acquire right principles regarding social justice. Entire cultures, otherwise advanced, can have thoroughly wrong ideas on vital matters like polygamy and racial discrimination. Many whites of goodwill in South Africa may not be aware of the horrors of *apartheid*. The same could be said about the attitudes of higher castes regarding the *Harijans* in India.

Hence, as we shall see later, the obstacles placed by psychic blocks and bad social atmosphere must be taken into account in assessing moral imputability. These factors are of paramount importance in moral education.

According to Vatican I and *Humani Generis,* in the present situation of man, divine revelation is practically necessary to overcome difficulties that impede "an easy, secure and unerring knowledge of religious and moral truths *per se* not inaccessible to reason."[32] In fact, many moral principles regarding social justice which today are rather universally accepted, at least in theory, actually became clear due to the leaven of the Gospel.

The grace of the Redeemer is always available to all people of goodwill in order to enlighten and strengthen them in the search for moral truths. Divine grace helps the knowledge of the natural law, but it is human reason that attains it.

History shows that even Christians guided by revelation and aided by grace find it difficult to come to a consensus on crucial matters. Hence the role of the living teaching authority in the Church.[33] Recent events have shown that the magisterium does not automatically dispel all difficulties. Still, it is to be accepted as a valuable guide in the right understanding of the natural moral law. Its mission is not restricted to Christians, but extends to the whole of mankind.

6. THE SALVIFIC SIGNIFICANCE OF THE NATURAL LAW[34]

The Gospel proclaims that one attains the Kingdom by serving Christ in one's needy brethren even when one does not explicitly recognize Him (cf. Mt. 25:35–46). In every genuine experience of personal love, in every practice of virtue or adherence to the norms of morality, one is implicitly touched by grace and drawn into the sphere of supernatural salvation. Every good act that is in conformity to the natural law is in fact an expression of the divine love which the Holy Spirit pours out into the hearts of men.

Divine revelation as expressed in the Bible has not resolved all moral problems, especially those of the modern world. Hence a believer cannot neglect to use the natural resources of his mind, although aided by grace, in order to discern the call of God in the complex circumstances of life today. One must recognize that it is the same God who enlightens our natural reason in order to know Him and His will and who speaks through His revealed Word for the same purpose of calling men to communion with Him and with each other.

When a man makes a proper response to the call of God expressed by his very nature, his response is in fact one made by a son of God through the gift of grace, even while it is a truly human act. The way toward sonship to God and brotherhood in Christ is in and through the human realities of life.

Since, in the *Logos* doctrine of John and in the Pauline theology of Colossians and Ephesians, Christ is seen as the center of creation as well as of redemption, the ultimate foundation of the natural law appears in a fuller light in Him. Hence the natural law has its place in a morality centered on Christ.

Reflection on the moral order is, as such, a human task. Still, the Christian believes that this reflection is carried on in the concrete order of grace, wherein the reflecting subject (the person in community) and the object of reflection (humanity in the individual person and community) are under the illuminating and transforming influence of the grace of the Holy Spirit. This is true even in the case of a non-Christian. But to the extent that a person corresponds with divine grace more explicitly, he is likely to come to a fuller and deeper understanding of morality. The explicitly doctrinal, sacramental and hierarchical economy of the Church are of special value in this respect. However, a Christian's religious complacency and pride may prove a grave obstacle. It can happen that non-Christians, or even unbelievers, who have an open mind and sincerely surrender themselves to the truth, may at times come to a deeper vision of certain moral insights—for instance, in the matter of justice.

Paul proclaims the demands of natural morality, like abstaining from the "passions of lust," as belonging to the *evangelium* (Gospel) of the Lord (1 Thess. 4:2). The Church has always included the natural order of creation in its Christian moral teaching. Since the eternal Word of God has really assumed our humanity and has become the archetype of all human perfection, the grace of Christ's Spirit within us invites us to loyalty to the order of creation. Fidelity to the principles of the natural law enables God's Word to dwell within us in a human way. "Being man" is concretely willed by God as ordered to "being under grace" or "being in Christ."

This is not to belittle in any way the newness and transcendence of the salvation brought by Christ. Since the whole of man's being is elevated to the supernatural order in Christ, one who lives in Christ always goes beyond the strictly natural level in his moral conduct, whatever the degree of explicit consciousness in this regard.

In the context of the original fall, because of which the demands of morality are often disagreeable to man, we can say that Christ has redeemed the natural law. The redeeming grace of Christ transforms the natural law from a "law of sin" to a law of life and salvation. Its fulfillment becomes, not a burden, but a loving response to the call of God. The grace of the Holy Spirit also helps in overcoming the darkness and blindness of sin, so that the demands of the natural law can be known with greater clarity and certitude.

Even some demands of the Gospel—for instance, those in the Sermon on the Mount and the call to bear the cross—may look unreasonable to carnal man. They may look meaningless from a purely natural point of view. But divine grace helps to see that such demands are not against the true natural fulfillment of man but, in fact, help in gaining authentic human development.

Hence, there should be no opposition between the "law of Christ" and the "natural law." The opposition is, rather, between "carnal" man, i.e., fallen man inasmuch as he has not been penetrated by the saving grace of Christ, and "spiritual" man, or man inasmuch as he is moved by the Spirit. The law of Christ brings to fulfillment a purely natural ethical order. At times some purely human values may have to be sacrificed for the sake of following Christ. This is because of the limited condition of man, in which he is unable to achieve all human values at the same time. It may also be due to a special call from God: for instance, to renounce marriage in order to realize its values in a deeper and more universal manner.

Grace presupposes man as an incarnate person living in a world of people and things. Hence the norms derived from his being are more than just the object of human, philosophical reflection. Their observance is a *preambulum,* a starting point for faith and Christian love. It is also an implicit acknowledgement of God's saving will. In this sense, the whole of natural law is taken up into the evangelical ethic, although its details might not be explicitly revealed in the Bible. As the holiness of God is the ultimate ground of the obligatory value of natural law, its absolute validity becomes clear in the personal dialogue of grace.

The content of the natural law is not modified by grace, but it acquires a deepened significance in the reciprocal love between God and man. The natural virtues become qualitatively different as the embodiment of the theological virtues of faith, hope and charity, and serve to further the theological life of grace.

Natural law by itself has no power to justify. But we have seen how human nature has been intrinsically elevated and transformed by grace. Historic man, created in and for Christ (Col. 1:15–16), is called to community of life with the Blessed Trinity through Christ. Therefore, just as human nature is the substratum of the supernatural reality of man, so the natural law derived from it is a means of attaining his supernatural destiny. Each exigency of the natural law represents an intrinsic expression of man's supernatural vocation. It indicates, however inadequately, the manner in which a child of God, justified by the mystery of Christ, should live.

Christian life consists above all in the exercise of the divine *agape,* which is a participation in the inner life of the Trinity. The natural law points out the *human way of realizing this charity.* As Christ is the exemplar of all human existence, the natural law indicates, although imperfectly, the way one should personally imitate and follow Christ.

Thus, in the present order, the natural law contributes to the supernatural destiny of man. "If you would enter life, keep the commandments" (Mt. 19:17).

7. THE ROLE OF THE MAGISTERIUM

It is within the ecclesial community that the Christian comes into saving contact with God. It is within this community that he lives out the demands of his calling. The whole Church is called upon to ponder over the mystery of God's plan for mankind and the world in Christ. However, the learning process goes on, not only within the Chruch, but also in dialogue with all people of goodwill.

The Christian attains moral truth by openness to the Spirit, by using his natural reason enlightened by divine grace, by good living, and by mutual sharing of views. The communal nature of experiencing and grasping truth in the Church has been called *sensus fidelium* (the sense of the faithful), which deserves the highest respect.

The role of the *magisterium* (the teaching authority of the episcopal college with the Pope at the head) is to promote this corporate learning process. Since the natural law regulates the human way of living out the faith, it comes under the direction of the hierarchy, whom the Holy Spirit has placed as shepherds over Christ's flock (cf. Acts 20:28). In protecting the treasury of faith, the Church's magisterium also has the right and duty to instruct her members concerning the fundamental values and norms of human life.

Although the faithful alone are directly bound by the proclamations of the magisterium, the moral teaching of the Church is addressed to all people of goodwill, since the Church is the "Mother and Teacher" of all peoples.[35]

Recent popes have repeatedly asserted that the teaching authority of the Church is competent to interpret even natural moral laws. For instance, *Humanae Vitae* of Pope Paul VI declares: "Jesus Christ, when communicating to Peter and to the Apostles His divine authority and sending them to teach all nations His commandments, constituted them as guardians and authentic interpreters of the moral law, not only, that is, of the law of the Gospel, but also of the natural law, which is likewise an expression of the will of God, the faithful fulfillment of which is equally necessary for salvation."[36] According to Vatican II, it is the duty of the Church as teacher of truth "to declare and confirm by her authority those principles of the moral order which have their origin in human nature."[37]

The magisterium is not to be understood as a form of ecclesiastical brainwashing. It is a *service of truth* to the faithful (and humanity at large) under the guidance of the Holy Spirit. It is normally exercised by fostering reflection in the whole body of the faithful and by prudent supervision, although at times authoritative pronouncements may be called for. Because the search for truth is a corporate process, everyone, particularly those who have the charism of holiness or truth in a significant way, has a role to play.

Vatican II emphasizes this point, although in the context of freedom in relation to civil authority: "A sense of dignity of the human person has been impressing itself more and more deeply on the consciousness of contemporary man. And the demand is increasingly made that men should act on their own judgment, enjoying and making use of responsible freedom, not driven by coercion but motivated by a sense of duty. . . . This demand for freedom in human society chiefly regards the quest for values proper to the human spirit. . . . The Vatican Synod takes careful note of these desires in the minds of men. It proposes to declare them to be greatly in accord with truth and justice."[38]

It is not entirely accurate to indentify the magisterium with "the Church" in this matter. Still, because of the special authoritative role of the hierarchy, such an identification is frequently made and perhaps cannot be altogether avoided. The expression "teaching Church" as opposed to the "learning Church" is also ambiguous. It may imply that some in the Church have only to teach and not learn. Such a conception contradicts the corporate nature of the learning process in the Church.

The role of the magisterium is not merely to authenticate the mind of the majority in the Church. It cannot be restricted to taking an opinion poll or just counting noses on a particular subject. It is, rather, to test the authenticity of the religious and moral experience of the Christian people in the light of the living Word of God and tradition enlivened by the grace of the Spirit. That the opinion of the majority of Christians at certain times or in certain places on specific issues may be erroneous can clearly be seen from recent history regarding racial equality, social justice and world poverty.

Competent theologians perform their particular service of investigating moral truth, evolving doctrinal syntheses, mediately and immediately preparing hierarchical statements, as well as loyally interpreting them to the faithful. But they do not constitute a sort of paramagisterium in rivalry with the hierarchical magisterium. Their opinions, while having their proper value, do not enjoy the same authority as the pronouncements of the hierarchy.

It is of paramount importance to make a clear distinction between the *canon laws* enacted by Church authority in its role of governing the society of the Church and the *moral teachings* regarding divine natural law. The latter, being the immediate expression of God's will imprinted in the very order of creation, cannot be altered by Church authority. Pope Paul VI makes this clear in *Humanae Vitae*: "Of such laws the Church was *not the author,* nor consequently can she be the arbiter; she is *only their depository and their interpreter,* without ever being able to declare licit what is not by reason of its intrinsic and unchangeable opposition to the true good of man."[39] However, the Church can and ought to revise the formulations of her teaching when there is manifest need for doing so.

Since natural law is, as such, knowable by the light of human reason, it is clear that reasoning does play an important part in the formulation of the teachings of the magisterium in this area. In fact, the popes have generally appealed to reason to support their declarations. But it cannot be said that a particular teaching is worth only as much as the rational arguments given. If so, there would be no difference between the pronouncements of the magisterium and the writings of theologians. Even Charles A. Curran, who is well-known for his critical stance regarding certain teachings of the magisterium, admits that "reason alone is not an absolute and self-sufficient norm for the teaching Church in considering specific problems."[40] *Humanae Vitae* affirms that obedience to the teaching authority of the Church is due "not only because of the reasons adduced, but rather because of the light of the Holy Spirit, which is given in a particular way to the Pastors of the Church in order that they may illustrate the truth."[41]

This may pose a lot of difficulties in practice. For instance, in the case of contraception a significant portion of the Church, among both theologians and ordinary faithful, found it difficult to accept the argumentation of *Humanae Vitae,* which rejected the opinion of a clear majority of the papal commission appointed to study the question. Pope Paul VI declared that the work of the commission, for which he expressed profound gratitude, did not dispense him from a personal examination of this serious question. Therefore, he said that, "having attentively sifted the documentation laid before us, after mature reflection and assiduous prayer, We now intend, by vitue of the mandate entrusted to us by Christ, to give our reply to these grave questions."[42] Hence, the binding force of the teaching seems to be based on the special assistance of the Holy Spirit for the exercise of the charism of guiding the faithful in attaining to truth.

As the functioning of the magisterium is conditioned by various factors, there can be defective presentation of moral insights. That is why the magisterium itself revises its pronouncements from time to time. A good example of this is the teaching on religious liberty. At times it can happen, as seems to be the case of *Humanae Vitae,* that the norm or principle proposed may seem clear but that there may be *moral conflict* in practice. Hence, there would be need for careful interpretation of what exactly is affirmed by a particular document and how its teaching is to be put into practice taking all the moral values involved. To evade such a task would only result in the polarization of the Church into those who are for and those who are against a particular teaching. It would also lead to bitterness and polemics in some, and indifference to Church teaching in others, as we are witnessing today.

The pronouncements of the magisterium can be infallible teachings, in the form of *ex cathedra* statements of the pope or solemn definitions by an ecumenical council. It is obvious that a member of the Church has to give unconditional assent of faith to these. The teaching could be about morality.[43] However, it is a much debated question whether the magisterium can infallibly propose norms of the natural law which are not explicitly found in divine revelation.[44] Bishop Grasser, the official spokesman of the doctrinal commission at Vatican I, declared that it was the explicit intention of the commission not to include in the definition of papal infallibility those matters not belonging directly to the deposit of faith.[45]

However, in fact, there has never been a single infallible definition regarding specific moral questions. The only case of anything like a solemn definition on a particular moral issue is that concerning usury in Lateran II and subsequent councils. Still, in spite of the solemnity of the language, many hold that this was only a disciplinary decree.[46] It is also difficult to establish that a particular moral teaching is infallible from what has been called "the ordinary and universal magisterium." As regards *Humanae Vitae,* it is widely known that Msgr. Lambruschini, who was officially delegated to present the encyclical in Rome, clarified at the outset that it was not an infallible pronouncement.

"Not infallible" evidently means "reformable"—that is, "open to revision"—but to take it as "doubtful" might minimize the value of the document. Between absolute certitude obtained from an infallible teaching and a doubt, there is *moral* or *practical certitude,* which can be had from a clear and emphatic intervention of the magisterium. Infallibility excludes every possibility of error. Moral certitude excludes doubt or proximate fear of error, though not every possibility of error.

Concerning the assent due to non-infallible teaching of the pope, Vatican II declares: "This *religious submission (obsequium)* of will and mind must be shown in a special way to the authentic teaching authority of the Roman Pontiff, even when he is not speaking *ex cathedra.* That is, it must be shown in such a way that his supreme magisterium is acknowledged with reverence, the judgments made by him are sincerely adhered to, *according to his manifest mind and will.* His mind and will in the matter may be known chiefly either from the character of the documents, from his frequent repetition of the same doctrine, or from his manner of speaking.[47]

A sincere desire to be truly loyal does not rule out problems and difficulties. Religious assent does not foreclose study and discussion, since the teaching is open to revision.

As regards the *possibility of dissent,* the declaration of the Belgian bishops on *Humanae Vitae* may be usefully cited. After stating that "every doctrinal declaration of the Church . . . should be received with the respect and docility that the teaching authority established by Christ legitimately demands," they add: "Someone, however, who is *competent in the matter* under consideration and capable of forming a personal well-founded judgment—which necessarily presupposes a *sufficient amount of knowledge*—may, *after a serious examination* before God, come to other conclusions on certain points. In such a case he has the right to follow his conviction, provided that *he remains sincerely disposed to continue his enquiry.*"[48]

John Henry Cardinal Newman, the staunch defender of papal authority, has also spoken of the rights of conscience with regard to papal teaching: "When I speak of conscience, I mean conscience truly so called. When it has the right of opposing the supreme, though not the infallible authority of the Pope, it must be something more than the miserable counterfeit which, as I have said above, now goes by the name. If in a particular case it is to be taken as a sacred and sovereign monitor, its dictate, in order to prevail against the voice of the Pope, must follow upon serious thought, prayer and all the available means of arriving at a right judgment on the matter in question. And further, obedience to the Pope is what is called 'in possession,' that is, the *onus probandi* [burden of proof] of establishing a case against him lies, as in all cases of exception, on the side of conscience."[49]

The teaching authority of the hierarchy extends not only to the enunciation of general principles of the natural law but *also to particular applications.* Pope John XXIII explained in the encyclical *Mater et Magistra*: "It is clear that when the hierarchy has issued a precept or decision on a point at issue, Catholics are bound to obey the directions. The reason is that the Church has the right and obligation, not merely to guard the purity of ethical and religious principles, but also to intervene authoritatively when there is question of judging the application of the principles to concrete cases."[50] However, since such directives are based on a prudential judgment of Church authority in political and other fields, the possibility of error is greater and, hence, reasons for conscientious dissent may more easily arise. Perhaps it would be better to call such directives *pastoral guidance* rather than doctrinal teaching.

Indeed, Vatican II wants the overdependence of the faithful on the clergy for moral decisions in the temporal sphere to cease. "From priests, the laity should look for light and spiritual energy. However, they should not imagine that their pastors are always such experts that they can give an immediate and concrete answer to every problem, however complicated, that arises, or even that such is their mission."[51]

Vatican II has expressed the role of particular bishops regarding doctrinal teaching thus: "The bishops, teaching in communion with the Roman Pontiff, are to be respected by all as witnesses to divine and Catholic truth, and the faithful have a duty to concur in the judgment which their bishop expresses in the name of Christ on matters of faith and morals, and by an act of religious submission to make it their own."[52] In present-day circumstances this teaching role is better fulfilled collegially by episcopal conferences.

———o———

Notes to Chapter XI

1. Cf. Gerard Watson, "The Early History of Natural Law," *Irish Theological Quarterly,* 33 (1966), 74.
2. *Summa Theologica,* la-llae, 91, 2, 1.
3. *GS,* art. 79.
4. *GS,* art. 89.
5. *DH,* art. 14

6. *GS,* art. 51

7. No. 4.

8. No. 10.

9. No. 13.

10. Cf. Josef Fuchs, *Natural Law,* Dublin, Gill and Son, 1965. Ch, 3; James M. Gustafson, *Protestant and Roman Catholic Ethics,* University of Chicago Press, 1978, pp. 6–12.

11. *Theological Ethics,* Philadelphia, Fortress Press, 1966, Vol. 1, p. 698.

12. *Op. cit.,* pp. 210–11.

13. "Calvin and the Prospects for a Christian Ethics," *Norm and Context in Christian Ethics,* ed. by Gene H. Outka and Paul Ramsey, New York, Scribner's, 1968, p. 176.

14. Stanislaus Lyonnet, "Lex naturalis et justificatio gentium," *Verbum Domini,* 41 (2963), 238–42; Pierre Grelot, "L'idée de nature en théologie morale," *Vie Spirituelle, Supplément,* 20 (1967), 208–29.

15. C. H. Dodd, *op. cit.,* p. 79.

16. *GS,* art. 79.

17. Cf. Josef Fuchs, *Natural Law,* Ch. 3.

18. Cf. Enda McDonagh, *Invitation and Response,* Dublin, Gill and Macmillan, 1972, p. 36.

19. *Human Values and Christian Morality,* p. 143.

20. *Ibid.*

21. *Morality Is for Persons,* p. 150.

22. *Social Ethics: Natural Law in the Western World,* St. Louis and London, Herder, 2nd ed., 1965, p. 19.

23. C. H. Peschke, *op. cit.,* p. 106.

24. *Morality Is for Persons,* p. 154.

25. *GS,* art. 5.

26. Bernard Häring, *art. cit.,* p. 185.

27. Josef Fuchs, *Natural Law,* p. 145.

28. Denzinger-Banwaart, *Enchiridion Symbolorum,* nos. 1785 and 1806.

29. *Acta Apostolicae Sedis,* 42 (1950), 561.

30. *Acta Apostolicae Sedis,* 31 (1939), 423.

31. Cf. lla-llae, 1, 1, 3 and 45, 4.

32. Cf. Denzinger-Banwaart, no. 1786; *Acta Apostolicae Sedis,* 42 (1950), 563.

33. Cf. John J. Reed, "Natural Law, Theology and the Church," *Theological Studies,* 26 (1965), 40–64.

34. Cf. Josef Fuchs, *Natural Law,* Ch. 8; Edouard Hamel, *Loi Naturelle et loi du Christ,* Paris, Desclée, 1964, Ch. 1.

35. Cf. the significant title *Mater et Magistra* of the famous encyclical of Pope John XXIII.

36. Nos. 4 and 45; cf. Vatican II, *DH,* art. 14. For earlier texts see John J. Reed, *art. cit.,* pp. 40–64.

37. *DH,* art. 14.

38. *DH*, art. 1.

39. No. 18.

40. *A New Look at Christian Morality*, Notre Dame, Fides, 1968, p. 95.

41. No. 20.

42. No. 6.

43. Vatican I, Constitution *"Pastor Aeternus"* (*The Christian Faith*, No. 839); *LG*, art. 25.

44. Cf. Gerard J. Hughes, "Infallibility in Morals," *Theological Studies*, 34 (1973), 415–428.

45. Cf. T. Granderath, *Geschichte des Vatikanischen Konzils*, Freiburg-i.-B., 1906, Vol. III, p. 476.

46. Cf. footnote in Denzinger-Banwaart, 31st edition, no. 365.

47. *LG,L* art. 25.

48. *Catholic Mind*, 66 (1968), Oct., 54–55.

49. *A Letter to the Duke of Norfolk*, London, Pickering, 1875, pp. 63–64.

50. No. 239.

51. *GS*, art. 43.

52. *LG*, art. 25.

CHAPTER XII

Moral Absolutes and
The New Morality

1. REACTION AGAINST TRADITIONAL NATURAL LAW DOCTRINE

According to traditional doctrine, natural law is *absolute* and *immutable;* that is, there are certain norms, even with regard to specific matters like life and sex, which have these characteristics. In other words, there are certain types of actions which are *intrinsically evil.* Of late there has been a strong reaction against this position. The new trend, with its diverse forms, is often spoken of as the "new morality." Many factors have contributed to the rejection of absolute norms and the development of a more "open-ended" ethic:

a) *Excessive legalism and casuistry* in older authors. In the past, it must be admitted, too much emphasis was laid on abstract principles to the neglect of human values, concrete circumstances, and the need for personal response in moral decision. Moralists often indulged in too much rational argument bordering on sophistry and divorced from the sources of revelation. Even while quoting St. Thomas, they were unaware of the dynamic character of Thomistic thought. Thus, of late, many have been so repelled by the older, rigid approach that they have swung to the other side, throwing out, as it were, the baby with the bath water. A lack of firsthand acquaintance with classical authors at times makes the reaction more violent.

b) *Existentialist philosophy.* According to this, man is defined more in terms of his "creative freedom" than as a permanent essence of rational animal. In this perspective, there is no room for fixed norms valid for everyone and for all times. Similarly, modern thought is strongly imbued by *phenomenology,* which stresses the immediacy of experience. Nothing can be examined in itself, without reference to the plurality of concomitant phenomena.

c) *The evolutionary view of man and the universe.* The nature of man is not something determined once for all, but is constantly evolving. How can there be a place for absolute and immutable laws in this perspective?

d) *Cultural relativism.* Anthropology has revealed a very wide divergence in the mores of various peoples. A greater sense of tolerance and a more creative stance regarding one's own ethical positions are legitimate conclusions. But manifest aberrations like cannibalism, human sacrifice and ritual prostitution call for some caution in drawing too hasty conclusions. Moreover, contemporary anthropology is piercing through the surface of cultural difference and discovering the basic points of convergence.

e) *The controversy regarding contraception.* Undoubtedly this has been the single most powerful factor that has provoked a rethinking regarding traditional natural law doctrine. In the sixties, the problem of birth regulation for individuals and entire nations became so acute that people wanted to find an effective solution at all costs. At the time the discussion was at its height, the alternative of natural family planning was not so practically feasible. Hence, while many just disagreed with the Church's stance on contraception, others went further and denied the validity of all traditional absolute norms.

f) *The influence of Protestant theology,* which was first felt in Germany and then spread to other countries.

2. THE PROTESTANT BACKGROUND OF THE "NEW MORALITY"[1]

The new morality is characterized by a shift from absolute, immutable essences to order and relationship in the dynamic operations of life.

For Martin Luther, it is *faith*, transcending the purely human, that alone can enable a man to be good. The "orders of creation" of which he speaks have only a secondary role.

According to Bernhard Weiss and Albert Schweitzer, the eschatological proclamation of Jesus has relativized all human values. The complete transcendence of God and the complete sinfulness of man characterize the human condition. Hence they propose an *interim ethic based on compromise*. Killing a human being may be bad, but sometimes it may be necessary.

Following Søren Kierkegaard, many Protestant theologians deny man any capacity to love until he finds God again in Christ. Man's alienation from his fellowmen can be traced back to his alienation from God. Only the acceptance of God's word of pardon in faith gives him the security to accept and love his fellowmen. Thus, the basis of Protestant ethic lies, not in a fixed nature, but in a historical event, an encounter between God and man, a call of God in a particular situation demanding a response. Still, the understanding of a situation in which one encounters one's fellowmen requires human experience and reflection. Consequently, these theologians are led to accept that any situation we enter is structured by certain laws or patterns that mold such situations. Thus Emil Brunner and Helmut Thielicke invoke Luther's "orders of creation." Imperfect and sinful though they be, God wills them and works through them. Thus Brunner, for whom Christian morality is a response to God's will known in each unique situation, writes: "The meaning of the divine order of creation in marriage is that it is life in community of two persons of different sexes, a community which is complete, based upon the natural foundations of sex love, but only fulfilled in the recognition of the fact that by divine appointment they belong to each other."[2] But if in a given situation the structures do not serve God's command to love, then they are to be bypassed. "The knowledge of the commandment of love . . . in a concrete case, within the sinful reality, is able to break through what is required in a general way in the law formulated as a universal rule."[3]

According to Karl Barth, man himself cannot answer the ethical question; only Christ does. He does this by culture, through the human form of the ehtical question, to show men the dynamic implication of God's grace at work in their lives. The way is open for free, responsible and empirical thinking in the field of ethics. God's command is personal and spiritual in nature. It is characterized by the *"permission"* (in the sense of enabling) it bestows rather than by the actions it precludes.

Rudolf Bultmann, strongly influenced by existentialism, opposes legalism, formalism and complacency, and stresses personal responsibility and decision in the present moment of history in response to the needs of man. To live humanly is to be at every moment in a crisis of decision for the Kingdom of God. The value of a man lies in his decision now, not in the intrinsic value of his nature or some supernatural gift bestowed on him. Radical obedience demands commitment to God's will expressed in the circumstances of the moment. Each concrete situation confronts man with a unique expression of God's will and calls for a unique decision. No law or norm can embrace all specific instances; there are always cases unprovided for. Bultmann warns against false autonomy or trusting in the observance of the law to achieve righteousness. It is faith that opens to man the possibility of choosing the Kingdom of God. Faith is the obedient acceptance of a new self-understanding by which man perceives the call to decision in the present moment.[4]

The starting point of Dietrich Bonhoeffer's Christian ethic is the deliverance of sinners by the power of God at work in Jesus Christ. Ethics begins with total surrender, for which he uses the term *discipleship*. "This is not achieved by dint of efforts to become like Jesus. . . . It is achieved only when the form of Jesus Christ itself works upon us in such a manner that it molds our form in its own likeness."[5]

Paul Tillich is at one with the Catholic viewpoint in rejecting any dichotomy between reason-determined and faith-determined ethics. "The 'will of God' for us is precisely our essential being with all its potentialities, our created nature declared as 'very good' by God, as in terms of the creation myth."[6] From the fact that love is the source of moral norms, he derives the relativity of ethics. "For love is both absolute and relative by its very nature. An unchanging principle, it nevertheless always changes in its concrete applications. It 'listens' to the particular situation.''[7] He grants that there must be something immutable in the ethical principle. But there must also be a power of change within the ethical principle itself.[8]

Reinhold Niebuhr was concerned to avoid both relativistic nihilism and rationalistic legalism. He affirmed in man a natural structure of personality that expressed the basic human drives and processes. He rejected the view of Karl Barth that all moral norms are to be derived from scriptural revelation alone. He says: "The essence of human nature is love, which is to say that for man, who is involved in the unities and harmonies of nature, but who also transcends them in freedom, there can be no principle of harmony short of the love in which free personality is united in freedom with other persons."[9] In his eyes, the natural law tradition has ignored the transcendent possibilities of freedom in transmitting the determined structure of nature.

Paul Lehmann starts from the fact of the *koinonia,* the fellowhsip of those who believe in Christ as God and in His continuing work, with Scripture providing the basic vision of reality.[10] He finds special significance in the kingly role of Christ. The "political" activity of Christ is the achievement of the *koinonia,* making life more human and mature. He says that Christian ethics aims at maturity rather than morality. The individual grows into Christian maturity by joining with God to form a world where the conditions of such maturity are present to all men. All previous ethical systems failed to close the gap between the ethical claim and the ethical act due to their reliance on moral principles. This also created a false sense of righteousness. It is only a *koinonia* ethic based on love that realizes the primacy of God's activity in the concrete present. Within the broad context of the *koinonia* and the specific milieu of the situation, the Christian always determines anew what the dynamics of God's humanizing activity in the world requires.

Richard Niehbuhr, who was deeply impressed by the variety and value of the great world religions, severely criticizes the "biblicism" of Karl Barth, that seeks to derive ethical guidelines soley from revealed affirmations about God. He proposes a Socratic method starting from a phenomenology of moral experience which is presumed to be Christian. The key metaphor he suggests for uncovering the basic structure of all human action is *homo dialogicus*. The phenomenon of responsibility, or an intelligent reaction that has the quality of accountability, is at the heart of his thought.[11] In line with the findings of social psychology, he admits that the entire context of responsibility is shaped by the community. However, the Christian sees God's providential design in all the forces that press upon him for a response. In order to respond fittingly to this design, one must correctly anticipate and interpret these forces.

Joseph Sittler finds in the Scriptures, not so much principles of morality, as revelations of God's marvelous deeds that extend their influence into the present and provide a new context for life in the world today. "I love because I am loved." The Christian relives the life of Christ, which is an obedient relationship to God. Sittler criticizes the proponents of a love ethic that subordinates all the elements of the Christian life to love. According to him, it is *faith* or total commitment that is the adequate basis for Christian life. However, love is the task of faith in the world. There is no need of other moral principles. Faith penetrates the world of facts wth creative sensitivty, exposing the exigencies and opportunities of love. Ethical decision can never be wholly liberated from man's sinful situation. In heartbreaking choices, disvalue is often grasped along with love.[12]

Joseph Fletcher presents *situationism* as a middle course between antinomianism, which relies solely on the existential moment, and legalism, which is overlaid with rigid prefabricated rules and regulations. He employs ethical maxims only as guidelines or illustrations of the situation, but is quite ready to set them aside if circumstances demand an exception. The main preoccupations of his approach are personalism, positivism, pragmatism and relativism. The sole intrinsic good and absolute norm of Christian decision is *agape,* which is neither desire nor sentimental liking, but a gift of self. Everything else has value according as it can function in the service of love. Hence, *whatever is the most loving thing in the situation is right and good.* "Apart from the helping or hurting of people, ethical judgments or evaluations are meaningless. Having as its supreme norm the neighbor love commanded of Christians, Christian situation ethics asserts firmly and definitely:

*Value, worth, ethical quality, goodness or badness, right or wrong—
these things are only predicates, they are not properties. . . .* There is
only one thing that is always good and right, intrinsically good, regardless of the context, and that one thing is love."[13]

Although Fletcher emphazies that love is careful and calculating,
he is not able to provide a secure foundation for this determination,
since he assigns a very relative place to laws or ethical values. He is
not afraid of saying that *"only the end* [of love] *justifies the means."*
According to him, the antinomian is ruled by the id and the legalist by
the superego, while the situationist, whom he defends, is ruled by the
ego—how, he does not clearly explain. The situationist approaches a
moral decision "fully armed with the ethical maxims of his community
and its heritage."[14] But he insists that every rule has its exceptions.
Still, sometimes he slips in an absolute; for instance, "No unwanted
or unintended baby should ever be born."[15]

In his discussion on sin, Harvey Cox affirms that the Gospel must
liberate man from mythical taboos and humanize sex through the ex-
orcism of cultural conventions and false values.[16] Through such desa-
cralization, Christian ethics must recuperate its quality of being the
"good news" which invites men to exercise full responsibility for others
in a community of persons.

Paul Ramsey, who comes close to Catholic ethics, has severely
criticized one-sided contextualism or situationism. He condemns a wholly
future-oriented agape ethic that ignores the morality of the means in its
prudential calculus. He acknowledges the primacy of love, but points
out that love lays down its own directions determined by the needs of
the neighbor. Christian morality is "faith effective through in-principled
love." Christian agape must regulate not only the choice of goals but
also the conduct through which they are achieved.

Ramsey finds Catholic tradition guilty of a static conception of the
natural law and of being inflexible regarding the formulation of norms.
According to him, certain principles are discovered to have general
validity, so that failure to act in accordance with them would be contrary

to the requirement of love. Others are mere summary rules derived from love's past experience. There may be situations in which they no longer express what love requires. They should be open to review and radical revision.[17]

John A. T. Robinson recognizes a polarity between the old and the new morality. We should not fear a tension between the fixed and the free, for "God is in the rapids as in the rocks."[18] He himself, however, opts for a pure love ethic. The only ultimate norm is to open oneself to another unconditionally in love, being totally uncommitted in every other respect, but totally committed in this. In spite of a search for pure *"act-agapism,"* he has to yield to *"rule-agapism."* He is bound to conceded that some things can never conceivably be the expression of love. He speaks of laws as "the dikes of love in a wayward and loveless world."[19] Speaking of premarital sex, he says: "I believe the nexus between bed and board, between sex and the sharing of life at every level, must be pressed as strongly as ever by those who really care for persons as persons."[20]

3. SITUATION ETHICS

Situation ethics is not a monolithic system. It is a widespread trend that gives primordial importance to the situation and only a minor place to norms. Situationists hold that since the situation, in all its concrete apsects, is unique and unrepeatable and, therefore, not susceptible to generalization, general norms cannot have absolute normative value. The particular situation itself is the decisive norm of morality.

Situation is variously defined by different authors. Still, it may roughly be described as the concrete resultant of spatiotemporal and other factors in which the personal freedom of an individual person is involved. The elements of the situation would include the physical, the biological, the social, the historical, the psychological, the moral and the religious. They are to a great extent identical with the "circumstances" of the human act in classical moral theology. But they are considered, not merely as mitigating or aggravating factors, but as intrinsically determining the morality of the action. The situation itself could be called the objective ethical norm.

If the validity of general norms is admitted, it is said that they are not bindng in exceptional circumstances. They must not be considered categorical imperatives but mere guidelines giving a general orientation. They are to be ascribed only an *indicative* value. They are somewhat like the spokes of a wheel, which all tend to one center, the will of God; but they never meet, because at the center there is a vacuum in which God makes known His inscrutable will.

Thus, although suicide or abortion would be wrong in ordinary circumstances, situationists would deny that any general rule in such matters is ultimate and decisive. A man placed in a special situation— for instance, a spy with important state secrets in his mind, the revelation of which would jeopardize the security of the nation—may rightly come to the decision that his duty is to commit suicide if he cannot escape.

a) *Philosophical (existentialist) approach.* The human person has an absolute value that cannot be subordinated to anything else. The situationist, therefore, refuses to subjugate the original subjective impulse of freedom to any so-called objective precepts. These cannot be absolutety valid, since the moral act cannot be determined exclusively by its objective structure even if it is correctly evaluated.

Good and evil belong to the interior realm of freedom *before* belonging to its external expressions. Hence, whatever promotes creative freedom in a particular situation is moral, and whatever hampers it is immoral. It is not so much *what* I do that is ethically relevant, but the *interiority of the freedom with which* I do it.

b) *Theological approach.* Grace is a unique and strictly personal call of God in Christ. Man stands before a situation which must be evaluated as a summons from God, as the relevation of His sovereign will. Any *a priori* determination of moral norms would jeopardize God's absolute sovereignty. The example of Abraham's sacrifice of Isaac is often brought up in this context.

The objectivist would answer to this that God's will does not exclude but presupposes His own eternal essence, which He could not deny. Likewise, He could not deny the image of His essence which is man.

The situationist would grant that there is an objective moral law, but argue that it is insufficient to express man's unique personal relationship with God, apart from the fact that we cannot be sure to what extent the divine image is preserved in man's sinful nature. Further, an objective ethical system could not do justice to the creative element in morality. "Moral principles are *maxims* of general or frequent validity . . . . The situationist is prepared in any concrete case to suspend, ignore or violate any principle if by doing so he can effect more good than by following it."[21]

The objectivist would again counter that denying the absolutely normative character of all objective rules, instead of liberating the creative aspect of freedom, would only end up with an aimless impulse which, in the long run, would become destructive. Objective guidance in the exercise of freedom does not necessairly eliminate spontaneity of choice. Will the situationist accept this point?

While the objectivist is wrong in assuming that human nature remains static, the situationist is not able to explain how the situation is to be evaluated without objective norms. To leave the decision only to subjectivity might lead to utter perplexity or self-deceiving rationalization of one's emotional inclination. To those who think that love itself would be a sufficient criterion, Paul Ramsey answers: "The only volume needed [for ethics] would be one containing the single statement that love is the inner attitude having no significant expression because it has every expression, since anything and everything can count as its expression and the greatest variety of things can count as love in the same situation."[22]

Ramsey goes on to point out that situation ethics would be revealed as an arbitrary subjectivism or non-ethics "unless it takes the other turn and joins a community of ethical discourse that is seeking to determine what pieces of behavior count or do not count as loving—upon the basis of a prior proper exhaustive description of what was done or proposed to be done."[23]

Fletcher explicitly admits that behind the debate between classical morality and situationism lurks the realist-nominalist controversy of old.[24] He has no hesitation in standing behind the extrinsicalism of William Ockham.

Fletcher has rightly drawn attention to the need for flexibility and for avoiding the excesses of legalism. But the examples he gives to show the need for flexibility are mostly drawn from the abnormal and the unusual, which makes his case weaker. Besides, many of his solutions are rather hasty and arbitrary. When he approves of the seduction of the farmer's daughter in the play *The Rainmaker*[25] in order to save her from being "spinsterized," he seems to think that this is the only solution for sexual repression. There is no thought of the possibility of sublimation, not to talk of positive integration, with the grace of God. He does not seem to realize sufficiently the deep significance of human sexuality and the sanctity of human life. Otherwise, he would not have so easily approved of adultery and killing in the name of love.

The uniqueness of a moral situation cannot be denied. But, as Enda McDonagh very well points out, "this does not exclude it entirely from continuity with similar situations involving other people or the same people at different times. . . . If there is no continuity between human situations, if they share no common element at all, then there are no words to describe, indeed no way of recognizing them. . . . To deny this intelligibility is to deny one's right to discuss the situation at all and to opt out of all that is human discourse in morality."[26]

Situation ethics of the extreme form was condemned by Pius XII in his allocutions of March 23 and April 18, 1952.[27] Later, on February 2, 1956, the Holy Office issued an instruction against the ethical system, which holds "that the decisive and ultimate norm of conduct is, not the objective right order determined by the law of nature and known with certainty from that law, but a certain intimate judgment and light of the mind of each individual, by means of which, in the concrete situation in which he is placed, he learns what he ought to do." The document does not exclude the need for taking into account "according to the rules of prudence, the particular circumstances of the situation."[28]

The document certainly condemns pure subjectivism and relativism. It should, however, be understood according to the nuances that have appeared in later reflection by the Church. It was already clear then that God calls man, not only through universal laws, but also through the particular situation, subjective dispositions and the inspiration of the Spirit. Even when the universal law is respected, there would still be a vast range of possibilities, the choice among which would be governed by the situation and made through the virtue of prudence or right conscience. Take the case of a very sick man painfully hovering between life and death for a long time. The universal moral law would exclude only the direct termination of life. But the sort of treatment and care to be given, and even whether to terminate an extraordinary treatment, would have to be decided after taking into consideration all the circumstances of the case—the spiritual and temporal advantages of prolonging life, the financial state of the family, availability of persons to take care of the patient, etc. There could be no hard-and-fast rule about such choices. This was a common view even among older authors on medical ethics.

4. NEW TRENDS AMONG CATHOLICS

Here we shall briefly refer to some of the theologians who have contributed to the renewal of the natural law doctrine. We shall restrict ourselves to those whose writings are available in English or who are frequently referred to in English theological literature.

Karl Rahner has attempted to integrate the positive insights of situation ethics into the Catholic tradition. He has shown that the ''general essence'' of humanity and each man's concrete individuality permeate each other and, hence, there is no contradication between the two. There is no situation which would justify simply going against the absolute negative precepts of the natural law. For the rest, one must act as the situation demands. Natural law requires only that we should not in principle deny certain basic values, like justice and mercy. Which of these at times simultaneously unrealizable values is to be chosen will depend upon the situation. The decision is to be made in one's conscience with the light of grace.[29]

Peter Chirico starts from the fact that man is a free and intrinsically dynamic being. While he shares a common nature with other men, he has his own unique modifications. He is a creature of relation, and his moral stature is shaped by the age and culture in which he lives. The moral law is basically the *law of growth in love*. While there may be standard moral imperatives binding on all men that further specify the rules of love of self and love of neighbor, they can never completely express the law of growth of an individual man. Since no man is held to the impossible, no man can be considered morally responsible for not totally affirming all that he is here and now. A basic distinction must be made between the morality of basic intentionality and the morality of external acts. The moral imperatives are always binding as to the first, but it cannot be concluded that certain specific external acts must always be avoided because they are aganst the imperatives of the natural law. Christian morality is a *morality of tension* which recognizes that man is continually facing obligations that he cannot immediately fulfill but toward which he must grow.[30]

Francis Simons, the then Bishop of Indore, speaking from the background of his cross-cultural experience, was one of the first to ask for reexamination of some of the traditional absolutes.[31] He first pointed out that tradition did admit some exceptions—for instance, in the area of killing and lying—although there was an effort to maintain that they were really not exceptions. Can we, he asks, equate the purpose of an organ or a function with a moral obligation? Do purpose and obligation always coincide? His questions and remarks seem to have had a considerable influence on the rethinking of moral absolutes in recent years.

Archbishop Denis E. Hurley, of Durban, has proposed the "principle of overriding right" to mitigate the rigors of absolute laws.[32] He starts from classical cases like this: "If someone attacks me, my right to life clashes with my duty to respect the life of my assailant, and my right predominates." Then he goes on to ask whether the predominance of a right in such a clash may not be generalized into a principle: "When the infringement of an obligation is necessarily involved in the exercise of a proportionate right, the obligation ceases." He thinks that vexed problems like that of contraception could be resolved in this way. The right to conjugal union would override the duty to keep the marital act open to life.

Robert O. Johann employs a relational model and seeks to strike a balance between mere conformity to preestablished norms, which he feels leads to crippling automation, and the excessive depreciation of rules. He insists that morally authentic personal choices always involve, at least implicitly, the adoption of a principle of conduct. "To be concerned, therefore, about rules of behavior is not to be morally hidebound. It is an effort, rather, to bring out the full implications of our choices and to see if, then, we still want to make them."[33]

N. D. O'Donaghue derives a theory of exceptions, or a *rule–reality tension*. "It may happen that a man's nature is so out of alignment with the law of proper fulfillment, or that the circumstances are so weighted against the way of nature, that the immediate insistence on the rule may literally do more harm than good."[34] It is not clear whether O'Donaghue is speaking of the subjective or the objective level.

Martin Nolan and others *extend the scope of the principle of totality*. According to them, the total good of the human person, including his solidarity with the community, may justify the sacrifice of an organ, function, or life itself. Thus there would be "no external mode of behavior that is, inevitably, moral or immoral."[35]

Herbert McCabe views ethics as *language and communication* which perceive meaning in terms of the ways of entering social life and as ways of being with each other.[36]

Franz Bockle agrees that scientific ethics must propose binding statements concerning the content of moral obligation insofar as we can recognize structures essential to the nature of man. However, these can be only very general and, to a high degree, abstract determinations. When we come to more concrete guidelines, considering the changing conditions of mankind, it is not enough to hold on tenaciously to earlier insights and formulations, but we must always seek anew the meaning of existence in the world of everyday reality.[37]

Germain G. Grisez starts from the first principles of practical reason as enunciating that good should be pursued. But in order to determine the goods that man should seek, one must examine all the basic tendencies and inclinations of man. He admits that man is endowed with basic tendencies prior to acculturation and free choice of his own, but only empirical enquiry can determine what these inclinations are. Such an investigation leads him to vigorously defend traditional Catholic teaching on contraception and abortion.[38] His analysis shows that the main traditional Catholic positions are not as *a priori* or as bereft of empirical support as is often made out. However, he does introduce some flexibility in the application of traditional principles.

Nicholas Crotty, considering moral norms as only empirical generalizations, rejects the classical distinction between direct and indirect as morally irrelevant.[39] According to him, it matters little to a man whether he expires as a result of direct or indirect activity. A love-centered ethic must be concerned with the actual implications and consequences of our behavior (*consequentialism*). Any action can in principle be the most loving response in a given situation. Moral rules can be only rules of thumb, which cannot be absolute. Crotty makes the interesting point that ''we need to be repentant not only of the sinfulness we bring to our conflict situations but of the very existence of these situations and the confusion, clash, and incompatibility of the moral values in any given response to them.''[40]

Felix Podimattam, too, rejects the validity of the distinction between direct and indirect voluntary. He logically concludes from this to the redundancy of the principle of the double effect. According to him, the object, the motive and the circumstances are *premoral* before their reference to right reason, which is the ultimate moral determinant. Again, only right reason can decide which right predominates in a conflict of duties. He distinguishes between ''intrinsically'' evil acts like debasing a person and ''internally'' evil acts like killing. The first cannot be justified under any conceivable circumstance, while the second may be. Thereby, he concludes to a large relativity of the natural law that would give room to prudential judgment and creative response to God's will.[41]

Josef Fuchs had for a long time upheld the validity of moral absolutes. However, in a study published in the organ of the Pontifical Gregorian Univeristy, he makes a significant shift in his position. He now distinguishes between *premoral evil* and *moral evil*. Killing, wounding, deceiving, sterilizing, etc., are only premoral evils. They, become moral evils only when they are "taken up into one's intention." This happens when there is no proportionate reason for causing the premoral evil. Traditional moralists held that certain activities were morally evil *ex objecto,* in the sense that no good intention could ever justify them. Now, Fuchs affirms that "a moral judgment of an action may not be made in anticipation of the agent's intention, since it would not be the judgment of a human act." Traditional absolutes presume that no possible circumstance or intention could justify certain modes of action. But since such an advance judgment cannot be founded, there can be no exceptionless norm of action. Certain universal norms suffice for ordinary use in practical living, though they are not absolute.[42]

However, Fuchs is forced to concede that there are certain norms "to which we cannot conceive of any kind of exception, e.g., cruel treatment of a child which is of no benefit to the child." When Fuchs wants to include the ultimate intention of the agent, he expands the notion of "one human action" to the point where human language will no longer sustain the unity.[43]

Bruno Schuller speaks of *"nonmoral values,"* like life, health and wealth, and "moral values," like justice, truthfulness and fidelity, which are predicated directly of the person. Thus, one must always be just. On the other hand, norms dealing with nonmoral values necessarily have an exception clause built into them. According to him, all nonmoral values must be judged "teleologically"—that is, from their consequences—and not "deontologically," or unconditionally.[44]

Fuchs, Schuller and such others could be identified with the movement toward a *consquentialist ethic,* although some of them would decline the label as appearing too close to classical utilitarianism.

Louis Janssens speaks of *ontic evil,* which may not be intended as a final end, but only as an intermediate end, oriented toward a higher end.[45] In a more recent article, he draws attention to the fact that premoral values like life, health, knowledge, etc., and disvalues like death, sickness, ignorance, etc., are inseparably connected in our conduct. He then states: "In the situation when premoral values are unavoidably connected with premoral disvalues which are inseparably blended, we ought to choose the alternative which indicates our preference for the lesser premoral disvalue."[46] He suggests that moral norms which refer to premoral disvalue should imply only descriptive language like *killing, falsehood,* etc., and not morally qualifyng terms like *murder, lie,* etc. Then he affirms that all such norms are only relative. We may depart from them for a proportionate reason.

Peter Knauer proposes a new understanding of the principle of the double effect.[47] His contention is that moral evil consists in the permission or causing (he does not distinguish between the two) of physical evil which is not justified by a commensurate reason. While in the past the terms *direct* and *indirect* were tied too closely to physical causality, he would call the effect indirect and hence justifiable whenever there is commensurate reason. The time-honored principle "The end does not justify the means" would apply only to moral evil used as means. This looks like a radical breakthrough; but it is no more than a studious and labored rejection of moral absolutes, which others, as we have seen above, have done in a more straightforward way. He does not seem to have contributed to clarity in the current discussion by ascribing to traditional terms a meaning that they cannot bear. It would have been much better to have admitted that, in his perspective, the distinction between *direct* and *indirect* is irrelevant and, consequently, the principle of the double effect redundant.

John G. Milhaven calls for an *epistemological approach* based on empirical evidence.[48] He develops a love ethic based on a proper evaluation of the consequences of our actions in the light of love.[49]

Charles E. Curran proposes a *relational-responsibility* model for ethics, as it allows one to incorporate the best elements of the teleological model of man-the-maker and the deontological (essential) model. He also proposes a *"principle of compromise"* based on the sinful situation of man arising ultimately from the presence of sin in the world.[50]

He would be slow in affirming that all values apart from final intentionality are premoral. "In some cases I would readily agree that the evil is premoral (e.g., contraception), but in other cases the social dimension of sin so affects reality that there is the necessity of accepting some moral evil as a consequence of the presence of sin in the world. It seems to me that those who deny this fact or say that the values in all cases are only premoral have too individualistic a view of sin and repentance. The reality of sin in the world affecting man in all his relationships serves as the basis for a theory of compromise, which realizes that in the presence of sin man ought to do things which should not be done if sin were not present."[51]

Thus, he says that certain sinful situations may force one to do things like abortion, which one would not do under other, ideal conditions. Still, there remains the difficulty of deciding which compromises it is reasonable to make. Curran warns against a too immediate consequentialist approach, which would identify the moral judgment with the findings of empirical sciences and neglect the *creative and transcendent aspects* of any truly human and Christian moral theory. "One who is planning the future of our cities must have not only the relevant sociological data but also a creative intelligence which can attempt to form new ways for men to live together in cities."[52]

Enda McDonagh has evolved a *morality of responsibility,* built upon reflection on the experience of the moral call in the human situation with interpersonal, social and historical dimensions. He goes from the experience of the "ought" to "is," not the other way around.[53] Faced with a problem such as abortion, the Christian response should not be simply to say: "You shall not." The first reaction must be to examine what can be done for the neighbor in need. The moral reason must be applied with a *sense of proportion* with regard to both the extent of the evil and the circumstances of those responsible. Our commitment is, not to an abstract value, but to persons. However, "persons" may not be confined to one's own immediate friends and acquaintances. The whole human community must be kept in mind.

Richard A. McCormick acknowledges the decisive role of *consequences* in moral theology, but he also realizes the importance of Christian intentionalism and ethics, in the light of which consequences are to be weighed and evaluated.[54] He acknowledges that he finds himself at home with the conceptual directions being taken by Fuchs, Schuller, Knauer and Janssens. He thinks that it is the *significance or meaning of an act,* and not merely immediate consequence, which generates concrete moral norms and contains the seed of their limitations.[55] Replying to John R. Connery's criticism of Schuller, he says that traditional morality "in the sharpening of forbidden killing down to direct killing 'of an innocent person' '' has implicitly admitted that killing is not wrong "independently of whatever reasons the agent might have had."[56]

5. ST. THOMAS AQUINAS AND MORAL ABSOLUTES

Nowadays, absolutists and relativists both appeal to St. Thomas to defend their respective positions. Hence it would be worthwhile to examine his thought briefly.

At first sight, St. Thomas seems to uphold certain negative moral absolutes—that is, certain physically defined actions which may never be used as means, even for a good cause. Thus, on the basis of natural reason, he condemns fornication, direct killing of an innocent person, taking another's property, divorce and polygamy. "The end of the act itself [fornication] by its nature is disordered even it the person acting could be intending a good end. The end does not suffice to excuse the act, just as is clearly the case with one who steals with the intention of giving alms."[57]

However, confronted with certain biblical passages and not having modern tools of interpretation, he is bound to provide some explanation. This he finds in God's sovereign freedom in dealing with man and things human. Thus, God could command Abraham to kill the innocent Isaac, ask Hosea to be united with a harlot, order the Israelites to despoil the Egyptians and permit polygamy and divorce. "That which a man does at God's will, obeying His command, is not contrary to right reason, although it seems to be against the common order of right reason. . . . Therefore, Abraham did not sin in willing to kill his innocent son, because he obeyed God, even though this, looked at in itself, is commonly contrary to right human reason. Thus Hosea did not sin by fornicating on divine command. Nor should such intercourse be properly called fornication, although it is termed fornication in reference to the common course of events."[58]

Such "dispensations" are possible because, in the mind of St. Thomas, the order to be observed by men is not binding on God, who is the author of the moral order. Still, St. Thomas sees a difficulty: how can God contradict Himself by going against the order of justice founded in His own divine essence? He grants that "the precepts of the decalogue themselves, inasmuch as they contain the quality of justice, are immutable."[59] Still, he notes that in the examples cited above the order of justice is not violated, since God is the master of human life and the other values involved.

St. Thomas seems to provide an intrinsic reason for the exceptions in the distnction between the *primary* and the *secondary precepts* of the natural law. "As for its first common principles (*prima principia communia*), here natural law is the same for all in requiring a right attitude toward it as well as recognition (*secundum rectitudinem et secundum notitiam*). As for particular specific points, which are like conclusions drawn from common principles, here also natural law is the same for most people (*ut in pluribus*) in their feeling for and awareness of what is right. Nevertheless, either the desire or the awareness may be lacking."[60]

Putting the same matter in another way, he says: "The just and the good . . . are formally and everywhere the same, because the principles of right in natural reason do not change. . . . Taken in the material sense, they are not the same everywhere and for all men, and this is so by reason of the instability of man's nature and the diverse conditions in which man and things find themselves in different environments and times."[61]

But St. Thomas is not quite clear as to which precepts belong to the primary or to the secondary aspects of the natural law. Besides, he has stated that only on the authority of God may values like human life be disposed of. God has, however, transferred a certain authority to man. He has given man dominion over all external things to use them for his benefit. He has also empowered civil authority to condemn a criminal according to the law.

Some, therefore, are asking whether, at a time when man has come of age and is "condemned to freedom," we might also conclude that God has transferred such an authority to the heart of man himself. This is indeed a big supposition when basic values like human life and sexuality are involved. Would St. Thomas himself have dared to draw the conclusion?

———o———

Notes to Chapter XII

1. Cf. John G. Milhaven and David J. Casey, "Introduction to the Theological Background of the New Morality," *Theological Studies,* 28 (1967), 213–244.
2. *The Divine Imperative,* London, Nisbet, 1937, p. 350.
3. *Ibid.,* p. 354.
4. Cf. Christopher Kiesling, "Bultmann's Moral Theology," *Theological Studies,* 30 (1969), 225–248.
5. *Ethics,* p. 185.
6. *Morality and Beyond,* London, Collins, 1964, p. 16.
7. *Ibid.,* p. 37.
8. Cf. *Ibid.,* p. 86.
9. *The Nature and Destiny of Man,* London, Nisbet, 1941, pp. 57–58.
10. Cf. *Ethics in a Christian Context,* New York, Harper and Row, 1963.
11. Cf. *The Responsible Self,* New York, Harper and Row, 1951.
12. Cf. *The Structure of Christian Ethics,* Baton Rouge, La., Louisiana State University Press, 1958, pp. 74ff.
13. *Situation Ethics,* Philadelphia, Westminster Press, p. 60.
14. *Ibid.,* p. 26.
15. *Ibid.,* p. 39.
16. Cf. *The Secular City,* pp. 205–216.
17. Cf. *War and the Church Conscience,* Durham, N. C., Duke University Press, 1961, Ch. 1 and 8; also *Deeds and Rules in Christian Ethics,* New York, Scribner's, 1967, Ch. 5 and 6.
18. *Christian Morals Today,* London, SCM Press, pp. 8ff.
19. *Honest to God,* London, SCM Press, p. 118.

20. *Christian Morals Today,* p. 32.
21. Joseph Fletcher, *Christian Responsibility,* Philadelphia, Westminster Press, pp. 31–32.
22. *Deeds and Rules in Christian Ethics,* p. 211.
23. *Ibid.,* p. 217.
24. *Christian Responsibility,* p. 34.
25. *Situation Ethics,* p. 13.
26. *Gift and Call,* Dublin, Gill and Macmillan, p. 31.
27. *Acta Apostolicae Sedis,* 48 (1956), 144–45.
28. *Acta Apostolicae Sedis,* 44 (1952), 270–78; 413–19.
29. Cf. "On the Question of Formal Existential Ethics," *Theological Investigations,* Vol. II, Ch. 7; for a brief synopsis of Rahner's work in the field, cf. James Breshanan, "Rahner's Christian Ethics," *America,* 123 (1970), 351–54.
30. Cf. "Tension, Morality and Birth Control," *Theological Studies,* 28 (1967), 258–85.
31. Cf. "The Catholic Church and the New Morality," *Cross Currents,* 16 (1966), 429–45.
32. Cf. "A New Moral Principle: When Right and Duty Clash," *Furrow,* 17 (1966), 419–22; "In Defence of the Principle of Overriding Right," *Theological Studies,* 29 (1968), 301–09.
33. "Rules and Decisions," *America,* 117 (1967), 61.
34. "Towards a Theory of Exceptions," *Irish Theological Quarterly,* 35 (1968), 217–32.
35. "The Principle of Totality in Moral Theology," *Absolutes in Moral Theology,* edited by Charles E. Curran, Washington, Corpus Books, 1968, p. 245.
36. Cf. *What Is Ethics All About?,* Washington, Corpus Books, 1969.
37. Cf. *Fundamental Concepts of Moral Theology,* New York, Paulist Press, 1968.
38. Cf. *Contraception and the Natural Law,* Milwaukee, Bruce, 1964; *Abortion,* New York, Corpus Books, 1970 (with R. Shaw), *Beyond the New Morality,* University of Notre Dame Press, 1974.
39. Cf. "Conscience and Conflict," *Theological Studies,* 32 (1971), 208–32.
40. *Ibid.,* p. 215.
41. Cf. *Relativity of Natural Law,* Kotagiri. Theological College, 1970; "The Principle of Nullifying Right or Obligation," *Vidya Jyoti,* 40 (1976), 434–446.
42. "The Absoluteness of Moral Terms," *Gregorianum,* 52 (1971), 415–58.
43. Richard A. McCormick, "Notes on Moral Theology," *Theological Studies,* 33 (1972), 76.
44. Cf. "Notes on Moral Theology," *Theological Studies,* 34 (1973), 61–62.
45. Cf. "Ontic Evil and Moral Evil," *Louvain Studies,* 4 (1972), 112–56.
46. "Norms and Priorities in a Love Ethic," *Louvain Studies,* 9 (1977), 207–38.
47. Cf. "La détermination du mal moral par le principe du double effet," *Nouvelle Revue Théologique,* 87 (1965), 356–76; "The Hermeneutic Principle of Double Effect," *Natural Law Forum,* 12 (1967), 132–62.

48. "Towards an Epistemology of Ethics," *Theological Studies,* 27 (1966), 223–241.

49. *Towards a New Catholic Morality,* Garden City, N.Y., Doubleday, 1973.

50. *Catholic Moral Theology in Dialogue,* University of Notre Dame Press, 1972, pp. 209–19.

51. "Moral Theology: Present State," *Theological Studies,* 34 (1973), 446–467.

52. *Ibid.,* p. 452.

53. *Invitation and Response,* Dublin, Gill and Macmillan, 1972; *Gift and Call,* 1975.

54. "Notes on Moral Theology," *Theological Studies,* 33 (1972), 96.

55. "Notes on Moral Theology," *Theological Studies,* 36 (1975), 91–92.

56. *Ibid.,* p. 98.

57. *De Malo,* 15, 1, 3: *Summa Theologica,* Ila-Ilae, 64, 6, 7; 154, 2; 66, 3, 5; *Supplementum,* 65, 1; 67, 2.

58. *Summa Theologica,* Ila-Ilae, 154, 2, 2.

59. *Summa Contra Gentes,* 3, 128, 3.

60. *Summa Theologica,* Ia-Ilae, 94, 4.

61. Cf. John G. Milhaven, "Moral Absolutes and Thomas Aquinas," *Absolutes in Moral Theology,* edited by Charles E. Curran, pp. 154–85.

CHAPTER XIII

Moral Values in Conflict Situations

1. VALUE ETHICS

The foregoing exposition of current trends among Protestant and Catholic writers, taken together with the principles of renewal of moral theology, makes it clear that the natural law should be understood in a more dynamic way than it has been in the past. While the genuine elements in traditional doctrine should be preserved, due importance should be given to the dynamism of love and the uniqueness of the situation.

Vatican II has proposed a more personalistic view of the natural law. Speaking of the responsible transmission of human life, it affirms that the moral aspect of any procedure should be determined by objective standards. "These, based on the nature of the *human person* and his acts, preserve the full sense of *mutual self-giving* and human procreation *in the context of true love.*"[1]

The Council clearly retains the concept of the natural law. But it has brought out its personal dimensions by stressing the finality of a free subject with its interpersonal relationships and personal ends. The aspects of mutual self-giving and the context of true love are not considered mere subjective elements. They enter into the objectivity of the human act. Thereby, the way is open to develop a morality of human values and personal growth.

Natural law, as Louis Monden puts it, "is a dynamic *existing reality,* an ordering of man towards his self-perfection and his self-realization, through all the concrete situations of his life and in inter-subjective dialogue with his fellow man and with God."[2]

The vexed problem of moral absolutes discussed in the last chapter will be closer to a solution if law is seen as an *expression of a value*. We have already seen that, underlying the demand in a law, there is a value. And this must be brought out.

Value in ethics is some reality that man spontaneously recognizes as possessing an intrinsic worth. It is the object of an original emotional intuition, or, more properly, of a spiritual intentionality. Max Scheler refers to value as the person himself offering and accepting love. It arises from an intuitive comprehension of the most fundamental tendency of the person. He insists that each moral value has a peculiar splendor and that it brings joy. Genuine virtue is not self-perfection, but openness to a hierarchy of values in response to the language of God spoken in all His words and works and finally in His incarnate Word, Jesus Christ.

Value is the beauty and authority of personal and personalizing relationships. The life of Christ is the highest manifestation of human value. Union with Him enables the realization of all earthly values as mediations of the supreme value of love. Through Him we attain the transcendent value that is God. While love gives meaning and fullness to other values, these in turn manifest the genuineness of love. Scheler emphasizes the fundamental principle of an ethics of value, which is the sacrifice of the lower to the higher. Man's desires are not from true love if they lead to the betrayal of higher values. For example, exploiting friendship for gain, manipulating prices to the detriment of the poor, and similar things, are an inhuman reversal of values.

Seinsethik (ethics of being) and *Wertethik* (ethics of value) both have their strong points. The first stresses the objectivity of ethics but tends to be impersonal; the second brings out the importance of personal relationships better but may lead to subjectivism. So, instead of being set in opposition, they should be synthetized. *Wertethik* will lead to the hierarchy of values in deciding on the moral righteousness of an action, while *Seinsethik* will be more sensitive to the violation of any basic norm of truly human activity.

We should here note that *value* in ethics is, not merely what is immediately or empirically perceived, but what is experienced in the depths of the personality with its transcendent and communal dimensions. The moral agent realizes that the killing of a man not only draws reprobation or penal sanction but violates the basic tendency of man toward the good, since respect for human life is somehow a participation in the absolute good. The particular value of respect for human life, which may also be called the moral object, is a specification of the basic tendency toward the good.

A weakness of much of consequentialism is precisely that it does not go deep enough. "A consequentialist model, especially when it depends on the findings of the behavioral sciences, seems to be too similar to the technological view of man. Today people are rightly reacting against such a model of human existence. There is also the danger of seeing man primarily in terms of his productivity and contribution to life and society. These are important considerations, but they are not the ultimate reasons for the values we give to human existence."[3]

The person himself is the basic value, the center of values. He is also the bearer of value. The attributes and dispositions which realize in the person the openness and unity that constitute his personality may be called moral virtues. They are, as it were, refractions of the basic value.

Value calls for a norm in order to express it and protect it. "A norm of morals is not an arbitrary restraint interfering with liberty, but a summons and invitation to the exercise of liberty, arising from the value in the object, an invitation to man to preserve and nurture value in freedom."[4] Traditional morality tried to express moral values in terms of fixed moral norms. In a static world with rigid modes of thinking and stable social structures, past formulations of moral norms seemed to be satisfactory. But in a fast-moving world, with ever new problems and ferment of thought, they need to be reappraised or refined.

Before the findings of modern psychology drew attention to the developmental dimensions of morality, it seemed sufficient to teach people of any age or stage of growth definite norms of morality. However, it is now clear that the human person comes to grasp moral value only gradually. Moral education would have to take into account this gradually *maturing process*. It should primarily aim at instilling genuine values in the minds and hearts of youth. Moral guidance should be concerned with helping a person to realize the values implied in a given situation.

Further, it is not enough to be preoccupied only with some values for which one feels special preference either through prejudice or because of a certain upbringing. All the values which contribute to community of love between persons need to be protected and fostered. The institutions and environment within which persons must live and grow should be the object of deep concern. We should wish, not only the growth of individuals, but also the development of economic, cultural, social and political life in such a way that these institutions provide an atmosphere in which personal liberty, justice and truth can flourish.

2. THE VALIDITY OF MORAL ABSOLUTES

There would not be any conflict in a hypothetical, perfectly ordered world in which everything is properly arranged and reason can easily perceive this order. In such a world, moral values and duties would never really conflict, and there would be a moral decision which could simply be called good. But that we are not living in such an ideal world is clear from a cursory reflection on the human situation.

The effect of sin in human life is manifested by conflict situations. The overly rationalist approach of the manuals minimized, when it did not largely ignore, the existence of conflicts of values in moral decision. The discussion on the "perplexed conscience" was reduced to a brief note, often in small print.

As Dietrich Bonhoeffer remarks, responsible action "has not to decide simply right and wrong and between good and evil but between right and right and between wrong and wrong."[5] In fact, the same moral act may involve two or more values. It may be morally impossible for the individual to posit the external act in such a way that it corresponds to all the values involved.

Confronted with such a situation, there are now mainly *three views or trends* among Catholic theologians:

1) There are some absolutes whose deliberate violation is always sinful. They are mostly in the spheres of human life and sexuality. Here, the conflict is ignored or an attempt is made to minimize it. The number of those defending this position is dwindling. But it is far from being altogether abandoned. This view may be called absolutist.

2) There are no externally defined absolutes. Killing, extramarital intercourse, etc., are only "physical," "premoral" or "nonmoral" disvalues. They acquire their moral significance only in relation to human intentionality in the given situation. Here, the moral conflict is effectively eliminated, although there would still remain the task of carefully weighing the relative values, since it is generally accepted that a physical or premoral disvalue may be chosen only in order to avoid some more serious evil. This position may be called relativist, situationist, contextualist, or consequentialist. There is a wide variety of defenders of this position, and some of them may vigorously decline one or the other of these labels. The opinions are so varied, and in many cases so nuanced, that a whole volume would be needed to do justice to them. Still, we hope that the brief expositions of several authors in the last chapter has given a fair idea of the general trend.

3) There are moral absolutes; e.g., certain types of actions always entail *moral evil*. However, in some conflict situations it may be a *lesser evil*. To put the matter positively, there is a moral obligation always to preserve certain values; but in conflict situations, one may have to be sacrificed for the sake of another, which is higher or more urgent. Here, the moral conflict is squarely faced. The solution of choosing the lesser moral evil (or the higher or more urgent good) is certainly not neat or comfortable, but it seems to be the only one that does justice to all the aspects of the problem. It reflects fully the reality of the human condition.

First, we shall see why moral absolutes must be admitted. We must start by noting that a moral norm is not so much an extrinsic limitation arbitrarily placed by religion or society, as an intrinsic demand of love.

A person-centered morality cannot *a priori* exclude an absolute moral norm. This implies only that the essential nature and the basic values of man are inviolable. The human person is called to tend to God, not only by explicit relationships with Him, but in and through the moral act itself, which specifies the basic dynamism of love. The concrete specifications of our moral activity are—immediately—not external, physical structures or biological laws. They are the attitudes or intentionalities one adopts toward the personal significance discovered in these external values. Thus, *life* is a premoral value, but *respecting life* is a moral value; *death* is a premoral disvalue, but *killing* is a moral disvalue.

Hence, to affirm moral absolutes regarding certain basic human values like life and sexuality does not necessarily imply a physicist or biological view of the natural law. Those who make such remarks may themselves be revealing an overly spiritualistic or disincarnate view of man. They may be implying, without being aware of it, that man is merely spirit and that the morality of his activity is determined wholly by his spiritual intentionality, whereas, in fact, man is essentially an incarnate spirit and, hence, his earthly life and other basic values have a determinant role in his moral life.

It is certainly difficult to discern which laws in particular are absolute. None is to be so characterized unless it is conclusively proved. The difficulty in ethical argumentation arises from the need for penetrating the intelligibility, and not merely the empirical reality, of things. From the fact that hair grows on the male face, it does not follow, as Epictetus of old argued, that men are obliged to grow a beard! Hence, one of the crucial questions in bioethics is to determine how far man is bound to respect his biological integrity or what is the limit of his power over his life and vital functions. It is not enough, for instance, to argue to the unlawfulness of contraception merely from the fact that conception takes place normally through the act of coitus. One would have to show why precisely such a positive interference with the procreative dynamism of the marital act always goes against the natural moral law or objectively violates a basic human value.

The contention of those who hold that there are moral absolutes is that some modes of human activity are such that they cannot be positively and internally taken up into the dynamism of love. Thus, one may want to show his love for a terminally ill patient by giving him an injection which will cause him to die without pain. The act may seem only a material procedure that could be justified by the intention of relieving him of the agonizing pain of further survival. But in reality, with its intrinsic finality of causing death (*finis operis*), it is a direct attack on the most basic value of that person, his life itself, whatever might be the ultimate motive (*finis operantis*) of the agent. This point will, however, make no sense to one who fails to see the difference between the objective intentionality of the act and the subjective motive.

Man inherits certain constants which moral reflection has disengaged from experience. These constants do not impede genuine creativity, for they call for realization in action, in the particular time and place where man is. Hence, to go directly against one of the fundamental human values is to violate in varying degrees an actual or potential aspect of personhood. From this we can see that to defend ethical absolutes is not necessarily to yield to legalism, but to defend the person and his inalienable rights. Without some absolutes, the intrinsic good of the human person would not be safe from invasion and suppression under some pretext or other. The human person might become just a commodity or means to achieve some other objective.

One could argue that several lives are more important than one life. From this, one could conclude that it is right to shoot a prisoner in order to induce him to reveal vital information that may save many lives in one's own camp. But if human life is considered a basic value in which every man participates, we should not so easily weigh lives against one another. Unfortunately, this was done in the case of Hiroshima. According to a cold calculation, it seemed that dropping an atom bomb on a whole town would induce such fear in the "enemy" that he would surrender and many precious lives of "our boys" would be spared. That Hiroshima and Nagasaki are not isolated aberrations is revealed by the whole logic of the so-called "nuclear deterrent."

What is behind the time-honored principle "The end does not justify the means" is that the violation of certain basic values of the human person cannot be positively justified by saying that thereby any good result would be achieved. While it is true that persons must not be sacrificed to an abstract principle or moral code, it is equally true that the interests of the human person are not positively promoted by violating the values that constitute his basic dignity.

A case which is becoming increasingly important is that of torture of prisoners or kidnapping and ill-treatment of hostages. There is no lack of rationalizations for such procedures. The modern world is swinging back and forth from violent indignation at such horrors at one time to quiet acquiescence at another. If such evils are not seen as absolute, they are likely to spread. One wonders whether the consequentialist has an effective answer to those who find justification for them in the name of the cause they are sincerely defending.

Regarding sexual intercourse, Richard A. McCormick admits that, since it is clear from experience and reflection that it calls for the marriage relationship, it is legitimate to speak of the marital act in the value-laden sense.[7] If one were to realize that coitus is a sign of total mutual self-gift, then the persons involved must already be in such a relationship. Taking into account the social dimension, this, in practice, means marriage. It would be irresponsible to perform the act outside the relationship. Thus premarital or extramarital intercourse is in reality a countersign that cannot be reconciled with the criterion of genuine love.

John A. T. Robinson, although regarding the exclusion of premarital sex only as a "working rule," concedes that "outside marriage, sex is bound to be the expression of less than an unreserved sharing and commitment of one person to another."[8]

While discussing Robinson's view, Paul Ramsey affirms that "in and from love, there *are,* or there may be, unbreakable rules, and the question to be relentlessly pressed is what these rules are."[9] He calls them "simple corollaries or implications of permanent love."[10]

Ramsey relates how the authors of a pamphlet entitled *Towards a Quaker View of Sex* were led from "Christian love embodied in an act" to "Christian love embodied in a general rule." Though they wanted to exclude proposing an absolute rule, they were led to admit: "There are some things of which one can say that it is so inconceivable that they should ever be an expression of love . . . that they are for Christians always wrong."[11]

Too many absolutes may have been held in the past. It may also be true that certain absolutes were formulated with limited understanding or with a defective perspective. Better understanding in a changed perspective would, then, call for new nuances or refinements. "You shall not steal or take away another's property" is perennially valid. But the determination of what belongs to someone is not easy. For instance, when land reform and similar "socialistic measures" were first proposed, many Christians were inclined to oppose them as going against the human right to private property, without sufficiently examining the foundations and the relative nature of such a right. Land reform looked to them like legalized robbery.

Moral principles applied to new situations give occasion for deeper insights into moral values, and this new knowledge in turn provides a more accurate and enriched expression of the principles of morality. For example, the principle of the equal dignity of woman as a person compared to man has been realized as she emerged from the home into wider fields and proved her capacities. Thus it might be said that "the more exact determination of ethical norms is the work both of reason and experience."[12]

Hence, we must not legalistically cling to outmoded expressions of norms which may have been badly conceived or forget the primary law of love and the call to creative responsibility. On the other hand, in the name of loving motivation, we should not neglect the basic demands of the human vocation expressed in genuine moral norms. Not everything can be justified in the name of love. Some actions may be essentially destructive of love. Both approaches lead to mediocrity: a Pharisaic self-righteousness or yielding to superficial values in the name of love.

3. SOLUTION IN CONFLICT SITUATIONS

What the classical authors had to say regarding the solution of moral conflicts, although in low key, is strangely ignored by many in the current discussion. They spoke of a *perplexed conscience* as the state of mind of one who has two alternatives set before him, each of which seems to be sinful. Some of the authors liken this to a scrupulous conscience that is in constant dread of sin. But others, like Henry Davis, the best known among the older English moralists, make it clear that the perplexed conscience is not the same as a scrupulous conscience.[13]

In the predicament of being faced with sin in either alternative, or what we would now call "moral evil" on either side, Davis suggests the following practical rules culled from St. Alphonsus de Liguori and others: 1) one should first consult prudent people; 2) "if this cannot be done and perplexity remains, he should *choose that which seems the less of two evils.* No sin will then be committed because he is not a free agent." As an obligation to do wrong would be subversive of morality, "he may be assured that in avoiding what appears the greater evil and choosing the less he is doing right and, therefore, doing a good action."[14]

Similarly, Edward Genicot says that "if one seems to be placed between two alternatives, of which one has necessarily to be chosen, and there appears sin on either side, he ought to choose what seems to him the lesser evil (*eligere debet id quod minus malum videtur*)."[15] He goes on to provide the basis for this solution: "No one sins unwillingly or is bound by the impossible." He presumes that all other means to avoid the evil have been exhausted.

The older authors always add that the conflict is only apparent and is only on the subjective level. They are also prone to think that such a conflict is a rare event and often arises from error or a scrupulous bent of mind. This is natural, given the self-assurance with which they handled moral problems. But now it is clear that moral conflicts, especially in today's complex world, are real and frequent.

The French bishops have applied this principle to the interpretation of *Humanae Vitae*.[16] They have no hesitation in accepting the teaching of the encyclical. They also note that many couples have been able to conform their conjugal life to the norm of always keeping the marital act open to life. However, speaking of those who experience veritable agonies in this matter, they state: "Contraception can never be good. It is always a disorder, but the disorder is not always culpable. It happens, indeed, that spouses see themselves confronted with a veritable conflict of duties. . . . On the one hand, they are aware of the duty of respecting openness to life in every conjugal act; they may judge in conscience that they have to avoid a new birth or put it off until later, and they are deprived of the resource of relying on biological rhythms. On the other hand, in what concerns them, they do not see how they can presently renounce the physical expression of their love without menacing the stability of their home."

Expressing the matter in another way, they say: "On this subject we shall simply recall the constant teaching of morality. When one has an alternative choice of duties, and, whatever may be the decision, evil cannot be avoided, traditional wisdom makes provision for seeking before God which duty, under the circumstances, is the greater." The spouses are asked never to "forget or despise any of the duties in conflict."

They do not see the conflict as a rare event. "The feeling of being quartered between contrary obligations is met, under one aspect or another, in the existence of almost all households: that it is necessary to reconcile the physical and moral good of one spouse with that of the other, the good of a child with that of his parents and even of his brothers and sisters, or community involvement with the requirements of the home. There, too, grave choices are often imposed."

The bishops then remark: "This is, in sum, the painful experience of the human condition. . . . As Christians, we are not unaware that it is a whole world which, despite its participation in the resurrection of Christ, is not delivered from contradiction and death."[17]

The Belgian bishops put the matter succinctly: "In dealing with the concrete application of certain directives of the moral order, it can happen that, because of particular circumstances which appear to them a conflict of duties, some of the faithful sincerely believe it is impossible for them to conform to these directives. In this case, the Church asks them to seek loyally the mode of acting that will permit them to adapt their conduct to the given norms. If they do not succeed at first, they should not consider that because of this they are separated from God's love."[18]

The Italian bishops point out that marriage ethics cannot be reduced to the one single point of the openness of the marital act to fruitfulness. "Nevertheless, it, too, must be safeguarded as an indispensable element of perfection and fullness, and [the couple] cannot but acknowledge in this norm, at once humble and sublime, the *metà ideale* (ideal goal) to which they are pledged by their dignity and conjugal vocation."[19] The teaching of the encyclical is "an essential element for the formation of their conscience." They must always strive to retain the moral norm proclaimed by the encyclical, and failure to do so would be a moral evil. But the bishops grant that "there are *laws of growth* in goodness, and that at times one passes through stages which are still imperfect, though with the aim of loyally transcending them in a constant effort toward the ideal."[20]

Similarly, Karl Rahner, in commenting on the encyclical, remarks: "It is basically possible to think that an 'ultimate' norm is formulated here. It is not precisely clear by this whether its moral obligation is 'possible of realization' by each individual or by each social group in every historical situation."[21]

The primary norm of Christian morality is total love of God expressed in love of self and neighbor. Other universally binding moral imperatives that further specify this love can never adequately express the law of growth of a particular individual. As no one is bound to the impossible, no one can be personally held responsible for not actually realizing in every moral act all the moral values implicit in the situation.

As regards basic human intentionality or man's desire and will toward basic values, certain moral absolutes are always binding inasmuch as there is the obligation to strive toward their maximum realization. However, the same moral choice may involve two or more values, and it may be virtually impossible for the individual to posit the external act in such a way as to correspond to all the values involved. As Peter Chirico expresses it, "tension morality" recognizes "that man is often faced with a combination of imperatives of such nature that the accomplishment of one makes morally impossible the accomplishment of one or more of the others. In short, tension morality recognizes that there is always—whether consciously realized or not by the person involved—a tension between what one is ultimately to do and what he actually can do here and now."[22]

Here, Chirico refers to the established doctrine that each just man is given sufficient grace for the observance of God's commandments. According to him, the thesis "refers to the fact that the just man always receives from God the power to avoid every true personal mortal sin. It does not say that the just man is always able to live up to the objective imperatives of the law."[23]

Even *Humanae Vitae* recognizes that the divine law regarding birth regulation "demands serious engagement and much effort—individual, family and social effort."[24] What is the individual to do when, through no fault of his, the social effort is lacking?

Chirico very clearly presents the attitude the Christian must adopt in face of the inevitable tensions in moral life.[25] 1) The Christian must identify the basic moral values in the situation. 2) He must *affirm every one of them,* without picking and choosing, and must have a true desire of realizing them all. 3) Even in the external order, he must make every effort to implement all the values. He can never acquiesce in the violation of some value. When he cannot achieve all of them, he must realize at least the more basic and primary ones. 4) He must recognize in the tension situation his constitutive weakness. Still, he has no reason for despair. He need not be afraid of committing personal sin, which is willful infidelity to God's will, when he does not always succeed in keeping all the objective norms because of the conflict situation. 5) Ultimately, each situation must be seen as a challenge to grow.

This approach to moral decision calls for much more moral maturity than is displayed by those who see only one end of reality. Not only must one know moral norms, but one must be able to see the underlying values, determine the hierarchy of values in a conflict situation, and come to a serene and considered decision. He must sincerely regret the loss of particular values, while at the same time not yielding to paralyzing guilt feelings when he has done whatever is in his power.

We may recall here what Vatican II has to say about moral education of young people. They "have a right to be encouraged to weigh moral values with an upright conscience, and to embrace them by personal choice."[26] This goes far beyond merely teaching them moral norms.

There are some who speak of a "generalized conflict situation"— for instance, regarding birth control in poor, overpopulated countries. The concept would be acceptable if it meant that a very large number of people experience a conflict or that the conflict arises due to a general inquitous social situation. But it should not be understood to mean that in such a situation the moral norm simply does not bind and that, therefore, compulsory sterilization would be legitimate. Nor should it be understood in such a way as to justify imposition of quotas by civil authorities on nurses and others for motivating candidates for sterilization. Those affected by the quotas would not be justified in using any means to fulfill them merely to save their job or other interests. It is true that they, too, would be in a conflict situation, but they would have to weigh carefully the relative values involved.

What this kind of impersonal approach can lead to was tragically shown recently in northern India. The poor people rightly resented others, at any level, deciding for them in a matter that is of the utmost personal importance for them. However, when quotas were required, it would have been licit for those affected to motivate people to plan their families, explain to them the relative merits of different methods, and give the authorities the names of those who freely chose a particular method.

We may add that, unless we hold that artificial contraception is intrinsically evil or that there is a moral absolute in the matter, it would be very difficult to prove that the measure could not be legally imposed in order to counter the enormous national problem of overpopulation. In fact, the warning of the Pope has proved prophetic: "Who could blame a government for applying to the solution of the problem of the community those means acknowledged to be licit for married couples in the solution of family problems? Who will stop rulers from favoring, from even imposing upon their peoples, if they would consider it necessary, the method of contraception which they judge would be most efficacious? In such a way, men, wishing to avoid individual, family, or social difficulties encountered in the observance of the divine law, would reach the point of placing at the mercy of the intervention of public authorities the most personal and most reserved sector of conjugal intimacy."[27]

In order to mitigate the rigors of moral absolutes, some traditional theologians distinguish between abstract moral principles and flexible pastoral practice. Thus, according to a discussion appearing in *The Clergy Review,* Sean O'Riordan attributes this approach to Fr. Visser, one of the drafters of the recent Vatican Declaration on Sexual Ethics.[28] It seems, according to Visser, that moral theology is primarily concerned with abstract principles, while the pastoral ministry is concerned with persons and, hence, must manifest flexibility and compassion. Such an approach, which is rather widespread, is good neither for moral theology nor for pastoral practice—the first would be lost in abstractions, and the second would yield to gross pragmatism. O'Riordan himself remarks: "The personalist type of moral theology is only working out in a theoretical way what the good pastors have instinctively known and done."[29] Indeed, there is great need for bridging the gulf between speculative moral theology and pastoral theology and practice. Any flexible pastoral approach should be solidly grounded in sound principles which are based on the nature of the human person. Otherwise, the pastor may be too much led, to use O'Riordan's expression, by "instinct."

It may appear to some that the distinction between choosing a lesser "premoral" evil and a lesser "moral" evil is only a quibbling with words. Some pragmatic person may say: "After all, we need not observe moral laws strictly!" Or, in the matter of family planning: "After all, it is allowed to use contraceptives!" But, in fact, respect for moral values seems to be much greater when we see that the conflict is at the level of moral values. When a moral disvalue (disorder, evil) is chosen, it is done regretfully (not with scrupulosity), and the desire of avoiding it and of conforming to the objective norm are all the greater.

This has been amply verified in practice in the matter of contraception. Those who have held that it is only a premoral evil, on the whole, have been much less eager to promote natural family planning. On the other hand, those who have held that it is a moral evil have been keen on fostering an approach to family planning which has now proved to be the one most conducive to human dignity and marital harmony. Indeed, the goal or ideal of keeping the marital act open to life must be constantly kept in mind, lest the marriage close in on itself or people lapse into what has been called a "contraceptive civilization," which is far from contributing to the quality of life that is the ostensible purpose of all family planning.

On the other hand, traditionalists may find that the solution of choosing the lesser evil is an astute twisting of the divine law. This is perhaps because they are not willing to see all the aspects of a moral problem or all the values involved in a given situation.

Others are not comfortable with choosing an evil, even though it may be a lesser evil. This feeling is certainly understandable. Some of the difficulty would be removed if the principle were to be presented in a positive way: namely, "In a conflict situation, one must choose the greater or the more urgent value." But there is need of facing the sinful situation of man, in which evil enters into human existence in insidious ways. In a purely individualistic conception of life, we could neatly separate good from evil. But the individual human person is immersed in a social atmosphere where good and evil commingle. He can only try to avoid evil as much as possible and regret that it is inextricably mixed with his good actions. As Nicholas Crotty remarks, the Christian at times may have to weigh the good and evil consequences of his action with the realization that his action will entail some evil which must be recognized and deplored.[30] In Christian life, there should be no place for Pharisaic self-complacency nor for anxious scrupulosity.

If one is to act responsibly in conflict situations, one must be initiated in the use of *preference-principles* for value assessments. Some of these may be mentioned here: 1) Other things being equal, a higher value deserves priority over a lower value. 2) One must prefer the more urgent option, but in such a way as to make apparent one's continual preference for the values which in themselves are higher in degree. 3) At times one must give preference to a more basic value, even while continuing to acknowledge the higher as higher; e.g., one must feed a starving man before preaching to him. 4) The common good is to be preferred to the good of the individual, with great care, however, to avoid the danger of collectivism. 5) Other things being equal, one should prefer the good of those with a special claim to one's responsibility. 6) The degree of probability of realizing a value in one's action must be taken into account. 7) The attainment of a value in the long run must be weighed. 8) The influence of one's action on the conduct of others must be considered (principle of generalizability). 9) At times, one has to ask what would happen to society if everyone were to perform a similar action in a similar situation (principle of universalizability).[31]

A Christian will carry on such an evaluation in a spirit of prayer. The rational reflection will be part of a wider spiritual discernment, since what is ultimately at stake is the discovery of God's will in the given situation.

The principles mentioned above are well accepted also by most of those who deny moral absolutes. Hence, these cannot be called laxists, although we have pointed out the limitations of their approach.

The French bishops in their declaration on *Humanae Vitae* bring out the *growth aspect* of Christian morality, which is a constant striving after the ideal in spite of ambiguities. Full Christian maturity is the culmination of a long and laborious process. Real progress does not consist in immediately resolving all doubts and acquiring a sense of self-righteousness. Louis Monden wonders "whether, in many of our contemporaries, the sympathy for situation ethics is not the expression of a very profound resistance to the unconditional character of the total donation to God's love, which forces one out of every natural shelter; whether it does not mean an anxious effort to keep one's vital decisions within one's autonomous power."[32]

While such a charge should not be too easily made against those who are sincerely striving to give a more personal and responsible tone to Christian ethics, one should also ask whether it is not more in accordance with the realities of human existence to acknowledge that we are imperfect and involved in a sinful situation. The primary aim of an adopted son of God is, not to "settle accounts" with God, but to surrender oneself more and more in faithful love to the merciful Father.

What is needed above all is openness to grace and the desire to grow in love. In an ideal adult conscience, "the compass of love would point the direction so unfalteringly that the external law is no longer needed. In such a man the law has been so fully assimilated, its deepest inspiration is so much a matter of personal experience, that it has become a conscious instinct and an infallible power of discrimination."[33] Then the "Love and, what you will, do" of St. Augustine finds its fullest application. But, till that stage is reached (if ever it is fully reached in this world), conscience needs the prop of the law. Genuine maturity implies the humble acknowledgement of what has remained infantile in ourselves, and of the pedagogical need of the law.

Notes to Chapter XIII

1. *GS,* art. 51.
2. *Sin, Liberty and law,* London, Sheed and Ward, 1965, p. 89.
3. "Moral Theology: Present State," *Theological Studies,* 34 (1973), 452.
4. Bernard Häring, *Law of Christ,* Vol. I, p. 227.
5. *Ethics,* p. 61.

6. Among those still defending the position, see William E. May, "Sterilization: Catholic Teaching and Practice," *Homiletic and Pastoral Review.* 77 (1977), Aug.–Sept., pp. 9–22; Thomas Dubay, "The State of Moral Theology," *Theological Studies,* 35 (1974), 482–506; John R. Connery, "Morality of Consequences: A Critical Reappraisal," *Theological Studies,* 34 (1973), 396–411; Timothy E. O'Connell, "The Question of Moral Norms." *American Ecclesiastical Review,* 169 (1975), 377–88.

7. "Notes on Moral Theology," *Theological Studies,* 33 (1972), 83.

8. *Christian Morals Today,* p. 42.

9. *Deeds and Rules in Christian Ethics,* p. 35.

10. *Ibid.*

11. *Ibid.,* p. 16.

12. Joseph de Finance, *Ethica Generalis,* Roma, Pontificia Università Gregoriana, 1963, p. 188.

13. *Moral and Pastoral Theology,* London, Sheed and Ward, 8th ed., 1959, Vol. I, p. 72.

14. *Ibid.*

15. *Institutiones Theologiae Moralis,* Louvain, Museum Lessianum, 17th ed., 1951, Vol. I, n. 54.

16. No. 15; see *The Catholic Mind,* 67 (1969), Jan., 47–64.

17. For a good elaboration of this document, cf. Gustave Martelet, *l'Existence humaine et l'amour,* Paris, Desclée, 1969. The author is widely credited with a major role in the preparation of the encyclical. At an international congress held at Milan in June 1978 to commemorate *Humanae Vitae,* Martelet explained that the encyclical called the use of contraception a "disorder" which would not be sinful if the couple acted in good conscience and had tried their best to obey the encyclical in the circumstances of their life. Arthur McCormack, who reports on the congress, says that this attitude was generally adopted by the participants. See *Tablet,* 232 (1978), 676.

18. *The Catholic Mind,* 66 (1968), Oct., 55.

19. *The Catholic Mind,* 67 (1969), April, 61.

20. *Ibid.,* p. 64.

21. "On the Encyclical *Humanae Vitae,*" *The Catholic Mind,* 67 (1968), Nov., 35.

22. *Art. cit.,* p. 272.

23. *Ibid.* See also Maurizio Flick and Zoltan Alzeghy, *Il vangelo della grazia,* Roma, Pontificia Università Gregoriana, 1964.

24. No. 20.

25. *Art. cit.,* pp. 273–74.

26. *GE,* art. 1.

27. *Humanae Vitae,* no. 17.

28. "The Declaration on Certain Questions Concerning Sexual Ethics," *Clergy Review,* 61 (1976), 229–37.

29. *Ibid.,* p. 234.

30. See *art. cit.,* pp. 212–19.

31. Cf. Bernard Häring, *Morality Is for Persons*, pp. 136–37; Louis Janssens, "Norms and Priorities in a Love Ethic," *Louvain Studies*, 6 (1977), 207–38; Richard A. McCormick, "Notes on Moral Theology," *Theological Studies*, 33 (1972), 88–99.

32. *Op. cit.*, p. 109.

33. *Ibid.*, 102–103.

CHAPTER XIV

The Christian and Canon Law

1. THE NATURE AND FUNCTION OF CHURCH LAW

Although the Church is a community of love, the Spirit Himself being her primary inward principle of guidance, her character as a human society calls for a certain amount of order, which positive law seeks to obtain. The New Testament itself validates the existence of law in the Church when 1) it witnesses to stable ministries in the Church; 2) it speaks of the power "to bind and to loose" (Mt. 16:17–19; 18:18); 3) it describes the regulation of Christian life in apostolic communities.

There should be no opposition between the *charismatic* and the *juridical* elements in the Church. Pope Pius XII declared that it is "a calamitous error which invents an imaginary Church, a society nurtured and shaped by charity, with which it disparagingly contrasts another society, which it calls juridical."[1] More recently, Pope Paul VI has expressed the need for law in the Church very strongly: "A community without law, far from being or ever being able to be, in this world, the community of charity, has never been and will never be anything else than a community of the arbitrary."[2]

For those who have an integral vision of the Church, the real question is not "Should there be Church law?" but "What kind of law should the Church have, and in what spirit should it be observed?"

Vatican II has provided the key to the understanding of Church law. In its Decree on Priestly Formation, the Council directed that "in the explanation of canon law and Church history, the mystery of the Church be kept in mind, as it was set forth in the Dogmatic Constitution on the Church."[3] There it is said: "Christ, the one Mediator, established and ceaselessly sustains here on earth His holy Church, the community of faith, hope and charity, as a visible structure. Through her He communicates truth and grace to all. But the society furnished with hierarchical agencies and the Mystical Body of Christ are not to be considered as two realities, nor are the visible assembly and the spiritual community, nor the earthly Church and the Church enriched with heavenly things. Rather they form one interlocked reality which is comprised of a divine and a human element."[4]

Law in the Church will bear a certain analogy to laws in other human societies. However, inasmuch as the Church is a unique community of salvation, her law must manifest a corresponding salvific character. As Charles E. Curran puts it, "The positive law of the Church, like all other externals in the Church, has a sacramental character. The law must be a sign of the inner reality of the Church, which is above all a community of love. The whole purpose of the law of the Church must be to build up the Body of Christ in truth and love. Canon law should strive to create the climate in which the Church and its individual members can better respond to the call of the Spirit."[5] The uniqueness of the ecclesial reality must be brought out even in the terminology used. Thus marriage is not a contract in the purely legal sense. It is better spoken of as a covenant of love. The laws regarding marriage should be formulated with this concept in mind.

Church law plays the positive role of drawing attention to some demands of the Christian vocation. It provides for the spiritual well-being of the faithful and determines the manner in which the relations between the faithful are to be lived. It must not stifle the freedom of the members. "The law is not meant for the law's sake . . . but is at the service of truth, justice, patience and charity."[6]

It should be clear that law has only a *subsidiary role* in the Church. The Christian has been freed from living under the economy of the law. He needs the external formulations of the moral law only inasmuch as he is not yet able by himself to discern the law of God imprinted in his heart. Likewise, he needs the guidance of human law only inasmuch as human weakness prevents him from discerning spontaneously the needs of common life in the ecclesial community. History shows that particular positive laws had to be enacted when the ebb of Christian life was low. As long as the faithful understood the centrality of the Eucharist in their lives,there was no need for a law about annual communion. Too many prescriptions stifle initiative and freedom. Hence, the ideal is, not as many laws as possible, but as few as are necessary.

Thus, ecclesiastical legislation must be wholly characterized by its purpose: to foster the creation of a Christian community or fellowship in virtue of the Christ-event, to regulate duties, to protect rights, to counteract abuses and social evils, so that "man, by both the protection and the command of laws, may share in the truth and grace of Christ, and live, grow and die in a holy, pious and faithful manner."[7] As St. Gregory the Great declared: *"Salus animarum est suprema lex"* (The salvation of souls is the supreme law).

According to St. Thomas, the law must be *an ordering of reason.*[8] The voluntaristic concept of Duns Scotus and Francis Suarez gives the impression that the obligatory force of human law depends on the arbitrary will of the legislator, when in fact law must correspond to the *common good:* it must reflect the needs of the community here and now.[9]

The will of the superior cannot simply be identified with the will of God. The role of the superior or the legislator is to mediate the will of God by promoting the good of the community. Hence, the meaning of the law depends upon the good to be achieved.

Here it is necessary to say something about the nature of authority in the Church. The dynamic presence and power (*exousia*) of the risen Lord is the ultimate source of authority in the Church. The manner of exercising power should be after the pattern of Jesus. "You know that those who are supposed to rule over the Gentiles lord it over them. . . . But it shall not be so among you; but whoever would be great among you must be your servant. For the Son of man also came not to be served but to serve" (Mk. 10:42,45). Authority in the Church is a function of service (*diakonia*). The superior or legislator must see himself as the servant of the community, humbly conforming himself to the call of the Spirit so as to order the life of the community according to its spiritual destiny. Pope Paul VI made this quite clear: "The exercise of authority in the Church, with the particular powers that come from the very will of Christ, in the context of evangelical love, for which every manifestation of love is a response to the will of Christ, is a responsibility of service to the community."[10]

Those in authority should inspire the spirit of obedience in their subjects by themselves being an example of obedience to the will of God. They should facilitate the response of obedience by their attitude of love and service. As Bernard Häring puts it: "The bearer of authority must not only examine his conscience again and again if in his pastoral leadership he is alert in his obedience to God and readiness to serve those entrusted to his care. He must also constantly renew the ways and means, the entire style in which he fulfills his office to see how he can better serve and represent the humility of Christ to them."[11]

The role of authority is not so much to enforce obedience by every means as to lead to *mature autonomy* and a courageous spirit of initiative in the people of God. Jesus said: "No longer do I call you servants, for the servant does not know what his master is doing, but I have called you friends, for all that I have heard from my Father I have made known to you" (Jn. 15:15). All those who have authority in the Church should cultivate this attitude. Jack Dominian has provided a good exposition of the difference between genuine exercise of authority and pernicious "authoritarianism."[12] The latter is a "system" of rules and regulations without any sense of intimacy and personal meaning. It is bred by an "authoritarian mentality" that is itself the product of narrow-mindedness, prejudice and insecurity.

2. THE RENEWAL OF CANON LAW[13]

All Church law has a *provisional* character because of the pilgrim nature of the Church.[14] In spite of the extraordinary legal acumen of great canonists like Gratian of old and Gasparri of late, canon law has always been defective. It has been imperfectly formulated and been subject to the contingencies of history. Besides, a technically perfect law is not necessarily a good law if it loses flexibility and creativity. We could cite the pungent remark of Denis F. Callaghan: "The Code of Canon Law, if anything, did its job too well!"[15]

The present Church law is largely based on Roman civil law, although it has absorbed some elements from other sources and, to a certain extent, has been inspired by the Christian spirit. Some limitations have crept in because of this one-sided dependence. Pope Paul VI himself acknowledged this: "It is unfortunately true that the Church, in the exercise of her power . . . has down the centuries borrowed from civil legislation certain serious imperfections, even methods which were unjust in the true and proper sense, at least objectively speaking."[16]

The concept of equality has been a positive feature of Roman jurisprudence. Still, some are asking whether certain principles from the common law prevalent in Anglo-Saxon countries could not be usefully introduced, such as the supremacy of law binding all agencies of government in order to avoid any arbitrary measures, the rule of evidence, equal protection of all members, and observance of what is called "due process of law." One may add that this broadening should also include elements from other legal traditions, including those from non-Western countries.

The present law bears some traces of the absolutist and feudal mentality of past ages. Now, many would wish that the democratic conception be admitted. While this is legitimate up to a point, it should not be forgotten that the Church is a unique society and that the democratic model may not adequately represent her nature. Hence, the law should be derived more from the peculiar nature of the Church herself. Accordingly, Pope Paul VI gave the following direction to a group of canonists: "Your first concern will not be, therefore, to establish a juridical order modeled on civil law, but to deepen the work of the Spirit, which must be expressed also in the Church's law."[17] Hence, the importance of the contribution of theology to the renewal of canon law should not be minimized.

The communal emphasis in the self-understanding of the Church, according to Vatican II, indicates *shared responsibility*. It is to be expressed in episcopal collegiality, the collaboration of the clergy, and the active role of the laity. The law must make it clear that the laity are not merely persons bound by duties nor objects of the ministrations of the clergy, but are subjects of rights and hence have their own proper part to play in the life and apostolate of the Church. There is need for trust in the goodwill and capacities of the laity. From the call to responsibility at every level follows the principle of *subsidiarity*. This means that a higher authority leaves to a lower what the latter can do well. In fact, the power of dispensing from universal laws has now been almost entirely transferred to the local bishops. It is highly desirable that decision-making power also be transferred to the bishops whenever it can; or, rather, that their right to shepherd their flock according to local needs and conditions be fully acknowledged, always in communion with central authority.

This brings up the point of *pluralism*, which is deeply embedded in human experience. Though the Church, as an eschatological community, transcends space and time, still she is immersed in the various human cultures to which her members belong. Vatican II has brought out the idea that the universal Church is the communion of local Churches.[18] Hence, law that seeks to promote the common good of the Church must take into account the traditions and social conditions of the different regions of the world where she lives. Some, therefore, have suggested that the universal law of the Church should comprise only general directions or broad principles, while further specifications are left to regional or local authority. However, the rapidly increasing mobility of people would require a certain degree of uniformity, lest there be total confusion.

In order to meet the needs of the faithful effectively, due account should be taken of the findings of contemporary *human sciences*—of psychology, for instance, in marriage jurisprudence. There is also need for systematic *social research*, for example, on the causes and effects of mixed marriages. As a function of practical reason, lawmaking requires close attention to concrete experience as well as general principles.

A radical *simplification of procedure*, in order to approximate legal action to pastoral care, would be desirable. Thus, there is a proposal to reduce the time limit for completing marriage cases. The prescribed time limit should be strictly kept in order to avoid undue hardship to innocent parties. Legal clarity and security have a limited scope compared to the rights of the individual person. Canon lawyers should not forget their primary pastoral role while displaying their legal acumen.

There should be no trace of discrimination against women. They should be accorded proper representation in the process of the renewal of Church law and given full participation in Church life.

The common law of the Church must foster, and not hinder, the life of various institutions, societies and associations in the Church. Canon law should provide only the broad framework within which they can make their proper contribution to the Church and wider society. The charism of the new "basic communities" which are now springing up in order to provide intimate fellowship amidst the impersonal structures of modern society, ought to be respected even while providing them with some sense of direction. Similarly, due autonomy of Catholic centers of learning should be safeguarded.

The promulgation of new laws ought to be preceded and accompanied by *proper education* of the clergy and the laity. This will be facilitated if all, according to their function and competence, are invited to take an active part in the legislative process. Wide consultation will give a sense of involvement and responsibility to all. A certain process of experimentation before the final formulation of laws could be useful, as in the case of the renewal of the liturgy and the recent legislation on mixed marriages.

However, there is no such thing as a definitive formulation for all time. Rather, there should be an inbuilt procedure for a *continuous revision* in the light of new needs and new experiences.

One of the persistent demands made of late is that Church law should include the full range of regulations and procedures for due process of law. The Church, it has been urged, should be the protector of the dignity and rights of the individual members of the people of God, not merely because of the present democratic trends in the world, but especially because of the very values the Church is called to promote in the world. Far from merely reflecting the respect for human rights in civil law, the Church ought to show the way in defending these rights within her fold. Hence, many have called for such provisions as an independent and impartial judiciary, the right to a speedy and public hearing, the right of counsel and cross examination, the right to appeal and the right of recourse from inequitable administrative decisions. Some of these points have been incorporated in the draft of the new Code. However, while there is certainly need for due process of law, there should not arise a spate of litigation that might further embitter relations among various persons in the Church.

The reform of canon law has important ecumenical implications.[19] Already the norms for mixed marriages and for spiritual sharing with non-Catholics have been considerably relaxed.[20] In the draft of the new Code, the binding force of laws on non-Catholics has been restricted.

However, the problem is deeper than that. Different Church traditions have different conceptions of law. The *Roman Catholic* conception has been primarily derived from the *hierarchical structure* of the Church. Because of this juridical basis, canon law can have at least an analogical relationship with civil law.

The *Orthodox* agree on the need for a definite order in the Church and, in fact, tenaciously hold on to a great number of canonical rules. But, according to them, the order flows out of the *sacramental community,* whose real creator is the Holy Spirit, and its function is, above all, to protect the sacramental mystery. Hence, there is no basis for the development of a legal system derived from a "divinely ordained structure" of the Church. The sacramental event itself must determine the life of the community.

According to the *Reformed* Churches, it is *God's saving Word,* above all, that is the source of Christian life. As the Gospel cannot be comprehended in juridical categories, the erection of a juridical system runs the risk of making law into an independent entity in its own right. Law must be clearly subservient to the proclamation of the Word.

The insights of the Orthodox and Reformed traditions could be useful complements to the Catholic tradition, as has already been recognized by Vatican II and the draft of the new Code. On the other hand, while the Catholic view may tend to legalism, the Orthodox view may tend to ultraconservatism, and the Reformed Churches have never succeeded in evolving a satisfactory Church order. Hence, the different traditions have much to learn from each other.

3. THE OBLIGATION OF CANON LAW

The obligation in conscience to observe the laws of the Church rightly understood follows from Christ's establishment of the hierarchy in the Church and, more directly, from the duty of the faithful to contribute to the common good of the ecclesial community. While civil law is concerned primarily with the external performance of the duty enjoined, the legislation of the Church is primarily directed to the spiritual good of her members. Hence, although the legal obligation of canon law seems to relate directly to the external act, it would be very wrong to think that it is enough to be satisfied with the external performance and neglect the interior motive and disposition.

Although the Code itself is discreet about the matter, canonists generally hold that certain laws, like participation in Sunday Mass, are binding under grave sin. First, it should be made quite clear that grave sin cannot be a penalty or punishment, since it is the reality of the breaking of man's relationship of love with God. Sin as such cannot be used as a penalty. Hence, the expression ''binding under mortal sin'' can only mean that the ''matter'' of a certain law is grave. The Church can point out that a certain obligation is serious; but whether one actually commits sin or not by missing Sunday Mass will depend on the extent of deliberation, as traditional moral theology itself recognizes.

Grave sin, as we shall see later in detail, is a change in the fundamental option of the person in a particular choice. The expressions "grave matter" and "light matter" can indicate the greater or lesser importance the Church attaches to a particular action. Still, the mere observance of the law is not an infallible criterion of holiness. Legalism can easily lead to mediocrity, if not to Pharisaism.

To determine in the concrete whether the matter of a law is grave, it is necessary to consider the words of the law, its object, its purpose, the circumstances, the sanction (if any), and its customary interpretation. In determining the gravity of an obligation, one should not put too much stress on the will of the legislator in a voluntarist sense. One must attend more to the importance of the matter, since the role of the human legislator is precisely to determine what is conducive to the common good.

In the past, each *single violation* of certain laws was considered grave. Now there is a trend to consider only *habitual violation* as seriously sinful. This view has been officially admitted in the matter of fast and abstinence. "Grave obligation does not refer to each of the days of penance. . . . He sins gravely against the law who, without excusing reasons, omits a quantitatively or qualitatively important part of the penitential practice prescribed in a general way."[21] Many would like this conception to be extended to Sunday observance as well. They would admit, however, that a single violation would be grave if it implied contempt of legitimate authority.

Because of the obligation in conscience, positive law has a moral dimension. Still, the distinction between *merely human regulations* and *moral norms,* which immediately express the basic values of man, must be carefully maintained. Much of the conflict between rigid legalists and extreme situationists arises from the neglect of this distinction. The saying of Jesus: "The sabbath was made for man, and not man for the sabbath" (Mk. 2:27) refers directly to the external regulations regarding the observance of the sabbath, and not to the fulfilling of the dynamic orientation of the human person toward the worship of God.

There is a classical axiom which says, *"Finis legis non cadit sub lege"* (The intention of fulfilling the purpose of the law does not come under the law). It is correct if understood to mean that one has fulfilled the Sunday obligation if one participated devoutly in the Eucharistic celebration without knowing at the time that it was a Sunday. But it would be wrong to take it to mean that one has sufficiently fulfilled the precept by fasting out of miserliness or by abstaining from meat because one likes fish. The Church's law is meant to serve the order of grace. "The external obligation of human law may never be severed from the law of the grace of Christ, which always invites the sentiment of man's heart."[22]

It is true that, if proper disposition was lacking, one is not always obliged to perform the act again, unless the human act was entirely missing or unless the very validity of the act depends upon the intention—e.g., in the case of an oath or of marriage consent. Still, there is always the obligation to repent of one's neglect and to assume the proper attitude that was lacking when the act was performed.

Overemphasis on the legal obligation should not be used as an evasion from the difficulty of instilling the importance of the liturgy or of mortification in the Christian life. It is not enough to get the people somehow to "hear" Mass. There is need for conducting the celebration in such a meaningful and attractive way that people come willingly.

Generally speaking, one cannot observe a law before the legal time for its fulfillment. This may be done only inasmuch as it is permitted by lawful authority—e.g., participating in the Mass on Saturday evening where there is such a permission. Once the time assigned has elapsed, one is not strictly obliged to perform the work—e.g., to assist at Mass on Monday because one could not do so on Sunday. However, one would be well advised to do so.

If one cannot perform the precise external duty prescribed, the spirit of the law would demand that something else be done in its stead. Thus, one should not altogether fail to celebrate the Lord's Day just because one is unable to go to Mass. Some other form of worship should be performed.

4. FREEDOM FROM THE LAW

A positive law is not based on the permanent nature of man, but on changing circumstances. The legislator simply cannot foresee all the possible contingencies that might arise. Hence, positive law essentially admits of exceptions. Otherwise, the letter of the law might go against the deepest intention of the law or cause injustice to individuals. "The written code kills, but the Spirit gives life" (2 Cor. 3:6).[23]

The law is meant as a form of guidance for Christian life, and not as its ultimate basis. To find security in the meticulous observance of the letter of the law would be to substitute the worship of an idol for the worship of God. It may be the sign of Pharisaic self-righteousness. Many Jews of Jesus' time succumbed to this temptation, nor is every Christian free from it. Scrupulous observance of external practices is no guarantee against lamentable self-deception, against failure to recognize the true God of the covenant. An unreflective conformism to the letter of the law may also betray an indolent attitude that shirks mature choice. With this background, we can briefly discuss some practical points.

a) A law *ceases to bind* not only if it is expressly abrogated by the legislator, but also if it loses all meaning and purpose for the community and even becomes positively harmful. Thus, an *obsolete law* ceases to bind even before it is formally abrogated. However, this should be manifest and not merely seem so. The hierarchy of a region would be specially competent to declare that a particular universal law is no longer necessary and hence without further binding force in the region. A consensus among prudent people in the area would also be an indication of this.

b) *Moral impossibility* simply *excuses* one from observing a human law. The intention of the law cannot be to urge its observance in spite of disproportionate difficulty or relatively grave harm to the individual or the community. Likewise, a positive law does not bind when it would hinder a correspondingly greater good. Thus, everyone knows that one who has to care for a seriously ill person and cannot at the same time assist at Sunday Mass, is excused from the latter obligation. Jesus went beyond the sabbath rules in order to heal the sick (cf. Mt. 12:10–13). He asks us to go beyond mere formalism to the deepest intention of the law, which at times requires that we omit its external prescriptions in order fulfill its real purpose.

However, the common good may sometimes require an extraordinary sacrifice in the observance of the law. Similarly, one may have to fulfill an obligation flowing from a state that has been freely undertaken, even when it would imply great difficulty—for instance, a pastor regarding ministrations to the dying.

The excusing causes are to be weighed by applying the principle of *epikeia*. A voluntanistic idea of *epikeia* would refer to the "will of the legislator." The individual is supposed to presume the goodwill of the superior. St. Thomas, on the other hand, affirms that it is rather a virtue, a part of the virtue of justice, closely allied to prudence.[24]

Some writers understand *epikeia* as a principle of interpretation by which one imagines that the legislator does not wish to insist on the observance of the law in difficult circumstances. This seems to be too voluntaristic a conception and is now being generally abandoned. There is no need for invoking the supposed benevolence of the legislator. The very nature of human law implies that it cannot bind under disproportionate difficulty.[25]

At first sight, it may seem that the idea of *epikeia* would foster anarchy. But it must be noted that it is not an attempt to evade the true demands of the law but, rather, to fulfill its true spirit.

The Code itself provides that in a *positive doubt of law*, ecclesiastical laws are not binding.[26] This is true as regards the moral and legal obligation because of the general principle of probabilism. The canon declares, moreover, that it is also true as regards the validity of acts. Even invalidating and incapacitating laws are not binding if a doubt of law exists. In a *positive doubt of fact*, the canon grants to ordinaries the power to dispense, provided the law is one from which the Holy See is wont to dispense.

As *epikeia* is linked to prudence, the canon law course cannot be merely an exercise in scholarly interpretation. It must also be an initiation into the *art of prudent discernment,* noting that using *epikeia* is ultimately listening to the voice of the Spirit.

Agape should always remain the fundamental attitude of the Christian. *Epikeia* is not a way of self-indulgence, but a *liberation for service.* Hence, its proper exercise needs a spirit of maturity and self-sacrifice, lest it lead to abuse. Still, *abusus non tollit usum*—i.e., abuse cannot constitute a sufficient reason to reject the time-honored principle of *epikeia* in Christian life.

Ecclesiastical authority, instead of being frightened at *epikeia,* should itself promote its proper use. According to Bernard Häring, it would itself fail in the virtue if it did not lead the faithful "gradually and according to their capabilities to that degree of maturity which eventually allows them to make a judgment proceeding from a confirmed virtue of *epikeia.*"[27]

c) At times there is reason to be free from an obligation, but it does not seem quite sufficient. Then, an authorized person can grant a *dispensation.* This provision presumes that people are not always able to judge for themselves the sufficiency of the reason for a simple excuse. If they were trained better to understand the exact significance of the law, there would be less need for having recourse to dispensations. However, a mere spirit of "permissiveness" or imagined maturity would not justify failure to have recourse to authority.

The canonical institute of dispensation has a strong flavor of voluntarism. It looks as if the dispensing authority is exercising some form of superior graciousness, reminiscent of feudal times. Therefore, it should be clear that he is not free to grant or deny dispensations arbitrarily. All who have the dispensing power are bound to use it according to the best interests of the faithful.

In order to prevent abuses, the Code has provided that a dispensation obtained by offering false reasons from an authority below the legislator is not only illicit but also invalid.[28] Should the motivating reasons cease to exist entirely, the dispensation also ceases.[29] Here we see that dispensation has an objective basis.

It is good to distinguish dispensation from *permission,* which is authorization to perform an action when the law prescribes the need for such authorization. Permission is "according to the law" and, hence, may be presumed when the competent authority cannot be approached, while a dispensation, being "against the law," cannot be presumed. The practice of requiring permission to do what is otherwise good and approved by the law needs to be curtailed in order to foster maturity in different sections of the people of God.

d) *Commutation* is a form of dispensation with a condition. It is a substitution of another work granted by competent authority—for instance, to adopt some other prayer in place of the breviary. Increasingly, such matters could be left to the decision of the person himself, with the help, where necessary, of a spiritual guide.

e) *Privilege* in the strict sense means a general disposition granting to some persons a right that is contrary to or beyond the common law. Privileges seem to have little meaning in today's world of fraternal equality. Many privileges connected with certain associations or offices may even be a source of scandal. While it may not be possible to do away with a longstanding and widespread practice immediately, this whole matter needs to be reconsidered.

———o———

Notes to Chapter XIV

1. *Mystici Corporis,* no. 63.
2. Allocution of 28 January, 1972, *Acta Apostolicae Sedis,* 64 (1972), 203.
3. *OT,* art. 16.
4. *LG,* art. 8.
5. *A New Look at Christian Morality,* p. 127.

6. Pope Paul VI, Allocution of 28 June, 1971, *Acta Apostolicae Sedis,* 63 (1971), 140.

7. Pope Pius XII, Allocution of 17 October, 1953, *Acta Apostolicae Sedis,* 45 (1953), 688.

8. Cf. Ia-IIae, 91, 4. "Reason" here is understood in the context of faith lived in the ecclesial community. Church law cannot be understood just as another form of civil law.

9. The idea of human law as a function of the common good will be explained more fully in the chapter on civil law.

10. Allocution of 28 January, 1971, *Acta Apostolicae Sedis,* 63 (1971), 135.

11. *Christian Maturity,* New York, Herder and Herder, 1967, p. 42.

12. *Authority,* London, Burns and Oates, 1976, pp. 7–15.

13. Cf. *A Pastoral Guide to Canon Law,* ed. by George J. Dyer, Dublin, Gill and Macmillan, 1977; "The Role of Law in the Church," *The Jurist,* 27 (1967), 163–181; Ladislaus M. Orsy, "Quantity and Quality of Laws after Vatican II," *The Jurist,* 27 (1967), 385–412; J. D. Conway, "Law and Renewal," *The Jurist,* 26 (1966), 413–425; James A. Coridan, "The Future of the Law," *The Jurist,* 34 (1974), 154–167.

14. This is in sharp contrast with the older image of the Church as a perfect society, with a perfect legal endowment.

15. In George J. Dyer (ed.), *op. cit.,* p. 2.

16. Allocution of 28 January, 1971, *Acta Apostolicae Sedis,* 63 (1971), 139.

17. Allocution of 17 September, 1973, quoted in George J. Dyer (ed.), *op. cit.,* p. 12.

18. Cf. *LG,* art. 13.

19. Cf. Lukas Vischer, "Reform of Canon Law: An Ecumenical Problem," *The Jurist,* 26 (1966), 395–412.

20. Cf. *The Ecumenical Directory* of 1967 and the Motu Proprio *Matrimonia Mixta* of 1970.

21. S. Congregation of the Council, February 20, 1967. See *Acta Apostolicae Sedis,* 57 (1967), 229; also *Clergy Monthly,* 31 (1967), 57.

22. Bernard Häring, *The Law of Christ,* Vol. I, p. 275.

23. *Summa Theologica,* IIa-IIae, 120, 1.

24. *Ibid.,* 120, 2.

25. Edouard Hamel, *op. cit.,* Ch. 3.

26. *Codex Iuris Canonici,* Can. 15.

27. *Christian Maturity,* p. 72.

28. *Codex Iuris Canonici,* Can. 84, 1.

29. *Ibid.,* Can. 86.

CHAPTER XV

Civil Law and Morality

1. THE RELATIONSHIP BETWEEN LAW AND MORALITY

However much people might differ regarding the concept of morality, all would admit that some human acts make a person good and others make him bad. Before we even talk about it, we experience this in the depths of our heart or our conscience. On the other hand, there can be no civil society without laws. The relationship between these two norms of human activity, internal and external, is becoming ever more important in today's world.

We tend either to exaggerate or to minimize the link between civil law and morality. In the first instance, there is danger of human life being cramped by excessive legalism, or of people being led to violate basic human values because of improper laws. In the second, there may be excessive individualism, leading to anarchy. Hence, we shall try to clarify the main problems involved in the relationship of law to morality.

In traditional society there was no clear distinction between moral and civil law. Both were handed down by tradition and were ultimately given a divine sanction. The Torah of the Hebrews or the Dharma of the Hindus comprised a whole way of life determined by the respective world view of the two religions. But there was a latent duality in either inasmuch as there was an unchangeable core and a developing jurisprudence according to the needs of the times.

Jesus brought out the distinction clearly, insisting on absolute obedience to the commandments of God (Mt. 19:16–19; Mk. 10:17–19; Lk. 18:18–20), which in turn could be reduced to the one commandment of love of God and neighbor (Mt. 22:34–40; Mk. 12:28–34; Lk. 10:25–28). That all other rules and regulations are of relative importance He affirmed by declaring: "The sabbath is for man, not man for the sabbath" (Mk. 2:27).

During the "Christian ages" in Europe, the distinction between moral and civil law, though always theoretically upheld, was not much recognized in practice because of a largely theocratic form of government. But with the rise of secularism on the one hand, and of the depreciation of the natural law by the reformers and philosophers on the other, legal positivism arose. Civil law was divorced from its religious and moral basis. It became a self-enclosed and self-sufficient system regulated by legal precedent or the arbitrary will of the rulers. The bitter fruits of this sundering of law from morality were borne in the horrors of the Nazi regime. The Nuremberg tribunal which was set up to try Nazi war criminals had difficulty at first establishing criteria for judgment when the defendants pleaded that they had only followed orders. This and the whole traumatic experience of the past decades led to a revival of interest in the natural moral law and in the need for deriving civil law from it.

More recently, various factors—like reaction against the rigidity of traditional natural law ethics among Catholics, and the vast divergence of opinion regarding the demands of morality in most countries of the world—have led to a new tension regarding the relationship of civil law to morality.

2. THE NATURE AND FOUNDATION OF CIVIL LAW

Man living in society needs to be governed by positive human laws. Their function is 1) to insist on the observance of certain divine natural laws affecting the good of society—e.g., not killing; 2) to determine the divine laws by making them more concrete—e.g., defining the amount of taxes to be paid or the requirements of a valid contract. In the present human condition, effective civil authority implies the power of coercion or the right to compel people to obey the necessary laws.

Hence, civil laws are founded on the divine law. "There is one lawgiver" (Jas. 4:12). Their purpose is to procure the *common good* according to the particular nature of civil society, which is finally meant to foster the spiritual good of man.

The common good is more than the sum total of the interests of individuals. As man is social by nature, the community to which he belongs has a good which surpasses his private good, although it cannot go against his basic dignity and rights. Every individual has the obligation of contributing to the common good, since it is by the procurement of the common good that the conditions for his personal development will be fostered.

Authority in society is a necessary instrument by which the different elements of the societal organism conspire to a common end in order to achieve the full development of each individual in the community. It is a service to the community, as is implied by the title "minister" applied to the chief executives of the nation.

Ultimately, all authority is a sharing in the sovereignty of God. "There is no authority except from God" (Rom. 13:1). But this is not to be understood in the sense of the "divine right" of kings claimed by certain absolute monarchs of the past. As human authority is wholly for the interests of the common good of the people, its power immediately proceeds from the people. They transfer that power to the rulers by democratic election or at least by tacit consent. But once the rulers have obtained legitimate authority, the people have to respect and obey their just ordinances, since the wisdom and love of God's royal dominion expresses itself through them. "Therefore he who resists the authorities resists what God has appointed, and those who resist will incur judgment. . . . for he [who is in authority] is God's servant for your good" (Rom. 13:2,4).

Especially in a democracy, the citizens must obey willingly but at the same time preserve inner freedom: "Be subject for the Lord's sake to every human institution. . . . Live as free men, yet without using your freedom as a pretext for evil; but live as servants of God'' (1 Pet. 2:13,16). There are special difficulties in a postcolonial era. Those who rightly resisted the unjust and oppressive colonial regime may have grown used to the habit of resisting all authority. Others, who perhaps allied themselves with the colonial rulers or profited from colonial structures, may not yet have reconciled themselves to the transfer of power and, hence, may still be hankering after the "fleshpots" of bygone days and be suffering from cultural alienation.

One's obedience must not be uncritical. St. Peter asks subjection as "free men." Citizens do not fulfill their responsibility merely by going to the polls. They have to collaborate actively in achieving the common good. They must be vigilant that their representatives carry out their duties faithfully. If anything is commanded that is against their conscience, they must resist as best as they can. Here the words of Peter apply: "We must obey God rather than men" (Acts 5:29).

Proper obedience to human laws is an aspect of the following of Christ. Civil laws indicate a certain minimum mode of expressing love of neighbor. Thus, they objectively contribute to the building up of the Kingdom of God.

But while human authority reflects God's sovereign dominion, we often make the painful discovery that its bearers are not always wise and perhaps are even mediocre and selfish. The rules and ordinances emanating from them are far from perfect. Then we ought to reflect that "the imperfection of human laws and the consequent burden often weighing so heavily upon men are a part of the Cross of Christ which we must share with Him."[1] The very imperfection of human laws should direct our attention to what lies beyond them, to the basic human values which they are meant someway to reflect. "A people gets the rulers it deserves" is an old adage. When an existing political structure is found to be inadequate to procure justice and the welfare of the people, it is necessary to ask whether there is something deeply wrong. Unless the evil is cured at its root, it would be vain to try to do patchwork, however useful this might be at the moment.

3. CHARACTERISTICS OF GOOD CIVIL LAW

The purpose of civil law being to provide for the genuine common good of society made up of individual men, it should not go against the basic values of man. Hence it must be within the limits of divine natural law. A law manifesting racial or other discrimination, or one imposing an intrinsically evil act would be invalid. We have already noted that if sterilization were not an evil as such, one would be hard put to show that the state could not impose it in critical circumstances.[2]

When a law is immoral, citizens should resist it by all available means and try to get it repealed. But in the meanwhile, an individual may submit to it if he experiences a conflict of duties and conscientiously judges that it would be a lesser evil.[3]

While it is beyond the competence of the legislator to enact a law prescribing something contrary to morality, it may under certain circumstances be legitimate to pass legislation tolerating and regulating evil behavior in order to prevent a greater evil. Some would accordingly justify the tolerance of prostitution in certain definite areas with sufficient hygienic measures if there is no other way of containing the evil. St. Augustine said: "Take prostitutes out of man's life, and you will steep the world in lust."[4] Today, many would suggest that the evil of prostitution be combated with more vigorous measures supported by an effective educational and rehabilitational program.

The distinction between the demands of morality and the expediency of positive civil legislation to enforce them should be clearly drawn. The purpose of civil law is, not to prevent every positive violation of the moral law, but to adopt such measures as will in the concrete provide an atmosphere favorable to morality and protect the citizens most effectively from moral corruption. Thus, the British Parliament rightly repealed the penalties against homosexual acts in private between consenting adults. The law as it stood caused too much interference by the police into the private lives of citizens and was a frequent source of blackmail of the innocent. Cardinal Heenan said on the occasion: "It may be that the civil law cannot effectively control such acts [private acts which affect the common good] without doing more harm to the common good than the acts themselves. In that case, it may be necessary in the interests of the common good to tolerate without approving such acts.''[5]

In a pluralistic society with sharply different points of view regarding the permissibility of divorce, the best that can be done is to limit the evil. Care should be taken to see that the enactment is not understood as encouraging divorce or in any way weakening the family bond. The Church recently tried to prevent a divorce law from being passed in Italy, presuming that it was not only against the true interests of the people but also against the national ethos. The subsequent referendum proved that the majority of Italians had moved away from Christian tradition in this area.

A similar problem arises in the case of abortion. If large numbers and even most of the people in a country think it is morally acceptable, the democratic pluralistic state would find it very difficult, if not impossible, to repress the evil. Too rigid a law would make the evil go underground, innumerable illegitimate abortions taking place in the most improper conditions and thus resulting also in maternal deaths. The State would be in a veritable dilemma whether to legalize abortion or not, apart from the fact that the legislators themselves might be of the view that abortion is justified under certain circumstances. Christians and others who are convinced that abortion is an abominable evil should try to convey their point of view to the general public and the legislators. They should show that there is a question not only of the interests of the woman, family or society, but also of the right to life of a human person, however undeveloped. Since the fetus is helpless, there is all the more reason why the state should protect its rights. They should likewise attempt to see that the abortion bill does not become so permissive as to positively increase the number of abortions. They should also strive to remove the causes that lead people to seek abortion. Beyond this, it would be unrealistic to expect the state to prohibit all abortions, just as it would be to impute bad motives to those who favor legalization of abortion in definite circumstances.

Whenever it is expedient to frame legislation tolerating a moral evil, it would, under certain circumstances, also be licit to cooperate in passing it and then in executing it—as when a magistrate grants a divorce. This is only material cooperation, which would be justified whenever there is a proportionate reason. The Christian legislator should make it clear that he does not approve of the evil of divorce. If the bill is too permissive or his cooperation would cause grave scandal, he should oppose it.

The fields of civil law and morality converge but do not coincide. Civil law as such does not make an action good or bad. It only takes a stand that favors the common good in a particular situation. As a result, whether it rightly or wrongly tolerates certain actions like abortion, it does not thereby follow that the actions become morally permissible. How often do we find people saying, "Abortion was wrong before; now it is right because the law permits it." Such laws are not meant to be doctrinal declarations but practical measures regarding certain aspects of life in order to procure the maximum common good or the minimum evil in the given circumstance. We may wonder whether the fanatical moralizers who want the State to repress all moral evils (as they see them) may not be adding to the confusion. Once the impression is created that the role of the State is coextensive with morality, if the State legalizes a certain action which till then was a crime—i.e., removes the penalty against it—people conclude that the action has become permissible.

What is forbidden by morality is *sinful* and what is forbidden by civil law is a *crime*. Many sinful acts are also criminal, but crime and sin are not identical. Lying is sinful but, as such, is not a crime; but if it involves fraud or a libel, it can also be a crime.

There is an area of private morality which is matter for individual conscience (enlightened by the Church and moral preceptors). The State should not intrude in this area without necessity. Legal restraints are justified only when the common good demands them.

Still, law and morality cannot be separated, since they both deal with the quality of human life. Law must keep close to the moral sense of the community, which must inspire it, since police surveillance alone will not be sufficient to provide the atmosphere conducive to morality.

From the basis that law must truly contribute to the common good, further conditions for its validity may be derived.[6] It must be possible of observance and not be too onerous to the average citizen. Extraordinary situations may demand imposition of heroic sacrifices. This is how conscription is defended in some countries, though its justification may be questioned, considering the type of wars that have been fought of late. The obligation of voluntary soldiers to go to the front may be more easily understood.

The law must be really useful. From this point of view, one may question the advisability of prohibition laws unless they are backed up by strong public opinion. Otherwise, they may only lead to widespread illicit distillation and sale, besides causing loss of excise revenue to the State. The law must be enforceable without undue cost and effort. "If anything serves to bring law into disrepute, it is having laws on the statute book and not enforcing them. If anything makes for injustice in a legal system, it is trying to enforce laws which cannot and should not be enforced."[7] Unless a particular law somehow reflects the community's moral sensitivity and is supported by broad consensus, it will become ineffective or too onerous. The experienced moralist John J. Lynch, referring to the total ban on the sale and use of contraceptives, remarks: "Especially is this true of prescriptions which positively provoke to violation because of the fact that they outrage the sincere convictions of a large segment of the populace."[8]

This does not mean that the immediate consent of the people is an essential requisite for the validity of civil laws even in a democracy. *"Vox populi, vox Dei"* is true only to this extent: the consent of the governed is required solely in the radical and remote sense that the people designate their legislators and have it within their power to replace them if these do not reflect their will.

In order to achieve greater involvement and observance, the law must be prepared with as much participation of the people as possible.

In all legislation, distributive justice must be maintained. For instance, the tax burden must be spread according to the capacity of each group to pay. Concessions and subsidies of every kind must be equitably distributed.

Lastly, the law must be clear and easily understandable. If it is not precise, then rich people especially will find endless loopholes with the help of ingenious lawyers. Through the ages, jurists have developed an esoteric jargon so that at times even the legislators do not comprehend what they are enacting. Even the minister introducing a bill and the opposition leaders calling for its rejection may have to rely too much on the brief prepared by some specialist in their entourage. The ordinary man is completely baffled and at the mercy of lawyers.

4. OBLIGATION IN CONSCIENCE

By His unequivocal declaration concerning the poll tax: "Render therefore to Caesar the things that are Caesar's" (Mt. 22:21), Jesus affirms the obligation to submit to civil authority. Paul confirms the same: "For there is no authority except from God, and those who exist have been instituted by God. . . . Therefore one must be subject, not only to avoid God's wrath but also for the sake of conscience. For the same reason you also pay taxes, for the authorities are ministers of God" (Rom. 13:1, 5–6).

Vatican II deplores the attitude of those Christians who "make light of social laws and precepts, and do not hesitate to resort to various frauds and deceptions in avoiding just taxes and other debts due to society."[9] The Council "exhorts Christians, as citizens of two cities, to strive to discharge their earthly duties conscientiously."

We have to obey civil laws, not just because those in authority make them, but because they have the *right* to do so. Obeying a government is like obeying a pilot—the word *government* being derived from the Latin word for steering a ship. The particular "pilots" come to a position of authority because they are chosen by some accepted legal procedure. But the reason there is a governing authority in the community at all is that it is demanded by the very social enterprise of life—that is, in order that the community may preserve and develop itself harmoniously.

Since law is an instrument of social order, it is not right for politicians to make laws and decisions that will best suit them or have some other purpose than the common good. They must act responsibly, or "respond to," the objective demands of the social order. If they pass a law that is manifestly against the common good, one ought not to obey the law except to avoid a greater evil to oneself or one's family. But if the law is basically good, though not the best in the circumstance, one has to obey it, while yet trying to have it improved.

Though it is evident that there is an obligation to obey just civil laws, opinion in the past was divided on the nature of the obligation. According to defenders of the so-called *penal law* theory, civil laws bind, not directly in conscience, but only to pay the penalty for transgression. This, they claim, is sufficient to assure the common good.

But recent theologians like Josef Fuchs and Bernard Häring rightly reject this theory.[11] They point out that there could not be an obligation to pay the penalty without the prior obligation to observe the law. In the words of Häring, "The obligation does not flow from the attitude of the lawgiver or the summons he may direct to the conscience, but from the agreement of the law itself with justice and right."[12] Even the legislator could not lay down the principle that the citizens are obliged in conscience only to pay the penalty. It is not the arbitrary will of the legislator but the demands of the common good that is the source of obligation. The legislator merely determines the extent of the obligation.

Historically, the theory of penal law first arose from the Constitutions of the Dominican and other ancient Orders, in which it was declared that the rules, not otherwise obligatory, did not bind in conscience.[13] But religious rules are on an entirely different plane. They are the explicitations of the life of the counsels and, hence, appeal directly to generosity. The declaration was made in order to free the religious from undue fear of sin, so that they might respond to the rule out of pure love. Moreover, a defective concept of sin as mere violation of the law underlies this whole approach.

Another important influence in the formation of the penal law theory was the preoccupation of theologians in countries like the Netherlands to lighten the burden of conscience arising from harsh laws, especially regarding taxation, imposed by the Spanish regime.[14] However, such a problem is better resolved by the prudent application of the principle of *epikeia*. A human law generally cannot bind under an unduly great difficulty. When a disadvantage clearly outweighs the good intended by the law, it frees one from its binding power. The judgment concerning the excuse is made by the person himself if necessary, with the guidance of others, through the virtue of *epikeia*, which is an aspect of the virtue of prudence.

According to the clear mind of Vatican II, a Christian should be prompt in paying taxes and other dues unless a proportionately grave difficulty excuses him. Taxes should not be understood as a mere burden imposed from without, but as a necessary contribution to the common good. When one pays taxes, one is not deprived of one's possessions by an alien body, but brings his share to an enterprise that will also benefit him, at least in the long run.

The State must see that the rich are made to perform their duty in spite of their enormous power to evade it. The judiciary should not be prone to decide in their favor due to the quibbling of lawyers who receive fat sums for their services. The lawyers must not be overkeen in enriching themselves by specializing in helping the affluent in tax evasion. The middle class often feel that they have to make up for the wrongdoing of the powerful rich class. But they should realize that they are very much better off than the vast numbers of the poor, whose lot cannot be improved unless the State has sufficient resources at its disposal. Instead of grumbling, they could help in detecting tax evasion on the part of the rich.

These days, there is a lot of talk about the considerable number of destitutes, who are living far below the subsistence level. Is it really possible to improve their lot substantially without the middle and upper classes contributing their share? That a part of the funds is frittered away at various levels is no excuse. If this exceeds the margin of human weakness, it is the duty of those who have the education and influence to see that this does not happen, instead of indulging in negative criticism.

5. FUNDAMENTAL RIGHTS

This expression can be understood in two ways: 1) basic *human rights* flowing from the very nature of man; 2) rights that are explicitly acknowledged by the Constitution or through constant jurisprudence. Fundamental rights in the second sense are derivative; that is, certain rights are legally recognized because they preexist on account of the moral values inherent in the human person. Hence, human rights in the first sense belong to the divine natural law.

Some of these rights are absolute and, therefore, may not be violated in any way—e.g., the right to life and dignity. "Every human being, even the child in the mother's womb, receives its right to life *directly* from God, not from its parents, nor from any human society or authority. Therefore, there is no man, no human authority, no science, no 'indication,' whether medical, eugenical, social, economical or moral, that can show or give a valid juridical title for a deliberate and *direct* disposing of an innocent life."[15] There is, here, the qualification of "innocent." However, it is increasingly felt that capital punishment is barbaric and is not an adequate means of safeguarding the social order. The death of a man in self-defense could be explained by *indirect killing*. The last classical exception of the legitimacy of killing in a just war is being more and more questioned.

The fundamental right to *human dignity* would be violated by racism, caste prejudice or by torture, which could never be justified by any superior good like the need for obtaining urgent information.

Other fundamental rights may never be taken away, but their exercise is subject to the common good. Vatican II clarifies this, especially in the case of *religious freedom:* "Injury is done to the human person and to the very order established by God for human life, if the free exercise of religion is denied in society when the just requirements of public order do not so require."[16] The only limiting factor would be the right of others.

The Council goes beyond the total neutrality (bordering on indifference) of the American Constitution, which excludes, for instance, State aid to religious schools and prayer in public schools. Government has not only to safeguard religious freedom but "also to help create conditions favorable to the fostering of religious life, in order that the people may be truly enabled to exercise their religious rights and to fulfill their religious duties."[17] Such active and sympathetic neutrality is better reflected in the secularism which has been enshrined in the Constitution of India.

The Council makes it clear that "the right to religious freedom is exercised in human society; hence its exercise is subject to certain regulatory norms. . . . Society has the right to defend itself against possible abuses committed on the pretext of religious freedom. It is the special duty of government to provide this protection. However, the government is not to act in arbitrary fashion or in an unfair spirit of partisanship. Its action is to be controlled by juridical norms which are in conformity with the objective moral order."[18] It is evident that things like ritual prostitution should be forbidden. The government may keep an eye on funds which are supposedly meant for religious purposes but may be misused, especially by religious groups that have no clearly defined authority. But this should not in any way lead to interference in the religious affairs or even the legitimate social activity of the particular community.

In this context, the Council makes a general statement: "In the use of all freedoms, the moral principle of personal and social responsibility is to be observed. In the exercise of their rights, individual men and social groups are bound by the moral law to have respect both for the rights of others and for their duties toward others and for the common welfare of all."[19]

The right to *free speech,* including the free use of mass media, is of considerable significance for human development. It is basic to the proper functioning of a democracy. But this right is not absolute, since it may clash with the rights of others to their good name, to correct information, etc.

The right to *private property* as proposed by the Church Fathers and enunciated in Vatican II and *Populorum Progressio* of Paul VI is considerably different from what often passes for the Christian view on the matter. The Church rejects the one-sided position of liberal capitalism, which defends the absolute right of property of the haves, and the Marxist view, which denies all private ownership of land and the means of production with a view to bringing about equality among all.

Vatican II first stresses the *common destination* of material creation. But "ownership and other forms of private control over material goods contribute to the expression of personality. . . . Private ownership or some other kind of dominion over material goods provides everyone with a wholly necessary area of independence, and should be regarded as an extension of human freedom."[20]

However, "by its very nature, private property has a social quality deriving from the law of the communal purpose of earthy goods."[21] In using his goods, "a man should regard his lawful possessions not merely as his own but also as *common property* in the sense that they should accrue to the benefit not only of himself but of others. For the rest, the right to have a share of earthly goods sufficient for oneself and one's family *belongs to everyone.*"[22]

Moreover, "the right of private control is not opposed to the right inherent in various forms of public ownership. Still, goods can be transferred to the public domain only by competent authority, according to the demands and within the limits of the common good, and with fair [not necessarily equal] compensation."[23] "It is a further right of public authority to guard against any misuse of private property which injures the common good."[24] The Council, therefore, calls for land reform and measures to make the goods of this earth available to all.

The Christian doctrines of the human person as *imago Dei*, of the incarnation, the resurrection and eschatology, provide a profound basis for human rights. The Pontifical Commission for Justice and Peace recently sent out a working paper wherein the whole matter of human rights is very well treated and some pastoral guidelines are proposed.[25] Since many current discussions turn round the topic of private property, it would be instructive to note how this document brings out its essentially social quality and inherent limitations: "Private ownership, insofar as it provides everyone with a wholly necessary area of independence, both for himself and for his family, should be regarded as an extension of human freedom and as a right which is, not absolute or unconditional, but limited. In fact, by its very nature private property has a social quality, deriving from the law of the communal purpose of earthly goods as ordained by the Creator; earthly goods should in equity find their way into the hands of all men and all peoples, and should never be used to the detriment of the common good."[26]

It is lamentable that so many Christians, some even not so well off, are prone to adopt the viewpoint of vested interests, for whom the right to private property means unmitigated ownership of goods actually in possession. If the right of *everyone* to have a share in earthly goods is to be effective, there is need for redistribution of wealth on a vast scale. If this is not brought about peacefully, the poor masses would be tempted to take to violent means. We may recall here the warning of Pope Paul VI to businessmen during his visit to Bogota in August, 1968: "Do not forget that certain great crises in history would have taken other directions if the needed reforms with courageous sacrifice had anticipated in good time the explosive revolts of desperation."[27]

The fundamental rights of man, based as they are on the natural law, have a long history. The first important elaboration seems to come from ancient Persia. It received furher development in Greece and Rome.[28] In Eastern thought, the stress is more on the duty of respecting the rights of others.[29] Thereby, human rights are balanced by the need of responsibility. Now we have the Universal Declaration of Human Rights adopted by the United Nations in 1948.

A difficulty arises from the fact that in this imperfect world the rights of some clash with those of others. On principle, "everyone has a right to existence, to bodily integrity and well-being, to everything necessary to maintain a decent standard of living, such as food, clothing and shelter, means of subsistence and any other services indispensable to social security."[30] It would be vain to think that this can be brought about without curtailing the rights of those who have, by fair and foul means, amassed a vast amount of wealth and so control the levers of power.

Everyone has the right to express his ideas and opinions freely. But what happens if a few powerful people capture the ownership of newspapers? What about the right of others to express their views freely? And what about the right of everyone to be correctly informed about public events?

The great Lacordaire once remarked: "Between the rich and the poor, between the weak and the strong, it is liberty that oppresses and the law that frees." Without going so far, we should realize that it is not easy to balance the rights of some with those of others. The fundamental rights in which the destitute are immediately interested are for food, clothing, shelter and employment, while the haves are keen on hanging on to their possessions and the right to mold public opinion according to their narrow interests. There is, indeed, in practice a tension between the most basic needs of the poor and what have been termed "bourgeois liberties." These latter have not to be despised. In fact, we have to strive to see that all possess them. But, in the meantime, the few who possess them cannot be allowed to hinder the most basic needs of those who live below the subsistence level.

6. CENSORSHIP

Censorship is the imposition of legal restraint upon the production, publication, sale, screening and performance of any book, magazine, newspaper, photograph, play, movie, radio or TV broadcast. It implies the power to make such restrictions effective through sanctions against those who evade them. Simple control, on the other hand, implies the use of parental, academic or other nonlegal pressures like advice, boy-cott and public criticism.

Censorship is a limitation on the natural right to speak and com-municate in other ways with others. Hence, the general rule in this area should be: the maximum of freedom and a minimum of governmental intervention. The burden of proof for any restriction is on those who impose it. Still, censorship remains a necessary prerogative of legitimate authority, since the rights of others have to be protected.

The question of censorship reveals the tension between individual rights and social responsibility. The first is stressed by liberalism or optimistic naturalism and is well expressed by L. T. Hobhouse: "To try to form character by coercion is to destroy it in the making. Per-sonality is not built up from without but grows from within, and the function of the outer order is, not to create it, but to provide for it the most suitable conditions of growth. Thus, to the common question whether it is possible to make men good by an Act of Parliament the reply is that it is not possible to compel morality because morality is the act or character of a free agent."[31]

The above passage expresses a valid insight, but it does not take into account the practical difficulty of protecting the right of others to truth. The most basic right in this matter is not so much freedom to express one's thoughts as the right to have correct information in order to be able to arrive at the truth. Commenting on the above statement of Hobhouse, Yves Simon pithily remarks: "The point is, precisely, that good habits possibly determined by coercion are to be numbered among the conditions under which morality can develop."[32]

Here we must note the distinction between mere freedom of choice and the more complete freedom of human fulfillment in society. That the first is not an end in itself has been well expressed by Jacques Maritain: "Freedom of choice is the *material* element in moral action (and this includes social action, the mode of action of the good citizen), since only free acts are capable of being regulated by moral rules. . . . It is reason that gives form and measure. An act is not of more value in morals because it contains a greater measure of freedom; on the contrary, to act for the pleasure of acting, soley to exercise one's freedom, is apt to be a sign of moral debility."[33] He goes on to say that the philosophy of unlimited freedom of choice "suffers from an unconscious form of hypocrisy, for it ignores for the benefit of man in the abstract all the heavy and severe burdens that lie on man in real life, the fact being that a limited number are enabled to enjoy this kind of freedom only by oppression of their fellows. The essential value of social justice and the common good are forgotten."[34]

St. Thomas had already anticipated the question: "Laws are passed to ensure the smooth running of the commonwealth. Unrestricted rights are not allowed in any civil constitution. Even in a democratic State, where the whole people exercises power, rights are not absolute but relative, though, from the equal liberty of all subjects under the law, the State may be described as predominantly equalitarian. The statutes passed by a democracy may be just, not because they reach pure and perfect justice, but because they fit the purpose of the regime."[35]

As regards the press, where the circulation of dailies is controlled by a handful of people belonging to vested interests and having unbridled freedom not only to express their views but also to manipulate facts, the freedom of the press becomes an illusion and the poeple's right to be correctly informed is just ignored. Thus, the press is controlled, if not censored, by a group whose aims may be totally at variance with the interests of the poor and starving masses.

What is the solution in such a situation? Government control is far from ideal, because it can stifle the democratic process.

The best solution seems to consist in the diffusion of ownership carried out carefully, and in giving greater influence to the working journalists in the policy of the newspaper. Multinationals already have too much power in developing countries and, therefore, should be prevented from getting a hold over the media also, lest the freedom of these countries become totally illusory. Diffusion of ownership of big newspapers is essential for bringing about any meaningful freedom of the press.

Censorship is inimical to the authentic development of man whenever it unduly limits his freedom, whenever it narrows the range of his individual decision and personal choice, whenever it blocks his access to any worthwhile idea. The offenders against this freedom can be the government or press barons manipulating news and views for their selfish interests. While one reacts against the intervention of government in spite of its popular backing, one should not forget about attempts to control the expression of thought in devious ways by vested interests who are out to exploit the poor. It can never be sufficiently emphasized that prior to the right to publish is the right of the people to get accurate information and thus be able to make considered decisions.

Censorship of books and periodicals may concern the expression of religious and political views or the manifestation of obscenity. Regarding religious views, the democratic State may bar only such material as will hurt the religious sentiments of other groups and thus violate public order. Even the expression of atheistic views is to be permitted, provided it is done with restraint and does not hold religious beliefs to ridicule and thus offend the feelings of the believers.

There should be no restriction on the dissemination of political ideas as such. Only when the publication of certain items immediately leads to grave public disorder may the State intervene. Still, the existing regime has no right to prevent change of social and political structures if the people desire to move in that direction. Such suppression will only produce frustration and a bloody explosion at a later date. The government is obliged to keep the people sufficiently informed of the nature, scope and purpose of the nation's international commitments. When the people pay the taxes and fight the wars, they have the right to ask why and to be answered truthfully. The American people are now realizing that they were taken for a ride in many grave instances, like the Vietnam war, and are demanding that the suppression of vital information cease.

Regarding *obscenity,* all are agreed that children should be protected from material that could deeply and permanently disturb an average child, with his lack of experience and immaturity of judgment.

Really mature people may have the right to read or view whatever they judge best for them. But, apart from the difficulty of preventing certain literature from falling into the hands of children, mere physical adulthood does not necessarily make people mature. Hence, a certain degree of censorship of obscene literature would be in order. But obscenity is a very difficult concept to define. The Supreme Court of the United States laid down a classical test in the famous Roth decision of 1957: "whether to the average person, applying contemporary standards, the dominant theme of the material taken as a whole appeals to prurient interest." Later the court added a further qualification: "and the work wholly lacks redeeming social significance." There are many elastic terms in this definition, but it is a fairly satisfactory norm. Much depends on the judgment of the censors, who should be neither too Puritan nor too libertine in outlook.

It is obvious that legal censorship should be backed by social control through various citizens' organizations and, even more so, by an educative process. But it is unhealthy to have a coterie of repressed individuals who attempt to protect others from dangers from which they themselves suffer because of their own immaturity or traumatic experiences.

Obscenity in movies and television has a special import because of the more powerful impact these media have on the mind and imagination.[36] But the basic principles are the same. Censorship should not concentrate too much on elements like the amount of nudity or the presence of "dirty" words. It is more important to "ask whether the material and the manner in which it was presented debase sex, inspire in the viewers a false philosophy of the nature and purpose of life, and corrupt their concept of the worth of human beings."[37]

The problem of depicting *violence* in movies has increasingly engaged the attention of critics in recent years. While some hold that it helps as a catharsis for violent emotions, others point out the danger of violent feelings being aroused or the techniques of crime being learned through the mass media. There is need for restraint in the depiction of violence. Some would wish to extend the term *obscene* (literally, "repulsive,'' ''indecent'') to violence, vicious defamation and whatever is offensive to morality. In fact, *Webster's New Collegiate Dictionary* includes ''abhorrent to morality or virtue'' among the meanings of *obscenity.*

The theme as such does not make a movie good or bad. Vatican II has clarified the point: ''With the help of the media of social communication, the narration, description, or portrayal of moral evil can indeed serve to make man more deeply known and studied, and to reveal and enhance the grandeur of truth and goodness. Such aims are achieved by means of appropriately heightened dramatic effects.''[38]

An increasingly important area of censorship concerns regulations regarding the *labeling* and *advertising* of products. *Caveat emptor,* or ''Let the customer beware,'' may have been valid when social structures were simple and the customer could inspect the product personally. But today in a highly complex society, when products originate in distant places and are so packaged that they cannot be inspected, it is impossible for the customer himself to verify the truth of the claims made for them. Hence, necessary restrictions should be made to defend the interests and even the life of the buyer. For instance, no drug should be allowed to be advertised as a remedy for cancer unless it has been proved clinically effective. It would also be proper, especially in poorer countries, to restrain business from provoking too many artificial needs which cannot be met without the diversion of national resources from the most basic necessities of life. If manufacturers or traders are allowed to advertise the merits of cigarettes, they ought to be required to note the hazards of cigarette smoking on the package. It would also be right to limit the advertising of liquor and such things.

The foregoing discussion shows the need of developing sound ethical thinking based on human values. The current confusion in this field needs to be cleared up, and a large consensus achieved. Then the proper scope of civil law should be understood: it is not coextensive with morality, but must be based on moral values; it should not offend against these values, but must produce the atmosphere most conducive to the moral living of persons in society.

The fundamental or human rights of persons must be recognized through constitutional or other means. The State must strive to extend these rights to every citizen. In the process, the exercise of these rights by some people who might have obtained unfair advantage to the detriment of others may have to be curtailed. This should not be done in any party spirit or to further some narrow interests.

Legal provisions must be supported by enlightened public opinion and by a vast educative process concerning human values, both individual and social.

Thus, the close relationship as well as the distinction between civil law and morality will become clear. Civil law will become a service for the development of individual persons as well as of the human community.

———o———

Notes to Chapter XV

1. Bernard Häring, *The Law of Christ*, Vol. I, p. 268.
2. Ch. XIII, 3. Cf. also Antony Cordeiro, "Compulsory Sterilization: Moral Aspects," *Bulletin of the Indian Federation of Catholic Medical Guilds*, 4 (1976), 62.
3. Cf. George V. Lobo, "Pastoral Aspects of Family Planning," *Vidya Jyoti*, 41 (1977), 18–28.
4. *De Ordine*, IV, c. 4.
5. See *The Furrow*, 22 (1971), 358–9.
6. Cf. Josef Fuchs, *Theologia Moralis Generalis*, Pars la, Roma, Università Gregoriana, 1963, pp. 117–19; P. Benenson, "The Natural Law and Statute Law," *Concilium*, 3 (1967), nos. 5, 24–29.
7. Denis O'Callaghan, "Law and Morality," *The Furrow*, 22 (1971), 358.
8. "Notes on Moral Theology," *Theological Studies*, 22 (1961), 236.
9. *GS*, art. 30.
10. *Ibid.*, art. 43.
11. Josef Fuchs, *Theologia Moralis Generalis*, pp. 123–28; Bernard Häring, *op. cit.*, pp. 270–71.
12. *Op. cit.*, p. 271.

13. Cf. Jean Tonneau, "Les lois purement pénales et la morale de l'obligation," *Revue de Sciences Philosophiques et Théologiques,* 36 (1952), 30–51.

14. Cf. V. Vangheluwe, "De lege mere poenali, Inquisitio historica," *Ephemerides Theologiae Lovanienses,* 16 (1939), 383–429.

15. Pope Pius XII, *Discourse to Italian Midwives,* Oct. 29, 1951, *Acta Apostolicae Sedis,* 43 (1951), 838.

16. *DH,* art. 3.

17. *Ibid.,* art. 6.

18. *Ibid.,* art. 7.

19. *Ibid.*

20. *GS,* art. 71.

21. *Ibid.*

22. *Ibid.,* art. 69.

23. *Ibid.,* art. 71. Later it is said: "Compensation must be reckoned in equity after all the circumstances have been weighed." Equity is different from the exact equivalent or the "market value."

24. *Ibid.* Note that the vigilance of the State extends also to private property. No one can say, "This belongs to me, so I can do whatever I want with it."

25. *The Church and Human Rights,* Vatican City, 1975. Cf. *Vidya Jyoti,* 39 (1975), 452–62.

26. No. 38, par. 13.

27. *The Tablet,* Aug. 31, 1968, p. 873.

28. See J. O. Hertzler, *The Social Thought of the Ancient Civilizations,* London, McGraw-Hill, 1936.

29. See *Human Rights,* A Symposium by UNESCO, London and New York, Allen, Wingate, 1949; O. J. Hertzler, *op. cit.*

30. *The Church and Human Rights,* no. 37, par. 4.

31. *Liberalism,* New York, Holt, 1911, p. 143.

32. *Nature and Functions of Authority,* Milwaukee, Marquette Univ. Press, 1940, p. 54.

33. *Freedom in the Modern World,* London, Sheed & Ward, 1935, p. 32.

34. *Ibid.,* p. 40.

35. *Commentary in V Ethics,* Lect. 2.

36. Cf. Pius XII, *Miranda Prorsus,* Encyclical on Entertainment Media, Sept. 8, 1957, *Catholic Mind,* 55 (1957), 539–570.

37. Kyle Haselden, *Morality and the Mass Media,* Tennessee, Broadman Press, 1968, pp. 107–8.

38. *IM,* art. 7.

CHAPTER XVI

The Mature Christian Conscience

1. INTERIORIZATION vs. EXTERIORIZATION

Scripture describes moral life as a dialogue or covenant relationship between God and His people. The call of God in the heart of man, asking him to respond to the divine gift of salvation, has been referred to as "conscience" in Christian tradition. But we see a remarkable development both as regards the reality and the concept of conscience, first in one direction and then in another.

In the beginning of salvation history, conscience appears as extrinsic and collective. God first speaks in a theophany, which gradually gives way to angelophany, and then human prophets become the bearers of God's Word. The great prophets of Israel call attention to interior dispositions and personal responsibility (Jer. 31:29–30; Ez. 14:1–8). They also foretell a time where God will imprint His law in the inmost *heart* of man (Jer. 34:33–34; Ez. 36:26–27).

Jesus effectively brings about this interiorization of moral responsibility by giving His Spirit. He stresses the primary importance of the inward dispositions of man's heart, compared to mere external observance. Paul uses the Stoic term *syneidesis* to express the notion of conscience as the inner director of human activity. "When Gentiles who have not the law do by nature what the law requires, they are a law to themselves, even though they do not have the law. They show that what the law requires is written on their hearts, while their conscience also bears witness" (Rom. 2:14–15; cf. 13:5 and 1 Cor. 10:25).

Finally, commenting on Paul, the Fathers of the Church explicitate the interiorization of conscience. It now becomes the voice of God speaking through the very heart of man.[1]

St. Thomas himself speaks of *synderesis,* or the quasi-innate habit of the first principles of the moral order, which guides the moral function of *syneidesis*. But with the later Scholastics, we see the start of a reverse process.[2] While they defined conscience as the subjective faculty of reason, they began to stress the mediation of law. Their thinking was increasingly affected by sterile intellectualism and the nominalistic tendency to extrinsicism. Meanwhile, moral theology became more oriented to solving confessional cases than to illuminating the path to Christian perfection. The famous controversy regarding probabilism in the seventeenth and eighteenth centuries, while it had the laudable goal of defining the right of freedom, in fact led to moral extrinsicism. According to the doctrine of "extrinsic probabilism," a head count of "approved authors" often seemed to decide what was morally right or wrong. By and by, there was a practical confusion between the divine natural law and positive human law.

Consequently, "formation of conscience" in pastoral practice largely meant the extrinsic teaching of moral precepts in catechesis and having one's "doubts of conscience" resolved by the confessor. In order to help the confessor in this task, there was practice in solving "cases of conscience" during priestly meetings or through clergy reviews. Little attention was paid to the personal disposition of the person or to his emotional state. The natural law and canon law were simply intermingled, with little thought to the primacy of the law of charity. Examination of conscience came to mean the comparing of one's conduct with a list of obligations.

Although the Church has always upheld the principle of the primacy of conscience on the subjective level, in practice it has been considerably downplayed. Vatican II sought to restore the balance. In one of its most significant passages, it declares: "In the depths of his conscience, man detects a law which he does not impose upon himself, but which holds him to obedience. . . . For man has in his heart a law written by God.

To obey it is the very dignity of man; acording to it he will be judged. Conscience is the most secret core and sanctuary of a man. There he is alone with God, whose voice echoes in his depths. In a wonderful manner conscience reveals that law which is fulfilled by love of God and neighbor."[3]

Thus the Council presents conscience in no uncertain terms as the personal center of communion with God. It is the preconceptual recognition of the absolute call to love. The Council also draws attention to the fact that love is the basic direction of conscience and, hence, of morality.

Conscience is not a ready-made source of moral knowledge. Its dynamic nature is brought out by references to the "search for truth" which Christians are called upon to make with the rest of mankind.[4] This is quite different from an automatic application of preconceived principles.

A mature conscience presupposes genuine freedom. Vatican II declares that "the gospel has a sacred reverence for the dignity of conscience and its freedom of choice."[5] In the context of the formation of youth, the Council affirms that "children and young people have a right to be encouraged to weigh moral values with an upright conscience and to embrace them by personal choice."[6]

Thus, the Council brings out the dignity and primordial importance of conscience in Christian moral life. As conscience is not given to us ready-made at birth, it has to be gradually developed.

2. CONSCIENCE AND THE SUPEREGO

Very early in life, the child's psyche develops an automatic censor. At first, the child's conduct is regulated from without, from the pressure of reality, especially of society, which, by means of taboos, controls the impulses of the primitive human drives. External norms are in turn introjected by the psyche. It is an interesting phenomenon to notice that when a mother repeatedly asks a child not to touch something, the child will come very near to doing so, but at the last moment will withdraw, saying to himself: "Don't touch." In the beginning, the mother's presence is necessary to make the prohibition effective. By and by, it works even in her absence.

In this way, the child absorbs early in life, by a quasi-automatic process, modes of behavior that are acceptable and not acceptable to society. He develops an instinctive response to various behavior patterns. This largely unconscious mechanism, called "superego" by Freud, is, unfortunately, often mistaken for conscience by Freudians and others. This is a grave misunderstanding. The superego belongs to the "pre-conscience," while conscience implies consciousness and freedom. Conscience, in fact, corresponds to the sphere of the "ego."[7]

The superego as such is amorphous, since it results from a blind incorporation of environmental values, customs and demands. There can be a "criminal superego" formed by the incorporated images of criminal parents or of a criminal environment. There can also be a "virtuous superego," which, if too rigid, can be a merciless taskmaster. It can appear in the form of masochism (hatred of self) or sadism (hatred of others). Medieval flagellations, the cruelty of the Inquisition or the murderous Holy Wars demonstrate how far the superego may be removed from the conscience, how far its demands may be from true holiness.

The commands and prohibitions of the superego do not arise from the perception of the intrinsic goodness or badness of the action contemplated. Their sole origin is in the need to maintain the approval of authority figures, who can at times be visualized very realistically. Thus the nineteenth-century Swiss author R. Toepffner recalls his experience: "For a long time I was unable to distinguish the inner voice of my conscience from that of my teacher. When my conscience spoke to me, I thought I saw it before me in a black cape, with a teacher's form and glasses sitting on its nose."[8]

The superego produces guilt feelings, the spontaneous anxiety of being threatened by a mysterious force (the remnant of parental threats of punishment) for having strayed beyond safe boundaries. The person experiences a feeling of isolation, of helplessness and loss of self-value. There is then an instinctive urge to escape retribution and break out of the isolation. Hence, the tendency to look for magical rites and formulae to placate the angered powers. There may be the direct approach of confessing to some authority figure or of seeking punishment, which can even lead to accident proneness.

All this is very different from genuine contrition, which is a personal experience of wounded love. Instead of calling for retribution, it seeks reconciliation. In place of preoccupation with the past, it is oriented toward the future. John Glaser points out the difference in this way: "The superego is static; does not grow, does not learn; cannot function creatively in a new situation—merely repeats a basic command. It is past-oriented: primarily concerned with cleaning up the record with regard to past acts." The conscience is "dynamic: an awareness and sensitivity to value which develops and grows; a mind-set which can precisely function in a new situation. It is future-oriented: creative; sees the past as having a future and helping to structure this future as a better future."[9]

The superego, then, is a prepersonal function of control and censorship. It is necessary in the life of an infant as a step on the way to the development of conscious perception of values. It also has a place in the life of an adult, since it relieves a person from having constantly to decide in routine life situations. But it must be integrated into a mature conscience. Otherwise, we have infantilism, or even neurosis when the superego is too severe—i.e., when there is too great a disproportion between the guilt experienced and the value in question. With this background, it would be useful to distinguish *three levels of conscience*.[10]

a) The first is the *level of instinct*. Here, in fact, we are in *preconscience*. On this level, *law* comes from without, from the pressure of reality, and especially of society, which, by means of taboos, controls the impulses of the primitive drives in man. Although these controls are introjected and felt as binding, they are experienced as alien and even hostile. *Sin,* on this level, is experienced as a material transgression of some prohibition or taboo. The ensuing guilt feeling is irrational. It is the spontaneous anxiety of being threatened by a mysterious power for having strayed beyond safe boundaries. *Contrition* becomes the instinctive urge to escape retribution, and it looks for magical rites and formulae to placate the angered power.

b) On the *moral (rational) level, law* is the function of self-development corresponding to the aspirations of the inner self appearing as absolute demand or moral obligation. Here, conscience is the power of discovering what will promote authentic self-realization. There is *sin* when one freely acts against the dictates of reason. *Contrition* is the acknowledgement of and regret for this deliberate deviation, together with the active will for amendment. Here, we are already on the level of conscience and morality proper. But this level is still largely impersonal.

c) On the *religious level, law* is the invitation to go beyond the growth of one's individual being toward a loving self-donation. In fact, it entails a higher and deeper self-realization. Obligation becomes "vocation," whose specific forms are in the line of the counsels and beatitudes. Conscience on this level is love itself as a power of discovering what can promote union with God and neighbor. It acts by connaturality rather than mere rational insight. It is the working of the grace of the Holy Spirit. *Sin* is the *refusal to love,* to be for the other. *Contrition* is the awareness of infidelity to love, with a confident appeal to the loving mercy of God.

These levels are not separate from each other as if they were three storeys. The lower is implicitly present and active in the higher. The higher rests on the lower levels as on a substratum, assuming them into itself and imparting a new and higher meaning to them. The growth of human psychic life proceeds from instinct to spiritual self-development and culminates in religious self-donation. Hence, we must give due importance to each level of the conscience. We must explicitly attend to the hidden workings of the unconscious and the various defense mechanisms it sets up. These should be properly integrated into the rational conscience, which, in turn, must be assumed into love.

3. PASTORAL IMPLICATIONS

1) The distinction between the impersonal pressure of the superego and the personal call of God in the depths of the conscience is very important for an authentic religious life. The tyrannical rule of the superego calling for inexorable retribution can easily be transferred to God, causing a grave distortion in religious upbringing.

Gregory Baum expresses this very clearly: "The idea of God as judge on a throne, meting out punishment, corresponds to a self-destructive trend of the human psyche. . . . The person who is dominated by his superego—and no one is able to escape it altogether—has the accuser, judge, and tormentor all wrapped in one built into his own psychic makeup. When such a person hears the Christian message with the accent on God the judge, he can project his superego on the divinity and then can use religion as an instrument to subject himself to this court and, unknown to himself, to promote his own unconscious self-hatred."[11]

2) The superego produces automatic guilt feelings whenever a taboo has been violated. The same is purged with equal certainty when a purificatory rite is accomplished. Thereby one is led to think that the transition between grace and sin, and vice versa, can take place with great frequency and rapidity. Here we have the root of misconceptions regarding sacramental confession, which can be reduced to an automatic purificatory ritual instead of being a means of genuine reconciliation.[12]

Much of the disaffection toward confessional practice can be understood as a reaction to the trivialization of grace and sin and a consequent banal fluctuation between one and the other. The reaction has its positive aspect, since it can be a step toward a meaningful approach to the sacrament. There is no use merely lamenting the diminishing number of confessions. What is needed is to deepen the moral conscience and, thereby, inculcate a genuine sense of sin as a deliberate alienation from love of God and neighbor, and of contrition as a new experience of God's loving mercy bringing about a radical change of heart.

The vicious circle between failure, remorse and purgation is especially true in the area of sexuality—for instance, in the matter of masturbation. The superego is ineffective in overcoming the urge to masturbation. The disproportionate guilt feeling which often accompanies compulsive masturbation only causes deeper frustration and a fixation in the matter. The fear complex leads to further falls. Mechanical confession to a priest seen merely as an authority figure brings only temporary relief and sets the stage for a repetition of the process. There is need for breaking out of the cycle by cultivating a positive attitude and deepening inner freedom.

3)   Unfortunately, much of traditional pastoral guidance has been directed to confirming the tyranny of the superego. As John W. Glaser remarks: "The superego is far more infallible as a tormentor of failure than as a source of effective motivation."[13] A certain type of clericalism may find satisfaction in paternalistic domination instead of pastoral inspiration. Even if this were effective in keeping the person on the right path for some time through a superimposed authority, there will be a breakdown as soon as the imposition for some reason weakens.

4)   There are some who look back with nostalgia on the certainties of bygone days and bewail the confusion that one now sees around. The superego has suddenly lost its traditional props, and the primitive drives of the id have broken out. Some would want to restore the authority of the superego in order to lock up the destructive forces of the id. But this would be a vain enterprise in the present situation even if it did not mean a regression. The only effective way of handling the problem is the development of a mature conscience.

5)   We should also note that when people have for a long time been kept under the rule of the superego through authoritarian imposition, it does not help to tell them suddenly: "Follow your conscience." This would only lead to complete disorientation. A mature conscience cannot be developed in a day. There is need of a patient and progressive deepening of moral values and a gradual initiation to moral autonomy. Those who suddenly swing toward uncontrolled autonomy should reflect that criticism of conventional morality may come from conscientious

insight or from an adolescent reaction against the domination of the superego. Besides, total autonomy is an illusion, since one's conscience is always influenced by society. Those who claim to have liberated themselves from authoritarian norms must ask themselves whether they have not fallen prey to a new conformism to current fads.

6) Christianity has rightly extolled the virure of obedience to God and His representatives on earth. But there are grave dangers in an obedience that is not free and enlightened. The thousands of ordinary individuals who took an active part in the extermination of Jews in Nazi Germany maintained that they were only obeying orders.

Stanley Milgram, in experiments conducted in the Interaction Laboratory of Yale University, has shown that otherwise good people can be induced to inflict meaningless pain on others under pressure from an instructor. Their readiness to be cruel was greater when the physical proximity to the victim was reduced.[14] Commenting on the results of this investigation, Jack Dominian remarks: "A combination of blind obedience, rigid application of law and impersonality are a most dangerous triad, which contemporary society has to guard against as industrialization encourages the growth of amorphous human complexes."[15]

Social life demands a sense of conforming activities of a collective nature. However, the danger of too much conformity must be noted. It tends to diminish genuine interpersonal encounter. The mechanical gestures performed in the older liturgy were often a conditioned response instead of being a communitarian worship of God "in spirit and in truth" (Jn. 4:23). Such a response can be equally found in mass political meetings, where many of the participants do not understand what is going on. There is only a *pseudo-mutuality* that does not foster true community.

Those who are brought up in blind obedience or conformity to what is thought to be good can later be pressurized or manipulated to take part in what is manifestly evil. Hence, the importance of deepening a free and personal response of conscience. If the Church is going to have a really profound influence on society, she must form persons who are capable of such a response.

Christians are known to be supporters of law and order in society. This is good if it means fostering a sense of mutual respect among citizens and cooperation with legitimate authority in bringing about the common good. But it should not imply slavish obedience to the powers that be and perpetuation of evil structures, especially those involving the exploitation of the poor. "Christians must support the rule of law and legitimate authority but, at the same time, they must encourage educational principles which will arm the citizens with the means of ensuring that authority acts as a source of service to the community and not as a source of irresponsible power which moves from service to coercion, from care to subjugation, from encouragement of maturity to that of immaturity."[16] The Christian community itself should offer an example of this life.

7)   Law, we have seen, has a place in Christian life as a definite direction safeguarding basic values (natural law) or the common good (positive law). But presenting morality as mere fidelity to a series of laws entails the danger of creating a formalistic mentality that does not touch the heart. In such a perspective, one will judge his conduct only in relation to very external and material criteria. One's conscience will be clear to the extent he materially discharges his obligations in accordance with the fixed model proposed to him.

When moral requirements appear to be situated on a different plane from that of human values, voluntary response will be lacking. If the subject is required to perform certain actions in pursuance of purely ascetic principles which cannot awaken affective response, there will then be want of spontaneity and enthusiasm. Indifference or rebellion will sooner or later set in. Making demands at an inopportune moment, when psychological preparation is inadequate and without sufficient encouragement, will cause frequent failure. The subject will feel excessively guilty and helpless. This may lead to despair and anguish, or to rebellion and deceit.

The reaction to demands imposed from without is one of opposition, for decision is then determined by the moral pressure another individual exerts and not by inner direction or spiritual attraction. The fact that he identifies good with certain clear instructions prompts the subject to consider that good conduct resides in material conformity to certain regulations and not in the rightness of the choice involving his personal destiny. In the static world of the past, mere external observance may have contributed to a certain peace and harmony; but, today, youth has to face new challenges. Hence the need for inner conviction.

We must, therefore, communicate moral values to youth and at the same time encourage them to make personal decisions. Only if they are helped to discover moral truth by themselves can their decisions be truly responsible. Only if they learn to think for themselves will moral doctrine be assimilated.

We must guard against the danger of putting a premium on submissiveness, being pleased with those who give external assent to our teaching and being suspicious of those who are inclined to think for themselves. We need to trust the latter, so that they can be gradually helped to reflect by themselves. We have to help the young to be honest with themselves, and we have to examine how much they really believe in what is handed down to them and how much they accept on authority for the moment.

There is need for positive experiences in order to have a favorable start in the moral life. For instance, instead of prematurely obliging a child to observe the ceremonial of a greeting or a farewell, he must first experience the joy of meeting a person. When he meets a stranger, the child's first reaction is to remain aloof. But if the other approaches him gently, he begins to respond; his confidence returns, smiles are exchanged, a friendly sign is made, and at that time the desire to be polite takes on a real meaning for him.

It is on the occasion of experiencing a relationship with another and in the very heart of that relationship that the awareness of a relationship with God is born. However, that which at first is experienced only obscurely needs to be brought to light. The incidents which depict Christ in His relationships with His Father and with men will afford a model of right behavior. Then the Lord's teaching, elucidated by the parables, could be offered to the child as an invitation to follow the example of Christ. For instance, if he is learning to experience joy in giving pleasure to others, the following words of Jesus could be suggested: "Insofar as you have done it to the least of my friends, you have done it to me" (Mt. 25:40).

4. THE CORPORATE DIMENSION OF CONSCIENCE

Though *con-science* (*syn-eidesis*) literally means "knowing with"— namely, "being witness of oneself"—and refers directly to the personal dimension of the moral life, the word could also be understood to mean "knowing together," or a *partnership in discerning the will of God*. Though each person is ultimately responsible for his decisions and actions, still he must act in solidarity with his brethren. Moral doctrine is largely the tested wisdom and experience of the whole Christian and larger human community.

Christian morality is often clarified through the lived experience of the faithful. Every Christian, in whom the Spirit of Christ dwells and operates, has to be involved, under the guidance of the hierarchy, in clarifying the Christian response to the demands of the Gospel regarding various areas of life.

Nowadays many feel that there is a conflict between the magisterium and their conscience. This is caused by the notion that the teaching authority of the Church is an external imposition on the autonomy of the conscience. It should, rather, be understood as a *service of guidance*. This will happen if the Church herself is regarded, not primarily as a juridical institution, but as a Spirit-filled community in which the hierarchy has a charism of love to guide the people of God in discerning the will of God.

The teaching of the magisterium does not dispense the faithful from exercising their own responsibility. Vatican II has a very significant text on this matter: "Laymen should know that it is generally the function of their well-formed Christian conscience to see that the divine law is inscribed in the life of the earthly city. From priests they may look for spiritual light and nourishment. Let the layman not imagine that his pastors are always such experts, that to every problem which arises, however complicated, they can readily give him a concrete solution, or *even that such is their mission.* Rather, enlightened by Christian wisdom and giving close attention to the teaching authority of the Church, let the layman take on his own distinctive role."[17] This is a clear call to Christian maturity. The role of the magisterium is, not to substitute for conscience, but to be an inspiration for it.

5. THE FORMATION OF CONSCIENCE[18]

From what has been said so far, it may be gathered that the rightly formed conscience is characterized by the following four attitudes:

1) It is *rational,* able to assess people and situations calmly and without prejudice. It is able to grasp moral values and know how to pursue them in a given situation. It is cognizant of right moral principles, their precise value and their relevance to various situations.

2) It is *autonomous,* able to reach decisions freely, though in communion and dialogue with others. It is able to assess the value of authority as a means of fostering union. But it does not make decisions merely with awe of authority or with a feeling of weakness and dependence.[19] The mature person is able to take a personal stand on vital issues in the face of opposition.

3) It is *altruistic,* is influenced by the needs and interests of one's fellowmen, is able to sacrifice self-interest for the sake of others. As Vatican II puts it, mature conscience "reveals that law which is fulfilled by love of God and neighbor."[20] Love provides the basic direction for moral action.

4) It is *responsible,* able to accept responsibility. It is not misled by mere sentiment for oneself or others. It is able to accept the short-

term and long-term consequences of one's decisions. It is able to take reasonable risks for a worthy cause.

No one expects a child to exhibit any of these four traits of maturity. We can expect him to be irrational, dependent, self-centered and timid. But it is through the correct handling of these infantile characteristics that moral maturity will finally emerge.

Different schools of psychology propose their own theory of personality. They are not necessarily exclusive. Rather, they shed light on different aspects of human personality. Their findings could be used to foster the growth of a mature conscience.

1) *Freudian theory*. Freud postulates a mental structure comprised of *id, ego* and *superego*. The *id* is the aggregate of the individual's primitive emotional strivings, which are unorganized and pleasure-seeking. The *superego* is the sum of the introjected social norms and works an an automatic censor for the primitive drives. The *ego* is the reality principle, which organizes the forces of the id through perception, memory, thought and action. However, there is the need to see the ego as a more conscious principle than Freud himself recognized and avoid the confusion between the conscience and the superego.

The id and the superego would be on the level of the preconscience, while the ego would be the principle of conscience proper. Formation of conscience would mean the proper development of the three dimensions of personality. The emotions of the child must be properly developed through the experience of love and acceptance. The refinement of the aesthetic sense will also contribute to the right orientation of the feelings. It is also the best way of helping the child face literature and movies when he is later exposed to them.

The superego is properly cultivated by means of loving discipline. If sufficient discipline is lacking in early years, there is the danger of permissiveness and, in extreme cases, of psychopathy or pathological insensitivity to social values. If early discipline is too rigid, the child will develop a fearful and authoritarian conscience leading to the pseudo-virtues of the unconscious.[21] Excessive guilt feelings may lead to neurotic scrupulosity. Social pressures must be replaced by loving social control or influence. Thus, a mature personality open to community will develop.

The ego should be cultivated by the inculcation of right moral values, attitudes and principles. In the past, there was an overemphasis on rational and abstract principles to the neglect of human feelings. This often led to the reinforcement of a rigid superego. Now, there is a tendency to neglect the rational aspect of morality, which, if unchecked, may lead to superficiality.

Besides these elements, the Christian will recognize the inspiration of the Holy Spirit. Learning how to recognize His movements in the heart and how to discern His call from the promptings of the evil spirit is a most important aspect of the formation of conscience.

Erik H. Erikson has enriched Freudian theory by expanding the concept of superego into a much broader range of experiences than Freud acknowledged.[22] According to Erikson, the child goes through a sequence of developmental possibilities which must be realized and adequately responded to by the parents. He sees growth in terms of specific crisis periods which have a positive and negative polarity. The result of the interaction with the periods is built into the life structure of the growing person. At first, it is the question of trust or mistrust because of the total dependence of the child. The development of basic trust is most vital for later life. Then, when the child is learning to walk, feed and so on, there is the polarity of autonomy or a sense of shame and doubt. The child has to acquire self-control without loss of self-esteem.

2) *Cognitive theory.* This gives more importance to intellectual development. According to Jean Piaget, the faculty of knowing is the key to human growth.[23] He provides a detailed description of how the child's assimilation enlarges as his relationship with the environment develops during the first twelve years or so.

Piaget distinguishes two principal stages. The first is *heteronomous,* characterized by moral realism and adult constraint. The child regards duty and the value attached to it as self-subsistent. The authoritative restraints imposed on the child foster ego-centrism. In the second stage, peer-group cooperation fosters *autonomy and mutuality.*

From this it follows that moral development requires social relations. Mature morality is not imposed from without, but evolved from within through free and equal social interaction. There is need for a shift from unilateral respect, hitherto directed to authority figures, to *mutual respect.*

L. Kohlberg has developed Piaget's theory further.[24] He describes three levels, each with two stages. The first is termed premoral, and its two stages are: conformity with those who have power to punish (till age 7) and the point of view of satisfying needs and obtaining rewards (7–10). There is as yet no sense of personal responsibility to others.

At the second level (10–13), the other does exist, but it is very largely authority that has to be pleased and respected. In the first stage here, the child is moved by the anticipation of praise and blame; in the second, morality is based on respect for authorities and on a sense of obligation to maintain social order. There is the desire to avoid the censure of authorities and the resultant guilt feelings. So, at this second level, the motivation is desire for social approval and respect for law and order. There are many who do not go beyond this level of "conventional morality."

The third level (13–16) is one of self-accepted moral principles. One begins to have respect for the rights of others. Moral principles are accepted in order to maintain reasonable self-respect of others. In the last stage, moral decisions are made in terms of autonomous principles of conscience. The primary motivation is the need to be consistent with one's own moral principles and thus avoid self-condemnation.

Kohlberg also emphasizes the need for interaction with social environment. What basically stimulates moral development is social role-taking: i.e., reacting to the other as someone like oneself. There is need for presenting stimuli which are sufficiently incongruous to stimulate a tension, and sufficiently congruous to be assimilated.

3) *Behaviorism.*[25] By studying a simple psychological activity like salivation, Pavlov showed that new experiences can be learned. The stimulus of food brings about the response of salivation. Instead of food, other associated stimuli, like the clatter of dishes, can produce the same response.

According to the classical conditioning theory, if a neutral stimulus is immediately followed by an unconditioned stimulus (*US*) for a sufficient number of times, the first will elicit from the organism a response similar to the one elicited by *US*. It now becomes a conditioned stimulus (*CS*). For instance, a dog will pull back its paw at the sound of a buzzer if this has been followed by an electric shock. Similarly, if a socially undesirable activity of the child is immediately followed by a strong pain-inducing stimulus, the activity will itself evoke a conditioned fear complex. Conscience, in this perspective, appears as the conditioned anxiety response to certain types of situations and actions.

According to a modified version of the theory called "instrumental learning," conscience is a phenomenon acquired through the instrumentality of rewards and punishments—e.g., a rat can be taught to push a bar and obtain food or turn off a switch and avoid a shock. In the case of the child, the process is facilitated by the cognitive faculty, which enables him to represent to himself the consequences of the act.

For the behavioral school, conscience is the result of the accumulation of the appropriate learned conditioned responses. This theory illuminates the process of socialization. It brings out the importance of applying the proper rewards and punishments in child rearing. It reveals what in fact happens in a large sphere of the educative process. But—neglecting rationality and autonomy, as it does—it is a far cry from a mature conscience. The factors of maturation, rationality, autonomy

and interpersonal relationships are downplayed. Behaviorism may be
the key to producing desired automatons, but not mature human persons.
Brainwashing, deprogramming and the like are some of the horrors that
follow from overly enthusiastic adherence to this approach.

4)   *Identification theory.*[26] This combines psychoanalytic insights
with the learning theory. Conscience is conceived of as a special type
of self-control resulting from the child's internalizing parental values
through the process of role-taking. The stronger and faster the identification, the stronger and faster will be the development of conscience.
Hence the need for a satisfactory emotional relationship between child
and parents.

Punishment does contribute to altering behavior. But the quality
of the relationship between the punishing agent and the recipient is a
key factor. Punishment is far more effective when the agent is held in
high esteem.

When severity is interpreted as unfair or excessive by the child,
then it can easily become counterproductive and foster the spirit of
revenge. In the absence of an affectionate bond, severe punishment can
also foster a vicious circle by the child resenting the infliction and, at
the same time, continuing to perform the undesirable act in order to
draw attention which is not provided in any other way. A punitive or
authoritative policy fails because behind the "bad" or "stubborn" child
is a despairing and confused individual who knows no other way of
attracting the attention of the source of love and protection.

Basing himself on recent empirical findings, Jack Dominian rightly
concludes: "From all this, it can be seen that attempts to shape human
behavior which rely on the most elementary observations of blind obedience and fear of punishment, emanating from and applicable in the
first years of the child's life, are totally unsuitable for influencing behavior later on when the growing person's and adult's autonomy, sense
of equality, altruism, aggressive make-up and loving response make a
formidable array of deterrent factors in the response to, or threat of,
punishment."[27]

Hence, the formation of conscience implies much more than conditioning to good behavior or communication of the knowledge of the moral law. It is the gradual unfolding of the human personality, making it aware of its potentialities and opening it to interpersonal relationships with God and neighbor. Formation of a mature conscience must take into account the nature and dignity of man with his transcendent vocation and, at the same time, the findings of positive sciences. It implies the deepening of personal autonomy and, correspondingly, a communitarian perspective. A mature conscience today must be able to face the inevitable uncertainties and risks of life. There is no easy solution to problems of conscience. Neither self-will nor neurotic anxiety has a place in Christian life. One must be able to respond with courage and hope to the call of God as expressed in the signs of the times.

6. THE PRIMACY OF CONSCIENCE

The voice of conscience, being the immediate perception of the divine will, is *to be followed always,* even when it is defective. Paul makes this clear in the case of meats offered to idols. The "weak" person, who acts against his persuasion that he should not eat such meats, stumbles (Rom. 14:21–23); his conscience is defiled (1 Cor. 8:7).

Thus, conscience is the *supreme subjective norm* of morality. It is *right* when its dictates correspond to the objective moral order; it is *erroneous* when it fails to do so. This can happen because the practical judgment is bound up with the exercise of human reason, which is fallible. Still, whenever the practical judgment is *certain,* it must be followed. These days, some bring in conscience only when a matter is not clear. According to the constant tradition of the Church, conscience is *always* to be followed *in every circumstance.*

As Vatican II points out, "conscience *frequently errs* from *invincible ignorance* without losing its dignity."[28] In it, the voice of God is heard imperfectly. The call to self-donation or moral rectitude is perceived, but the particular mode wanted by God is misunderstood. When the error is totally inculpable, there is no personal fault or sin in following an erroneous conscience.

According to St. Thomas, one even sins by not following one's erroneous conscience. He has given some shocking examples. "Conscience obliges in the sense that whoever acts against his conscience has the will to sin. Consequently, if someone believes that by not fornicating he commits a mortal sin, he chooses to commit a mortal sin by not committing the act. And therefore he does sin mortally."[29] Again: "To believe in Christ is good in itself and necessary for salvation; but the will does not tend thereto, except inasmuch as it is proposed by the reason. Consequently, if it be proposed by the reason as something evil, the will tends to it as something evil."[30]

These examples show that the primacy of conscience as the subjective norm of morality is an age-old principle in the Church. It may have been obscured in practice by authoritarianism; but it has never been denied. The modern tendency to belittle the objective aspect of morality and, hence, the need for forming a right conscience arises to some extent from a reaction to the practical neglect of the binding force of conscience.

Regarding *culpably erroneous* conscience, Vatican II declares: "The same cannot be said of a man who cares little for truth and goodness, or of a conscience which by degrees grows practically sightless as a result of habitual sin."[16] A culpably erroneous judgment of conscience is accompanied by a warning as to the need of dispelling the error by altering one's whole attitude toward truth and goodness. In such a state, it seems that one who follows his conscience would sin because of his culpable negligence. But he would equally sin by not following his conscience, since it is always binding.[32] The only way out of the impasse is for the person to purge his negligence and arrive at an inculpable judgment of conscience. Bernard Häring explains the matter as follows: "Viewed correctly, the culpably erroneous judgment is not really a verdict of conscience at all. The true judgment is not the superficial and confused voice of the misled man, but that deeper protest of reason, which in this instance warns and exhorts: 'Cleanse your conscience! Free yourself of the guilt of a darkened and confused conscience!'"[33]

Hence, we see the importance of forming a right conscience, in which the practical judgment coincides with the objective will of God.

As Vatican II states: "The more the correct conscience holds sway, the more persons and groups turn aside from blind choice and strive to be guided by objective norms of morality."[34] Again, in the Decree on Religious Freedom, the Council declares: "Every man has the duty, and therefore the right, to seek truth in matters religious, in order that he may with prudence form for himself right and true judgments of conscience, with the use of all suitable means."[35]

The Council also points out that "in the formation of their conscience, the Christian faithful ought carefully to attend to the sound and certain doctrine of the Church.[36] However, this does not dispense the Christian from a mature reflection on the doctrine and from applying it responsibly to his particular situation. The following of conscience is an *inviolable right* of the human person. Hence, it follows that:

a) One has the right not to be hindered from forming a right conscience. It is unjust to propagate error maliciously for selfish reasons.

b) Children and simple people should not be unnecessarily scandalized by the "enlightenment" of the learned (cf. Rom. 14:10–22:1 Cor. 8:9–13).

c) One who sincerely acts according to his conscience, even though erroneous, has the right not to be considered and treated as an evil person.

d) Everyone has the right to act according to his sincere persuasion and is not to be coerced to act against it. If he does not violate the rights of others, he should be allowed to go ahead. Exceptions are only apparent. In the case of suicide, for instance, the person is most often not in his right senses and, hence, is not in a position to form a true judgment of conscience. Besides, suicide, being an attack on the most basic value of life, offends against the common good and therefore could legitimately be prevented by others. Because others also have their rights, one cannot claim unlimited right to spread seditious or obscene literature which harms the common good. But, as we have already seen, censorship is to be exercised reasonably in order that the common good may be really fostered.

e)   It is unlawful to advise another to do something objectively wrong on the pretext that he will act in good faith because of his erroneous conscience. This would be formal cooperation in an evil act which is certainly culpable on the part of the one who knows that it is wrong. However, one may help another to discern whether a certain moral evil is a lesser evil in a certain situation. If the other is completely incapable of exercising such discernment, one may empathetically discern for him. Even in such a case, the choice should, as far as possible, be personalized by the other, since no one can substitute for the conscience of another. Such choosing for another should be done most sparingly in order to transcend authoritarian morality and in order to encourage moral responsibility.

f)   It is illicit to induce another to act against his personal conscience, which would in effect be to induce him to commit sin. Hence, grave questions arise like that of conscientious objection to war. It is a much discussed question whether it is lawful to force a person, through imposition of penal sanctions, to take up military service as a combatant if he is persuaded that all warfare is immoral. Some try to justify the coercion by saying that such people are in bad faith. But this seems to be a gratuitous assumption. Vatican II has declared: "It seems right that laws make humane provision for the case of those who for reasons of conscience refuse to bear arms, provided, however, that they accept some other form of service."[37] The Council makes no judgment on the objective moral claim of the conscientious objector.

7.   THE DOUBTFUL AND PERPLEXED CONSCIENCE

We have seen that a *certain* conscience always has to be followed. However, conscience is at times *doubtful* as to the lawfulness of an action, whether it suspends judgment or is inclined to one side but with the apprehension that the contrary may be true. There is a doubt whenever there are solidly *probable reasons* on either side.

The doubt may concern either the existence or the meaning of a moral principle (*doubt of law*) or the existence of a fact (*doubt of fact*). Thus, if one doubts whether therapeutic abortion is lawful, there is a doubt of law; if one doubts whether there is a fetus in a growth in the uterus, there is a doubt of fact.

The doubt may be merely *speculative,* concerning an ethical principle (for instance, whether an ectopic pregnancy may be terminated), or *practical,* concerning what is to be done here and now.

The basic principle regarding doubtful conscience is this: "In a practical doubt regarding the lawfulness of an action, one may never act." Otherwise, one would expose oneself to the violation of God's will. Paul remarks: "But he who has doubts is condemned, if he eats, because he does not act from faith [is not in good faith]'' (Rom. 14:23).

The action must be postponed until *practical certainty* is reached in some way. This could be achieved *directly,* by reflection or by consultation with experts and relevant books. The effort one is obliged to make is to be measured by the importance of the matter or the value involved. Excessive preoccupation would rob life of its joy.

If the doubt cannot be solved directly, one could try to attain practical certainty by having recourse to *reflex principles.* These are *rules of prudence* which do not resolve the speculative doubt but only indicate the practical step to be taken.

The most common reflex principles, especially in the matter of justice, are:

1) "In doubt, we must stand on that side where presumption [of right] stands." This will not do justice in all cases, but at least it guarantees that injustice is avoided in the greater number of cases.

2) "In doubt, the condition of the actual possessor is the better." After taking sufficient care to find the rightful owner, one may retain the object on the presumption that the possession gives him a good title until the contrary is proved.

3) "In doubt, the accused is to be favored; or the crime is not to be presumed, but is to be proved."

4) "In doubt, stand for the validity of the act—for example, the validity of the marriage consent." This principle should not be applied too rigidly, lest people be forced to continue unnecessarily in an unfortunate situation.

5) "In doubt, amplify the favorable and restrict the unfavorable." This applies mostly to positive law.

6) "In doubt, presumption stands for the usual and the ordinary."

7) "When a definite object is to be attained, the safer course must be followed." For instance, one may not use doubtful matter in a sacrament except in an emergency.

8) "A doubtful law does not bind" (*Lex dubia non obligat*). The reason is that freedom cannot be bound except by a certain obligation.

The last principle is the most important. Note that it directly applies *only to a doubt of law,* and not to a doubt of fact. Still, a doubt of fact can sometimes be reduced to doubt of law. Thus, one who doubts whether he has fulfilled a vow is not obliged to perform the action again, since such an obligation cannot be proved for certain.

There was once a vigorous controversy whether one had to choose the more probable opinion (probabiliorism) or could choose a solidly probable opinion even though the contrary seemed more probable (probabilism).[38] At present, the latter system—probabilism—is generally accepted in the Church. When it was first formulated in the seventeenth century, it met with strong resistance because some were prone to construe probability from flimsy arguments and the times were characterized by legalism; law seemed to have prime rights while freedom had to be demonstrated.

Probabilism does not mean that one may act according to his fancy or mere subjective inclination. Nor does it mean that we are to seek the easier path. It simply means that there is no strict obligation to follow a doubtful law. This leaves the way open to seek the most important value in the situation. For instance, when there is a serious doubt whether a particular type of operation is licit, the doctor may go ahead in order to care for the good of the patient. It is not merely "freedom from," but "freedom for" pursuing the good.

It should be noted that probabilism has a restricted validity concerning the presence or absence of negative moral absolutes. (If one denies the possibility of such absolutes, then probabilism makes no sense.) Hence, we must not concentrate on mere freedom from the law. The main preoccupation should be to seek the moral values involved in the situation as best as possible. Then probabilism will not become an astute tool for selfishness, but a means of exercising responsible freedom.

A probable opinion should be based on *solid reasons.* Simple people may depend upon the opinion of persons competent in the matter (*extrinsic probability*), although they should be encouraged and helped to reflect for themselves. If an ordinary person finds that experts contradict each other, it may be a sign to him that the question is doubtful. Extrinsic probability does not save the individual from personal reflection and decision.

Extrinsic probability, or the opinion of experts, is ultimately based on *intrinsic probability,* or the reasons they adduce. A mere claim of authority is not sufficient. It would lead to an authoritarian society, in which the ordinary man would have no active role.

One who accepts the doctrinal authority of the magisterium of the Church cannot consider an opinion which is directly contrary to the *clear and emphatic* teaching of the hierarchy as solidly probable merely on the authority of private doctors, whatever their renown. However, if the magisterium maintains silence in the face of such a contrary opinion for a considerable time, the opinion may be accepted in practice as probable. Besides, the teaching of the magisterium calls for interpretation. The proclamation of a certain principle may have to be taken together with other principles. In other words, there may be a concrete conflict of duties or conflict of values.

Then we have what is called a *perplexed conscience*—a state of conscience in which a person placed between two urgent duties fears that he will offend against a moral value whichever side he chooses. We have already explained that in such a situation, the person has to choose what sincerely seems to him the *greater duty* or the lesser evil.[39] We have also seen how the French bishops, in proposing this way of resolving the dilemmas of couples regarding family planning, called it "traditional wisdom."

8. THE SCRUPULOUS CONSCIENCE[40]

Scrupulosity is a painful condition in which the person suffers from an uncontrollable fear regarding the lawfulness of an act to be done or of one already done. This is not the same as a *tender conscience,* which has a horror of sinning but is not paralyzed by guilt feelings. On the contrary, the delicacy of such a conscience only spurs the person to creative love.

A scrupulous person is unable to decide for himself. Hence, in the past, the tendency was to decide for him. Now there is an growing understanding that what is needed is precisely the opposite: namely, to build up the latent freedom within the person so that he develops a genuinely autonomous conscience.

In the past, also, scrupulosity was looked upon as a wholly moral or spiritual problem to be treated by advice and spiritual direction. Now it is recognized as a predominantly psychic problem, although with religious overtones. To clarify the matter, it would help to distinguish scrupulosity in a broad sense from scrupulosity proper, which latter could be classified as a neurosis.

The first has two forms:

a) A *temporary emotional unrest and doubt* at some critical stage of life, e.g., puberty, first awareness of a special vocation, or an important step like religious profession or religious conversion. At such times, something like an attack of scrupulosity may appear. Generally, it is a crisis of growth and passes away leaving the person more mature if it is handled carefully with the help of a competent spiritual guide. While every encouragement is to be given, doubts about vocation should be taken seriously, lest there be reason to regret later.

b) *Scruple of compensation,* which may also be called a "Pharisaic conscience." It is a psychic reaction against tepidity or hidden compromise. When a person resists the call of God, the spiritual unrest repressed by the conscience may break out in the form of an obsessive preoccupation in some other area, generally of little or much less significance. Such a person may seek a kindly spiritual guide whom he expects to soothe his conscience. As Andreas Snoeck puts it, he "tries to obtain the *carte blanche* which the inner self has already granted him but which his conscious ego cannot bring itself to accept without the approval of some exterior authority."[41]

This is more a moral or spiritual problem, unlike the emotional illness of true scrupulosity. The role of the confessor or spiritual guide in this case is to bring the person to acknowledge the hidden compromise and see the unrest as an invitation to a real change of heart. Refusal of social obligations is one of the more frequent causes of compensatory scruples. Such people need to be confronted with their true obligations instead of yielding to anxiety over some petty matter.

Real scrupulosity is a *psychic or emotional sickness.* It is a type of neurosis that expresses itself in an anxious concern of a moral and religious nature. It is a form of *obsession with the stain of sin.* "It is the persistent, gnawing, unreasonable conviction that one has offended God or is about to do so."[42]

When faced with a moral choice, the scrupulous person is terrified at the prospect of sinning. After an action, he is inclined to examine it over and again to find possible aspects of guilt. He is impelled to purge the guilt by worrying or by repeated ritual acts like frequent and mechanical confession or other devotional exercises. At times, compulsive impulses are joined to the obsession of scrupulous ideas. The more they are suppressed by anxiety, the stronger they become.

For instance, a passing sexual thought may arouse anxiety, which in turn may awaken stronger obscene thoughts. The imagination is impelled toward them, and the fear gets worse—which, in turn, strengthens the thoughts. These may evoke physical pleasure at which the person panics and is now afraid of committing a sinful act. The consciousness is almost paralyzed. Next, the impulse will get stronger, and he may finally do what he feared. Then a whole cycle of remorse and purgation will start.

Together with an acute feeling of inadequacy, the scrupulous person manifests a certain amount of stubbornness. The complicated reasoning of many a scrupulous person in discovering sin where there is none does not spring from a spiritual understanding but is "only the loud rattle of an unconscious factor that has not been properly integrated into the personality."[43]

Different writers attribute the *genesis* of scrupulosity to different factors. Some would emphasize *innate predispositions*, both psychic and physiological. The first, according to Pierre Janet, is a psychic impotence or *psychasthenia,* a lack of psychic equilibrium that creates a feeling of insufficiency and insecurity. According to some, this in turn would be explained by an organic imbalance.

But *environmental factors* seem to be of greater importance. Scrupulosity can generally be traced to anxiety arising from a overreligious and overprotective upbringing which leads to a faulty development of the superego. Sexual or aggressive stimulation may cause anxiety arising from a severe punitive superego. A person may be so threatened by such basic urges that he acquires a guilt complex. He is impelled to expiate them by repeated ritual acts like confession. He is prone to displace feelings of hate and fear of childhood authority figures onto God. Faulty attitudes concerning God, morality, sex, etc., acquired during childhood, are a strong contributory factor.

Scrupulosity is by no means a sign or means of virtue. It has a cramping effect on personality development and spiritual progress. The imaginary fear of evil and the defense reactions against it result in flight from responsibility and from genuine human contacts.

As we have already remarked, blind obedience to the confessor or spiritual guide can at best afford temporary relief and security. It is a wrong approach to make the victim dependent on another because he is not yet able to decide for himself. Besides, scrupulosity is basically more an emotional problem than a lack of insight. For that reason, the person must learn to stand on his own. Any provisional dependence that may be needed in the initial stages should be based on confidence rather than on imposition of another's will. Any form of therapy must aim at developing the sufferer's autonomous judgment and free choice.

Too rapid a diagnosis of the condition and the presumption that one case is just like another often leads to stereotyped advice that hardly touches the fringe of the problem. The sufferer's complaint that the priest "cannot possibly understand my case" is, unfortunately, often not without foundation. The problem of each scrupulous person is unique and must be approached as such.

In the initial interviews, he should be invited to unburden himself as fully as possible. Thus, the spiritual guide will have a greater insight into the problem, and the sufferer will feel assured that his problem is being taken seriously.

Mere reasoning will not help. However, the scrupulous person may have misconceptions regarding sexuality, requirements about the integrity of confession, etc. These should be cleared up. He should be slowly helped to acquire positive attitudes regarding religion and life. As far as possible, the underlying cause of the anxiety and obsession should be uncovered. "The critical point in this counselling process comes in those sessions which attempt to relate past experiences and attitudes with present fears and anxieties. . . . He sees how early taboos against dirt, sex, disobedience, and so forth, have determined the kinds of response to similar situations in his present life."[44]

It is necessary for the spiritual guide himself to breathe a spirit of joy and peace. His whole bearing must represent the love of God. At times, it helps to confront the victim with the extreme misery and destitution of countless other people, but his obsession may be such that bringing up this point too early may be inappropriate.

Confession at rarer intervals should be suggested. The sacrament should not be allowed to be a means of magical release of neurotic tension. It should be seen as an act of worship and a joyous return to the Father in the ecclesial community. This can be achieved especially by participation in a communal celebration of the sacrament of reconciliation where the whole atmosphere is full of positive hope and joy.

———o———

Notes to Chapter XVI

1. Cf. Antonio Hortelano, *Morale Responsable*, Paris, Desclée, 1970, pp. 32–34.
2. Cf. Odon Lottin, *Psychologie et Morale au XII et XIII Siècles*, 4 t., Gembloux, 1942–1954.
3. *GS*, art. 16.
4. *Ibid.*
5. *GS*, art. 41.
6. *GS*, art. 1.
7. Cf. Gregory Zilborg, "Superego and Conscience." *Conscience*, ed. by Ellis Nelson, New York, Newman Press, 1973, pp. 210–23.
8. Quoted in John W. Glaser, "Conscience and Superego: A Key Distinction," *Theological Studies*, 32 (1971), 34.
9. *Art. cit.*, p. 38.
10. Cf. Louis Monden, *Sin, Liberty and Law*, New York, Sheed and Ward, 1967, pp. 4–18.
11. *Man Becoming*, New York, Herder and Herder, 1970, pp. 223–24.
12. Cf. George V. Lobo, *Renewal of the Sacrament of Reconciliation*, Allahabad, St. Paul Publications, 1976.
13. *Art. cit.*, p. 43.
14. *Obedience and Authority*, London, Tavistock Publications, 1974.
15. *Authority*, London, Burns and Oates, 1976, p. 19.
16. Jack Dominian, *op. cit.*, pp. 83–84.
17. *GS*, art. 43.
18. See William Kay, *Moral Development*, London, Allen and Unwin, 1972; E. M. Beck et alii (ed.), *Moral Education*. New York, Newman Press, 1971.
19. For the distinction between humanistic and authoritarian ethics, see Erich Fromm, *Man for Himself*, New York, Fawcett, 1970.
20. *GS*, art. 16.

21. John C. Ford and Gerald Kelly, *Contemporary Moral Theology*, Vol. I, p. 191.
22. *Identity, Youth and Crisis*, London, Faber and Fber, 1968.
23. Cf. J. H. Flavell, *Developmental Psychology of Jean Piaget*, Princeton, Norstand, 1963.
24. Cf. L. Kohlberg and E. Turiel (ed.), *Moralization Research*, New York, Holt, Rinehart and Winston, 1971; E. W. Beck et alii, *Moral Education*.
25. Cf. H. J. Eysenck, *The Structure of Human Personality*, London, Methuen, 1960; B. F. Skinner, *Beyond Freedom and Dignity*, Harmondsworth, Penguin Books, 1973.
26. Cf. R. R. Sears et alii, *Pattern of Child Rearing*, Evanston, Ill., Row Peterson, 1957.
27. *Op. cit.*, p. 49.
28. *GS*, art. 16.
29. *In Rom.* 14, Lect. 2.
30. *Summa Theologica*, Ia-IIae, 19, 5.
31. *GS*, art. 16.
32. Cf. St. Thomas, *De veritate*, 17, 4.
33. Vol. I, p. 156.
34. *GS*, art. 16. Cf. Helmut Juros, "Formation of Conscience and Ethics," *Concilium*, 1978, pp. 39–46.
35. *DPH*, art. 3.
36. *DPH*, art. 14.
37. *GS*, art. 79.
38. For the history of probabilism, cf. Philippe Delhaye, *The Christian Conscience*, New York, Desclée, 1968, pp. 221ff.
39. Cf. Chapter XIII.
40. Cf. Andreas Snoeck, *Confession and Pastoral Psychology*, Westminster, Md., Newman, 1961, Ch. 3; George Hagmaier and Robert H. Gleason, *Moral Problems Now*, London, Sheed and Ward, 1959, Ch. 7; Willibald Demal, *Pastoral Psychology in Practice*, Cork, Mercier, 1955, Ch. 4; Dermot Casey, *The Nature and Treatment of Scruples*, Dublin, Clonmore and Reynolds, 1948; J. R. M. Nolan, "The Problem of Scruples," *Priest and Mental Health*, ed. by E. F. O'Doherty, *ibid.*, 1962, Ch. 9; James H. VanderVeldt and Richard P. Odenwald, *Psychiatry and Catholicism*, New York, Mc Graw-Hill, 1952, Ch. 19.
41. Andreas Snoeck, *op. cit.*, p. 105.
42. George Hagmaier and Robert H. Gleason, *op. cit.*, p. 145.
43. Andreas Snoeck, *op. cit.*, p. 107.
44. George Hagmaier and Robert H. Gleason, *op. cit.*, p. 164.

CHAPTER XVII

Freedom and Responsibility

1. CHRISTIAN FREEDOM

The modern world is characterized by the striving for freedom. When this takes extreme or violent forms, some Christians seem to panic and oppose the whole movement of freedom. But the theme of freedom is central to the whole of Christian revelation.

In the Judeo-Christian tradition, the act of creation itself is pictured, not as an accident, not as something God had to do, not as a means of achieving some need, but as a sovereignly free act. Since man is made to the image of God, he somehow possesses a freedom that resembles God's creative freedom. As God's image, he shares in God's dominion over irrational creation. God offers a personal relationship which man is free to accept or reject.

Throughout salvation history God appears as a liberator. Thus, God frees the Israelites from the slavery of Egypt for a free service as His chosen people. The external bond of slavery was but a sign of the internal slavery of man. Fallen man, left to himself, is "sold to sin" (Rom. 7:14). Paul tells the Romans, "When you were slaves of sin, you were free in regard to righteousness. But then what return did you get from the things of which you are now ashamed?" (6:20–21).

However, Christ has now freed man from slavery to dishonorable passions. While sin has been radically conquered, still, man perceives the vestiges of slavery as long as he is in the flesh. But in the power of the Spirit he has the means of overcoming it. According to Paul, we have been saved from inner slavery, fear, the corruption of the surrounding universe and the subjection of our body (Rom. 8:14–24). These evils are fetters on creative existence.

Christ has also freed us from the yoke of the law. Though not lawless, the Christian is no longer "under law" (Rom. 6:15)—under any law understood as an externally constraining force. Rather, he now lives "under the law of Christ" (1 Cor. 9:21), which is the interior gift of the Spirit. The law of God no longer binds from without; it acts from within, as the appeal and claim of grace. The Christian is no longer overwhelmed by a multitude of demands which he cannot cope with, but interiorly hears the voice of the Spirit urging and enabling him to do what is right. The person who gives himself to the Spirit is truly free. "The Lord is the Spirit, and where the Spirit of the Lord is, there is freedom" (2 Cor. 3:17).

Accordingly, the law of sin and death is replaced by "the law of the Spirit of life in Christ Jesus" (Rom. 8:2). This liberation has a positive orientation. "Now that you have been set free from sin and have become slaves of God, the return you get is sanctification and its end, eternal life" (Rom. 6:22). It is also a call to service: "Though I am free from all men, I made myself a slave to all, that I might win the more" (1 Cor. 9:19).

This is quite different from the Stoic ideal of total autonomy or autarchy. It is the possibility of a radical dedication and gift of self. It is not self-assertion but surrender in love. There are two ways of escaping the constraint of the law: libertinism, on the one hand; and the spirit of the beatitudes, on the other. The first is not true liberation, since it brings psychological, social and spiritual disturbance. The second leads to inner spontaneity and peace. It makes us interiorly free to decide for God in love. The highest degree of freedom is the perfect love of God, in which man is freed from any resistance to the movements of the Spirit leading to service of God and neighbor.

The imminence of the Kingdom which Jesus announces means liberation from subjection to the rule of Satan, sin and death, from social and religious pressures, from the enslaving needs of an imprisoned self.

It is freedom from fear and anxiety. "Do not be anxious" (Mt. 6:25), says Jesus. It is freedom to care about God and His Kingdom. "Seek first his kingdom and his righteousness" (Mt. 6:33).

Christ Himself is supremely free because of the presence of the Spirit in Him.[1] He freely associates with the "sinners" and the "unclean," people who are to be avoided. His attitude toward the ruling class is completely free. He breaks down communication barriers. He is free from the fear of the unclean (cf. Mk. 7:15) and from petty regulations. He is free from the fear of natural forces, as is manifest in the scene of the stilling of the storm.

The secret of Christ's freedom is His total commitment to the Father, which gives him prophetic assurance. His life is not preprogrammed except to bring about the Kingdom of God. Hence, He is free from all narrow interests and from any anxiety about human approbation. Christ's sovereign freedom is fully revealed precisely when he surrenders His life freely to the Father. "No one takes it from me, I lay it down of my own account" (Jn. 11:18). This shows that true freedom and obedience are not contradictory if both are based on the spirit of love.

To the extent that a Christian shares in Christ's commitment to the Kingdom, he is free from any limited objective. Christian faith reveals the radical insufficiency of all earthly realities. The dialectical tension between the "already" and the "not yet" frees him from idolatrous expectations and imprisonment in limited objectives.

2. THE MEANING OF FREEDOM

Freedom can be understood on different levels:

a) On the *physical level*, it is the absence of physical coercion or constraint. This is enjoyed to the full by wild animals.

b) On the *social level*, it is the absence of social demands and restrictions and, hence, the facility to do as one pleases. This is merely external and, as such, is not an unqualified good. An unlimited freedom of this kind is undesirable for persons living in close relationships, since the social order would thereby collapse. What is important is the ability to participate in appropriate ways in social life by being able to direct one's relationships to personal perfection and the common good.

c) On the *personal level*, therefore, it is the spontaneous creativity of the human person determining himself. Inner determinisms or limitations block the individual from doing as he ought to do or what he desires to do from the depths of his being. True freedom, then, is self-determination, shaping one's own life according to one's ideals. Such freedom in man is initially found only in germ. It has to be developed through the exercise of the capacity of the will to tend to the good. So it is a *gift* as well as a *task*.

Antecedent factors certainly influence our action. Nevertheless, we are not entirely determined by them in every choice we make. At least sometimes we experience, not "It happened to me," but "I made up my mind." As W.H.M. Van Der Marck puts it, "A certain limiting and determination of human possibilities lies in the very nature of human inter-subjectivity. The possibilities open to man, or man's freedom, consist precisely in the fact that he himself is able spontaneously to choose a position regarding the human situation he faces. He can adapt himself to the inevitable, but he can also rebel against it. He can bow fatalistically under difficulties, but he can also try gradually to overcome them. . . . In other words, freedom does not consist in being able to design a world for himself; rather, it consists in being able to take up one's position for or against a world which, in a certain sense, is already designed and forces itself upon one."[2]

Truth is basic to freedom. As Jesus said: "The truth will make you free" (Jn. 8:32). Juan L. Segundo has expressed the importance of sincerity and authenticity for true freedom: "Liberty operates first and foremost in the realm of truth. It operates against bad faith and deceitful tendencies whereby we pass off, as our own, things that are in fact imposed upon us by the determinisms with which we work, think and feel.''[3] That is also why oppressive regimes have recourse to untruth in order to maintain their power.

Marxism looks for the social truth which lies buried in the structures that alienate man. Hence the importance of Marxist analysis, whatever be the limitations of Marxist thought in other respects. Sigmund Freud unmasks the real motive behind human conduct in order to restore man to the truth of his projected aims. He lays bare the workings of the superego, which he calls an ''alien land within.''[4]

Freedom belongs, not to isolated individuals, but to persons as members of a community. It is fostered in an atmosphere of solidarity, while it is stifled by impersonal collectivism. True liberation can be had only by shared responsibility. One member cannot be fully free unless he acknowledges the freedom of the others. The tyrant or slave driver paradoxically loses his freedom himself. A situation in which the elite classes enjoy a seemingly high degree of culture at the expense of servile work on the part of the masses is degrading to the elite classes themselves.

Some think that if we liberate individuals, then society will automatically be transformed. But, as Segundo points out, ''such a statement is based on an erroneous conception of man. It does not appreciate the fact that the individual can be truly liberated only in terms of his total human condition, i.e., with his social context.''[5] This is so, as the same author explains, because ''society is not the end result of juxtaposing already constituted individuals, and [because] from the start it is a system of human relationships and interrelationships that constitute the individual and form part of his total human condition.''[6]

Still, on the other hand, society cannot be liberated without the inner hearts of the people being freed from selfish tendencies. That is why very sudden revolutions are prone to establish even more oppressive tyrannies. Oppressive structures must be eliminated by a combination of individual conversion and the reshaping of structures and institutions, both of which are long and difficult processes.

Liberty is not merely a condition for morality; it is itself an important aspect of morality. This is very well brought out in a parable of Rodo's, *The Farewell of Gorgias*.[7] Gorgias' mother was so greatly attached to her son's innocence that she regularly obtained magic potions from a sorceress to ensure its continuance. One day when the supply ran out, she returned empty-handed to find herself confronted with a bitter old man who reproached her fiercely: "Your savage egotism has robbed me of my life, offering me instead a demeaning bliss. You have robbed me of ennobling action, illuminating thought, and fruitful love."

The mother tries to suppress the possibility of her son's choosing evil by suppressing his liberty and prolonging his infancy till the very end of his life. The son finally enjoys a few brief moments of adulthood and uses them to curse his mother for having deprived him of a free adult life.

Liberty is not merely the capacity to choose between good and evil. It is a value in itself which more than compensates for the possible evil that may result from a particular bad choice. Hence, there is need for taking prudent risks in life. "Not to risk, then, is to close oneself off from this realm in a definitive way. Risking oneself obviously entails trouble. And, while we cannot be completely sure about it, it would seem that being free and being a person is worth the trouble, whatever the end result may be."

Social structures, whether civil or ecclesiastical, are instruments to carry out the human project. But they should not be allowed to become mechanical and deterministic factors.

Today it is very important to withstand social pressures that create a feeling of being abnormal in those who do not conform to the majority. Thus, in some countries juveniles are impelled to indulge in sexual activity or at least brag about doing so in order to feel normal. In view of the widespread immature desire to conform, it is necessary to have men and women who dare to withstand the undesirable influence of the brute majority. On the other hand, it should be clear that true freedom is exercised in community by respecting the freedom of others and by supporting one another's growth. Today it is not dependence nor independence that is needed, but *interdependence*. Emphasis on freedom, although clearly based on the Bible, may frighten some people. But they should realize that without freedom there is no true moral life, since the moral act is essentially a freely posited act. Besides, it does not help to compel youth to do "the right thing," imagining that thereby they will be trained to do good. Today the elders may make a child do what they believe, rightly or wrongly, is "the right thing." But if his capacity for free decision has not been developed, tomorrow others will make him do what they want him to do, which may not be pleasing to the elders.

In this connection, Jack Dominian has given the example of the extermination of millions of Jews in Nazi Germany, which was actually carried out by normally "good" people who later pleaded as an excuse that they were only obeying orders. "On the surface most of them were ordinary people who would have been horrified to inflict violence on their neighbor, but obedience countered their spontaneous disinclination to do so into a series of actions which form part of the most appalling crimes in the history of mankind."[9] Dominian also refers to experiments carried out in the Interaction Laboratory of Yale University to show the dangers of unthinking obedience.[10]

The meaning of true freedom can be expressed in a schematic form:

(1) It is, first of all, freedom *from*. Basically, it is freedom *from our own inauthentic selves.* We need *inner liberation* from ignorance, fear, anxieties, evil inclinations, bad habits, prejudices, psychic compulsions, obsessions, and the like. Then we can think about freedom *from undue pressures from others,* like useless regulations, bad example, threats, unjust social structures, and so on. Inner freedom is most basic. Those who are perfectly free within themselves cannot really be touched by external pressures. Normally, however, external freedom is necessary for the growth of inner freedom.

(2)   Freedom *from* is not an end in itself. It is directed to freedom *for*. We should want to be free from undue constraints in order that we may be able to have care and concern for others.

True freedom, then, is the *capacity to give oneself to others,* to dedicate oneself spontaneously to the service of others.

3.   RELIGIOUS FREEDOM

The free exercise of religion is a freedom *sui generis,* since it raises the issue of man's relation to God, while other civil rights have to do only with man's relation to other men or to human society.

At the time of Vatican II, there were two main views regarding religious freedom.[11] The first was derived from the medieval conception of the theocratic state and from the post-Reformation principle *cujus regio ejus religio* (The religion of the prince has the dominant position). This view was expressed by the following scheme. *Thesis:* "Truth alone has rights." The Catholic religion is the only true one and, hence, it alone has the right to exist. Although the internal conscience of others has to be respected, religious error ought to be repressed by the State. This may not always be possible. Hence the *hypothesis:* "Error may be tolerated." This is a matter of course in nations that are predominantly non-Catholic. Even in those that are largely Catholic, legal "tolerance" may be necessary for public peace because of widespread pluralism.[12] This view was apparently supported by Pius XII as late as 1953: "That which does not correspond to the truth and the norm of morality has, objectively, no right to existence or to propaganda or to action. . . . Not to inhibit [error] by means of public laws or coercive methods can nevertheless be justified in the interests of a higher and greater good."[13]

The principle that error as such has no right to exist is perfectly true in the abstract. But, in the concrete, the view led to a lot of repression in so-called Catholic countries and weakened the voice of the Church when it proclaimed human freedom in other situations.

Hence, more recently, a second view developed for several reasons: a) the transition from the classical mentality, which was unduly preoccupied with abstract concepts, to historical consciousness; b) the transition from sacral society to secular society and the consequent understanding of the proper mission of the Church and civil authority; c) the realization that the "privileged" position of the Church and "protection" by civil authority in certain conditions only impeded her mission and involved her in many unchristian modes of behavior by unscrupulous leaders claiming to serve religious interests when they were really serving their own; d) the realization that some traditionally Catholic countries have been considerably dechristianized; e) widespread pluralism and the closer union of different peoples, cutting across religious differences; f) the imperative of the ecumenical movement and a better understanding of the positive values of other religions as well as of the true nature of the missionary task; g) the persecution of Catholics in some countries; h) accusations that the Church has a double standard when she is in a majority and when she is in a minority situation, and the consequent suspicion that an increase in her numbers could pose the danger of others being repressed; i) the experience—for instance, in America—of the Church thriving without official patronage; j) a better realization of human dignity and of the freedom proclaimed by the Gospel.

The second view, then, upholds the principle of religious freedom itself. Not only does it defend man's civil right to immunity from coercion in his search for religious truth, but it also upholds the right to profess his faith publicly and practice it socially.

This view was adopted by Vatican II in the Declaration on Religious Freedom. The Council claims that the Church has always supported the principle of religious freedom as befitting the dignity of man and as being in accord with divine revelation. This is true as far as the Church defended the doctrine that one has to embrace the truth freely and that no one may be coerced into the faith. The undeniable development of doctrine is glossed over. However, the Council makes a *mea culpa*, repudiating all past measures of coercion in religious matters: "In the life of the People of God as it has made its pilgrim way through the vicissitudes of human history, there have at times appeared ways of acting which were less in accord with the spirit of the gospel and even opposed to it.''[14]

The primary intention of the Declaration is to define religious freedom *in relationship to civil society,* as is clear from the subtitle ''On the Right of the Person and of Communities to Social and Civil Freedom in Modern Society.'' Besides, it is explicitly stated that ''it has to do with immunity from coercion in civil society.''[15]

However, the implication is broader. ''This freedom means that all men are to be immune from coercion on the part of individuals and of any human power, in such wise that in matters religious no one is to be forced to act in a manner contrary to his own beliefs. Nor is anyone to be restrained from acting in accordance with his own beliefs, whether alone or in association with others, within due limits.''[16]

The Declaration does not directly touch on the issue of freedom within the Church. On the contrary, it urges the faithful, in the formation of their conscience, ''to attend carefully to the sacred and certain doctrine of the Church.''[17] But the document cannot but be a stimulus to deeper understanding of Christian freedom in relation to the doctrinal and disciplinary authority of the Church.[18] In fact, another document, *Lumen Gentium,* declares that ''every layman should openly reveal to them [pastors] his needs and desires with that freedom and confidence which befits a son of God and a brother in Christ. An individual layman, by reason of the knowledge, competence, or outstanding ability which he enjoys, is permitted and sometimes even obliged to express his opinion on things which concern the good of the Church.''[19]

The document makes it clear that religious freedom does not mean indifferentism. ''It leaves untouched traditional Catholic doctrine on the moral duty of men and societies toward true religion and toward the one Church of Christ.'' The Council ''professes the belief that God Himself has made known to mankind the way in which men are to serve Him, and thus be saved in Christ and come to blessedness. We believe that this one true religion subsists in the Catholic and Apostolic Church, to which the Lord Jesus committed the duty of spreading it abroad among all men.''[20] It also warns against the inclination ''to use the name of freedom as the pretext for refusing to submit to authority and for making light of the duty of obedience.''[21]

Religious freedom is based on the fact that ''every man has the duty, and therefore the right, to seek the truth in matters religious, in order that he may with prudence form for himself right and true judgments of conscience, with the use of all suitable means.''[22] Ultimately, it has its foundation in the dignity of the human person in its full dimensions. Man, being intelligent and free, is a responsible agent in seeking and adhering to the truth.[23]

The exercise of religious freedom consists, first of all, in personal and voluntary acts. ''No purely human power can either command or prohibit acts of this kind.'' This is because a man is bound to follow the dictates of his conscience, by which he comes to know the imperatives of the divine will. And ''he is not to be forced to act in a manner contrary to his conscience. Nor, on the other hand, is he to be restrained from acting in accordance with his conscience, especially in matters religious.''[24] This applies also to joining the Church. As one's response to God in faith must be free, ''no one is to be forced to embrace the Christian faith against his own free will.''[25]

Since the right to religious freedom is based on the very nature of man, ''this immunity continues to exist even in those who do not live up to their obligation of seeking the truth and adhering to it.''[26] Consequently, this freedom goes beyond the subjective good faith of the individual. It is not for others to judge his good faith. Hence, religious freedom extends to unbelievers with good or bad faith.

The social nature of man requires that he be free to express his religion in a *corporate manner*. Religious enquiry is to be carried on with mutual dialogue. Besides, ''the social nature of man itself requires that he should give external expression to his internal acts of religion . . . that he should profess his religion in community.''[27] Hence, ''religious bodies also have the right not to be hindered, either by legal or administrative action on the part of government, in the selection, training, appointment, and transferral of their own ministers, in communicating abroad, in erecting buildings for religious purposes, and in the acquisition and use of suitable funds or properties."[28] The Council also asks that religious liberty be protected by effective constitutional guarantees.

This right extends to the establishment of educational, cultural, charitable and social organizations inspired by the religious spirit. Since the family is a society in its own right, parents "have the right to determine, in accordance with their own religious beliefs, the kind of religious education that their children are to receive."[29]

The Council does not favor the principle of establishment of a particular religion, although it does not condemn the arrangement, provided the freedom of individuals and of other religious bodies is guaranteed and there be no discrimination on religious grounds.[30] On the other hand, it does not approve of a complete divorce between the State and religion. Government ought to recognize the transcendent value of religion in the life of its people and "show it favor, since the function of government is to make provision for the common welfare."[31] It is "also to help create conditions favorable to the fostering of religious life, in order that the people may be truly enabled to exercise their religious rights and to fulfill their religious duties, and also in order that society itself may profit from the moral qualities of justice and peace which have their origin in man's faithfulness to God and to His holy will."[32]

Therefore, total separation between religion and State as it prevails in countries like the United States is far from the ideal. It leads to the forbidding of prayer in State schools and to discrimination against those people who want to send their children to religious schools. They have to pay the common taxes for education as well as fees in the private schools. A secular State should mean neutrality toward every religious group, but not indifference or depreciation of religious values on the part of public authority.

The Council repeatedly declares that the exercise of the right to religious freedom is not absolute. Since religion is to be practised in society, the right "is *subject to certain regulatory norms.*" Because of the exercise of their right, individuals, men and social groups are bound by the moral law to have respect both for the rights of others and for their own duties toward others and for the common welfare of all." While the principle should be that "freedom must be respected as far as possible," "society has the right to defend itself against possible abuses committed on pretext of religious freedom."[33] It is clear that no one should offend the religious feelings of others nor unduly disturb public order in the name of religion. Hence, there can be reasonable regulations regarding religious processions and the use of loudspeakers and the like. Manifest aberrations, like child sacrifice and sacred prostitution, have to be checked.

Because of the dialectical nature of freedom in society, there cannot be a clear-cut and uniform solution valid for all times and places. The inevitable tension between the rights of various groups has to be resolved by goodwill and dialogue between various religious communities. None should forget that religion is meant to glorify God and bring about fraternal unity among all men. As a result, there should be no fanaticism or partisan quarrels, which only debase religion.

Christians, according to the mandate of the Lord, and after the example of the Apostles, are called to share their faith with others and bring them to participate in the ecclesial communion. "However, in spreading religious faith . . . everyone ought at all times to refrain from any manner of action which might seem to carry a hint of coercion or of a kind of persuasion that would be dishonorable or unworthy, especially when dealing with poor or uneducated people."[34]

The State has the right and duty of preventing proselytism or forced conversion inasmuch as this violates the right of citizens or disturbs public order. But this should in no way lead to the prevention of genuine conversions. There should be full freedom, not only to *profess* and *practice* one's faith, but to *propagate* it by all fair means. It does not belong to a secular State to be worried about the fact that some change their faith, since, by definition, a secular State is supposed to be neutral with regard to religious groups. On the other hand, those religious groups who engage fervently in the propagation of their faith, for which they have every right, should be careful to see that their methods are aboveboard and that they do not bring about cultural alienation and divisiveness in the name of religion.

While it is wrong to take advantage of the poverty of people to allure them to an external change of religion, human advancement cannot be divorced from interior religion. If underprivileged classes see in Christianity, for instance, a possibility of a greater sense of human dignity, they cannot be blamed for wanting to join such a fellowship.

The right kind of religious freedom calls for proper formation. Therefore, the Declaration "urges everyone, especially those who are charged with the task of educating others, to do their utmost to form men who will respect the moral order and be obedient to lawful authority. Let them form men, too, who will be lovers of their freedom— men, in other words, who will come to decisions on their own judgment and in the light of truth, govern their activities with a sense of responsibility, and strive after what is true and right, willing always to join others in cooperative effort."[35]

4. MORAL RESPONSIBILITY

By the very fact that the gift of freedom is also a task, inasmuch as freedom is for service, the Christian vocation to freedom is also a call to *responsibility*. The very term means "response ability," or the "ability to respond to God's call."

Paul warns that God calls all men to account for their actions (cf. 2 Cor. 5:10). But since he also declares that "all are justified by his grace as a gift, through the redemption which is in Christ Jesus" (Rom. 2:23), the moral doctrine of responsibility must be understood in the context of God's gracious redemption. While man is *held* responsible, so he is also *made* responsible by God's grace. He is *enabled* to fulfill his responsibility. As Karl Barth puts it, "It is as He makes Himself responsible for man that God makes man, too, responsible."[36]

Christian ethics is the response to God's call in the present moment. Hence the importance of distinguishing mere *chronos* (time measured in years, months and days) and *kairos* (time of opportunity and grace, a moment of ongoing salvation history). The Christ-event has introduced an absolute newness in human history. It provides a basic perspective from which to judge human conduct, as He is the Omega-point of the final fulfillment, the dynamic center of orientation of all human aspirations.

Christian ethics is an *"interim ethics"* related to the *eschaton*. The paschal mystery of the death and resurrection of the Lord is expressed in the present hour of grace and decision. The judgment that will be manifest at the Parousia is already at work in the hidden voice of conscience. Only those who are ready to recognize the Lord's call in the daily events of life will be prepared to receive Him at His final coming. Hence the stress in Vatican II on reading the signs of the times.[37] Paul tells the Christian: "Awake, O sleeper, and arise from the dead" (Eph. 5:4) and bids him to "make the most of the time" (v. 16).

Consequently, the Christian is called to be alert to the needs of the time. He has the responsibility of bringing the light of the Gospel to current problems. He has to discern what is of permanent value in existing traditions and what is dated and needs to be changed. Without this discernment, he will miss the opportunity of responding to God's call at the present moment of history.

Bernard Häring has brought out very well the significance of the *kairos* for Christian morality. "A right understanding of the *kairos* and of God's constant presence excludes inflexible planning and routine as well as inactivity. The *kairos* awakens man's spontaneity, initiative, generosity, without allowing any estrangement from life. It is an urgent and dynamic appeal for an existential response while man must leave behind him all reckoning and human tradition which would hinder him from being outgoing, alert, ready for the real possibilities and needs. It means a call to authenticity, uniqueness, to being one's own self with others on every occasion. Without undue tension or timidity, one can then grasp the opportunities that never will return in this same form."[38]

The real world is the sphere where man must function as a Christian. This is the world which is to be conformed to Christ. "The world is the sphere of concrete responsibility which is given to us in and through Jesus Christ."[39] As Jesus Christ was "deputy" for God in the world, the Christian lives in deputyship, representing God before men and selflessly taking their needs upon himself. He is thus concretely inserted into the real world of concrete relationships.

As Christ, who was without sin, shared in the fellowship of human guilt (cf. 2 Cor. 5:21), the Christian, too, must share the guilt which is the inevitable consequence of involvement with the realities of human life and institutions, without, however, being overwhelmed by guilt feelings. He is not to condemn his brothers, but is to share their burdens and help them to lead a better life.

The moral response is ultimately a religious response, for each moral act is directed to the ordering and bettering of the human world as an answer to God's call and covenant. Moral responsibility is not only conformity to law, but commitment to the creation of a human community which is an image of the Trinitarian community in God.

Responsibility means that man responds to God by responding to persons, values and exigencies within the real world of experience. We have seen in Chapter XIII how man cannot be satisfied with choosing some values in a given situation but has to affirm all of them and try to realize them as best as possible even if this implies facing an agonizing tension. In the light of new problems and experience, he has to refine his moral norms. As Albert R. Jonsen writes: "The responsible man as decision maker is one who, while he admits that in great part established principle and rule suffice to order life, is aware that he well must view situations, with new exigencies. He is aware that the value which he accepts must be realized in new situations, amid new difficulties, with renewed energy and resourcefulness. He knows that he must continually endeavor to draw out of his personal and communal experience a new appreciation of the values."[40]

This is how moral principles were evolved in the past. A recent example of responsibly refining a moral principle is that of the per-

missibility of a woman's positively taking means to protect herself against
the danger of a pregnancy arising from forced intercourse. The case
arose on the occasion of alleged rapes at the time of the independence
of Zaire. Some Roman moralists declared that this was not against
traditional doctrine, since the malice of forbidden contraception consists
in voluntary intercourse accompanied by deliberate interference with
the procreative dynamism of the act.

We should also note that the admission of moral absolutes does
not minimize personal responsibility. Apart from the fact that a difficult
decision may have to be made regarding the choice of a lesser evil in
some circumstances, the moral absolutes still leave a vast scope for
responsibility. For instance, *Humanae Vitae,* after Vatican II, speaks
about responsible parenthood. According to the encyclical, besides respecting the woman's natural rhythm, this calls for (1) necessary dominion over the sexual impulse, and (2) responsible decision regarding
the number of children, taking into account the "physical, economic,
psychological and social conditions."[41]

The Mansfield Report issued by a study committee convoked by
the WCC International Mission Council also speaks in the same vein:
"The knowledge of the relation of sexual love to the procreative process
gives to the couple the power, and therefore the resonsibility, to lift the
begetting of children out of the realm of biological accident or 'fate'
into the realm of personal decision."[42] It should be noted in general
that the more the knowledge and power of man increases, the more the
scope of responsibility expands.

It must be said to the credit of situationists and contextualists that
they have strongly stressed personal responsibility. For instance, Joseph
Fletcher has devoted a whole book to this theme.[43] He insists on the
distinction between sentimental and discerning love, although he may
not have provided a fully satisfactory ground for the discernment. Quoting Phil. 1:9, he suggests four pillars for Christian ethics: 1) a prayerful
reliance upon God's grace; 2) the law of love as the norm; 3) knowledge
of the facts, of the empirical situation in all its variety and relativity
(he rightly decries the attitude: "My mind is made up, so don't confuse

me with the facts!''); and 4) judgment—i.e., decision, which is responsibility in humility.[44]

Likewise, Dietrich Bonhoeffer expresses the essentially responsible dimension of ethics as follows: ''When the deed is performed with the responsible weighing up of all the personal and objective circumstances and in the awareness that God has become *man* and that it is *God* who has become man, then this deed is delivered up solely to God at the moment of its performance.''[45]

Thus we see that obedience and responsibility are interlocked. The ultimate reason for both is the filial relation of man to God, which is perfectly realized in Jesus Christ, who stands before God as the one who is supremely free. ''To say that man is responsible is to say that he has been freed to enter into the world and work for the realization of Christ therein; it also means that he is bound, obliged to do so.''[46]

Vatican II has stressed the place of responsibility in Christian life. For instance, the Council invites religious to practice obedience in the spirit of mature responsibility. ''Realizing that they are giving service to the upbuilding of Christ's body according to God's design, let them bring to the execution of commands and to the discharge of assignments entrusted to them the resources of their minds and wills, and their gifts of nature and grace.''[47]

The personal nature of responsibility needs to be stressed. Responsibility for a thing or a cause has value only when it is directed to the good of persons. Otherwise, things or ideologies will become the masters of man and lead to material preoccupations or fanaticism. Enda McDonagh rightly describes the nature of the moral call basically as an interpersonal situation, a situation involving two personal centers or poles, whether individuals or community groups. The moral response, according to him, has three phases: first, the recognition of the other as source of a moral call—e.g., to feed the hungry; second, respect for the other's call; and third, the response itself.[48]

From such an analysis, the distinction between *reacting* with passion and *responding* with reason becomes clear. The first is totally impersonal, while the second is a communion of persons.

Modern psychologists have made a big contribution to the understanding of responsible moral life. For instance, Erich Fromm distinguishes between "humanistic" and "authoritarian" ethics.[49] The latter denies man's capacity to know what is good and bad; it is based on awe of authority's magic power and on the subject's feeling of weakness and dependence. The content of such an ethic is primarily seen in terms of the interests of authority, although the subject derives considerable benefit from the easy security it brings him. Thus, a teacher may call a pupil good if he does not cause trouble and is a credit to him. The "good" child may be very insecure, wanting only to please his elders, while the "bad" child may have genuine interests which do not please them. There is no room for responsibility in such a conception.

The importance, then, of developing moral responsibility cannot be sufficiently stressed. Germain Grisez and R. Shaw have proposed a good program for such formation under what they term "modes of responsibility":[50]

1)   Right moral orientation calls for consistent commitment to the realization of basic purposes with which one could identify to such an extent that the free actions by which one realizes them would in fact constitute him as the person he is. Moral responsibility rules out a primitive spontaneity that yields to inclinations not in harmony with fundamental life-purposes. Spontaneity should be in line with one's basic commitment to good and not determine one's commitment.

2)   One must have an open and inclusivistic attitude toward all the fundamental human purposes as they refer to himself and others. Parents and school teachers should not forget how they felt when they were on the other side of the fence.

3)   Another mode of responsibility is willingness to see others develop, and not be on the defensive in order to protect one's own

position. The teacher should be ready to see a pupil surpass him, allowing him to be different and develop in different ways. There should be willingness to accept responsibility for the needs of others even when there is no explicit obligation.

4)   There is need for detachment from any specific and limited good, so that its want of realization does not shatter one's hopes. This is akin to ''Ignatian indifference.''

5)   This should go together with fidelity to one's ideals even while seeking to realize them realistically and amidst difficulties in the way. This is a balance between the immoral extremes of fanaticism and non-involvement.

6)   Fidelity does not mean rigidity. There should be a continual effort to explore new ways of better serving the basic goals. Utilitarianism is to be subordinated to basic value.

7)   Social duties become moral responsibilities to the extent that they flow from our insertion into a particular community based on justice.

8)   When there is a conflict between one's duties as a member of different communities—for instance, the family and business—every effort should be made to resolve the conflict; and, if it still remains, one must choose that which is more urgent and important, in dialogue with the persons concerned.

9)   It is never right to act directly against any one of the fundamental human goods, since these goods make up personhood and are themselves ends of human action, and, as such, cannot be treated as means to other ends—e.g., abortion, torturing a child. Directly violating life amounts to using a human person as a means to an end.

Pseudo-ethical theories seize upon one or other of these modes of responsibility to the exclusion of others. They go wrong, not because they sponsor false principles, but because they pursue some unilaterally.

5. THE PARTICULAR VOCATION

We have frequently referred to the "gift call" or vocational structure of moral life. Each person is born into a particular family, grows up in a particular way and is endowed with particular gifts in order to fulfill a particular destiny within the overall human and Christian destiny. It is a call to become this particular human being. The call comes afresh at each moment through each situation. Now the question is whether this should be understood as a call to isolated responses in each situation, using the initial endowment of self-creativity, or whether God Himself calls people to a permanent state. The problem of vocations today goes further than merely trying to find better means of promotion, recruitment and discernment. The radical question of the permanence of vocation needs to be answered.

Scripture provides abundant examples, both in the Old and in the New Testament, for an affirmative answer. That God Himself specially intervenes in our lives is clear from the sudden illumination we get, for instance, when we meditate on a particular biblical passage. Besides, there are stable ministries and charisms in the Church. Hence, it is proper to conclude that God may call a person to this or that permanent state of life. It is possible to imagine that God would be content with whatever choice we make in good faith. It is also true that someone may have to do the best he can with a particular wrong choice when later he incurs certain obligations to do so. But this does not exclude God's initial calling to a definite state of life.

In the past, there may have been some too hasty decisions regarding vocations, or a refusal to see that one might not be fitted to carry on with a way of life one had chosen. There was also the threat of damnation held out to those who "lost" their vocation. But this is no reason now to swing to the opposite side and deny God's call to a permanent state of life. We should take note of Paul's mind. According to him, God calls each one in a specific way and determines the state of life in which the call of faith comes. Once one has heard the call, he is to remain in that state. "Let everyone lead the life which the Lord has assigned him" (1 Cor. 7:17).

The further question of the degree of permanency is a difficult one. First, it is clear that, within a vocation, there is a large number of possibilities. In fact, every member of a religious community has a unique role to play and a unique way of attaining perfection within the overall charism of the institute.

Then, one vocation could be combined with another; for instance, a religious could also be a teacher or a nurse. This should not, however, be a mere external juxtaposition. The teaching mission must receive a special modality from the fact that it is exercised by a religious, while the religious life itself receives a special tone from the teaching mission.

Now, could a vocation for a particular person be a temporary one? To some extent it can be. For example, a marriage can end due to the death of the partner. However, the Church insists that a consummated sacramental marriage is indissoluble, even though there are painful instances of marital breakdown. We should also be slow to affirm that religious vocation, which is a call to total commitment to God and the community, can be temporary. Of course, the time of formation is a time of discernment. But once a final commitment is made *with due discernment,* one should not easily give in to doubts. That the theory of "temporary vocation" is not very conducive to peace of mind has been shown in many a case. If proper discernment was not made before final profession, then there is good reason to make it later.

I am not denying the very possibility of a "temporary vocation." It may well be that a certain religious clearly feels that God is now calling him to another way of life, in which he could be committed more deeply to the very same values which up to now he was trying to realize in his present vocation. But this is not easily to be thought of, lest there be no stability and peace of mind.

At times, the problem arises because a religious feels that he is not given the opportunity of performing a service toward which he is strongly drawn. For instance, a religious may feel that God wants him to do social work, while his superiors ask him to teach. Most of such problems could be solved by deeper discernment and mutual dialogue.

It may also be that the religious could see in the school situation itself great possibilities of social service—e.g., by developing the social consciousness of the students and teachers, by initiating them into social service, by actively supporting social projects, and so on.

The Christian life itself is a vocation or call to sanctity. Still, this is to be lived out in more particular vocations, which are not restricted to the priesthood and religious life. Vatican II declares that laymen should know "that it is generally the function of their well-formed Christian conscience to see that the divine law is inscribed in the life of the earthly city."[52] They have to fulfill this role in their family life and in the particular profession they are called to. Married people are called to found the "domestic Church."[53]

The clerical and religious vocations have a special place in the Church. Bishops, priests and deacons are specially called to be ministers of word and sacrament. Religious, by their vocation, have to present word and sacrament, "not so much in what is said or done immediately, but in the style of life, as the sign manifest in the acceptance of the evangelical counsels or the vows. These are an announcement to the world of its call to the fulfillment of its true meaning."[54] They have to witness, by their very life, to the eschatological realities. As Vatican II points out, God "calls some to give clear witness to the desire for a heavenly home and to keep that desire green among the human family."[55] By sacrificing—for the sake of the Kingdom—some earthly values (or at least certain forms of realizing them) and by living in a close community, they are to be signs of the fulfilled community of mankind.

The divine call first comes as a summons to see human values. A particular human value or way of life becomes a "vocation" when it is clearly perceived as a personal appeal from God, who is worthy of all love. Though the divine intiative is to personal communion of life with the all-holy God, still He makes use of natural, intramundane factors, but in such a way that these become the experience of His free and generous offer of grace.

6. COMMAND AND COUNSEL

Traditional moral theology distinguished between the "command that binds" and the "counsel that invites." The command was supposed to imply an *unconditional obligation,* so that its deliberate violation would be a *"sin."* The counsel was supposed to be *only an invitation* or suggestion which did not strictly oblige. Its fulfillment would be a work of "supererogation," and its refusal would be only a *"positive imperfection."* The counsels were supposed to be of two kinds: first, the so-called "evangelical counsels," or "higher means" offered to those who wished effectively to tend to perfection so that they might attain it in an easier and more secure fashion; second, particular inspirations of the Spirit going beyond the strict requirements of the universal divine commandments.

There is no doubt that the Holy Spirit, through the Gospels and in each one's heart, issues invitations which are beyond the law. Still, the traditional conception seems to introduce an unnecessary dichotomy into the Christian life. First of all, God's commandment is itself a gift before it is a demand. To one moved by the Spirit, it corresponds to the heart's deepest dynamism and, hence, is not felt as an outward constraint.

On the other hand, the radical demands of the Sermon on the Mount are addressed to all who would gain entrance into the Kingdom. (See especially the beatitudes and the call to "be perfect as your heavenly Father is perfect" in Mt. 5:48.) Everyone owes God the full response of love in proportion to the talents bestowed on him.

Consequently, the so-called "evangelical counsels" are addressed to every Christian. But the concrete mode of living them out is different for different people. If all must have the spirit of poverty, some are called to literally renounce everything as a condition of discipleship (Mk. 10:21). Jesus praises the decision to renounce marriage "for the sake of the Kingdom" if one receives a call to do so. As Rudolf Schnackenburg says: "The distinction between commandments and counsels is not formally recognizable as such in the Gospels, but was made clear only later in the Church; still, it has a biblical foundation."[56]

Yet it is another matter to say that a command is binding and a counsel is only inviting. Some would defend such a view by citing 1 Cor. 7:38: "He who marries his betrothed does well, and he who refrains from marriage will do better," and from the fact that Paul says that he has no command of the Lord regarding virginity and is giving only his own opinion (7:25). From the whole tenor of 1 Cor. 7, it is clear that virginity is a special charism in the Church. But, from the larger scope of Paul's ideas on charism and vocation, it does not seem to follow that the response to a counsel is a matter of choice in the sense of "take it or leave it."

As John W. Glaser points out, Paul recommends virginity as better only in general. But he does not say that for the individual to whom the call is addressed it is only a recommendation. In Paul's thought, a charism is not a mere ornamentation added to the Mystical Body. Every gift is a call and, hence, is given for the building up of the Body of Christ. He links the variety of *charisms* to the variety of *diakonias* in the Church (cf. 1 Cor. 12:4–5).[57]

Karl Rahner has drawn attention to the fact that Paul's teaching does not support the classical theological distinction between *gratia gratum faciens* (grace that makes the recipient himself intrinsically holy and pleasing to God) and *gratia gratis data* (grace which is given only "gratuitously" to someone for the benefit of others, but which does not sanctify the recipient). "On the contrary, he only sees or only envisages the case when the charismata both sanctify the recipient and redound to the benefit of the whole Body of Christ simultaneously and reciprocally."[58] Hence, there is no room for an invitation which could be rejected without rejecting the person inviting.

It might happen that the individual call of God is not certain. But when it comes with certitude, there seems to be a clear obligation to follow it. Referring to the example of the rich young man (Mk. 10:17–20), Schnackenburg writes: "This account must not be understood as though Jesus offered two ways to a man honestly seeking and striving for the Kingdom of God, an ordinary one of the commandments and an extraordinary one of renunciation of earthly possessions. Jesus' intention regarding that rich man was a single one from the start. . . . He left the man no choice."[59]

Similarly, when Paul says that if one cannot live as a virgin or widow he may marry without sinning (1 Cor. 7:36–39), he is not saying that a clear call to virginity is a "mere counsel" which one is free to accept or reject. He is implying that the very inability to live as a virgin or widow is a sign that such a state in life is not the one to which this individual is called. A call may be more excellent *in itself,* but it is not to be counselled to everyone, since each has his own vocation.

The obligation of following the counsels refers not only to a stable way of life but also to each inspiration of the Spirit. In fact, the Christian, whatever his state of life, is bound to tend to perfection by making the best use of the talents or charisms given to him (cf. Mt. 25:14–29). This does not contradict the spirit of freedom, since true freedom is fulfilled only by uniting one's will with that of God.

However, this view that one is concretely bound to follow the individual call of God just as much as the universal law addressed to all, should be cautiously proposed to people, since, otherwise, it could lead to undue anxiety of conscience. Besides, those who still think that sin is only the "violation of the law of God" will not understand that rejecting a clear counsel could also be sinful. The matter will become obvious only if sin itself is understood as an offense against the love of God by rejecting His call.

Moreover, the obligation of following the counsels or inspirations of the Spirit should not be proposed in a legalistic manner. It is more a question of openness to the call of God, of a right attitude of accepting His grace. The Christian should always be attentive to the promptings of grace and try, not to do the most perfect thing in itself, but to cooperate as fully as possible with the action of the Holy Spirit in his heart, without giving way to nagging anxiety.

To fall short of the Gospel ideal without any deliberate fault on one's part could be called "mere imperfection." However, "to lag behind the Christian ideal consciously and deliberately, to neglect consciously and deliberately actions which one clearly recognizes as most conformable to one's spiritual condition, is more appropriately termed, not a mere imperfection, but sin.[59] On the other hand, to talk of performing something which lies beyond the strict requirements of the universal law and to which one clearly feels called as a work of supererogation sounds Pharisaic. The Christian who loyally coooperates with God's grace and uses all his gifts in the service of God and neighbor will, according to the Gospel saying, consider himself as "an unworthy servant" (cf. Lk. 17:7–10).

The sinful nature of refusing God's clear inspirations has a bearing on the "sufficient matter" for sacramental absolution. Many confessors are prone to think that they must extract some "sins" from the penitent even when he has already confessed that he has not been responding to the inspirations of the Spirit. Their view is that it is not enough to confess "imperfections" but "sins," meaning to say that some offenses against the *commandments* must be confessed. They unduly stress the distinction between commandments and counsels and contribute to a minimization of the Christian obligation to respond to the call of God, whether it comes through a rule or through a counsel.

———o———

Notes to Chapter XVII

1. Rudolf Pesch, "Jesus, a Free Man," *Concilium,* 10 (1974), No. 73, 56–70.
2. *Toward a Christian Ethic.* Westminster, Md., Newman, pp. 46–47.
3. *Grace and the Human Condition,* New York, Maryknoll, 1973, p. 33.
4. *The Ego and the Id,* New York, Norton, 1962, p. 38.
5. *Op. cit.,* p. 37.
6. *Ibid.,* p. 37.
7. Cited by Juan L. Segundo, *op. cit.,* pp. 42–43.
8. *Ibid.,* p. 45.

9. *Authority*, London, Burns and Oates, 1976, p. 16.

10. *Ibid.*, p. 17.

11. John C. Murray, *The Problem of Religious Freedom*, London, Chapman, p. 196.

12. Cf. Maurice Bevenot, "Thesis and Hypothesis," *Theological Studies*, 15 (1954), 440–46.

13. Allocution "Ci Riesce," *Acta Apostolicae Sedis*. 45 (1953), 788–89. The harsh condemnation of religious freedom in proposition 15 of the *Syllabus of Modern Errors* of Pius IX (1864) is to be understood as a reaction to the doctrinaire rationalism and religious indifferentism of the time. This document also condemns the interference of the "lay State" in religious affairs.

14. *DH*, art. 12.

15. Art. 1.

16. Art. 2.

17. Art. 14.

18. Cf. John C. Murray, "The Declaration on Religious Freedom: Its Deeper Significance," *America*, 114 (1966), 592–93.

19. Art. 37.

20. *DH*, art. 1.

21. Art. 8.

22. Art. 3.

23. Cf. art. 2 and 9.

24. Art. 3.

25. Art. 10.

26. Art. 2.

27. Art. 3.

28. Art. 4.

29. Art. 5.

30. Art. 6.

31. Art. 3.

32. Art. 6.

33. Art. 7.

34. Art. 4.

35. Art. 8.

36. *Church Dogmatics*, Edinburgh, T. and T. Clarke, 1957, Vol. II/2, p. 57.

37. Cf. *GS*, art. 4.

38. *Morality Is for Persons*, pp. 111–12.

39. Dietrich Bonhoeffer, *Ethics*, p. 212.

40. *Responsibility in Modern Religious Ethics*, Washington, Corpus Books, 1968, p. 210.

41. No. 10. Cf. *GS*, art. 50.

42. See R. Fagley, *The Population Explosion and Christian Responsibility*, New York, Oxford University Press, 1960, p. 231.

43. *Christian Responsibility*.

44. *Ibid.*, p. 28.

45. *Ethics*, p. 234.
46. Albert R. Jonsen, *op. cit.*, p. 131.
47. *PC*, art. 14.
48. Cf. "The Structure and Basis of Moral Experience," *Irish Theological Quarterly*, 38 (1971), 3–20.
49. *Man for Himself*, London, Routledge, Kegan and Paul, 1949.
50. *Beyond the New Morality*, University of Notre Dame Press, 1974, pp. 108 ff.
51. Cf. Paul M. Quay, "God's Call and Man's Response," *Review for Religious*, 33 (1974), 1062–99.
52. *GS*, art. 43.
53. *LG*, art. 11.
54. Enda McDonagh, *Gift and Call*, p. 111.
55. *GS*, art. 50.
56. *Op. cit.*, p. 50.
57. See "Commands-Counsels: A Pauline Teaching," *Theological Studies*, 31 (1970), 275–87.
58. *The Dynamic Element in the Church*, Freiburg, Herder, 1964, p. 55.
59. Bernard Häring, *The Law of Christ*, Vol. I, p. 50.

CHAPTER XVIII

The Responsible Human Act

1. THE DETERMINANTS OF THE HUMAN ACT

Man exercises his responsibility through particular acts which express his fundamental option or the basic direction of life. The "human act" (*actus humanus*) is to be distinguished from an "act of man" (*actus hominis*). The first is an action posited with spiritual insight, with personal knowledge and free will. The second comprises all biological processes, like breathing; sensory impulses, like feeling pain; as well as spontaneous psychic reactions that precede the activity of intellect and will, like the first movements of anger and sympathy.

Only the human act is the subject of moral value, although the exercise of the human act depends to a large extent on the involuntary conditions and reactions of man. The human act is "the person in act," although it never exhausts the capacities of the self in a given instance.

The human act has a *cognitive element,* since man cannot will without knowing, even though his knowledge itself depends upon his willing. Still, it is primarily the *volitive element* that constitutes the human act. While a human value is perceived through the intellect, it is personalized through the will.

Today, the importance of *emotions,* or the affective element in moral activity, is being realized. In the past, it was frequently said that "feelings don't count." But modern psychology has revealed that feelings do count, and count a great deal. However, the primacy of the intellect and the will in moral activity should not be lost sight of. Besides, human emotions, unlike animal instincts, have a rational component. An emotional response is not just an automatic reaction to a stimulus, but is affected by one's vision of life.[1]

There are three determinants of the human act:

(1) It is, first of all, specified by its *moral object*. This is not to be understood merely in its physical or biological entity (*material object*) but as a value, inasmuch as it is perceived as somehow affecting the moral integrity of man or somehow leading to the final end (*formal object*). Thus, abortion is not merely the expulsion of a fetus, but the termination of unborn human life. Progesterone is a contraceptive when used, not to treat a pathological condition, but directly as a means of preventing conception. It is of vital importance to note carefully that what is here considered is, not the *finis operantis* (the subjective motive of the particular agent), but the *finis operis* (the objective nature of the moral action).

(2) *Circumstances* are particulars of the human act that affect the moral object as defined above. They are relevant if they increase, decrease or modify the good or evil quality of the act; e.g., if a poor man gives alms, then the action is nobler. The fact that someone is married further specifies a wrong sexual act (simple fornication becomes adultery).

(3) *Subjective motive,* or the end intended by the particular agent; e.g., alms given either out of kindness or to show off; an abortion performed to prevent the birth of a defective child or in order to save the reputation of a girl.

There are three main views regarding the relevance of these elements, corresponding to the position adopted regarding the existence of moral absolutes. According to traditional Catholic teaching, there are some moral objects that are *intrinsically evil;* i.e., such acts are always morally evil, irrespective of the circumstances and the subjective motive of the agent. Thus, induced abortion is always evil under whatever circumstances and for whatever cause it is performed. According to the exponents of the so-called new morality, the complete moral object cannot be divorced from all the circumstances and the actual motive of the agent. We have also seen that there is an intermediary view which would admit that some moral objects are intrinsically evil but in such a way that, in a conflict situation, one may at times have no other alternative but to choose them as a lesser evil.

This last position, which has been adopted in this work, does somewhat weaken the strength of "intrinsically evil." It introduces some relativity into the absolutist principle. But it does not imply a watering down of the demands of Christian morality. It is more a question of trying to safeguard all the values in a given situation as fully as possible.

If, then, intrinsically evil acts are admitted, the following would be the approach to judge the morality of an act:

a) Examine first the morality of the moral object itself. If this is evil, then there would be no way of positively justifying it by examining the circumstances and the motive. Still, it may be that the moral object is a lesser evil to be chosen regretfully and with the desire of adopting a different course of action as soon as possible.

b) If the moral object is good, circumstances can augment the moral value or goodness of the act. If it is bad, circumstances can aggravate the evil on the same level without changing its nature—for instance, hurting a weaker man; or they can also change the species of the moral act, or, rather, add another species of malice—e.g., sacrilege in an unchaste act by a religious.

c) A good motive can *never positively justify* an action that is intrinsically evil; but an evil motive can vitiate a good action—e.g., giving a present in order to seduce a girl. If the motive is gravely sinful, the whole action becomes vitiated; if it is only venially sinful, then the action becomes a venial sin if no other end is intended; if some good end is also intended, the action becomes partly good and partly bad— e.g., helping the poor out of kindness as well as vanity.

It should be noted that *Humanae Vitae* in a key passage declares: "To justify conjugal acts made intentionally infecund, one cannot invoke as valid reason the lesser evil."[2] It goes on to say that "it is not licit, even for the gravest reason, to do evil so that good may follow therefrom." But the encyclical does not say what is to be done in a real conflict of duties or when one is faced with a veritable moral dilemma. It does not resolve the problem of a perplexed conscience. However, traditional wisdom, as we have noted, does provide a principle for such an eventuality.

2. THE FUNDAMENTAL OPTION

A person-centered approach leads to the question of the fundamental option—that is, self-commitment of the person beyond individual acts. Scripture draws attention to this by emphasizing the place of the "heart" or the core of personality in the moral life (cf. Mk. 7:18–23). God looks not only at man's deeds but at his heart. He calls Israel, above all, to set right its heart, its basic direction.

The personal ego, or the unity of the self, is more than the sum of individual acts and aims. These are intermittent expressions of the ego. While individual moral acts and aims are the object of moral knowledge and volition, the human person is also conscious of himself as a subject without necessarily reflecting on himself as object. He can commit himself in freedom without realizing himself in action as an object.

Hence, besides *freedom of choice* (*libertas arbitrii*), man has a *basic* or *transcendental freedom* which, in the words of Josef Fuchs, "enables us not only to decide freely on particular acts and aims but also, by means of them, to determine ourselves totally as persons, and not merely in any particular area of behavior."[4] This is moral freedom in the highest sense.

Because the human person is by nature oriented toward others, self-realization in openness toward others is the true moral commitment of his basic freedom; withdrawal into isolation is negative self-commitment. Ultimately, basic freedom is the capacity to place oneself unreservedly as a person before God and one's fellowmen. The person's self-commitment transcends individual choices or the sum of them. "It underlies them, permeates them, and goes beyond them, without ever being actually one of them."[5]

Still this *fundamental option* must not be understood as an absolutely definitive commitment. A person can never grasp and engage the totality of himself categorically as an object. Hence, in our pilgrim state, the fundamental option is always imperfect and precarious. It constantly needs to be confirmed and strengthened. Similary, in the negative use of our basic freedom through grave sin, all the possibilities for good are not absorbed and, hence, conversion still remains possible.

Superficial inconsistencies with the basic option toward the good, in what are called venial sins, weaken the basic freedom and pave the way for a negative basic choice. On the other hand, a sinner's repeated striving toward the good prepares the ground for radical conversion of heart.

The moral worth of a choice depends more on the basic free self-disposal of the person than on the form of the particular act. This may also be expressed by saying that it is love that gives the ultimate significance to any act of virtue, since, as we have seen, the primary virtue of love is specified through other virtues. The same is true of the relationship between "sin" in the singular and "sinful acts" in the plural. In the New Testament the sin of pride, or the self-sufficient rejection of God as the source salvation, is presented as the basic sin.

The regular performance of good acts increasingly integrates the various layers of man's being with his fundamental option toward the good, so that this is strengthened. Hence, there is interdependence between basic freedom and freedom of choice.

In distinguishing acts that are fully human (*actus perfecte humani*) and those that are not (*actus imperfecte humani*), it is necessary to refer, not only to the clarity of knowledge and degree of freedom of choice, but also the activation of basic freedom. What is called "light matter" is generally presumed to be a small proof or offense against love; but it may be an occasion for the activation of basic freedom, so that the act could be "seriously" good or bad.[6]

By concentrating on external acts or on conformity to external patterns of behavior, we have too long sought a certain *moral security* instead of the *commitment of faith*. "What will people say?" or "How shall I fulfill my minimal obligations?" are often the preoccupations of many Christians. Sunday Christianity or the religion of mere observances is a parody of the true religion which Christ came to instill in our hearts.

We are too prone to judge people from their external conduct without giving sufficient thought to their possible motives or dispositions. Though we cannot fully penetrate the heart of another man, we should make due allowance for inner goodwill when we witness behavior which, unfortunately, falls short of objective standards. On the other hand, while being ever ready to trust in the goodwill of others, we should not too easily be taken in by an outwardly meticulous or sanctimonious conduct which may be a cover for selfishness or mediocrity.

In the past, there has been a tendency to atomize morality by concentrating excessively on the rectitude of individual acts (act-centered morality). Now there is a tendency to swing to the opposite extreme and minimize the importance of individual choices. But, as Josef Fuchs points out, "the basic, free self-realization of the subject always takes place in particular acts related to an object distinct from the person as a whole. The spiritual person can only attain basic free self-realization when he emerges from his spiritual unity into the physically conditioned diversity of his development in space and time to which his personal freedom of choice is directed."[7]

Since the fundamental option is expressed in particular acts, these should not be neglected. A one-sided stress on the former would lead to subjectivism and moral relativism. We must take into account the interdependence between a person's fundamental option and his individual acts. Moral acts should not be thought of in isolation from the totality of the personality. Individual acts express only inadequately the basic self-commitment. The exact fulfillment of external duties is not a guarantee of inner rectitude. It may only be a front for self-right-eousness or manifest a stifling mediocrity that is satisfied with the minimum.

There are peak moments in one's life which call for orientation of one's whole personality—for instance, marriage and religious profession. These are opportunities for basic self-disposal of the person. Still, it can happen that the basic commitment does not coincide with the exact moment of the external solemnity, but may take place on some other occasion.[8] Today the importance of *motive* and *purpose* are rightly stressed, since these flow directly from the person's self-commitment. But the objective nature of the action performed should not be ignored, since the personal call is precisely to respond to the concrete invitation of the Spirit as it generally comes to us through the demands of the situation and the norms basic to the nature of man.

The whole person is the subject of moral activity. Man is not a pure spirit imprisoned in a body or just united with the body, but is essentially an *embodied spirit* or *animated body*. Hence in the moral life, the entire being of man is involved to a greater or lesser degree. There should, therefore, be no dichotomy between one's fundamental option and one's concrete individual actions.

When a moral choice is capable of changing the subject's basic direction, it may be called a *critical response*. If it is in line with the subject's basic direction, it will confirm it in a serious way.[9] *Subcritical responses* lack this ability to change the basic direction. They may express and deepen it or prepare for a change.

Regarding the critical response, Enda McDonagh rightly warns against the conception of "some grand dramatic choice" that would not do justice to the gradual, historical, mainly implicit formation of the basic orientation. He explains the actual process thus: "The subject's basic orientation is the fruit of his historical responses, responses over a time, which together have been predominantly in one direction in such a way and to such a degree that the subject has acquired this kind of settled disposition. . . . It presupposes a certain centering of the person, his unification and polarization to the degree that one can speak of him, as a whole, as having one moral direction.''[10] Likewise, a change in the basic orientation will be the culmination of a process which may not be adverted to until it is over.

From this it is clear that it is most unrealistic to conceive of sin and grace as rapidly alternating states in a mechanical way. A good boy is suddenly taken unawares by, say, a sexual temptation and immediately falls into mortal sin. Then he runs to confession and is immediately restored to the state of grace. Such a way of thinking leads to depersonalization. Perhaps it is not entirely right to attribute the fault to the old manuals, since they defined a human act with all its concomitants. However, their overemphasis on individual isolated acts led, in practice, to this conception.

The idea of the fundamental option has very important implications for moral education. Such education should not consist merely in training people to perform good acts. Rather, it should concentrate on evoking the right basic response to the call of God and on strengthening such a response. Everything else should be seen in this context.

It should be noted that, for the non-Christian, the first right basic choice is the way to justification. It is equivalent to what is called "baptism of desire." Hence the importance of preparing non-Christian children to make such a right choice by providing the proper atmosphere to respond to the call of God.

3. THE IMPUTABILITY OF INDIRECTLY WILLED ACTS

According to classical morality, there is a vital difference between an effect that is directly willed (*voluntarium directum*) and one that is only indirectly willed (*voluntarium indirectum* or *in causa*). The latter is not intended as an end or as a means, but is only foreseen to result from a directly willed action. Thus, a motorist who takes a peg of whiskey may be directly willing a little enjoyment, but he may also foresee the danger of a traffic accident. This foreseen side effect is an indirectly willed effect of his action.

An indirectly willed evil effect is imputed to the agent whenever he *could have and should have avoided it*. This follows from the most basic moral principle: "Good is to be done, and evil to be avoided." A man is obliged to avoid the evil effects of his actions as far as possible. If he permits an evil effect which he could and should have avoided, then he is certainly responsible for it. The more certain and immediate the foreseen effect is, the greater is the imputability.

The distinction between directly and indirectly voluntary effect seems to be universally admitted in spontaneous discourse. The directly willed killing of a man is strongly condemned by all. But it is recognized that deaths will flow from dangerous sports, from running of big industries, and so on. These deaths are blamed on the promoters or managers only when reasonable precautions are not taken to avoid them. The accidental killing of noncombatants, such as children, is tolerated, while the direct killing of even a few children in order to lower the morale of the enemy is strongly condemned. At times, it is true, the distinction gets blurred in the heat of war. Thus Hiroshima, which was not an important war target, was destroyed by the first atom bomb in order to reduce casualties on the Allied side. Similarly, the Americans had recourse to "carpet bombing" of North Vietnam in the hope of bringing the war to a speedy end. But such acts met with vigorous opposition even on the American side.

From the foregoing analysis, classical moral theology has derived the *principle of the double effect*. It spells out the conditions under which an indirectly willed effect may be permissible or not imputable to the agent.

a) The *moral object may not be evil in itself*, like direct abortion or extramarital intercourse. It should be noted that the "moral object" as defined above is either good or evil, never indifferent.

b) *The good and evil effect must proceed at least equally directly from the act.* Thus, the hemorrhage in a pregnant uterus may be controlled by the use of ergot, which stops the bleeding but may also endanger the life of the fetus. Similarly, morphine administered for the purpose of relieving pain may endanger the life of the patient. This is quite different from trying to maintain the beautiful soprano voice of boys by means of castration, as was commonly done in Italy for two centuries. In other words, the immediate effect must not be solely evil; the good effect should not physically result from the evil effect. This is an explicitation of the first condition that the moral object must not be evil in itself.

c) The intention of the agent must be good; i.e., the *agent may not intend or approve of the evil effect.* It would not do to say that morphine is for relieving pain, though in fact the death of the patient is being sought. This would be a malicious subterfuge.

d) *There must be a proportionately grave reason* in order to permit the evil effect. A graver reason is required 1) the graver the evil effect, 2) the more certain it is, 3) the more proximately the action leads to the evil.

Briefly, the principle could be stated as follows: "Undertaking an action from which a good and an evil effect are foreseen is permissible if the action itself is not evil, if the bad effect is not intended, and if there is sufficiently grave reason to permit the evil effect."

This principle is justified on the score that, otherwise, life would become paralyzed, since evil effects flow from a great number of good and well-intentioned actions, against the will of the agent. Ambiguity and an element of risk are, unfortunately, part of the human condition.

It should be clear that the principle of the double effect has real validity only when one admits moral absolutes or the concept of intrinsically evil acts. If all the circumstances and the subjective intention (*finis operantis*) are included in the moral object, then there is no sense in the distinction between direct and indirect voluntary. Thus, most of the exponents of the new morality are logically led to deny the relevance of the distinction and, consequently, the validity of the principle. The only exception some of them would make would be in the matter of scandal. They frankly admit that the principle is redundant, since any object before the determination of the agent's intention can only be a physical or premoral evil and may therefore be intended for the sake of a proportionate good end. Some make minor clarifications. For instance, Richard McCormick asks: "Would it not be better to say that it is legitimate to intend a disvalue *in se sed non propter se?*" (in itself, but not for itself).[11]

There are a few who nominally retain the principle but give it a sense that is completely at variance with its original significance. Thus, Peter Knauer extends the principle even to those acts in which the good is mediated through the evil effect. The action would be legitimate, provided the good produced is commensurate with the evil through which it is attained.[12] He would apply this to extramarital intercourse, the direct killing of an innocent person, and so on.

Knauer has every right to hold his opinion regarding the existence of moral absolutes, but his extending the traditional principle to an entirely different moral stance is like "putting new wine into old wineskins." Certainly it does not contribute to clarity in moral discourse. Similarly, it is not at all helpful to speak of an "indirect effect" just because there seems to be a proportional reason. Those who deny moral absolutes would do well also to reject the validity of the principle of the double effect and, more basically, the distinction between direct and indirect voluntary. The matter is complex enough, and an inappropriate use of terms only creates more confusion.

We have noted that the distinction between direct and indirect voluntary is the keystone of traditional ethical reasoning. It has sure validity inasmuch as one accepts moral absolutes. But too mechanistic an application of the distinction may lead to strange results. For instance, in traditional medical ethics it was admitted that if there was danger of rupture in the case of a nonviable tubal pregnancy, the whole damaged tube could be removed with the fetus inside, but the tube could not first be opened and the fetus removed even if thereby the tube could be salvaged. The second procedure was supposed to be direct killing of the fetus and hence not permissible, while the first was only indirect killing and hence could be justified by applying the principle of the double effect.

However, such reasoning seems too abstract and leads to incongruous results. By removing the tube, not only would the fetus surely die, but the tube also would be lost; whereas if the fetus were shelled out, there would be a possibility of salvaging the tube. Besides, in the process of excising the tube, as soon as the blood vessels are clamped, the fetus already loses its life and, thus, the death of the fetus is in fact prior to the excision of the tube.[13]

This is one of several cases which point to the need for a certain flexibility in applying the principle of the double effect. Even a conservative ethicist like Germain Grisez admits that the manualists' handling of the principle overstressed the physical causality of the act.[14] He would maintain that when an act with two effects (one good and one evil) is posited, if no other act intervenes between the action posited and one or other of the effects, then the effects should be said to be produced with equal immediacy. In such cases, then, the good effect may be considered as the sole object of the direct intention, while the evil is considered as merely permitted. Thus, he would allow abortion to save the life of the mother, because here the removal of the fetus produces the good and the bad effect with equal immediacy. But one could not justify the commiting of adultery by a mother aiming to be released from a concentration camp in order to succor her children, because here the good effect would not be present in the act that is adulterous but in a distinct subsequent human act.

Further, the principle of the double effect should be taken together with that of choosing the lesser evil in conflict situations. Albert R. Di Janni has explained this point well. He differs from Bruno Schuller and others in affirming that such acts as homicide are more than premoral evils. They have a negative *moral* meaning. Death is clearly a nonmoral evil, but the willful causing of death should retain at least a minimal negative *moral* index. To treat it as a mere nonmoral evil would be to lean too much in the direction of situationism. He would then classify such acts "as morally intrinsically evil, but in a *weak* sense."[15] They would not be disallowed, whatever the consequences; they may become morally "tolerable" in some situations. They would then be the source of "creative regret." The distinction between direct and indirect voluntary would be morally valid because it usually generates conclusions which coincide with the conclusions generated by the more basic dignity/welfare/value distinction. Similarly, the principle of the double effect would retain its validity, but it would have to be applied with a degree of flexibility. Paul Ramsey, too, adopts a similar position.[17]

Here we may briefly deal with the cognate *principle of totality*. Originally, this was restricted to the somatic aspect of life. "Any treatment including the excision of an organ is licit if it is necessary for the saving or well-being of the whole individual organism." This was the principle justifying surgical procedures.

But a major breakthrough came with the question of organ transplants from living donors. Those who considered this licit held that it would be justified, not by the principle of totality, but by the so-called "principle of charity."[18] This was not a very accurate way of speaking, since, as we have explained, charity is the all-comprehensive value that determines the entire moral activity of man, and not merely a few isolated areas. So, gradually, it became clear that the principle of totality would have to be extended to include the total well-being of the person. Thus, for instance, the donation of an organ for transplantation could be motivated by sacrifice for another which would result in spiritual fulfillment for the donor.

Many theologians now want to give the principle of totality the widest application. For example, Bernard Häring affirms: "The main criterion is the principle of totality, not a totality of mere organic function, but a perspective of wholeness that considers the total vocation of man." He then defines this all-embracing concept as follows: "The dignity and well-being of man as a person in all his essential relationships to God, to his fellowmen and to the world around him."[19]

Expressed in this way, the principle might provide a good sense of direction. But it would become merely a formal principle. It would not determine what exactly in each matter "conduces to the dignity and well-being of man as a person in all his essential relations." It would still leave open the question whether there are some actions that necessarily violate basic human values—e.g., the direct termination of life. Thus, *Humanae Vitae* first asks: "By extending to this field the application of the so-called 'principle of totality,' could it not be admitted that the intention of a less abundant but more rationalized fecundity might transform a materially sterilizing intervention into a licit and wise control of birth?"[20] Then the encyclical itself answers: "To justify conjugal acts made intentionally infecund, one cannot invoke as valid reason . . . the fact that such acts would constitute a whole together with the fecund acts already performed or to follow later."[21] If contraception were only premoral and not intrinsically evil, then the principle of totality would apply. But whether it is so or not has to be discussed otherwise, and not by simply invoking this principle.

4.   RESPONSIBILITY FOR THE ACTIONS OF OTHERS

Our actions may have good or bad effects on the moral behavior of others. Moral problems arise especially with regard to bad effects through *scandal* and *cooperation*.

a)   *Scandal* is an action (good or bad) or an omission which induces another to evil; that is, it becomes a temptation or an occasion of sin to one's neighbor. We cannot be indifferent to the effect of our actions on others, even when we think that what we are doing is right.

St. Paul made this clear while speaking about eating meat offered to idols. One who has a strong, enlightened faith does no evil by eating such meat. "I know and am persuaded in the Lord Jesus that nothing is unclean in itself" (Rom. 14:14). However, "If your brother is being injured by what you eat, you are no longer walking in love. Do not let what you eat cause the ruin of one for whom Christ died" (v. 15). One is bound to take note of the weakness of another's conscience. That is why St. Paul admonishes those who are puffed up by their "knowledge." One who, in his weakness, thinks that eating such meat is sharing in idolatry may be induced to offend against his faith by seeing the behavior of those who are supposedly enlightened (cf. 1 Cor. 8:1–13).

On the other hand, we cannot desist from every good action just because it might scandalize some people; otherwise, life would become impossible. Hence, applying the principle of the double effect, actions that are good in themselves, but nevertheless give scandal to others, need not be omitted if the omission would entail proportionate harm or inconvenience.

This refers to simple *scandal* or *"scandal of the weak."* But *"Pharisaic scandal,"* malicious use of another's behavior in order to do evil, is simply to be ignored. Another form of Pharisaic scandal that deserves contempt consists in manifesting great pretended shock at the behavior of others.

Is it permissible to *counsel another a lesser evil* in order to prevent a greater evil? According to traditional authors, it would be licit if the person is determined to do evil in any case and the lesser evil proposed is included in the greater evil intended—e.g., ransacking a house instead of setting fire to it. It would not be licit if the evil suggested is in a quite different line or to a different person, unless this latter cannot be reasonably unwilling. Some would make a case for counselling contraception to a woman who regularly resorts to abortion and is unwilling or unable to practice natural family planning.

b)   *Cooperation* is understood as any concrete help given to another in the commission of what one judges to be immoral. Cooperation is *formal*, either 1) when one who is aiding the principal agent fully agrees with the latter's intention, or 2) when the cooperator performs, under the direction of the principal agent, an essential part of the immoral action—e.g., an assistant surgeon taking part in an abortion. Formal cooperation is never right, since it implies explicit or implicit approval of the evil or partakes of the malice of the action of the principal agent.[22]

In *material* cooperation, what the cooperator does is not in itself evil; but he recognizes that his action is used by another to do something evil. The common example is that of a nurse assisting at an illicit operation. Material cooperation is licit when there is a *proportionate reason*. In the case of the nurse, the factors to be weighed on one side would be: How bad is the operation? How frequently does she have to cooperate? How proximate is the cooperation? How necessary is it? That is, would noncooperation effectively dissuade the surgeon from performing the operation? Is there any scandal involved? Factors to be weighed on the other side would be: financial loss, especially if she is the sole support of the family; professional disability—e.g., in the matter of promotion; the interests of the patient—e.g., if, after the removal of the appendix, the surgeon goes on to perform tubal ligation; and loss of opportunity to do good by having to leave the particular medical facility. As far as possible, scandal should be removed by suitable explanation. If the cooperation could be avoided by individual or joint protest, there is an obligation to so protest.

Similar judgments should be made in other matters. The responsible person will avoid the extremes of simply getting involved in the evil actions of others, and of running away in horror from his duty just because it implies material cooperation with evil. It should also be noted that material cooperation is more permissible when the principal agent is in good faith regarding the morality of his actions.

5. THE VALUE AND LIMITS OF CASUISTRY

Casuistry was traditionally used as a powerful aid in the formation of moral judgment. It dealt with a "case" (*casus*), not a concrete situation. A "case" is a "typical situation" involving a certain determined combination of circumstances, and the "solution" is valid only to the extent that the precise combination of circumstances is verified. A "concrete situation," on the other hand, refers to that absolutely unique, nonrecurring combination of circumstances occurring in actual life.[23] Here, because of its uniqueness, prefabricated judgments cannot be made. The conscience has to grapple with the issues at stake and discern the morality of the action at the given moment, in the light of Gospel orientations and general ethical principles.

Casuistry in the past dealt mostly with the application of general moral principles, like that of the double effect, and generally concluded that such and such a *type* of action was "not sinful" or at least "not gravely sinful." Whether an action was "allowed" or "not allowed" was its main concern. It seldom discussed the way of discerning what was most in accordance with the Gospel ideal or the Christian vocation, which, after all, is the real will of God. Casuistry also took for granted that there are negative moral absolutes. It mostly examined the scope of these absolutes and their applicability to the "case" at hand, though it often went further and discussed the "pastoral" aspects of the problem.

When casuistry was overdone, it led to rationalism, legalism and minimalism, as well as excessive rigorism or astute permissiveness, according to the temperament of the people concerned. When it was used moderately, it was a helpful guide to the solution of life problems.

With the widespread denial of moral absolutes, casuistry seems to have fallen into disrepute. Still, some modern situationists, like Joseph Fletcher, have developed a new form of casuistry. His whole book on *Moral Responsibility* is a discussion of a string of cases. He repudiates the attempt to anticipate or prescribe real-life decisions in their existential particularity. He proposes many extreme cases of extramarital intercourse and the like and, rejecting any absolute prohibitions, discusses how Christian love should be at work in evaluating them. Whatever one might say about his excessive situationism, he manifests a keen sensitivity to the immediate moral values involved. He and other like-minded authors are less perceptive of the *long-range* implications of many of the actions they discuss.

It seems that there is need for combining the best elements of traditional and recent casuistry. As we have seen, moral absolutes cannot simply be rejected, and classical moral principles like that of the double effect do have a definite value. Hence, there could be a moderate role for a casuistry of right and wrong, provided it did not lead to legalism or minimalism. It should also take into account the tension aspect of morality and not neglect any of the moral values implied in the situation.

It should go on to discern the most perfect thing to do in a given situation. For instance, it is not enough to say that this is a case of direct abortion and, hence, not permissible; there is need to go further and see how best to meet the difficulty of the woman concerned.

Hence, moral casuistry must be combined with spiritual discernment. This is all the more necessary in matters like material cooperation and occasions of sin, where there are no moral absolutes.

Today, newer forms of moral training are evolving. One is the *"case method,"* which seeks, not to find a cut-and-dried solution, but to sensitize the participants to the moral values and issues involved. This, together with approaches like *role playing* and *value clarification,* is an excellent means of active participation and attitudinal change as well as a stimulus to right living. However, used exclusively, these methods may fail in building up consistent moral thinking. If, in the past, there was too much concentration on abstract principles, it is no reason to neglect clarity of mind regarding the moral life.

Notes to Chapter XVIII

1. This is very well brought out by John Powell in his book *Fully Human, Fully Alive,* Niles, Ill., Argus Communications, 1976.
2. No. 14.
3. Cf. Josef Fuchs *Human Values and Christian Morality,* Ch. 3; Eugene J. Cooper, "The Fundamental Option," *Irish Theological Quarterly,* 39 (1972), 383–92.
4. *Op. cit.,* p. 99.
5. Josef Fuchs, *op. cit.,* p. 96.
6. St. Thomas, *Summa Theologica,* Ia-Ilae, 89. 3.
7. *Op. cit.,* p. 99.
8. Cf. Jouis Monden, *Sin, Liberty and Law,* p. 36.
9. Cf. Enda McDonagh, *Gift and Call,* p. 62.
10. *Ibid.,* p. 64.
11. "Notes on Moral Theology," *Theological Studies,* 33 (1972), 75.

12. "The Hermeneutic Function of the Principle of Double Effect," *Natural Law Forum*, 12 (1967), 136–62.

13. Cf. George V. Lobo, *Current Problems in Medical Ethics*, Allahabad, St. Paul Publications, 1974, pp. 112–14.

14. Cf. *Abortion: The Myths, the Realities and the Arguments*, pp. 32–46. Cf. also Augustine Regan, "The Accidental Effect in Moral Discourse," *Studia Moralia*, 16 (1973), 99–127.

15. "Double Effect/Indirect Action," *Thomist*, 41 (1977), 363.

16. *Ibid.*, p. 372.

17. Cf. *The Patient as Person*, New Haven and London, Yale Univ. Press, 1970, pp. 144–64.

18. Cf. Gerald Kelly, *Medical Ethics*, St. Louis, The Catholic Association, 1958, p. 248.

19. *Medical Ethics*, Slough, St. Paul Publications, 1972, p. 42.

20. No. 13.

21. No. 14.

22. Some authors call participation in the evil action itself, but without explicit sharing in the evil intent, *immediate* cooperation.

23. Cf. Josef Fuchs, *Human Values and Christian Morality*, p. 41; Edouard Hamel, *Loi naturelle et Loi du Christ*, Ch. 2.

CHAPTER XIX

The Conditions for Free Response

1. THE NATURE OF FREE ACTIVITY[1]

It is a cardinal point of Christian doctrine that man is free. Unless this is admitted, man would not be responsible for his acts and, hence, would be incapable of virtue or vice; the whole edifice of morality would crumble.

The basic capacity of the will to choose freely may be called *philosophical freedom*. It may be defined thus: "Given the necessary conditions, man is capable of freely deciding whether to act or not to act, and of choosing between alternative courses of action." In other words, in every choice, the opposite course, even with great difficulty or repugnance, remains a possibility. The act of the will cannot be fully determined by any influence outside itself.

However, it must be recognized that there are limits to the actual exercise of human freedom inasmuch as it is an incarnate freedom, or freedom in a situation. It can be affected by various influences like fear, psychological and social pressures, or pathological conditions which prevent or inhibit the agent from taking the initiative in the formulation of his decisions and the execution of his actions.

Psychological freedom, then, is found to the extent that such impediments to the exercise of philosophical freedom are absent. It exists in varying degrees, according to the presence or absence of various factors in the functioning of cognition and will power.

The distinction between *conceptual* and *evaluative* knowledge is very important in understanding moral responsibility. The free decision of the will depends on the power of deliberation, the capacity to assess alternative courses of action. For this, mere conceptual (abstract, notional) knowledge is insufficient; evaluative (concrete, real) knowledge is necessary. This distinction has been clearly explained by John Henry Newman in connection with the assent of faith.

In order to be guilty of grave sin, one must actually *realize* the gravity of the action. For instance, a small child may "know" that a certain course of action is gravely sinful. But, normally, his mind will not have sufficiently developed to realize, appreciate, evaluate the gravity of the action, since he will not have matured enough to appreciate the value involved. He will not, normally, have the evaluative knowledge required for committing a grave sin. The same would be true for positing a "seriously good action," or a perfect act of virtue.

Likewise, a psychopath may exhibit a pathological inability to realize normal social obligations or to be sufficiently sensitive to the rights of others. He may be incapable of appreciating the ethical implications of his grave neglect of duty, persistent disturbance of peace, or even of revolting crimes like stabbing a child.

In the juridical field, some marriages have been declared null by the Roman Rota because of the absence of evaluative cognition. The decisions were given on the score that a person, even though otherwise intelligent, was incapable of realizing the gravity of the marriage commitment. This was admitted as far back as 1941 in a decision *coram Wynen.*[2] A series of decisions given by Felici from 1934 onward clearly distinguishes between the *cognitive faculty* and the *critical faculty.* "For a valid marriage, there is required that discretion of mind which permits the person to perceive the peculiar nature and force of the marital contract, and there is also required that strength of will which enables the person to give and receive the rights and duties of marriage."[3]

Evaluative knowledge is habitually present in the normal adult. It may be disturbed by some transitory impediment even while conceptual knowledge is present. One may be awake and aware that he is about to perform a certain action and even that the action is gravely evil, and yet he may not fully *realize* its seriousness because of some psychic stress or a particularly strong impulse of passion. Therefore, for an act to be fully responsible, the person must have evaluative knowledge, both habitually and at the moment of acting.

The human *will has no absolute control over the imagination or emotions.* Given the presence of certain stimuli, an emotional response or an impulse to do something about it follows. The will can control the voluntary seeking of the stimulus, but not directly control the ensuing feeling. It cannot, for instance, directly command the body not to feel pain or pleasure when such sensations are aroused by a stimulus. When the intellect recognizes that the pleasure is illegitimate or that the action toward which one is inclined is evil, the will can refuse to consent to the pleasure or the inner inclination, but cannot just wish away the sensation or inclination.

Even when there is evaluative knowledge of the gravely sinful nature of the external action toward which there is an urge, *the will cannot always fully control the executory powers* so as to prevent the external action from taking place. In some cases, the executory faculties may go ahead in spite of the contrary will. It is easier to admit this in the case of those suffering from a psychic abnormality. But it can also happen in the case of a normal individual when he is under especially severe psychic stress.[4] However, this should not be easily exaggerated. Pius XII repeatedly warned against a too ready presumption of instinctive dynamisms that would take away responsibility for one's actions.[5]

Could there also be a *more direct interference of the emotions on the will*? In other words, does not the psychological freedom of the will depend to some extent on healthy emotional functioning? Although it is difficult to explain it, such influence does seem to exist. This point is of great importance in the development of the emotions for a perfect moral life. It also has a bearing on determining the degree of consent to illicit pleasure. The voluntary in man does not exist apart from the involuntary sphere. In fact, it does not exist at all unless the latter has reached a certain degree of development. Therefore, it could happen that, in spite of sufficient evaluative knowledge being present, the freedom of the consent may be diminished, even substantially, due to the direct influence of the emotions upon the will.[6]

2. CLASSICAL FACTORS DIMINISHING IMPUTABILITY

a) *Ignorance.* There can be no imputability if there is no conscious advertence to the malice of an action. Hence, ignorance can diminish or take away culpability.

Ignorance is called *invincible* if it cannot be dispelled by the diligence called for by the circumstances or the importance of the matter. This completely takes away the voluntariness of the malice and, hence, its imputability also. Thus, if a person unknowingly and in good faith serves spoilt food, he is not culpable for the sickness caused.

Ignorance is *vincible* if it can be so dispelled. This does not take away culpability, as it is *voluntary in its cause* or is provoked by conscious negligence or even bad will. For instance, a priest or a physician who has willfully neglected his studies or further training cannot be excused from the evil effects that arise from his incompetent guidance. Nevertheless, vincible ignorance generally diminishes voluntariness and culpability, since actual insight at the time of acting is lacking. Usually, one does not foresee and consent to all the evil consequences of one's negligence. The greater the negligence, the greater also is the culpability. If the ignorance is *affected*—i.e., kept up deliberately in order to evade an obligation—then there is no diminishing of the guilt.

b) *Error* is false judgment or conviction. It arises from deficient education, bad company or misleading information. One is not responsible for the consequences of error made in good faith. But man is obliged to counter, as much as he can, the negative influence of forces that tend to misguide him.

c) *Inattention* refers to momentary deprivation of insight. If attention is completely lacking, there is no human act; but one is responsible to the extent that the act is voluntary in cause. Thus, one is not responsible for the damage caused in complete intoxication unless one somehow foresaw such behavior and could have checked oneself from getting drunk. Partial inattention lessens culpability to the extent that it affects the voluntariness.

d)   *Violence* is force brought to bear on someone against his will by an external agent—for instance, violence on a virtuous maiden. There is no imputability except insofar as the inner will may have consented or external resistance may have fallen short of the degree necessary and possible in the particular circumstance. While internal resistance of the will is always necessary, external resistance may not always be called for. It is required only to the extent that it is foreseen to be efficacious in preventing the action or forestalling scandal.

e)   *Fear* is mental trepidation due to an impending evil. (Anxiety is a haunting trepidation whose cause is not clear or which is disproportionate to the known cause.)

Fear as such does not take away imputability, although it generally lessens it in proportion to the intensity. Thus, for instance, the threat of torture does not by itself justify the denial of faith, nor does fear of death justify running away from the battlefield. But if the emotion of fear completely darkens the mind or paralyzes the will, there is no more imputability. The intensity of the fear depends, not only upon the stimulus, but also on the subjective state of the person. A special example of relatively grave fear is *reverential fear,* by which a person shrinks from opposing someone out of reverence or piety—e.g., a daughter regarding a marriage arranged by the parents against her will.

It is to be noted that civil and ecclesiastical law often invalidate acts that have been posited under the influence of grave fear, or they make such acts voidable at the instance of the party who has been affected. Church law invalidates marriages and religious professions entered into under the influence of grave fear unjustly caused, as well as marriage consent arising from reverential fear.

f) *Passion* (or movement of the sensitive appetite) that precedes free decision of the will diminishes imputability according to the degree of vehemence. A man is not responsible for the impulses of passion unless they are the effect of past voluntary action. He is guilty regarding an inordinate passion only to the extent that it flows from past sinful conduct and he has not done enough to overcome its influence. A passion which the will has deliberately fostered generally increases the voluntariness. Still, the actual sin committed under the spell of the passion is less grave than one committed with calm deliberation.

The passions or emotions as such should not be looked upon as mere negative or dangerous factors, for without them human existence and freedom would lack vitality and vigor. Freedom implies voluntary control over the passions. But such control cannot be accomplished by a mere defensive attitude. The passions must be directed to the good, *pressed into the service of freedom.* This is done by a process of *integration* into the total personality with its values.

Thus, the sexual impulse is not only not evil but positively good. In marriage, it must be made an expression of love. Outside the marital relationship, it must be integrated into the whole personality. There is no need to fear sexual arousal. It should not be anxiously repressed or violently suppressed, but must be calmly controlled according to a person's situation. The will must gain gradual dominion over the emotions through love.

g) A *good habit* arising from the deliberate performance of good actions augments the power of freedom for the good. Hence, education to "good conduct" should not be neglected. However, it should not be mere automatic conditioning, but a fostering of free choice for the good. The family and social environment play an important part in this process.

An *evil habit* acquired through involuntary acts diminishes culpability but calls for effort to overcome it through trust in God, self-confidence and counselling. If it is acquired through voluntary acts, it bears within itself the malice of previous sins until it is repudiated. Still, isolated evil actions committed under its influence are less culpable, since the power of freedom is diminished. But the obligation to get rid of it remains all the more.

3. THE INFLUENCE OF UNCONSCIOUS MOTIVATION

Freud has shown how the dynamic unconscious can cause compulsive behavior. Thus, he discovered that a patient's inability to drink water from a glass was referred back to the disgust experienced in childhood at seeing someone give a dog a drink from a glass. The theory of unconscious motivation may also be applied to attitudes, feelings and prejudices of normally healthy people. Thus, a student may dislike his new teacher because, unknown to him, she reminds him of a person he hated as a child. Even important decisions like choosing a marriage partner may be influenced by such a factor.

Depth psychology has, in this way, revealed how far human activity depends on the unconscious psyche and has pushed its boundary back to the earliest experiences of the child. These can leave behind lasting anxiety, inhibitions and defense reactions. The balanced tension between the instinctive impulses and the superego can be upset by permissiveness or rigidity in upbringing. Sudden shocking events may affect or even paralyze spiritual growth.

However, it would be illegitimate to conclude that almost all persons are so determined by the unconscious that their responsibility for their actions is well-nigh nonexistent. In 1952, Marc Oraison proposed the view that we must presume that, in the vast majority of cases, sexual lapses are only material sins and that hardly anyone is subjectively guilty of grave sin.[7] This is an exaggeration. The author may have meant to sympathize with the weakness of man; but such a view would remove the very basis of virtuous living through responsible human acts, and all our belief in the primacy of conscience would be illusory.

We may readily admit that there are many indeliberate phenomena, like dreams and involuntary lapses, that can be explained by psychic determinisms. Even the deliberate acts of the will may be influenced by the unconscious. But *to influence is not to compel*.[8] The dynamic unconscious is one of the factors which exert pressure on the human will without necessarily forcing it. Pius XII several times reaffirmed the principle of the normal person's responsibility for his acts. He declared: "That these psychic urges may exercise pressure on an activity does not necessarily signify that they compel it." Even in cases of mental illness, he insisted that the misdirected instincts should not be prematurely considered "as a sort of fatality."[10]

Hence, a balanced view should be adopted in this matter. The normal person is presumed to be capable of the highest virtue before God or of being guilty of grave sin. Still, allowance should be made for the functioning of unconscious psychic mechanisms that may reduce responsiblity. More positively, Juan L. Segundo suggests that "the decisive thing is to take advantage of the [unstable] situation of psychic equilibrium to enlarge and deepen our capacity for feeling and living the lives of others as neighbors. Herein lies the one and only possibility, ever limited, of defending our liberty, person and love from the inevitable doses of egotism that the law of minimum effort will inject into our every concrete act."[11]

Certain unconscious motivations are not so unconscious. Traditional ascetic literature was aware of the lack of "purity of intention" in a student of literature who reads a pornographic book, apparently for its style, but covertly for its salacious content. He knows his true motive but may not be willing to admit it to himself. He is rationalizing or, in plainer terms, deceiving himself. Hence, the automatic psychic mechanisms operating deep within the personality should not be confused with rationalizations that can be uncovered by a sincere examination of conscience, perhaps with the help of a spiritual director. When there are so-called "mixed motives," the imputability of sinful acts may be reduced, but not necessarily taken away.[12]

Responsibility for virtuous conduct may also be affected by unconscious factors in our psychic life.[13] Psychiatric literature has drawn attention to the possibility of seemingly virtuous conduct being based on unconscious influences of a far from virtuous kind. One may, for instance, think that he is practicing the virtue of penance, whereas he is actually deriving masochistic satisfaction from pain. Continence may really be the result, not of virtue, but of frigidity, revulsion or latent homosexuality. The "little way" may merely reflect an infantile attitude toward one's father. Such *pseudo-virtues* may be pathological symptoms of an underlying disorder capable of being explained in terms of neurotic character defect.

However, there is again need for caution in prematurely explaining all facility for virtuous conduct in terms of a pseudo-virtue. Besides, holiness is not impossible for a neurotic person if he tries to respond to God's love in spite of his psychic limitations. Still, it remains true that neurosis is a great handicap in spiritual progress. The pseudo-virtues often lead to self-deception and pride. The egocentrism characteristic of neurosis is far from being conducive to Christian love and generosity. Hence, when a pseudo-virtue is detected, it should be gradually rectified. When the person himself gains some insight into his condition, he should seek help to free himself from the unconscious determinism.

4. THE DIMINUTION OF FREEDOM THROUGH MASS SUGGESTION

Today, with the technological model of thinking, there is danger that man be looked upon simply as *homo faber,* a manipulator, not only of physical and biological nature, but also of his very humanity. The excesses of behaviorism are leading to the systematic manipulation of human conduct. In spite of all the talk about freedom, people are being increasingly conditioned by the dominant culture. While in dictatorial regimes this is done through overt means like threats and sanctions, in so-called free societies it is achieved more through suggestions, insinuations and all manner of subtle pressures.

We should beware, not only of conscious manipulation, but also of all forms of skilled operations that work on the unconscious and produce what Herbert Marcuse called the One-Dimensional Man. Fortunately, critical minds are developing a new awareness and sensitivity to systematic manipulation in all areas of life. There is urgent need of strengthening this movement.

Modern mass media—the press, radio, television, movies—are powerful means that contribute to the welfare of man. They can particularly foster true dialogue. But they can also be misused to achieve conformity to the values and attitudes desired from the mass by the vested interests who have an immediate profit motive or who constitute the privileged classes. We have already mentioned the illusion of freedom of the press when the majority of newspapers and magazines are controlled by a handful of people with selfish interests. Instead of the government controlling the press, it can happen that the press barons control the government and the electoral process by astute propagation of falsehood, suggestive headlines and well-contrived pictures. Truth is violated, not only by persistently propagating falsehood, but also by a clever suppression of facts. The manipulation of truth is especially pernicious in a poor country when the press is indirectly influenced by international monopolistic capitalism. Anarchists and sensationalists also have to bear their share of blame when they prevent honest dialogue by their excesses.

Entertainment may be used as an effective means of manipulation, since people approach it mostly for relaxation and "are seldom aware that a world view, or suggestion about behavior and life-style are being communicated."[14] It is a pitiable sight to see how educated people are made to adopt fashions, at times grotesque, according to the whims of a few "pace setters."

The fragmentation of modern life and massive exposure to undigested information dulls the mind and thus makes the public vulnerable to manipulation. The mind-changers have a field day when they deliberately project messages not corresponding to the realities of social existence. "Messages that intentionally create a false sense of reality and produce a consciousness that cannot comprehend or willfully reject the actual conditions of life, personal and social, are manipulative messages. When manipulation is successful, alternative social arrangements remain unconsidered."[15]

Bernard Häring calls for positive resistance to this evil. "What we need above all is education for discernment and the constant effort to detect manipulation and to check the mind-managers. We should all contribute to building up a widely held, profound and loudly articulated conviction that the manipulation of persons cannot be an instrument of rehumanization. We need clear and pure motives to communicate in mutual respect and, in the process of communication, to learn from and with all those involved.''[16] He also points out the need for genuine leadership in the process of liberation and humanization. The leaders should not attempt any kind of countermanipulation as, at times, happens in the case of religious and social reform, but promote genuine dialogue and coresponsibility.

The impersonal mass, impelled by mass propaganda, prejudice and suggestion, can be converted into a true human community only by the cultivation of personal liberty and the emancipation of the self from the delirium of the herd.

Young people, especially, need the environment of the group to find identity and security. But they must be educated to rise above group pressures and develop personhood.

Modern *advertising* techniques, which operate on the principle of ''hidden persuasion'' through working on the unconscious, pose a special problem.[17] Advertising could be a positive factor in informing the consumer and stimulating demand, and thus indirectly contribute to economic development. But it can also blunt the sense of responsible choice. ''The individual is rarely confronted at a level at which ability to reason and select has any relevance at all. In fact, much of persuasive advertising is designed to *reduce* the consumer's ability to choose rationally.''[18]

Some businessmen compare advertising and packaging to art and poetry, which deal with symbolic aspects of reality. The common purpose of both may be to persuade. However, the analogy is not entirely convincing, since the techniques of persuasion must be evaluated with respect to their social consequences. Advertising deals with symbols, but these symbols purport to be statements about concrete reality when, in fact, they are often false to reality. The inclination of the advertiser is to manipulate factual elements so that they often distort reality.

A certain amount of latitude is permissible in any mode of expression—for instance, hyperbole or evident exaggeration, which, however, must be kept within bounds. While it is justifiable to use a certain degree of persuasion, customers should not be treated as less than persons.

An advertiser can offend against human dignity by unduly using *subliminal stimuli*. It has been demonstrated that a considerable proportion of a group of people can be led to buy a product by flashing signs for a fraction of a second during the running of a conventional film. This will not be visible to the conscious sense, but will have its effect on the unconscious. There is also the more common device of using subtle allusions which escape the conscious mind but prove effective in persuading.

Häring points out that "advertising not only influences the purchasing of certain things but also creates a whole consumer mentality, creating new needs—especially artificial ones—and distorting in the hearts of many people their scale of values."[19] Poor people are often led to spend their meagre income on relatively unimportant products to the neglect of basic needs like food. The middle class are constantly induced to keep up with the Joneses by acquiring goods which they can ill afford. Through methods like hire-purchase, they are constantly saddled with debts. The worth of a person is made to depend upon what he buys or what he wears or what brand of cigarettes he smokes.[20]

Mass advertising tends to stereotype the capacity for emotional response and, thus, gradually lowers the level of personality. By constant association with a brand name, it leads to the devaluation of femininity and sexual love. Gradually the impression is created that woman is only an object to be used. By inducing youth to increase their sex appeal through use of cosmetics, sex is reduced to the level of an article in consumer society. To exploit sex for the sake of cheap gain is to debase this noble function, although to some extent feminine charm can add to the grace of life. Vulgar displays of nudity exploit femininity and treat woman as a thing. Take an advertisement for a soft drink: not only are the taste buds tickled by the color and sparkle of the liquid, but the bottle is put in the hands of a luscious, half-naked girl, so that the image of the product is associated with sexual satisfaction.

We may also remark that certain propaganda stunts to get maximum participation in church services may not conduce to real religious growth. There is need of avoiding manipulation in mass religious conventions and charismatic sessions.

It is vital for the fostering of genuine democracy to note that advertisers can manipulate the press by giving or withholding contributions according to the degree of editorial conformity to their narrow interests. Today, no mass-circulation paper can long survive without the patronage of advertisers. Even in the absence of open coercion, an editor will hesitate to print an unfavorable story about a company that contributes large sums by supplying ads.

———○———

Notes to Chapter XIX

1. Cf. Henri Widart, "Reflections on the Nature of Free Activity," *Psychology, Morality and Education,* ed. by Fernand Van Steenberghen, London, Burns and Oates, 1958, Ch. 2; Seymour Spencer, *The Good That I Would,* London, Darton, Longman and Todd, 1967; John C. Ford and Gerald Kelly, *Contemporary Moral Theology,* Westminster, Md., Newman, 1958, Vol. I, Ch. 10 and 11; Joseph S. Duhamel, "Moral and Psychological Aspects of Freedom," *Thought,* 35 (1960), 170–203; Rudolf Allers, "Irresistible Impulses: A Question of Moral Theology," *American Ecclesiastical Review,* 100 (1939), 208–19.
2. *Decisiones S. R. Rotae,* Vol. 33, pp. 145–56.
3. *Decisiones S. R. Rotae,* Vol. 48, p. 468.
4. Cf. John C. Ford and Gerald Kelly, *op. cit.,* 228.
5. Radio message of 23 March, 1952, On Right Formation of Christian Conscience in Youth, *Acta Apostolicae Sedis,* 44 (1952), 270–78; allocution of 13 April, 1953, to psychotherapists, *ibid.,* 45 (1953), 278–86.
6. Cf. Joseph S. Duhamel, *art. cit.,* pp. 190–92.
7. *Vie chrétienne et problèmes de la sexualité,* Paris, Lethielleux.
8. Cf. Joseph Donceel, "Second Thoughts on Freud," *Thought,* 24 (1949), 466–84; John C. Ford and Gerald Kelly, *op. cit.,* pp. 180–201; Roland Dalbiez, *Psychoanalytic Method of Freud,* New York, Longmans, 1948, Vol. II, 296–98.
9. Allocution of 13 April, 1953. *Acta Apostolicae Sedis,* 45 (1953), 279.
10. *Ibid.*

11. *Grace and the Human Community,* New York, Maryknoll, 1973, p. 147.

12. John C. Ford and Gerald Kelly, *op. cit.* pp. 191–94; E. Tesson, "Moral Conscience and Psychiatry," *New Problems in Medical Ethics,* ed. by Peter Flood, Westminster, Md., 1951 Newman, Vol. III, pp. 85–102; Charles H. Nodet, "Psychoanalysis and Morality," *ibid.,* pp. 103–17; F. Pasche, "Psychoanalysis and Moral Conscience," *ibid.* pp. 118–21.

13. Cf. Heinz O. Luthe, "What is Manipulation?", *Concilium,* 5 (1971), No. 7, 12–26.

14. Bernard Häring, *Manipulation,* Slough, St. Paul Publication, 1975, p. 21.

15. Herbert I. Schiller, *The Mind Changers,* Boston, Beacon Press, 1973, p. 1.

16. *Op. cit.,* p. 24.

17. Cf. Vance Packard, *The Hidden Persuaders,* New York, McKay, 1957.

18. James Halloran, "The Dangers of Advertising," *Doctrine and Life,* 12 (1962), 427–28.

19. *Op. cit.,* p. 25.

20. Cf. Thomas McMahon, "Manipulation and Consumer Goods," *Concilium,* 5 (1971), No. 7, 88–96.

CHAPTER XX

Sin: Negative Response to the Call of God

1. WHATEVER BECAME OF SIN?

Sin has had a bad press in recent times. There are several reasons why the sense of sin has been lessened in the modern world.[1]

a)   First of all, there is a reaction against past overemphasis on sin.

b)   Then there is the reaction against a legalistic, formalistic and juridical notion of morality and sin, against a focus on precise measurements regarding both the matter of sin and degree of guilt. "Is it allowed?" "Is it a mortal sin?"—such have often been the common preoccupations. People were provided with what looked like a sin-grid, a precise set of categories of failings for use in examining their conscience or preparing for confession. This seems artificial to many today. They protest against understanding confession as a private guilt-shedding process with little reference to social responsibility.

c)   People now are questioning the overemphasis on sins relating to sex and the concomitant negative view of sex. This is weakening the very notion of sin.

d)   The current stress on personal conscience, together with a false identification of this reality with "doing as I like," has taken away the very possibility of sin.

e)   A waning sense of God in certain quarters has brought about a correspondingly waning sense of sin.

f)   An unrealistically optimistic view of evolution and human progress would not admit of sin in man. Likewise, if all evil is viewed as an essential dimension of the evolutionary process, then sin as moral evil does not make sense.

g)   There is some confusion between irrational guilt feelings, which need to be shrugged off, and real moral guilt, which needs to be atoned for.

h)   Overemphasis on collective responsibility for evil structures in the world seems to leave little room for personal guilt. Similarly, too much stress on psychic determinisms minimizes moral responsibility.

However, sin cannot be just wished away. An eminent psychologist, Karl Menninger, in his thought-provoking book *Whatever Became of Sin?*,[2] while acknowledging the wide variety of factors that can lessen human freedom—like heredity, environment, instinctual drives and subconscious motivation—insists that there is still such a thing as moral responsibility and that the world would be a healthier place if we showed more concern for repentance and conversion from sin.

Throughout the Bible, we see sin as a mysterious reality at work in the world, a dark power that can be overcome only by God Himself. It is not restricted to religious factors. It extends to all forms of selfishness, deceit and exploitation.

Theologically, we cannot understand the history of God's love for mankind unless we see it as the love of the Creator for creatures who reject His love. "God shows his love for us in that while we were yet sinners Christ died for us" (Rom. 5:8). If someone kills a child, and the child's parents forgive him so deeply as to receive him into their friendship, he cannot presume on that friendship, but must realize he is a forgiven person. Even our faith in the resurrection will have little bearing on the reality of our lives unless we consider our continual resistance to the power of the risen Lord.

The Gospels make it clear that, concretely, Christ came into the world "to give knowledge of salvation to his people in the forgiveness of their sins" (Lk. 1:77). The angel explains the significance of the holy name of Jesus by saying: "You shall call his name Jesus, for he will save his people from their sins" (Mt. 1:21).

It is also striking that sin is never spoken of in the Bible except in relation to salvation. No sooner does Genesis speak of the fall of man than it holds out the hope of redemption, of the triumph of the "woman's seed" over the "serpent's seed." The Gospels speak of sin in terms of forgiveness by Jesus, who manifests the patience and mercy of God regarding sinners.

Thus, divine revelation and reflection on the human condition call for an admission of sin in the world. However, we must go beyond the old mechanistic and legalistic idea of sin.

2. SIN IN THE BIBLE[3]

According to Genesis, man is called to a free dialogue with God, an intimate converse "in the cool of the evening." But the serpent tempts him to a monologue, an urge to be satisfied with the echo of his selfish voice. "The primeval history of man is presented from the point of view of his original relationship to God as it breaks down in dramatic circumstances."[4]

The sin of Adam and Eve is not only the "original"but also the *typical* infidelity of mankind. It is what happens, not just to the first man, but to "Everyman." It is the pursuit of an inordinate aspiration (*hybris*) toward false moral autonomy. Wanting "to be like God, knowing good and evil" (Gen. 3:5) does not mean merely wishing to distinguish good and evil; rather, it is a proud claim to determine for oneself what is good and what is evil, without reference to the divine will. This is an inadmissible self-assertion of man against the Creator, a rebellion against God's right to be the sovereign master. Man defies God by abandoning his status as creature, by refusing to depend upon Him who gave him existence.

There are two prominent trees in the garden of Eden: the tree of the knowledge of good and evil and the tree of life (2:9). Man had time, according to the mythical Genesis account, only to pluck and eat from the first. Before he could eat of the tree of life, he was driven out of the garden.

Genesis describes sin as the breaking of a personal relationship with God.[5] Sin severs the relationship not only of dependence but also of friendship. The break in this personal relationship with God introduces a disharmony in human relationships. The attempt at self-fulfillment alienates Adam and Eve from each other. They yearn for each other while at the same time seeking to dominate each other. Whereas, before the fall, Adam saw Eve as a supreme gift from God, he now despises her as "that woman whom you gave." Having failed to supersede God, Adam and Eve experience weakness and insecurity. They are shamed by their exposure to each other as betrayers of God and, thus, potential betrayers of each other.

Man was called to share in God's dominion over creation. But the expulsion from the garden consequent on sin symbolizes man's loss of dominion over the forces of nature and heralds his subjection to their ravages.

The story of Cain shows that separation from God gives rise to separation from other men. Cain is the fugitive who flees from God, from his fellowmen and ultimately from himself. To be a sinner is truly to be a "vagabond," as Nod, the name of the place to which Cain fled, signifies (4:16).

In the account of the tower of Babel (Gen. 11:1–9), the sin of arrogance leads to a catastrophe. The common effort at usurping the sovereignty of God leads to confusion and alienation.

The same theme is developed by the prophets of the exile. Is. 3:21 describes the fall of the king of Babylon consequent upon his pride. Likewise, Ez. 28:1–19 portrays the downfall of the proud king of Tyre, who considered himself a god.

In the Book of Daniel there is an attack on the *hybris* of pagan kings. The great king Nebuchadnezzar, who set up a golden image of himself to be worshipped by his subjects, is brought low and compelled to honor the Most High. Antiochus Epiphanes, the little "horn" who raises himself up against God, is despoiled of his kingdom (7:24–27).

The gravity of sin assumes its full dimension only when placed in the context of the covenant between God and man, which is likened to the conjugal union. God has "known" Israel with an elective love (Amos 3:2; Hos. 13:5); so Israel must "know" Him. There is intimacy and the mutual dialogue of love. Because of God's special choice, they must be His people and are expected to act as such. Sin is the *rupture of the covenant bond,* the violation of the spousal relationship (Hos. 2; Jer. 3:1–5, 19–25; 4:1–4; Ez. 16:23–26). It is the rejection of a vocation, rebellion against the Lord who chose Israel as a son (cf. Is. 1:2–4).

Sin is "hatred" toward Yahweh (cf. Ex. 20:5; Deut. 3:9). It is the rebellion of a child against the goodness of a most loving father. In the episode of the golden calf (Ex. 32), Israel preferred a god within reach, a god whose anger could be appeased by sacrifices, a god who could be brought to man's way of thinking, a god who does not make ethical demands. The constant temptation of Israel is the refusal to believe wholeheartedly in Yahweh and surrender to Him.

While the alliance constitutes Israel as a unified people before God, sin "disassembles" the people of God. To "know" God is really to love one's neighbor, to take up the cause of the poor and the underprivileged. Sin disrupts the unity of the people. The prophets are extremely blunt in denouncing the cruelty of the war leaders, the luxury of the privileged classes, lying and treachery (cf. especially Amos, Hosea and Jer. 22:13–16).

The vocabulary used to describe sin is very concrete, mostly borrowed from human relationships.[6] The word most frequently used is *hata* (*hamartia* in the Septuagint). Literally, it means "to miss the mark." Morally, it denotes "to be led astray." It signifies, not simply a mistake in judgment, but a failure to reach the goal. In the context of the covenant, it means failing toward God. It is more than a transgression of a law; it is a break in the covenant relationship, in the pact of love initiated by God Himself. Note the poignant phrase in Ps. 15:4: "Against thee only have I sinned." Thus, sin is regarded as "folly." The sinner becomes foolish by his sin (cf. Jer. 8:8–9).

Awon refers to the interior state of the guilty man. It denotes the disorder which sin causes in the life of man. Sin is a great weight which continuously bears down on the sinner. Hence, the Hebrews attempted to transfer the burden of guilt onto a scapegoat (cf. Lev. 26:22).

Pesha signifies the revolt of the people against Yahweh and the consequent break in the alliance.

In the Old Testament, there is a legal as well as a spiritual aspect of sin. There are traces of a primitive notion of God, an autocratic, demanding, rewarding and punishing God, apparently more interested in laws and decrees than in people. There are catalogues of concrete actions that are transgressions. This conception is influenced by the primitive, premoral notion of "impurity." Note, for instance, the notion of "sins of ignorance" (Job 1:5; Lev. 4:2,27), of "hidden sins" (Ps. 90:8). Uzzah becomes guilty through a well-intentioned act (2 Sam. 6:6–8), giving the impression that sin is constituted by the material act. Such a conception leads to legalism. All who did not or could not observe the details of the law became sinners.

However, especially in the prophets, sin is presented as an injury done to the heart of Yahweh. It appears essentially as a violation of personal relationships. Even when Ezekiel and others speak about the "stain" of sin, the expression must be understood in the context of the poignant tragedy of sin, and not as a mere material blot.

Sin follows upon original innocence; i.e., the human condition is not evil in itself. Man's native weakness was a favorable ground for sin. Still, man freely succumbs to the serpent's wiles. The Bible, as opposed to much other religious literature, recognizes the devil's incitement as always external to the core of personality.

Sin brings with it the "wrath" of God (cf. Ps. 74:1), which means that, because of the alienation from God, sin produces loneliness and insecurity. Thus, sin and unhappiness go together. Sin is revealed through divine punishment, whether collective or individual (cf. 2 Kgs. 21:24). But punishment is meant to lead to conversion, which brings happiness.

One sin begets another. It is like a rust that eats into a person's soul and remains engraved in the sinner's heart. Sin, therefore, infects the heart of man. It creates a spiritual attitude which, in the course of generations, becomes connatural to man (cf. Jer. 17:1; 13:23). It is at times described as "hardening of the heart," a dulling of the moral sense, so that there is less and less reluctance to sin.

Sin ultimately leads to "death," both spiritual and physical. Death was not part of the original plan of God for man. "For God created man for incorruption, and made him in the image of his own eternity; but through the devil's envy death entered the world" (Wis. 2:23–24). By refusing to surrender to the Author of life in the very act of affirming himself to be the ultimate source of good and evil, man was cutting himself off from the very source of life. In this way, death entered into the world.

We may sum up the Old Testament teaching on sin in the words of Albert Gelin: "The Old Testament constitutes a massive denunciation of sin, which is seen as an offence against God. The doctrine of sin is not complete here, however; the New Testament alone, by placing before us God incarnate and crucified, will fully reveal the final logic of grace offered and sin committed. But already the Old Testament, with some gropings and hesitations, has placed before us the essential: on the supernatural level, sin is the refusal of God; on the level of conscience, it is the perversion of man. When a man refuses God, it is his own truth he refuses as well."[7]

The major theme of Jesus' message is: "Repent [*metanoeite, change your heart*], for the kingdom of God is at hand" (Mt. 4:17).[8] The coming of the Kingdom carries with it the urgent call to repentance and the offer of pardon through the Messiah. Due to the hostility shown to His teaching, Jesus refers to hardness of heart. The opposition of evil forces will culminate in the death of Christ, which, however, will be a victory over sin and death.

The call to discipleship implies conversion of heart. "The time is fulfilled, and the kingdom of God is at hand; repent and believe in the gospel" (Mk. 1:15). While sin implies resistance to the coming of the Kingdom in one's life, victory over sin is to be obtained through total adherence to the cause of the Kingdom that comes in the person of Jesus.

In the parables of mercy (cf. Lk. 15; Mt. 18:12–14, etc.), Jesus reveals the loving mercy of the Father. Sin itself is represented as a son's wandering from the father's home. Jesus Himself receives sinners with great love and delicacy at the risk of scandalizing the "righteous." "I am come not to call the righteous, but sinners" (Mt. 9:13). He makes Himself the suffering servant and sheds His blood, "the blood of the covenant, which is poured out for many for the forgiveness of sin" (Mt. 26:28).

Jesus calls us beyond the letter of the law to its spirit—that is, to its profound intention. Hence, sin is whatever goes against the call of God. True justice is in the inner man; so also is sin. "What comes out of a man is what defiles a man. For from within, out of the heart of man, come evil thoughts . . ." (Mk. 7:20–23).

Lack of belief is the most radical sin. "Every sin will be forgiven, but the blasphemy against the Spirit will not be forgiven" (Mt. 12:31; cf. Mk. 3:28–30). The "capital" sin is the refusal to recognize the power of God in Christ and to confess Him as the Messiah (cf. Jn. 8:24). Jesus condemns the hypocrisy, pride and obduracy of the Pharisees (Mt. 23). Exclusion from the Kingdom is the lot of the finally obdurate. But it is not for the disciple to anticipate the judgment (Lk. 9:54–56).

Jesus discerns in the moral and spiritual distress of the sinner a radical humility which opens him to the divine call to conversion. Through such humility, sinners become true clients of the Kingdom.

The Synoptics speak mostly of sin in the plural. The common meaning of the word *sin* as "transgression of the divine command" is accepted. But the Synoptics witness to how Jesus concerns Himself with leading the people away from a merely juridical, external understanding of sin. He points to the "heart" as the seat of the moral life. He makes it clear that it would be a great misfortune if sinners shut themselves off from God's loving design of salvation.

Forgiveness of sin was seen as an essential element of salvation by the primitive Church. In the apostolic preaching, the *kerygma* terminates in the call to conversion (cf. Acts 2:38; 3:19; 17:30; 26:20). Conversion implies radical renouncement, or the total gift of self, for the cause of the Kingdom. This should be manifested in moral integrity—the avoidance of sin—although it should not be forgotten that the struggle against sin is more a question of cooperating with grace than of human effort.

The social aspect of sin and repentance was strongly stressed in the apostolic community. The emphasis on the heart does not obscure the communitarian dimension of the Christian's vocation or failure to respond to it.

Paul and John see sin in close connection with Christ's saving activity. They speak mostly of "sin" in the singular. Behind individual sinful acts there stands a situation of evil that impels one toward particular sinful deeds.

Paul uses the sinful condition of Jews and pagans before Christ as the backdrop of his teaching on redemption through Christ. For him, sin is something universal, something in which every human being is involved.

The time before the Mosaic covenant is dominated by the sin of Adam. "As sin came into the world through one man and death through sin, and so death spread to all men because all men sinned—sin indeed was in the world before the law was given" (Rom. 5:12–13).

For the Jew, the law is good (Rom. 7:16), but, through it, man becomes aware of sin (7:7). "Sin, finding opportunity in the commandment, wrought in me all kinds of covetousness" (7:8). One of the functions of the law is to uncover sin (Gal. 3:19) by revealing the sinfulness of evil acts. So, "the law brings wrath" (Rom. 4:15), but the ultimate purpose is redemption.

The situation of the pagan is similar. He is formally guilty inasmuch as the moral law is written on his heart (cf. Rom. 2:14–15). His unfortunte state is described in Rom. 1.

The sinful acts of man are the expression of a force that is hostile to God and His Kingdom. "All men, both Jews and Greeks, are under the power of sin" (Rom. 3:9). Because of this, man is "sold under sin" (Rom. 7:14) and becomes prisoner of the "law of sin" (8:2). Paul stresses the tyranny of sin, from which Christ alone can save (7:2–25). Still, man cannot escape the personal responsibility for yielding to his sinful tendencies or not opening himself to the grace of Christ.

Christ has triumphed over sin. The death of Christ has radically changed the sinful state of humanity. We have been basically liberated from sin (Rom. 6:18–22). "The law of the Spirit of life in Christ Jesus has set us free from the law of sin and death" (8:2). Christ's victory over sin is renewed in each Christian. "How can we who died to sin still live in it? . . . We know that our old self was crucified with him so that the sinful body might be destroyed, and we might no longer be enslaved to sin" (Rom. 6:2–6).

In Paul, two lines of thought run together: on the one hand, the conviction that man is master of his decisions and, therefore, is responsible for them; and, on the other hand, the fact that the sinful deeds of the individual share a mysterious solidarity in the sinful situation of mankind. While sin tries to lord it over us like a despot and penetrates right into us, we are still free. We can resist and overcome sin by the indwelling Spirit of Christ taking possession of us.

Sin introduces a division within the self. "For I do not do the good I want, but the evil I do not want is what I do" (Rom. 7:19). Sin hurts the whole body of believers just as a wound in one part of the physical body hurts the whole body. "If one member suffers, all suffer together" (1 Cor. 12:26).

Sin implies an alienation from God which Paul calls "the law of flesh."[10] Hence, the moral life of a Christian implies a struggle against sin. But the spiritual combat must be understood in the context of a positive life of holiness, of bringing forth the "fruits of the Spirit" (cf. Gal. 5:16–26).

John speaks of Christ as one who came "to take away the sin of the world" (1:29). Sin is lawlessness, unrighteousness. It is loving darkness rather than the light. "The light has come into the world, and men loved darkness rather than light, because their deeds were evil" (3:19). John calls sin "fellowship with darkness" (1 Jn. 1:6).[11]

In John, too, we see behind sinful acts a mysterious reality that engenders them, a power which is hostile to God and His reign, and from which only the Son of God can free us. The whole world enveloped in darkness stands in opposition to the light of Christ.

The sinner hates the light "lest his deeds should be exposed" (3:20). Such blindness can be explained only by the perverse influence of Satan, "the prince of the world" (12:31). Sin is really slavery to the devil (8:24), being "of the devil" (1 Jn. 3:8), while "no one born of God commits sin, for God's nature abides in him" (3:9). Unbelief, shutting oneself to the light of God, is sin in its basic dimension.

Christ triumphs over "the sin of the world" and "the prince of the world" because He is one with the Father (Jn. 10:30). The disciple is made a sharer in His victory. "No one born of God commits sin, for God's nature abides in him" (1 Jn. 3:9).

3. THE NATURE OF SIN[12]

a)   At the *premoral* or *instinctual level,* sin consists of a *material transgression* of some socially imposed taboo. The ensuing guilt feeling is irrational. It is the anxiety of being threatened by a mysterious power.

Although a certain amount of automatic control derived from early childhood is part of normal life, this should not be allowed to develop too rigidly; and, in any case, there is need for going beyond this level. Otherwise, there will be infantile fixations or, when the guilt feelings become too powerful, morbid scrupulosity.

b)   On the merely *ethical (rational) level,* sin becomes the deliberate *violation of a law.* In fact, for centuries, a commonly accepted definition of sin has been that of St. Augustine: "To sin is to oppose oneself, by word, by desire or by action, to the Eternal Law."[13]

This conception has the advantage of being somewhat theocentric and including the aspect of freedom. But it holds the danger of conceiving of God as a human lawgiver, and of His will as an extrinsic imposition. As J. Regnier notes, "Man is not made for obeying under pain of death a 'potentate who gives orders.'"[14]

When this perspective of violation of the law is overstressed or when the interpersonal dimension of the law is forgotten, we have legalism, which pays attention only to the exterior act and neglects the inner spirit. Jesus strongly condemned the attitude of the Pharisees: "Woe to you hypocrites! for you cleanse the outside of the cup and of the plate, but inside they are full of extortion and rapacity" (Mt. 23:25).

If sin is understood primarily as a violation of the law, penance will appear as restoring the balance by inflicting compensatory or vindictive punishment on oneself, and confession as merely the fulfillment of a legal requirement. There is danger of gradually regressing to the previous instinctual level, confession then becoming a quasi-magical device by which the debit account one has accumulated before God is cleared up.

c) Hence, the *religious aspect* of sin must be brought out more explicitly. Sin then becomes a *failure in love,* a rejection of the personal call of God.

It must be clearly understood that the law of God is not something imposed from without (by a God who is a survival of the lords of the feudal era, whose commands, according to Karl Marx, alienated man by keeping him in slavery). The law of God is identical with the demands which His creation and salvation make upon us.

On this level, repentance is the awareness of infidelity toward love, together with a confident appeal to the mercy of God. It is essentially a personal dialogue with God, who gratuitously offers His forgiveness— or, rather, who has fore-given us in Christ.

Sin is an internal disorder, a *refusal to grow.* It hinders the progressive liberation of man from the slavery of the flesh in the Pauline sense. "The 'material' man, who has deliberately shut himself up in the prison of his own egoism, will, naturally, be incapable of this expansion, exactly as a habitual drunkard or debauchee becomes completely incapable of savoring the real intellectual and spiritual joys of life."[15] While the sinner has the illusion of freedom, he is in fact being enslaved; his authentic self is being destroyed. This point needs to be particularly brought home to modern man.

Thus, sin is not so much the violation of an abstract law, something like the categorical imperative of Kantian morality, as the *refusal to commit oneself to the process of salvation history.* As the divine normally comes to us in interpersonal relations with our fellowmen, an offense against God implies, directly or indirectly, an *offense against human and Christian brotherhood.* Christians would do well to ponder Trotsky's famous complaint against too individualistic a conception of sin: "Lenin and I turned to Christianity to seek the solution to the ills of humanity, but we found there only a prophylactic for the salvation of the individual, an art of abstaining from sin."

It would be helpful at this stage to discuss the psychology of sin. A certain Pelagian tendency, represented by humanists and liberal Protestants, and influenced by an overly optimistic view of human nature, considers all human acts as proceeding from unhindered freedom. The Reformers, on the contrary, stressed man's inherited propensity to sin— a propensity that would make actual sin almost a necessity. Luther, for instance, spoke of the "bondage of the will to sin." Augustine's formulation of the doctrine of original sin also seems to have influenced this view.

Liberalism rightly emphasizes man's capacity for self-determination, but it fails to take into consideration the weight of historical forces and social pressures on the individual. Depth psychology has shown how pervasive and potent is the influence of the milieu on human lives. Older generations were aware of the difficulty of mastering evil habits and impulses.

The individual is certainly placed under circumstances that allure him to sin from the earliest years of his moral development. However, this does not make sin inevitable. The capacity to overcome self-centeredness is present in him. By the grace of God, he can resist the movements of selfish passions or even lift himself out of the mire of sin if he has sunk into it. Therefore, it is necessary to maintain a balance between the capacity for self-determination and the inclination to sin.

Still, the question remains: If the will necessarily tends to its object— namely, the good—how can anyone choose evil? The sinner does not seek evil for its own sake. To say that sin is pure hatred or pure negation of love is an oversimplification. What the sinner does is to seek an evil under the guise of a good. If he thought it was the only good in the context, there would be no sin; at the most, it would be an error. But, often, a person is confronted with two goods: one apprehended as the real good, and the other as a partial good but looking more attractive. Sin consists in deliberately choosing the latter, in not resisting certain forms of covetousness despite the awareness that they are disordered.

The real good is somehow apprehended as submission to the will of God. But the temptation is to seek a good independent of God, so that to sin is to attempt to find fulfillment in a totally autonomous way. Even those who seemingly reject the notion of God still, in some way, apprehend a *good that is absolute*. If they reject this good, then they are in effect rejecting God, so that real sin is possible also for so-called atheists. In fact, even in a believer, the revolt against God is normally implicit, since the sinner does not want to lose God, who is the Sovereign Good, but turns inordinately to a limited good. Thus, faith is rejected through a false desire for self-sufficiency. The refusal of God takes place in the sphere, not so much of conscious knowledge, as of transcendental self-awareness. But there are objective criteria (or "conjectures," according to St. Thomas).[16]

It is the duty of every man to realize himself in freedom during his earthly pilgrimage. As long as he is not yet in full possession of his transcendent destiny, he can withdraw himself from the origin and support of his being. He can cease to will what, in his basic nature, he always desires. He can regard the true good as not good for him and can make absolute an illusory good, even while he knows in his heart of hearts that it can never absolutely satisfy him.

Love of self is a natural thing. But to sin is *to love oneself inordinately*—i.e., without being open to God and to one's fellowmen. In the full light of Christian revelation, we know that God comes to us as the source and goal of our freedom. Sin, then, involves not merely closing oneself against one's true destiny but rejecting the gracious offer of God. We refuse our true fulfillment in God and try to find it in our poor ego, when all the time God is calling us to intimacy with Himself.

Therefore, as Karl Rahner aptly puts it, even sin "is always a real piece of existential realization, of real self-fulfillment, a part of the way toward the real good (however the imagination baulks at this). One should say that the deeper and the more radical sin is, the more the sinner involves and achieves his own person in this, and the more he must realize (even though in a radically false direction) the possibility of his own existence."[17] It would seem that a positive and efficacious effort at conversion should include a *realization of the value the sinner has been seeking* so far the wrong way. Now, he should be helped to seek it the right way. "Change of heart" does not mean rejecting the value, but trying to achieve it in the proper way. This opens up a new perspective in pastoral counselling.

The spritual element in man is destined to rule over the bodily element, to order the natural inclinations toward their proper end. Sin is failure to dispel one's ignorance or to conquer one's weakness, so that the instincts come to dominate the spirit. In a more biblical perspective, to sin is *to allow the "flesh" to dominate the "spirit."*

Thus, sin can always be reduced to one of two factors: a) *pride*— i.e., refusing to be subject to God and not desiring to receive one's perfection from Him; or b) *"sensuality"*—i.e., not trying to permeate the body by the Spirit. This latter could be reduced to the former.

Ultimately, the cause of sin is the *limitation of man* in his present situation, in which he does not apprehend the Sovereign Good perfectly, but only in a fragmentary way. Sinfulness arises from man's defectibility and is aggravated by the sinful atmosphere and the inclination to sin with which he is born. But sin should not be identified with such human defectibility, since it presupposes *a free act.*

For a right understanding of sin, it is very important to distinguish between *moral guilt* and *psychological guilt feelings.* The first is the condition of one who has freely chosen to refuse to love God and neighbor, whatever the degree of feeling accompanying his refusal. Moral guilt is removed by repentance and divine forgiveness.

Psychic guilt is essentially irrational and is to be traced to the uncritical and infantile acceptance of norms from external sources, especially during early childhood. It is the product of the "unconscious conscience." The feeling of guilt when I am not morally guilty is misplaced and is damaging to the psyche. But when I am morally responsible for an evil choice, some guilt feeling is appropriate and beneficial, but it should not be disproportionate. A person who has committed sin but experiences no feeling at all may have hardened his heart. Preachers who want to bring their congregations to the experience of conversion tend to arouse in them a strong sense of guilt. This may be beneficial up to a point, as a first step in the process of self-realization and conversion; but it should not be done excessively, lest it arouse morbid guilt feelings.

Psychic guilt can be transferred from one condition to another. The self-condemnation I feel in connection with some trivial matter may be due to some deeper cause, which I am incapable of admitting even to myself. It may also be experienced as a sense of failure or inadequacy, of inability to live up to the standards one imposes on oneself—for instance, some ideal of competence or success which one irrationally feels obliged to attain. The remedy is self-acceptance.

Psychic guilt may respond to psychotherapy. The therapist's task is to help the sufferer recognize the hidden cause of his feelings and so learn to react to them appropriately. Thus, psychotherapy can free man from many undesirable repressions and obsessions that block freedom. Thereby, the conscious self can be expanded.

Freud, Hesnard and some other psychoanalysts have created confusion by wrongly identifying sin with irrational and unconscious taboos whose devastating consequences they observed in their patients. The true notion of sin has nothing in common with corrosive guilt feelings. As Ignace Lepp observes: "There does exist a morbid universe of failure, and psychotherapists together with moralists ought to fight against it. But not every sense of failure is morbid. When I feel guilty of a particular failure with respect to the human community, there can be no question of liquidating the guilt feeling; on the contrary, I must do whatever I can to make reparation for the fault."[18] In fact, each wound of sin, if not healed by genuine sorrow and readiness to change, puts man on the road to disintegration and slavery.

Sin arises from a wrong attitude deliberately fostered or a decision freely made. Consequently, when a man does something objectively evil out of ignorance, or when his outward behavior is in conflict with the demands of morality but the inward resolution is not involved, we have what is called *material sin*. This is sin only in appearance, since the vital element of deliberation is missing. Unfortunately, many simple people judge the existence and gravity of sin only from the external happening. For instance, a man once told his friends, "Thank God that He saved me from a serious sin. I tried to steal a large amount for a whole week but didn't succeed!" Such people must be helped to realize the importance of the *formal element* in sin—namely, the deliberate refusal to answer the call of God in a given circumstance.

However, the weight of external actions (which are often expressions of the inward attitude) as well as the social consequences of merely material faults should not be neglected.

The opposite of material sin is an outward act with a seemingly good meaning, but which is deliberately chosen to disguise one's sinful internal attitude. This is *hypocrisy,* which is severely condemned in the Bible.

4. THE EFFECTS OF SIN[19]

It is not so much that God punishes sin as that *the sinful state itself becomes a punishment to the sinner.* As the Bible emphasizes, sin is the worst form of *slavery.* To be "children of wrath" (Eph. 2:3) means to suffer the consequences of rebellion or brokenness in our relationship with God and neighbor.

What is called "the state of sin" or "habitual sin," which follows upon actual sin, should not be imagined in a juridical manner. It is not a debit account which has somehow to be settled. It is, rather, alienation from God and the community.

Sin also implies alienation within the sinner. It causes loss of self-respect, frustration and disintegration. It is a severe threat to the wholeness of the personality, since it represents a radical contradiction in one's innermost being. Hence, sin is nowadays rightly called a *spiritual sickness* requiring divine healing. In this perspective, the sacrament of reconciliation becomes a sacrament of spiritual healing.

Temporal punishment, which the Council of Trent declares is not fully remitted together with the remission of grave sin,[20] is not something imposed from outside. It means that the penitent's attitude is not always fully rectified immediately. The basic good orientation regained through repentance may still be affected by the remnants of wrong peripheral attitudes. Such a state calls for further purification, which is not without pain.

Sin ultimately *leads to death*. Sin is the refusal of divine life. "By turning away from God, who can fulfill him and in whom alone others can fulfill him, the human person goes down into utter loneliness; his nature is frustrated in the deepest finality. True, in this way man does not lose his being, but he gives up its fullness and meaning, and in this sense the word 'self-destruction' applies."[21]

According to Paul, death is the consequence and punishment of sin (cf. Rom. 5:12ff). Death, in his mind, is not so much the physical separation of body and soul as "eternal death" or alienation of the whole being from God, the unique source of life. The effect of sinful actions even on physical health, through deprivation of joy and peace in the depths of the personality, is being recognized more and more today.

Grave sin implies *loss of genuine love*—both supernatural and natural, since the two cannot be separated. Man, whose true existence depends completely on the love of God, is robbed of the proper foundation of his being when he lacks this love. Man turned away from God and turned in on himself is man apart from his authentic self. Hence, sinful man is, as such, incapable of any genuine love. However, through sorrow with the help of grace, a partial return is possible even before complete reconciliation. Besides, the sinner often retains certain good moral attitudes which, nevertheless, remain restricted or interiorly limited because of his lack of charity. As a result, the inability to love brings about incapacity for integral goodness. The integration of instinctual drives and powers into the total personality becomes impossible, since this can be brought about only through love.

Sin causes *loneliness and anxiety*. As Bernard Häring writes: "As he loses the grace and peace that come from God, he becomes all the more unable to transcend himself and to establish authentic relationships with others. The sin which damages his capacity to love, to listen, to accept others and to make them happy, destroys man in his inner core."[22]

This estrangement can be seen in the effect of Adam's sin (Gen. 3), in the confusion of tongues following upon rebellion against God in the story of the tower of Babel (Gen. 9:1–9), and in many other events.

Sin introduces an element of inauthenticity in human relationships. Illusion and deceit grip man. Thus, desire in unlawful sexual intercourse (which is a false sign) ends in scorn and disgust, at least when it is actually perceived as evil.

Hell, the final consequence of sin, is that uttermost loneliness in which man is definitively estranged from God and his fellowmen. We see this in the strong imagery of the New Testament. "The door was shut" (Mt. 23:10). "Cast the servant into the outer darkness" (Mt. 25:30). "Depart from me, you accursed" (Mt. 25:41). Dostoyevsky, in *The Brothers Karamazov,* says: "Hell is nothing else than the suffering of those who are incapable of love."

Medieval man envisioned hell as an imprisonment within the fiery womb of the earth. The *Spiritual Exercises* of St. Ignatius propose the following prelude for the meditation on sin: "To see with the eyes of the imagination and to consider that my soul is imprisoned in this corruptible body, and my whole self in this vale, as if it were in exile among brute beasts."[23] This picture gives an idea of the loneliness and degradation than sin brings.

Existentialists like Søren Kierkegaard have analyzed the new dimension that sin gives to the *anxiety* flowing from the human situation. Modern existentialism pays special attention to the undefined character of anxiety which acquires a special sharpness due to sin. Some current attempts to do away with ethical norms and thus mitigate the sense of guilt are increasing the undefined anguish of man. O. H. Mowrer has pointed out the moral basis of much of mental illness. According to him, if often arises because of "a hidden history of serious misconduct which has not been adequately redeemed."[24] He holds that "anxiety comes, not from acts which the individual would commit but dares not, but from acts he *has* committed but wishes that he had not."[25] The remedy would be none other than simple admission of one's misbehavior without any palliative, pretexts or alibis. Though this view may be an exaggeration, it does make a valuable point.

The alienation worsens with each unrepented sin. Scripture speaks of "bondage under sin" or "bondage under the devil." The same is implied by the domination of the "flesh" (as opposed to the Spirit) in some texts of Paul—e.g., Gal. 5:16–26; Rom. 7:14. One is "sold out to sin," so that sin becomes, as it were, a person that "dwells in me" (Rom. 7:20).

This is what is theologically called *concupiscence* (in the pejorative sense). Personal sin arises, in the first instance, because of selfishness and self-centeredness. But this in turn is aggravated through sin. There arises a stronger *inclination to sin,* to unintegrated behavior and egoistic action in conflict with love. We should note that concupiscence is found, not in the body as such, but in the whole being of man.[26] However, man's basic freedom is not totally lost. Otherwise, he would no longer be responsible, and conversion would be impossible.

5. MORTAL SIN, VENIAL SIN, SIN UNTO DEATH[27]

The Bible does not explicitly speak of the distinction between mortal and venial sin, but it provides some basis for the distinction.

The Old Testament mentions grave lapses for which one is cut off from God's people or which entail a separation from Yahweh (cf. Gen. 17:14; Num. 9:13; Jer. 7:9f; Ez. 18:5–18; 22:6–10). On the other hand, it says that "a righteous man falls seven times" (Prov. 24:16).

In the New Testament we find enumerations of sins that *exclude from the Kingdom* (1 Cor. 6:9–10; Gal. 5:19–21); or which are *deserving of death* (Rom. 1:24–32). On the other hand, it mentions lesser daily sins. In the everyday petition of the Our Father we are asked to pray: "Forgive us our sins." James states that "we all make many mistakes" (3:2). John warns that "if we say we have no sin, we deceive ourselves and the truth is not in us" (1 Jn. 1:8). John also speaks about "sin unto death" (1 Jn. 5:16) or sin against the Holy Spirit (cf. Mt. 12:32; Mk. 3:29).

The Church, both in her teaching and in her practice, has constantly maintained the distinction between grave and light sin, although it has not always been understood in the same way. The Council of Trent declared that all mortal sins must be confessed, but that there are sins which do not destroy the state of grace. Although not obligatory, it is commendable to confess these as well. The distinction is maintained in the new *Order of Penance.*

The distinction between mortal sin and venial sin is established in various ways. According to St. Thomas, mortal sin is a disorder concerning the end itself (*inordinatio circa finem*), whereas venial sin is a disorder concerning only the means (*inordinatio circa ea quae sunt ad finem*).[28] Mortal sin is turning away from God and turning to a creature, whereas venial sin is failure to direct a created object or intermediary goal to God, without, however, turning away from God. Venial sin is a *compromise,* somehow wanting God at the same time as one's selfish interests.[29]

Authors who stress the loving relation to God, see the difference between mortal and venial sin in the basic disposition of the sinner: whether his action is in *direct contradiction to love* or whether it only stands *outside the basic direction of love.* Franz Bockle explains venial sin as "a step *not* positively directed *toward* the goal, a step off the main road, but which leaves a man generally heading toward God."[30]

Many recent writers explain the matter in terms of the fundamental option. Mortal sin is an action that changes or is equivalent to changing one's fundamental option toward God or expressing an alienation from Him. Venial sin does not touch one's fundamental option. The person affirms God's will from the center of his personality, but rejects it from a merely peripheral dimension.

As Karl Rahner explains, the inconsistency of venial sin arises from the fact that man "is constructed, as it were, in layers starting at an interior core and becoming more and more external, and because (even free) activations can spring from many different layers . . . it is possible to do one and the same thing and have several, in themselves contradictory, motives and intentions for it."[31]

In fact, we must distinguish two levels of morality. We have *slight morality* on the peripheral or superficial level, which does not represent a total engagement of the person. Here we have daily good actions or venial sins. But the core of the personality, where man engages his freedom totally, is the area of *grave morality*. Here we have mortal sin.

Kevin O'Shea explains that mortal sin "can only happen at the very deep level in which man is present to himself wholly as a person, fully master of his freedom, fully face to face with the God of the covenant." He says that "this cannot happen in an ordinary isolated act, but only in the projected course of a human lifetime, climaxing in the personal position taken in death. It is not a matter of 'falling into sin' haphazardly, but of being, in one's life and inner personality, a 'sinner,' a man who is 'unto-sin-death,' and who thus enters death." But he adds that "beyond the consummating death-experience, there will be situations during *life* when a person will be master of his freedom, and will encounter the presence of the God of the covenant inviting him to communion, and will take a position."[32]

Mortal sin may also be compared to the complete breakdown of a marital relationship, and venial sin to ordinary family quarrels.

Grave or mortal sin does not necessarily mean an explicit or formal break with God. It is enough that the heart is seriously divided, that one fully deliberately refuses love in a serious matter. As the Dutch Catechism explains: "A serious break with God does not merely mean hatred of Him, but also the refusal of something which is essential for faithfulness of love. A husband offends his wife not only by hating her, but also by infidelity in what is essential to love."[33]

Because mortal sin affects the fundamental option, it cannot be a frequent occurrence in the life of an ordinarily good Christian. The transition between grace and mortal sin and *vice versa* is not like changing clothes. St. Thomas makes this point clearly: "Although grace is lost by one act of mortal sin, still grace is not lost easily, since for one who has grace it is not easy to perform such an act because of the contrary inclination."[34] There is a tendency to trivialize mortal sin in certain circles. The matter needs to be taken more seriously, and then we shall not see mortal sin at every turn. As Karl Rahner remarks: "Every mortal sin as such, regarded in itself, tries to integrate the whole of life into a *no* to God and, hence, is in itself the most terrible thing a man can do."[35]

The psychological experience of utter gloom after a fall and then of sudden sunshine after a quick confession, if it happens at relatively short intervals, does not indicate changes in the core of the personality or a transition from grace to sin and *vice versa*.[36] Turning away from God implies a major change in the core of the personality. Hence, a person normally trying to serve God is not likely to "fall into sin" by a single uncharacteristic choice. It is much more likely to be the result of a long chain of lesser faults which blunt the moral sensibilities, weaken the love of God, and establish the self more and more habitually as the center of moral choice. But actual mortal sin itself is a particular, conscious and free choice, a definite turning point in one's personal history. We see a similar process in marital breakdown. It can come about only as a result of an accumulation of minor misunderstandings and infidelities. Still, there is generally a particular point of decision when one partner or both are faced with a choice between total alienation and reconciliation, a choice which will formalize the growing estrangement or halt the drift apart.

Subsequent gravely evil acts spring from the evil basic option and do not require a further radical reorientation of the will. A person in the state of grave sin may perform acts that seem due to unselfish love but, in fact, may be due to respect for convention, a subtle form of selfishness or even habit. Just as in venial sin one seeks at a more superficial level of one's being an end which is inconsistent with the good embraced by the core of the personality, so also the apparently good actions of a person in the state of grave sin may be attempts at a more superficial level to seek a good which is rejected at the deepest level.

One of the main principles of *discernment of spirits* is that a choice made in accordance with the fundamental option will arouse a sense of well-being and calm, whereas that which goes counter to it will cause disturbance or remorse. Thus, if the option is good, anxiety and sadness will be evoked by a bad choice; if it is evil, disquiet will accompany a good choice.[37]

From the above discussion it will be clear in what sense one could say that mortal sin is *more a state than an act*. Mortal sin is an engagement of the total personality against God. The external act or acts could be termed mortal sin only to the extent that they *mediate* such an option. As Josef Fuchs explains, mortal sin is more a *disposition of self as a person* than an isolated act.[38] It is a state of being-in-rebellion or of alienation from God. It does not just happen in a split second.

Still, the state of mortal sin is brought about through a free act of the will; it is realized through a human act properly understood—not in the sense of merely material action, but in the sense of a commitment to evil. It is a *state brought about by a critical act*. The idea of grave sin being a state is not entirely new. Traditional morality clearly distinguished between *actus* (act) and *habitus* (state of guilt), although it was too easily assumed that a person could suddenly commit a mortal sin and that, if he died just then, he would be lost for ever.

Inasmuch as there is an element of human act, we can speak of the *species* and *number* of such acts. There is a distinct new mortal sin whenever there is the equivalent to a grave refusal of love or a turning away from God. When there is full advertence to it, a gravely sinful act may have two or more malices; e.g., in adultery, there is not only an improper use of sex, but also a violation of marital fidelity. When the Church requires that the species and number be confessed, what is meant is that all the serious ways in which one has deliberately offended God and the community be acknowledged. But this does not mean that meticulous enumeration of sins in a legalistic spirit should obscure genuine metanoia. A right balance should be struck between preoccupation with ''material integrity'' and too casual and vague an accusation.

In practice, it would be more helpful for the penitent to reveal his state of soul in simple and concrete language than to use technical labels for sins.

The distinction between mortal and venial sin is one not only of degree but *of essence*. Venial sin is not simply a small sin; it is sin only in an analogous sense, since only mortal sin is sin in the full sense. While, in mortal sin, the whole of the personality is engaged, venial sin is a *superficial act* in which the core of the personality is not involved. Failure to understand this point has led some to deny the distinction between mortal and venial sin, just because in both there is an offence against God.

However, the distinction should not give the impression that some sins matter and others do not—which would lead to moral minimalism and the lowering of moral standards. But, as Anglican Bishop Kenneth E. Kirk has pointed out, "Everything depends upon the emphasis and the direction in which the distinction is employed. It may help the man who is in danger of mortal sin to look upward, making the eradication even of venial sin his final ambition; such a result is evidence that the doctrine has been put to wise and fruitful use. Or it may lead him to look downward, and rest complacently in the fact that he is not as other men are; that leads direct to Pharisaism and spiritual stagnation."[39] Hence, venial sin should not be taken lightly. It decreases the fervor of charity and, when not checked, gradually paves the way for the tragedy of mortal sin.

It is not helpful to distinguish between venial sin and positive (voluntary) imperfection when the latter is understood as refusing to follow the inspirations of the Spirit in matters that are not strictly commanded by law. The latter is no different from venial sin when sin is understood at the religious level as an offense against the love of God.

Many recent theologians speak of a third kind of sin: *sin unto death*. Ordinary grave acts, though expressions of a fundamental option, do not constitute one's definitive and irrevocable choice. Man disposes himself through successive acts, and hence, meanwhile, conversion from the state of sin is possible through the grace of Christ. But there could be a choice, in a fully intuitive act, which is so total that, through it, man irrevocably chooses eternity for better or for worse. It is the supreme word of love or the final hardening of heart, the sin against the Holy Spirit. According to some, this is supposed to happen at the moment of transition in the very act of dying, since the final evil choice alone can determine eternal salvation or condemnation.[40] Bruno Schüller has raised serious objections against this "final option" theory.[41] According to him, it would reduce the importance of moral choice during one's lifetime and we would have to presume a special illumination at the last moment. These difficulties are not unanswerable, since good or bad actions during one's lifetime would prepare the way for the final choice, which need not be put at the very moment of dying.

The possibility of "sin unto death" should shake one's false complacency, but it should not create undue anxiety. Whoever is sincerely willing to seek gradual liberation from egoism and relies on God's grace can be certain of not meeting this final tragedy. The danger arises only when one simply refuses to be oriented toward the good or is determined to seek self-justification.

Since only the final hardening of heart can be said to be death-dealing in the fullest sense, some would reserve the term *mortal* only to this. They would call other provisional basic options toward evil simply "grave sins" or "serious sins." In fact, the new *Ordo Penitentiae* avoids the word *mortal* while speaking about integrity of confession. But the later Vatican Declaration on Sexual Ethics comes back to the term *mortal sin* in reference to extramarital intercourse and the like. Many, indeed, do not see any objection to this wider use of the term *mortal*, since a fundamental option toward evil in the course of one's life causes spiritual death and, if one dies unrepentant, eternal death also.

6.   THE DETERMINATION OF MORTAL AND VENIAL SIN

According to traditional doctrine, three conditions must be verified for inferring mortal sin: (1) grave matter; (2) full knowledge; (3) full consent. If any of these conditions is lacking, there would only be a venial sin. "Grave matter" means a moral object that substantially affects an important moral value.

Grave matter is not the same as mortal sin. It is altogether wrong to say that certain types of actions are mortal sins, since mortal sin presupposes personal involvement or full knowledge and consent. Traditional theology was well aware of the distinction between grave matter and actual (formal) mortal sin, though the distinction was often obscured in popular circles and even in catechisms. Misunderstanding of Latin expressions was also a cause of the confusion. Older Latin authors generally used to say that such and such a kind of action is *"mortale."* They only meant that the matter was "grave" or liable to lead to mortal sin. But the term was at times translated to mean actual mortal sin.

It is *incorrect to say that the main factor lies in grave matter.* People often confuse material with formal sin. When the material element if found, they feel that they are obliged to mention it in confession even if advertence and consent are lacking. They seem to be afraid of "falling into hell" as they might have "fallen into mortal sin" (hell being understood as an extrinsic punishment inflicted by an angry God).

The determining factor in mortal sin lies in the *personal turning away from God,* in the break in the love-relationship with Him, if one's whole personality is engaged in the evil. Hence, there should be no undue preoccupation with determining the exact dividing line between grave and light matter. What is more important is to seek the right orientation in life and genuine conversion of heart.

Still, the *determination of grave matter is not completely irrelevant,* for, normally, it is only in a grave matter that one is fully involved as a person and commits oneself in his basic stand in relation to God. On the other hand, man's fundamental liberty (by which he is able to dispose, not merely of his acts, but of himself) is generally not involved in a light matter. As Piet Schoonenberg explains: "From a practical viewpoint this means that the gravity or levity of the exterior action is a *sign* of the gravity or smaller depth of the fullness of our interior decision; a sign which reveals, but may also conceal. Stealing a coin generally does not put us before a central decision, whereas infidelity in marriage does."[42] Sean Fagan speaks of "catalogues of sins" as "warnings and indications as to the kind of behavior that can lead to the state of mortal sinfulness, spiritual death."[43]

Those who would deny even this qualified link between grave matter and mortal sin would be betraying an overly spiritual mentality in which the external expression of one's inner attitude would have little significance. In such a view, the sense of responsibility would be diminished instead of being increased. We may note here the observation of Karl Rahner: "Man must constantly achieve himself as a person in an 'intermediary reality' formed by the union of his animated corpo-reality and embodied spirituality together with their concrete, material and purpositional objectification, and by the external world of equally real persons and things as well as by the objectifications produced by 'external actions.' "[44]

Murder is not the same as a blow on the back. Moral theology attempts to arrange typical patterns of action according to their objective gravity. "Objectively gravely sinful" means that a particular deed in general is apt to challenge a man to make a fundamental decision with regard to God. However, the warning of Jesus that whoever even insults his brother shall be liable to hell fire (Mt. 5:22) should make us critical of such classifications. The external deed can be fully evaluated only in relation to a man's basic interior disposition. An act which seems small may at times proceed from utter egotism. On the other hand, an outwardly serious fault may not in fact flow from a basically wrong orientation. Hence due importance should be given to subjective dispositions.

As a result, we must avoid two extremes: the first, looking only at the gravity of the matter and thereby materializing sin; the second, entirely neglecting the importance of the matter involved and thereby spiritualizing sin excessively. The first leads to the unchristian attitude of self-justification, which finds security in stopping short of the brink of moral sin, while true security can be found only through unreserved trust in the Lord's mercy. The second seems to be an ill-considered reaction against the first. Sinful deeds on the surface of our life are *signs* of what is happening deep within. As the gifts of the Spirit spring ultimately from faith, so the "works of the flesh" stem from unbelief. The turning away from God in unbelief is realized and specified in individual human acts, each drawing its material from the manifold world of values where God is rejected in a wrongful attachment to creatures. By his sins man makes himself a sinner.

But, because external actions are *not univocal signs* of the inner disposition, we must be extremely cautious in judging the conduct of others. Definitive judgement belongs only to the Lord, "who tries the minds and hearts" (Ps. 7:9; cf. Acts 1:24). Even the confessor can only make a presumptive appreciation as regards the disposition of the penitent so that he may be the minister of grace and mercy. According to a well-founded tradition, a person who generally displays goodwill but is weak in some respect and renews his sorrow and purpose of amendment soon after falling, can be presumed not to have fallen into mortal sin.

In *assessing imputability,* the following questions would be useful:

a) *Did you realize fully* that it was a grave matter? This refers to sufficient (*evaluative*) knowledge, which at times may be lacking—even in an adult—because of psychic obsession or addictive urge with consequent mono-idealistic narrowing of consciousness to the single object of desire.

b) *Could you have resisted?* This has to do with the consent of the will.

A sincere negative answer to either of these questions reveals the certain absence of mortal sin. A positive answer to both gives a strong presumption of mortal sin, although not always certainty. In making a judgment about grave subjective guilt, the confessor has to rely above all on the enlightened testimony of the penitent's conscience.

The example of *alcoholism* could illustrate the matter of assessing imputabilty.[45] It is a condition with these traits: excessive drinking over a period of years; serious life problems, like disruption of family harmony; compulsion; inability to stop drinking without special help.

Responsibility for becoming an alcoholic exists only inasmuch as the pathological condition was foreseen and not prevented to the extent possible. In general, according to experts, the responsibility is small. The compulsive factor in the average alcoholic notably diminishes responsibility for getting drunk, so that grave imputability would be rare. When the craving comes on, evaluative cognition may be hampered or there may be the irresistible impulse to drink. During and after the drinking bout, the person may be overburdened by neurotic guilt feelings. However, he is responsible for doing something about his condition by seeking help. While the spiritual director might be lenient in judging the subjective guilt, the person must be encouraged to believe that he can overcome the habit. The underlying problem must be tackled by counselling, especially by group counselling—for example, in Alcoholics Anonymous groups.

7. THE SIN OF THE WORLD

The Bible emphasizes human solidarity with respect to sin and redemption. It was a free decision of Adam and of Eve as protoparents that introduced moral evil in the world. However, Adam and Eve are not solely responsible for human misery. Many subsequent personal sins are also the cause. We are all Adams and Eves when we sin. "We each do our part in a total process of wasting, spending, polluting, defiling, stealing, hoarding, exhausting and destroying."[46] The accumulated infidelities of man bring about an atmosphere of moral corruption and decay. Each individual sin inserts itself into the sinfulness of the human race. Each man is born into a world where there is a horrifying contamination of evil. The prophets' denunciation of collective blindness, group-egotism and the pursuit of a social life that betrays the covenant is more than ever applicable today.

According to Paul, "sin" and death reign over the world (cf. Rom. 5:12–24). John speaks of "the sin of the world" (1:29; cf. 1 Jn. 5:19). This is the mystery of iniquity which entered the world through the original fall and which dramatically unfolds itself down the ages. It works in each one of us, so that our personal sins could be considered its manifestations. The "original sin" is not simply the fact that each human being is inclined to follow the bad example of his predecessors; nor is it simply a quasi-ontological legacy. It derives from the basic solidarity of each individual with all other men, with the evil of corporate life. The chromosomes become bearers of sin through the unresolved conflicts of parents and communities as well as through the discords of social life into which infants are born and in which they grow up. The very atmosphere in which each person lives out his personal history is infected by an evil influence.

However, we cannot simply blame the situation for our moral failures. It will not do to hang all the weight of our corruption around the neck of poor Adam or to excuse ourselves by pleading helplessness. Each one of us is responsible for our partnership in the mystery of iniquity every time we fail to do the good we could or commit the evil we could avoid. We are also responsible for our lack of sorrow, for not recognizing the need for conversion and not accepting God's gift of redemption. "So understood, the sin of the world allows no excuse for evasion but becomes call to total communion, to an explicit changeover, to a constructive solidarity possible in Christ only."[47]

Indeed, Christ's redeeming grace is also present in us. "Where sin increased, grace abounded all the more, so that, as sin reigned in death, grace also might reign through righteousness to eternal life through Jesus Christ our Lord" (Rom. 5:20). Christ's saving solidiarity has reshaped the evil heritage of the past. "For our sake he [God] made him to be sin who knew no sin, so that in him we might become the righteousness of God" (Cor. 5:21).

In the words of Juan L. Segundo, Jesus encountered a world "turned into a lie, a frozen mental outlook incapable of deeper comprehension.''[48] We are now becoming aware of the reality of sin embodied in political, economic and social structures. Today, scandal is not only individual, it is even more the contaminating power of structures that seduce and enmesh the ordinary man.

Gregory Baum has exposed the manner in which unjust institutions falsify awareness. This ''social sin'' is made up of: 1) dehumanizing elements built into social, political, economic, and, at times, even religious institutions; 2) cultural and religious symbols that legitimate and reinforce these influences—for example, by persuading people that the source of evil is only in the hearts of individual men; 3) false consciousness that any questioning of the profit-oriented dominant culture is evil; 4) collective decisions made by the organs of the existing social structures which perpetuate and aggravate the dehumanizing trends.[49]

As the Canadian bishops remarked in a pastoral letter in 1974: ''The market is designed primarily to make profits, not to feed people.'' There is an inbuilt injustice in a situation in which ''the supply and distribution of food is determined mainly by effective demand, not by human need.''[50] Large-scale human misery is the consequence.

There is a dialectical relationship between personal and social sin. The unjust structures are first initiated on a small scale by people who have a limited and self-centered perspective. Then the repeated personal sins of some accentuate institutional discrepancies. These unjust structures are the bearers of social sin and will eventually modify the consciousness of the people and produce an alienating self-understanding. The powerful in society will be inclined to use these structures for their advantage, the resulting greed and superficiality being the sins of the rich. The underprivileged will be inclined to anger and despair, leading to the sins of the poor.

In order to meet this situation effectively, we must overcome the *privatization of sin*. We must be aware that preoccupation with ''bad thoughts,'' ignoring the effect of one's political options and social activities, could be responsible for the misery of countless people. An individualistic concept of justice might be the cause of the greatest injustice. Millions of abortions in crowded countries may be influenced by those who block immigration into countries where petty thefts may be rare. Collective prejudices and a poisoned public opinion are far worse than water and air pollution. As Herbert McCabe observes: "Men whose goodwill has been cultivated exclusively in immediate personal relationships amongst their families, friends, and acquaintances are quite frequently blind to large and devastating social injustice and to the agony of people whom they do not meet socially."[51]

It must be noted that because of its intimate solidarity with man, the material universe itself suffers and sighs under the frustration of evil. According to Paul, "creation was subject to futility, not of its own will" (Rom. 8:20). Each sin rejects the voice of the created universe as it sighs for redemption. Everyone who sins makes himself accountable for increasing the opaqueness of the world. He aggravates racism, caste-ism, neo-colonialism and all forms of collective intolerance. To quote Bernard Häring: "The truth that sin always involves the world created by God, and seeks to organize the good energies for solidarity with evil, is one of the most profound and most shocking reason for total conversion and constructive co-responsibility for the world in which we live."[52] An erroneous concept of sin as a stain on the soul to be washed out by penance fails to take seriously the impact of sin in the world, especially in human relations. It leads to the refusal to cooperate in the redemption. Similarly, an excessive preoccupation with avoiding transgressions of the law betrays a flight from responsibility and a scrupulosity caused by a profound alienation. Häring calls this a "sinful concept of sin."

Hence, there is need for reforming a one-sided ethic of conformity to the law that produces uniformity and enslavement under collective prejudice and fosters vague sentimentality instead of courageous com-mitment. Individual confession alone made in anonymity cannot break the pall of alienation. There is also the need for communitarian "revision of life," as well as a community celebration of reconciliation in which people gather to listen to God's Word, reflect on their sins—including objective involvement in the injustice of their group—and, together, seek means of renewing society.

A legalistic idea of sin also implies a security complex that ignores the fundamental call to growth. As the social milieu helps or hinders individual and communal growth of freedom, all opportunities should be used for freeing man from every form of alienation and for developing human conditions that foster the growth of mature freedom. Only a communitarian commitment to good can overcome solidarity in corruption.

We must be aware that sinfulness in the life and structures of the ecclesial community is all the more deplorable, since the Church's mission is to be the sacrament of holiness and salvation. "But if the salt has lost its taste . . ." (Mt. 5:13). Whatever makes religion irrelevant to life is itself a sin against the Church's mission of proclaiming the Gospel and helping all men to reach God. Thus, it is sinful to cling to past formulations and policies that do not correspond to available insights and shared experiences of the Church and humanity today. Häring, therefore, puts out the call: "We cannot rest with denunciation of discrete sins of individualistic behavior; we must attack primarily an individualistic vision of the world and of religion which causes so many sins of omission and of mistaken vision and of mistaken approaches to fundamental questions."[53]

Hence, the importance of environment must be given due recognition in pastoral theology and action. Salvation must take root in all the structures of the world. However, personal conversion should not be neglected. The root cause of sin in the core of one's personality, in the abuse of one's freedom, must be recognized. Sin must be tackled at both the personal and the social level. Only such a two-pronged thrust can win the battle.

———o———

Notes to Chapter XX

1. Cf. Sean Fagan, *Has Sin Changed?* Dublin, Gill and Macmillan, 1978; James P. Mackey, "The Idea of Sin in the Modern World," *Sin and Repentance*, ed. by Denis O'Callaghan, Staten Island, N. Y., Alba House, 1967, pp. 18–50.

2. New York, Bantam Books, 1978.

3. See Andrew Mayes, "The Nature of Sin and Its Origin in the Old Testament," *Irish Theological Quarterly*, 40 (1973), 250–63.

4. Gerhard von Rad, *Old Testament Theology*, London, Oliver and Boyd, 1962, Vol. I, p. 154.

5. Cf. L. J. Hayes, "Sin, the Non-relationship in Gen 2–11," *Homiletic and Pastoral Review*, 72 (1972), 42–49; Albert Gelin and Albert Deschamps, *Sin in the Bible*, New York, Desclée, 1964; Albert Gelin, *Key Concepts of the Old Testament*, London, Sheed and Ward, 1955, pp. 81–91; Ceslaus Spicq, "Men's Sin," *The God of Israel, the God of Christians*, New York, Desclée, 1961, pp. 149–63; Jacques Guillet, *Themes of the Bible*, Notre Dame, Ind., Fides, 1960, Ch. 4; Peter Riga, *Sin and Penance*, Milwaukee, Bruce, 1962, pp. 8–20.

6. Gottfried Quell et alii, "Sin," *Bible Key Words*, ed. by Gerhard, Kittel, London, A. and C. Black, 1951.

7. *Sin in the Bible*, pp. 32–40.

8. See Peter Riga, *op. cit.*, pp. 21–40.

9. See Jerome Murphy-O'Connor, "Sin and Community in the N. T.," *Sin and Redemption*, ed. by Denis O'Callaghan, pp. 18–50.

10. Cf. Eugene J. Cooper, "Sarx and Sin in Pauline Theology," *Laval Théologique et Philosophique*, 29 (1973), 243–55.

11. Cf. Eugene J. Cooper, "The Consciousness of Sin in 1 John," *ibid.*, pp. 237–48.

12. Cf. Piet Schoonenberg, *Man and Sin*, London, Sheed and Ward, 1965; Louis Monden, *op. cit.;* Henri Rondet, *The Theology of Sin*, Notre Dame, Ind., Fides, 1960; Peter Riga, *op. cit.*, pp. 41–62. J. Regnier, *What Is Sin?* Cork, Mercier, 1961; Eugene J. Cooper, "A Newer Look at the Theology of Sin," *Louvain Studies*, 3 (1971), 259–307; R. J. Tapia, "What is Sin?," *Thought*, 47 (1972), 211–24; Karl Rahner, "Guilt and Remission," *Theological Investigations*, Vol. II, pp. 266–81.

13. *Contra Faustum*, 22, 27 (Migne, *Patrologia Latina*, Vol. 42, p. 418).

14. *Op. cit.*, p. 37.

15. J. Regnier, *op. cit.*, p. 39.

16. *Summa Theologica*, Ia-IIae, 112, 5.

17. "Some Thoughts on a Good Intention," *Theological Investigations*, Vol. III, p. 155.

18. *Authentic Morality*, New York, Macmillan, 1965.

19. See Piet Schoonenberg, *op. cit.*, Ch. 2.

20. Denzinger–Banwaart, no. 840.

21. Piet Schoonenberg, *op. cit.*, pp. 68–69.

22. *Sin in the Secular* Age, Slough, St. Paul Publications, 1974, p. 60.

23. No. 47.

24. *Psychotherapy: Theory and Research*, New York, Ronald, 1953, p. 82.

25. *Learning Theory and Personality Dynamics, ibid.*, 1950, p. 537.

26. Cf. Karl Rahner, "The Theological Concept of Concupiscentia," *Theological Investigations*, Vol. I, pp. 347–82.

27. Cf. Denis O'Callaghan, "Mortal and Venial Sin," *Irish Ecclesiastical Record*, 107 (1967), 158–65; Kevin O'Shea, "The Reality of Sin," *Theological Studies*, 29 (1968), 241–59; Felix Podimattam, "What Is Mortal Sin?," *Clergy Monthly*, 36 (1972), 57–67.

28. Cf. *Summa Theologica*, Ia-Ilae, 88, 2.

29. See Prudent De Letter, "Venial Sin: Its Final Goal," *The Thomist*, 18 (1953), 32–70.

30. *Op. cit.*, p. 96.

31. "Some Thoughts on a Good Intention," *Theological Investigations*, Vol. III, p. 113.

32. *Art. cit.*, pp. 247–48.

33. *A New Catechism*, London, Burns and Oates.

34. *De Veritate*, 1, 9.

35. "The Comfort of Time," *Theological Investigations*, Vol. III, p. 154.

36. Cf. John W. Glaser, "Transition Between Grace and Sin," *Theological Studies*, 19 (1968), 271–72.

37. St. Ignatius, *Spiritual Exercises*, nos. 314–15.

38. "Sin and Conversion," *Theology Digest*, 14 (1966), 292.

39. *The Vision of God*, London, Longmans, 1931, p. 249.

40. Cf. Ladislaus Boros. *The Moment of Truth*, New York, Herder, 1965; Karl Rahner, *On the Theology of Death*, ibid., 1961.

41. Mortal Sin, Sin unto Death," *Theology Digest*, 16 (1968), 232–35.

42. *Op. cit.*, p. 36.

43. *Op. cit.*, p. 71.

44. "Guilt and Remission." *Theological Investigations*, Vol. II, p. 272.

45. Cf. John C. Ford and Gerald Kelly, *op. cit.*, Ch. 13; George Hagmaier and Robert W. Gleason, *op. cit.*, Ch. 6 and 12; William C. Bier, *Problems in Addiction*, New York, Fordham Univ. Press, 1962; James Vanderbilt and Robert P. Odenwald, *op. cit.*, Ch. 20.

46. Karl Menninger, *op. cit.*, p. 222.

47. Bernard Häring, *Sin in the Secular World*, p. 202.

48. *Evolution and Guilt*, p. 55.

49. *Religion and Alienation*, New York, Paulist Press, 1975, pp. 201–22.

50. See *La Documentation Catholique*, 71 (1974), 1040.

51. *Op. cit.*, p. 163.

52. Bernard Häring, *op. cit.*, p. 62.

53. *Ibid.*, p. 115.

CHAPTER XXI

Reconciliation

1. THE CALL TO CONVERSION AND RECONCILIATION

The preaching of Jesus starts from an urgent call to conversion (Mk. 1:15). This *metanoia* implies total reconciliation, both personal and communitarian.

Made to the image of God and invited to communion with the Triune God, as well as to mutual fellowship and harmony with the whole of creation, mankind through sin broke away from this communion and harmony. Being alienated from the source of their existence, men and women became alienated from one another and from the cosmos. This tragic situation is graphically described by Paul in his letter to the Romans: "For although they knew God they did not honor him as God or give thanks to him, but they became futile in their thinking and their senseless minds were darkened" (Rom. 1:21). However, God "did not abandon mankind to the power of death but helped all to seek and find Him."[1]

Through an initiative of divine condescension, the Father has reconciled all the peoples who were, as Paul says, "separated from Christ, alienated from the commonwealth of Israel, strangers to the covenant of promise, having no hope and without God in the world" (Eph. 2:12). Paul goes on to say that "now in Christ Jesus you who were once far off have been brought near in the blood of Christ. For he is our peace, who has made us both one, and has broken down the dividing wall of hostility" (vv. 13–14).

Through the decisive Christ-event, our human nature has been restored and ennobled. By assuming our flesh, the Son of God has sanctified it. In Christ, the common Fatherhood of God and brotherhood of all human beings has been restored. By His death, corruption and death have been conquered. By His resurrection, our humanity has been basically glorified. As Paul puts it expressively: "He is the beginning, the first-born from the dead, that in everything he might be preeminent. For in him all the fullness of God was pleased to dwell, and through him to reconcile to himself all things, whether on earth or in heaven, making peace by the blood of his cross" (Col. 1:18–20). Paul marvels at the divine purpose which God set forth in Christ "as a plan for the fullness of time, to unite all things in him, things in heaven and things on earth" (Eph. 1:10).

Thus the love of God for sinful humanity is manifested in Christ Jesus, who is "the primary sacrament" of our encounter with God. The Father reestablishes communion of love with men and women through His Son. "In this the love of God was made manifest among us, that God sent his only Son into the world, so that we might live through him. In this is love, not that we loved God but that he loved us and sent his Son to be the expiation for our sins. Beloved, if God so loved us, we also ought to love another" (1 Jn. 4:9–11).

The meaning of reconciliation can be seen from the three main terms by which it is expressed in the New Testament:[2]

1) *Hilasmos,* a cultic term which seems to imply expiation more than propitiation. In propitiation, the action is directed toward God in order to change His attitude from one of wrath to one of goodwill and favor. In the case of expiation, on the other hand, the intention is rather to counteract the cause that brought about the breakdown in relationship. Thus, in Heb. 2:17, Christ is represented as performing an act whereby man is delivered from the guilt of his sin, not an act whereby God is propitiated. It is an action of God through His High Priest Jesus for the salvation of man.

2) *Apokatastasis,* a political term meaning "restoration." Yahweh will bring Israel back from exile into his own land (Jer. 16:15;

23:8; 24:6). Ezekiel draws a parallel between the eschatological restoration and its beginning in the first choice of Israel (16:60). The term is also used for healing, which is an important dimension of reconciliation (Mk. 3:5; 8:25; Mt. 12:13; Lk. 6:10). It is explicitly linked with repentance in Peter's speech at the Temple: "Repent therefore, and turn again, that your sins may be blotted out, that times of refreshing may come from the presence of the Lord, and that he may send the Christ appointed for you, Jesus, whom heaven must receive until the time for establishing all that God spoke by the mouth of his holy prophets of old" (Acts 3:19–21).

3) *Kattallage,* a secular term signifying improvements in a negative relationship. In Judaism, repentance and confession of sins are means by which reconciliation with God is sought. The New Testament makes it very clear that the subject of reconciliation is God. Thus Paul says that "God was in Christ reconciling the world to himself" (2 Cor. 5:19). In pagan religions, generally, the deity is the object of the reconciling work of man; the preoccupation is with placating an angry God. But according to the Christian revelation, it is God who takes the initiative in reconciling sinful man, who is incapable of reunion with God by himself. Paul emphasizes the divine initiative by saying: "For if while we were enemies we were reconciled (*kattellagmen*) to God by the death of his Son, much more, now that we are reconciled, shall we be saved by his life" (Rom. 5:10).

Reconciliation is an expression of the new situation that has been brought about by the death and resurrection of Christ. It is to end a relationship of enmity and to substitute for it one of peace and goodwill. According to Rom. 4:3–8, justification comes about when God does not impute iniquities to man, but reckons him righteous by faith. According to God's plan, Christ assumes the guilt of our sins so that "we might become the righteousness of God" (2 Cor. 5:21). Again Paul declares that "you, who once were estranged and hostile in mind, doing evil deeds, he has now reconciled in his body of flesh by his death, in order to present you holy and blameless and irreproachable before him" (Col. 1:21–22).

In his letter to the Ephesians, Paul conceives the work of redemption as breaking down the wall of hostility between mankind and God, between Jew and Gentile: "But now in Christ Jesus you who were once far off have been brought near in the blood of Christ. For he is our peace, who has made us both one, and has broken down the dividing wall of hostility, by abolishing in his flesh the law of commandments and ordinances, that he might create in himself one new man in place of the two, so making peace, and might reconcile us both to God in one body through the cross, thereby bringing the hostility to an end" (Eph. 2:13–16).

The need for human reconciliation is parabolic of man's need of reconciliation with God. Since man is made to the image of God, sin and reconciliation have an essentially interlinked horizontal and vertical dimension.

2.   THE ROLE OF THE CHURCH IN RECONCILIATION

The fruit of reconciliation brought about by the death and resurrection of Christ is "a new creation" (cf. 2 Cor. 5:17). While the paschal mystery has a definitive character, its concrete working out in the world is an ongoing process. This is now achieved principally in and through the Church, the Spirit-filled community of redemption, gathered by Christ from all peoples to be formed mystically into His Body.

The Church is not one more sect or religious group over against others. According to Vatican II, she "is a kind of sacrament or sign of intimate union with God, and of the unity of all mankind. She is also an instrument for the achievement of such union and unity."[3]

Paul defines apostolic activity as the ministry of reconciliation, which he expresses by different vivid terms: "All this is from God, who through Christ reconciled us to himself and gave us the *ministry* of reconciliation; that is, God was in Christ reconciling the world to himself, not counting their trespasses against them, and entrusting to us the *message* of reconciliation. So we are *ambassadors* for Christ, God making his appeal through us" (2 Cor. 5:18–20).

Since reconciliation is achieved through the whole *kenotic existence* of Christ culminating in His death, the mode and style of the Church's ministry of reconciliation is determined by the same kenotic character. Hence, this *kenotic pattern* is intrinsic to the ministerial activity of the Church. As a recent writer eloquently states, "In its praxis and enactment, the Church has to follow the kenotic path which was intrinsic to the act of reconciliation in Jesus and, therefore, remains determinative until its completion at the end of time."[4]

In His kenotic existence, Jesus "did not count equality with God a thing to be grasped, but emptied himself, taking the form of a servant" (Phil. 2:6–7). Thereby, Jesus revealed a God who is not merely loving, but who *is love* (cf. 1 Jn. 4:8). He also disengaged Himself from the power structures of this world and opted for the *anawim* of Yahweh (cf. Lk. 4:18f).

This has a tremendous consequence for the ministry of the Church. "If the Church wishes to be the sacrament of reconciliation to the world, it is imperative that she follows the same kenotic path, disengaging herself from 'power and glory,' and from the socio-economic, political, cultural and religious power structures of the world."[5] Especially in regions where the Church is a minority, there is a tendency to impress by building up a mighty institutional structure. While institutions have their value, a one-sided reliance on institutional power may go against evangelical witness and the role of the Church to serve humanity and not to dominate in any way.

On the other hand, the Church's sacramental ministry of reconciliation should not be overly spiritual, concentrating on personal failings and neglecting the areas of social justice. As Karl Rahner remarks: "It must not be forgotten that a great amount of injustice and lovelessness exists in the world, for which we are responsible, but which does not at all become discernible in the average everyday consciousness of man and of society. . . . [Penitential devotion] should be an opportunity for each community of Christians to face the injustices within its own group, injustices which the real bourgeois society frequently accepts in a blasé manner and simply as a matter of fact."[6]

While the Church strives for justice and reconciliation in the world, she has herself constantly to pass through a process of inner renewal and a self-reflective kenosis. In His self-emptying, Jesus became completely transparent to the Father, drew Himself out of Himself and reconciled the world to God. The Church, too, has constantly to pass through this process of self-reflective kenosis. By purifying herself of all divisions and structures that hinder her mission, and gaining a self-understanding of herself as the sacrament of union with God, she has to gain a transparency that will enable her to play her true reconciliatory role in the world. The Church herself, then, stands in need of reconciliation in order to be the sign and means of reconciliation in the world today.

We will therefore trace the main elements of tension and crisis within and without the Church that urgently call for reconciliation.

3. ELEMENTS OF TENSION AND CRISIS IN THE CHURCH

1) *Conservatives vs. Progressives.* There is a strong polarization in the Church today between both these groups. The two tendencies arise from opposite perceptions of reality, from two attitudes toward the movement of transformation that is taking place in the world in all spheres. The conservative mentality seeks security and the defense of established values and structures, while the progressive seeks change and progress. As such, both have their validity, provided they are based on love for the truth and zeal for the glory of God and the good of the people. Both have their role in balancing each other. There is definitely need for renewal without losing genuine traditional values. But the conservative position is often marked by a manifestation of personal insecurity and the desire of controlling others, while the progressive position may often be a blind reaction to it. Hence, on both sides, there is need for critical self-awareness, the discovery of the motive force behind one's own position and openness to the values embodied in the opposite position.

2) *Sacral vs. Secular.* While primitive man saw the sacred in every stone, brook and plant, gradually there arose a distinction between

the sacred and the secular. More and more areas of human life began to be transferred to the secular sphere, so that now for many people the secular seems to have entirely supplanted the sacred. The solution is not in restoring the old conception, which tended toward magic, but in seeing the sacred as the sanctification of the secular by the presence and activity of the Spirit of God.

3) *Immanence vs. Transcendence.* In the past, there was a tendency to consider God as "out there." Now, in a way, as a return to some ancient conceptions, many are inclined to find God in nature, especially in the innermost depths of the heart of man or in human activity. This is right as long as the divinity is not absorbed into the earthly sphere, and all idea of otherness and mystery is not lost. The stress on immanence or transcendence has tremendous consequences for spirituality and for mutual acceptance in the Church.

4) *Static vs. Evolutionary.* The traditional conception stresses *being,* or the static aspect of reality. Now, the emphasis is on *becoming,* or on the evolutionary aspect. In this latter vision, rapid change is taken for granted or even welcomed, while the traditionalist tends to hold on to the established views and modes of activity. In point of fact, change should be admitted and sought—without, however, losing the substance of older values.

5) *Faith vs. Reason.* Primitive man was largely influenced by faith in unknown powers and occult knowledge. Now, the scientific revolution has introduced the principle of reason and empirical verification. The recent critique of traditional Christian doctrines has led to a deeper understanding of the person and image of Christ. However, one-sided rationalization may lead to the "one-dimensional man" who accepts only what he can see through his senses and grasp by analytical reason. That this is totally unsatisfactory can be seen from the large-scale revival of magic and the proliferation of irrational cults. There is, then, a need for critical reflection on the truths of faith without yielding to rationalism or empiricism.

6) *Spirit vs. Matter.* Those with a dualistic mode of thinking tend to overstress the importance of the spiritual, leading to alienation, to

the neglect of one's essential secular duties, and even to injustice and oppression of the poor. Some react and swing to the other extreme, overstressing the temporal, thereby neglecting the ultimate meaning and goal of human life—a tendency which again can destroy the basic dignity of the human person. We must, then, seek a holistic vision of the human person and of reality in general.

7) *Prayer vs. Work.* The dichotomy between the spiritual and the material leads to separation between prayer and work, some stressing the first and others the second. Frequenting prayer groups should not be an escape from earthly tasks, especially from the struggle to bring about a more just society. On the other hand, activism should not lead us to reduce human liberation to a merely temporal project which does no good to suffering people. Prayer and work must be seen as the closely related horizontal and vertical dimensions of human activity.

8) *Detachment vs. Involvement.* If "world" is understood in a good sense, Christians should be involved in all its concerns while steadfastly combatting the evil structures in society. Faith should not lead to alienation or to the shirking of one's temporal tasks, but should provide the right inspiration for them. Any truly religious withdrawal from earthly concerns should lead, not to despising them, but to having a deeper respect for and a greater influence over them.

9) *Denial vs. Fulfillment.* Jesus came that we "may have life, and have it abundantly" (Jn. 10:10). Self-denial cannot be a goal in itself. We are called to fulfillment, which realistically implies the denial of our evil tendencies and urges. A certain denial of good tendencies is meaningful only inasmuch as it leads to deeper fulfillment. Today there is need for completely abandoning the negative stance of Manichaeism and Jansenism regarding human values. But there is also the need for reviving the genuine spirit of Christian mortification (cf. Chapter VIII, 5). This inclines us to "put to death" whatever is evil in us, to be ready to pay "the cost of discipleship," and to be discerning in giving up whatever is good when this is necessary for achieving a higher good.

10) *Church as Institution vs. Church as Communion.* Vatican II has clearly expressed the renewed self-understanding of the Church as a spiritual communion of believers. But it has not totally rejected the institutional aspect. The inevitable tensions between the two aspects has to be faced. The danger of institutionalism must be neutralized by permeating the laws and structures of the Church with the spirit of love and service (cf. Chapter X).

11) *Universal Church vs. Local Church.* Earlier, dioceses were seen as administrative units of the monolithic universal Church. Now, Vatican II views the universal Church as a communion of local Churches. This has vital consequences for realizing the mystery of God's plan of salvation according to different regions and cultures. "Inculturation" in Christian life, worship and even the expression of faith, becomes not a mere peripheral issue but a requisite to the authenticity and catholicity of the one Church of Christ. However, every local Church should be open to communion with other Churches, and the genuine unity of faith should not be lost. There should be a healthy balance between unity and pluralism.

4. TENSION BETWEEN VARIOUS ECCLESIAL GROUPS

1) *Clergy vs. Laity.* One of the main aberrations which Vatican II set about to rectify was clericalism, with its suggestion of a superior caste dominating every aspect of life in the Church. The laity react to this implication either by being alienated from the Church, by being passive in the Christian life and the apostolate, or by various forms of anticlericalism. The Council proposed to remedy the situation by emphasizing the principle of love and service. Even while reaffirming the hierarchical structure of the Church, the Council stressed the basic equality of all the members of the People of God and their participation in the priestly, prophetic and kingly mission of Christ. It should be noted that the promotion of the laity will not come about merely by concessions on the part of the clergy, but by lay people themselves assuming their distinctive role and responsibility in the Church.

2) *Bishops vs. Priests.* Although the bishops alone make up the hierarchy or "sacred rule" in the Church, all the bishops and priests together form the presbyterium. Both sides must realize that they have been jointly called to the ministry, not for themselves, but for the service of God's People. They must renounce entirely the spirit of domination or rivalry. The bishop in the diocese should realize that his own ministry will be successful only if he obtains the full and willing cooperation of his priests. The priests must recognize that the bishop is the center of unity of the diocesan presbyterium and its chief animator.

3) *Priests vs. Religious.* Prior to any differentiation of function and roles, all the members of the Church form the one Body of Christ. Although it would be wrong to set up any opposition, religious life belongs more specially to the charismatic or prophetic aspect of the Church. Hence, the clergy should not seek to domesticate the charism of religious and use them to maintain obsolete power structures. Religious, on the other hand, should not tend to be alienated from the realities of the local situation or seek to withdraw themselves from legitimate ecclesiastical authority. Properties, institutions and local influence may be so many causes of friction and rivalry. Such problems can be solved only by total selflessness and common dedication to the Kingdom. Each group must respect the charism of the other and have only the glory of God and the good of His people at heart in all their undertakings.

4) *Bishops vs. Theologians.* Vatican II assigns to the preaching of the Gospel an eminent place among the duties of the bishops. "They are authentic teachers . . . endowed with the authority of Christ, who preach to the people committed to them the faith they must believe and put into practice. By the light of the Holy Spirit, they make that faith clear, bringing forth from the treasury of revelation new things and old, making faith bear fruit and vigilantly warding off any errors which threaten their flock."[7]

However, the pronouncements of the magisterium cannot be arbitrary. They presuppose corporate reflection in the Church which normally requires the help of exegetes and theologians. The services of theologians are normally used in the preparation of the pronouncements. But the theologians, with all their expertise, should not set themselves up as a parallel magisterium. A spirit of faith will make them submit to the guidance of the hierarchy even while helping the latter in fulfilling its function. A tension between theologians and bishops is natural when the first are conscious of their expertise and the second of their authoritative role. This again can be resolved only if both put themselves at the service of the truth and are docile to the inspirations of the Spirit. There is need for mutual respect and cooperation in order to serve the People of God in its penetration of the Christian mystery.

5. ELEMENTS NEEDING RECONCILIATION IN THE WORLD

1) *Disparity Between Rich and Poor.* Within most countries, especially the developing ones, the gulf between the rich and the poor is widening. There is a grossly inequitable distribution of power, wealth and opportunities. There is a glaring contrast in the cities between the wealthy capitalists in their palaces and the poor workers in the slums; in the villages, between the prosperous landowners and the landless laborers. The selfish interests of a few privileged and powerful groups express themselves in wrong attitudes which are finally embodied in unjust laws, policies, conventions and organizational structures of society that can only be termed sinful. In this context, the Church is called upon to make a clear option in favor of the struggle for the liberation of the poor and the oppressed.

2) *Inequalities at the International Level.* The contrasts at the local level are but a projection of the glaring disparity between rich and poor countries—a disparity which, to a large extent, is a legacy of colonialism. Although colonial rule has been almost completely ended, it has been replaced by a more subtle and insidious neocolonialism by which poor peoples are exploited and manipulated. International law, trade relations, diplomacy and even armed intervention are used to perpetuate the iniquitous relationship. The Church has its own share in the establishment and maintenance of colonial structures. However, there is now a widespread consciousness in the Church about the need

for combatting them. Today the Church should take a clear stand on global injustices and strive to bring about a just international economic and social order. The wasteful use of scarce resources by some affluent nations and the mad arms race which is going on at the expense of the poor need urgent attention. The Church, with its supranational character, has a unique role to play in this area.

3) *Ecological Imbalance.* According to biblical revelation, God alone is the Master of creation, man being its steward to whom the whole earth is entrusted so that he might wisely make use of it and transform it for the glory of its Maker. Hence, reconciliation should extend itself to tackling the problem of widespread and harmful exploitation of natural resources by a few countries at the expense of poor peoples and of future generations. Environmental pollution affecting especially basic resources of air and water should cause particular concern. *Octagesima Adveniens,* Paul VI's apostolic letter of May 14, 1971, declares: "Man is suddenly becoming aware that by an ill-considered exploitation of nature he risks destroying it and becoming in his turn the victim of this degradation. Not only is the material environment becoming a permanent menace—pollution and refuse, new illnesses and absolute destructive capacity—but the human framework is no longer under man's control, thus creating an environment for tomorrow which may be intolerable. This is a wide-ranging social problem which concerns the entire human family."[8]

Christians cannot be indifferent to this vital problem. They must do everything to reverse this destructive trend, especially by recalling the basic truth of God's dominion over creation and its primary destination for the good of the whole human family.[9] According to Paul's cosmic perspective, the material world, in solidarity with mankind, is to share in its liberation (cf. Rom. 8:19–22). Consequently, the Church is to involve herself in the restoration and transformation of the whole universe.

4) *Racism, Časteism and Tribalism.* The separation between rich and poor nations is, to a large extent, drawn along racial lines. The "white man's burden" of the colonial era has become the white man's

advantage. In South Africa, there is an inhuman oppression of the so-called inferior races by a minority regime supported by more powerful white nations. In some other countries, like the United States and the United Kingdom, there is more or less open discrimination against non-white races. In India, there is the age-old stratification of caste, which leads to the oppression of lower castes and bitter rivalry among the others. Likewise, many countries of Africa are suffering from internecine warfare between different tribes, which prevents cooperation and development whether on the national or the regional level. The Gospel message comes to proclaim the basic equality of all human beings. The Church, because of its Catholic nature, is called upon to be a strong element of reconciliation and healing in this context. This presupposes that she herself is free of the virus of racism, casteism or tribalism.

5) *Totalitarianism.* A large number of oppressive rightist and leftist regimes holds the greater part of the human population in tyrannical subjection. Human rights are grossly violated even in so-called democratic countries. In recent times, Church documents have called for a vigorous defense of these rights. Individual Christians and ecclesial communities must be fearless in upholding the dignity of the human person, made to the image of God and redeemed with the Blood of Christ.

6) *Political and Economic Corruption.* In many democratic countries, the political scene is a sad spectacle of instability, of divisions and of endless wrangling. Political activity has ceased to be a service of the people and has become a selfish seeking for power and advantage. The media are used by powerful groups to further their own vested interests, so that it is difficult for the average person to arrive at the truth.

Economic corruption has become all-pervasive and reached frightening proportions. In the business world, profiteering, bribery, hoarding, black-marketeering and tax evasion are rampant. Corruption has penetrated deep into the administrative machinery. Even well-meaning Christians find it hard to avoid contagion or being sucked into this whirlpool of corruption.

In this situation, the Church, as "the salt of the earth and the light of the world" (Mt. 5:13), is called upon to give an example of selfless service in her administrative setup and to make her policies and financial deals fair and entirely free from any trace of corruption. Individual Christians, too, must set a high example of integrity in political and business life.

7) *Labor Problems.* One of the areas of life that is particularly full of tension, discord and strife is that of labor. Work is often treated as merchandise; and the human person, the subject of work, is degraded. In many places, there is the evil of "bonded labor," not far different from slavery, and the exploitation of women and children as cheap labor. In this situation all should heed the call of Pope John Paul II to recognize the primacy of the person over labor and the priority of labor over capital.[10] The Church should strongly defend the rights of workers, worker solidarity and the dignity of human labor. More attention should be paid to the world of labor, especially the unorganized sector, in which fair wages and just working conditions are continually denied. Church-related institutions must give the example of just remuneration and decent working conditions.

6. RECONCILIATION AND CONFLICT

In this situation of widespread conflict and oppression, three positions are possible: 1) a *blind struggle* to redress injustices without any consideration of means or consequences; 2) a *benevolent neutrality,* an expectation that everything will be alright provided we use patience and kindness; 3) striving after *reconciliation,* but being ready to face any tension involved.

1) If there is no spirit of reconciliation, we have a "justice that becomes injustice," in the words of the Pope.[11] "Then justice itself falls victim to other negative forces such as jealousy, hatred and even cruelty. Then the desire to destroy an enemy, to limit his freedom and even to reduce him to total dependence becomes the chief motive of action. This is contrary to the nature of justice, which strives rather to establish equality and balance between rival parties."[12]

2) The case for benevolent neutrality is based on several mis-understandings:[13] a) that conflicts arise only because of personal mis-understanding and that there is always equal blame on both sides (two unwarranted assumptions); b) that one can in fact be neutral in any case of conflict (whereas such neutrality would be beneficial to the oppressor, as it enables the status quo to be maintained); c) that tension and conflict are necessarily worse evils than injustice and oppression (yet the history of Israel shows that God actually commands His people to resist tyranny and oppression, and Israel is condemned for attempts at compromise).

The figure of Jesus as Prince of Peace is often misunderstood. Surely, He came to bring peace. Still, this peace is not one of com-placency in the face of injustice, but of actively bringing about order and justice—which may require struggle.[14] A certain amount of conflict is inevitable. Jesus Himself declared: "Do you think I have come to give peace on earth? No, I tell you, but rather division" (Lk. 12:51; Mt. 10:34 has "sword" instead of "division"). In fact, His uncom-promising stance provoked the opposition of the vested interests of the time and ultimately brought about His violent death. Jesus clearly dis-tinguishes between the peace which He brings and the peace which the world wants (Jn. 14:27). The first is based on truth and justice, while the one which the oppressive elements in the world would have is that which compromises with the truth and covers up injustice. Jesus did not hesitate to highlight existing conflicts in order to bring about a more genuine peace. Likewise, Mary in her Magnificat proclaims that God "has put down the mighty from their thrones, and exalted those of low degree; he has filled the hungry with good things, and the rich he has sent empty away" (Lk. 1:52–53).

There is no evidence that Jesus adopted a posture of neutrality in the conflict between the rich and mighty, on the one hand, and the poor and lowly, on the other. In no uncertain terms, He declared the latter blessed and cried "woe" on the first. The apostolic letter, *Octagesima Adveniens* affirms that, in teaching us charity, the Gospel instructs us in the *preferential respect* due to the poor.[15]

3) However, Jesus sought the reconciliation of all people of His time. He came to demolish the dividing line between Jew and Gentile, slave and freeman, male and female (cf. Gal. 3:28; Col. 3:11).

We must distinguish between personal animosities and structural conflicts that exist between the oppressing class and the oppressed, between the rich and the poor. While the Christian must be resolutely engaged in redressing evils, this does not mean that he should hate the rich and the powerful and want to destroy them as people. The privileged should be pulled down from their thrones, from their structural position in society that enables them to oppress the poor. If today we want to be on God's side, we must decidedly support the cause of the poor. This is not only for the sake of the poor, but also for the sake of the rich who are morally and spiritually poor because of their involvement in injustice. By oppressing their fellowmen, they disfigure the image of God within themselves.

Hence, confrontation and conflict do not necessarily imply personal hatred. At times it may be the only way to free the rich from the sin of injustice in which they are caught up and, hence, the only effective way of loving them.

7. CONVERSION OF HEART

We have seen the vast program of reconciliation which the Church today is called upon to perform. But we have also seen in the last chapter the dialectical relationship between the personal and the social dimensions of sin. Unjust sinful situations and personal failings play upon one another and aggravate one another. However, personal conversion is in itself more basic.

Although the call to conversion in the Old Testament is generally addressed to the people of Israel as a whole, each individual Israelite is clearly asked to respond personally. This is manifest from the very terms used. For instance, in Ezekiel we have: "A new heart I will give you, and a new spirit I will put within you; and I will take out of your flesh the heart of stone and give you a heart of flesh" (36:26). In spite of the communitarian dimension of the New Testament message, sin and reconciliation are primarily personal. "What comes out of a man is what defiles a man. For from within, out of the heart of man, come evil thoughts . . ." (Mk. 7:20–21). The coming of the Kingdom is a call to *metanoia* (cf. Mk. 1:15), or a radical change in the depths of man's heart, and a faith commitment to Christ, through whom the Good News comes.

Indeed, one of the most specific elements of the Christian message is, in the words of Pope John Paul II, "the truth about the human person, truth that is revealed to us, in its full extent and depth, in Christ."[16] From this point of view, it is necessary to restore the *sense of personal sin* which is being obscured by contemporary unchristian values as well as by a one-sided emphasis on the social dimension of religion and life. However, care should be taken not to revive the morbid sense of guilt and scrupulosity from which many Christians suffered in the past.

It should again be noted that the initiative for repentance and conversion of heart comes from God. "God shows his love for us in that while we were yet sinners Christ died for us" (Rom. 5:8). It is not the works of penance that effect the inner change of heart but God's gracious gift. Human effort is only the sign of man's willingness to abandon inordinate attachments and turn his heart wholly to God.

8. THE MYSTERY OF MERCY AND FORGIVENESS

In a wounded world, to human persons with wounded hearts, God's love is revealed as one of mercy and compassion. God appears, above all, as a God of *hesed* (literally "graciousness" and translated as *eleos* in the Greek Septuagint and *misericordia* in the Latin Vulgate). It reflects Yahweh's will to save. It is characterized as His *emet,* or fidelity, and it is most frequently associated with the covenant. Yahweh preserves His covenant fidelity to those who "walk before Him" (cf. 1 Kgs. 8:23). While the *hesed* of Yahweh calls for fidelity on the part of man, it is in itself unconditional. It is more enduring than the response of man and is a forgiving attribute which seeks to maintain or restore good relations even when man attempts to destroy them.

Yahweh revealed Himself to Moses as "the Lord, a God merciful and gracious, slow to anger, and abundant in steadfast love and faithfulness, keeping steadfast love for thousands, forgiving iniquity and transgression and sin" (Ex. 34:6–7; cf. Num. 14:19; Jer. 3:12). Israel's infidelity breaks the Sinai covenant of love; but, far from resigning Himself to this, God Himself takes the initiative for a new and eternal covenant (Jer. 31:31–34; Ez. 36:60–63).

Jesus, whose very name means "Yahweh is salvation," came to reveal the Father's merciful love to sinners, in order to bring about a perfect and definitive reconciliation. The parables of mercy in Lk. 15 manifest a mercy that seems surprising, unreasonable and even shocking. Jesus Himself shocked the pious by associating Himself with those who were written off as fallen or sinners. To their angry outbursts Jesus replied: "Those who are well have no need of the physician, but those who are sick. Go and learn what this means, 'I desire mercy, and not sacrifice.' For I came not to call the righteous but sinners" (Mt. 9:12–13). Jesus did not give up anyone as a hopeless case. He saw the potentialities of good in people and evoked them by His merciful love. For instance, the Samaritan woman (Jn. 4), Zacchaeus (Lk. 19:1–10), and the sinful woman (Jn. 8:1–11) all experienced the concern of Jesus for human dignity. As John Paul II makes it clear in *Dives in Misericordia*, "Those who experience mercy do not feel cast down but rather are found again, as it were, and 'esteemed' again."[17]

The merciful love of the Father is finally revealed in the Cross of Christ, in the unparalleled way in which Jesus loved sinful humanity. "For our sake he [the Father] made him [Christ] to be sin who knew no sin" (2 Cor. 5:21; cf. Jn. 3:16). "Christ loved us and gave himself for us" (Eph. 5:2).

The humanity of Christ is the primordial sacrament of redemption since it is the sign that effectively manifests and communicates the salvific love of God. We have perfect assurance of God's pardon in the

Passion of Christ. God loves us with an unconditional love. Our waywardness does not change His loving and accepting attitude. "God shows his love for us in that while we were yet sinners Christ died for us" (Rom. 5:8).

God does not wait for us to return. He has already forgiven us— or, better, *fore-given* us in Christ. We have already been accepted. Now we have only *"to accept that we are accepted."* The sacrament of reconciliation is the celebration of the "fore-given" love of the Father through Christ.

The forgiving love of God calls us to forgive our neighbor. One who does not forgive from the heart remains closed to the experience of God's forgiving love.

The New Testament—particularly, the Sermon on the Mount— stresses the attitude of *mutual forgiveness*. One of the most expressive beatitudes is: "Blessed are the merciful, for they shall obtain mercy" (Mt. 5:7). One is first to be reconciled to one's brother before offering his gift at the altar (5:23).

Mutual forgiveness appears as the most characteristic virtue of the disciple of Christ and the son of the heavenly Father (5:43–48). The much quoted passage: "Be perfect, as your heavenly Father is perfect" has little to do with divine omnipotence or omniscience. Jesus wants us to share the divine perfection by imitating the goodness of the Father toward the just and the unjust, toward His friends and His enemies. He, therefore, wants us to love our enemies and do good to those who persecute us. There is nothing special in loving those who love us and saluting only those who salute us. Even the much despised tax collectors and Gentiles do that. Indeed, the history of religions indicates that it is only in Christianity that this virtue of mutual forgiveness stands out clearly. Whether Christians regularly practice it is another matter.

Again we are asked to pray: "Forgive us our debts, as we also have forgiven our debtors" (6:12). God's forgiveness is unconditional, but it will have no effect on us unless we are ready to forgive and be reconciled with those who have offended us. So Jesus insists: "If you forgive men their trespasses, your heavenly Father also will forgive you; but if you do not forgive men their trespasses, neither will your heavenly Father forgive your trespasses" (6:14–15). Forgiveness of sins is not a mere declaration but an effective return to the Father. It is a reconciliation and a restoring of bonds, just as sin is an alienation. This necessarily implies also a return to one's brethren, who are the images of God and children of the Father in Christ. That is why we are told: "Judge not, that you be not judged" (7:1).

This theme is clearly brought out in the parable of the two sons, where there is a strong contrast between the attitude of the father welcoming his wayward son and that of the elder son, who rejects his brother (Lk. 15:20–32). Again Jesus brings home the lesson of mutual forgiveness in the parable of the unforgiving servant, which ends with the strong warning that, as the man who would not forgive his fellow servant was delivered over to the torturers, "so also my heavenly Father will do to every one of you, if you do not forgive your brother from your heart" (Mt. 18:35). Not forgiving one's brother or sister is, in effect, rejecting God. Alienation from one's neighbor implies alienation from God. Reconciliation with one's neighbor implies reconciliation with God.

9. THE SACRAMENT OF RECONCILIATION

Reconciliation involves a radical break with the past and becoming "a new creation" (2 Cor. 5:17). This newness is first realized in baptism. In what is apparently a baptismal homily, Peter declares: "By his great mercy we have been born anew to a living hope through the resurrection of Jesus from the dead. . . . Having purified your souls by your obedience to the truth for a service of love of the brethren, love one another earnestly from the heart" (1 Pet. 1:3,22).

But, due to the weakness of human nature, this basic reconciliation with God and with one another has to be constantly renewed. The sacrament of reconciliation is the celebration of the "fore-given" love of the Father through Christ. It is the liturgical expression of the experience of being forgiven and accepted which gives ecclesial assurance of divine pardon.

When Christ was on earth, He used various words and gestures to heal and forgive sins. Now the risen Lord communicates His saving grace through the sacraments of the Church. They are not mere things or empty gestures, but are the personal encounters with Christ through which we personally experience His saving grace and respond to it.

In sacramental confession, the human dialogue with the priest symbolizes our dialogue with God to which we are graciously called. It is a sharing in the paschal mystery of Christ, a dying to the old self and a rising to a new life of holiness and grace.

The sacramental union with the mystery of Christ's death and resurrection opens our eyes to see all human realities as God sees them and as they are directed to our final fulfillment in Him. All the evil in the hearts of men and in the structures of the world is judged. It is recognized for what it is and, thereby, the way is opened for a radical act of fidelity in union with the total self-surrender of Christ. The call to detachment from selfishness is also a call to commitment to the building up of the Kingdom of God.

It is also very important to understand the role of the Spirit in the sacrament of reconciliation. The Spirit Himself creates the first stirrings of repentance and an openness to God and to others. Forgiveness of sins itself is not so much a juridical act or a mere declaration of God through the priest that the penitent's sins are forgiven. It is an interior transformation of heart fulfilling the prophecy of Ezekiel: "A new heart I will give you and a new spirit I will put within you" (36:26). Thereby the penitent is moved to commit himself to live, no more "according to the flesh with its desires," but according to the inspiration of the Spirit to bring forth the fruits of "love, peace, patience, kindness, goodness, faithfulness, gentleness and self-control" (Gal. 5:16–23).

Important consequences follow from this. Firstly, the whole process of sacramental confession, whether on the part of the confessor or on that of the penitent, must be understood as a truly "spiritual" activity—that is, disposing the heart to the action of the Holy Spirit. The spiritual gift of reconciliation, often experienced in charismatic gatherings, must be clearly linked with the sacrament of reconciliation. The new-found interest in the Holy Spirit, far from diverting the faithful from the celebration of the sacrament, should help in renewing the manner of celebration.

One of the common difficulties of people regarding confession to a priest arises from an overindividualistic understanding of the whole economy of salvation. The work of conversion and reconciliation is not only a matter of individual relationship between the penitent and God. It also has an essentially social dimension. It is not, as we have seen, the result of individual human effort, but of the grace and gift received in and through the community of love which is the Church. The confession of sins must be understood as the humble submission of one's conduct to the judgment of the priest representing God and the community. This judgment is not one of condemnation, but of healing and salvation. The confessor exercises it by kindly welcoming the penitent, by proclaiming the Word of God, giving wise counsel and encouragement, and finally by proclaiming pardon in the name of God and the Church. Sacramental absolution is the effective sign used by the Church to reconcile the sinner to herself and to God. We should not isolate it, however, from the wider responsibility and activity of the whole Church which leads up to the final sacramental reconciliation.

The sacrament, then, must be understood as the *sanctification of daily reconciliation*. It is not an isolated exercise of piety to be accomplished in a few moments, but rather the high point of the entire effort of the Church to renew the life of the faithful with God's grace. It is not a substitute for real reconciliation in daily life, but the culmination of the continual movement of reconciliation through the ministry of the Church. It deeply affects the whole of a person's life and is vital to the whole Church in her continual striving for purification and renewal. Indeed, it affects the whole world by releasing an energy of integration and healing.

Sacramental confession is not merely a verbal recital of our faults. It is a manifestation of our changed attitude to God and His people. It is an act of worship by which God is praised, His justice and holiness acknowledged, and His mercy proclaimed. In this way, confession becomes a proclamation of faith in God's loving mercy, a true participation in the sacred liturgy of the Church.

Admission of moral guilt dispels the darkness of sin. "God is light and in him there is no darkness at all" (1 Jn. 1:5). A humble avowal before God and His Church counteracts the dark power of sin and casts light into the hidden recesses of the conscience. Thus it opens the soul to the rays of light and the love of God. Confession before the visible Church releases the sinner from his solitude and enfolds him in the solidarity of truth. The dialogue with the priest offers an evangelical light for one's particular situation and ensures a depth of conversion. Confession also brings about the interior freedom by which one becomes capable of living out one's Christian vocation and thereby makes one's whole life a liturgy of praise of the Lord.

. The sacrament of reconciliation not only restores a grave sinner to grace but also enables the faithful Christian to deepen his or her baptismal commitment, to transcend the limits which the "flesh" tries to place on the road to Christian perfection. Thus, it becomes a powerful means of growth in spiritual maturity and in union with one's neighbor. In this way, frequent confession enhances the effort to live out to the full the implications of baptism, through which we are conformed to a new life of holiness that is manifested by a life of charity and fraternal service.

These fruits will be forthcoming only if there is a proper understanding of the sacrament and a meaningful celebration. There is particular need for stressing the right idea of sorrow as a confident turning to God, and not a morbid guilt feeling which retards genuine spiritual growth and, in its extreme form, leads to paralysis of the psychic and spiritual life. True sorrow for sin should imply an inner experience of God's merciful love, a joyous homecoming and a reestablishment or deepening of one's loving relationship with God and one's fellowmen.

It should also imply a readiness to repair the scandal or damage caused, as well as a firm commitment to renew the structures of social life, beginning with the family and the neighborhood.

————o————

Notes to Chapter XXI

1. *The Roman Missal*, Fourth Eucharistic Prayer.
2. See *Dictionary of New Testament Theology*, ed. by Colin Brown, Vol. 3, Exeter, Paternoster Press, 1978, art. "Reconciliation," pp. 145–76.
3. *LG*, art. 1.
4. G. Pattery, "Reconciliation: The Bearing of Paul on the Synodal Theme," *Vidya Jyoti*, 46 (1982), 451.
5. *Art. cit.*, p. 452.
6. *Penance Today*, New Jersey, Dimension Books, 1974, pp. 34–35.
7. *LG*, art. 25.
8. No. 21.
9. Cf. Vatican II, *GS*, art. 69 and 71.
10. Encyclical *Laborem Exercens*, September 14, 1981, nos. 6 and 12.
11. John Paul II, encyclical *Dives in Misericordia*, November 30, 1980, no. 12.
12. *Ibid.*
13. Cf. "Reconciliation or Conflict: The Christian Dilemma," *Doctrine and Life*, 33 (1983), 36–37.
14. See pp. 67–69.
15. No. 23.
16. *Dives in Misericordia*, no. 1., (summarizing the encyclical *Redemptor Hominis*, March 16, 1981).
17. No. 6.

Moral Guidance Today

With the current ferment in moral theology, a pastor would be hard put to determine what he has to say to people who approach him for guidance. Gone are the days when he could give pat answers to every question. This situation is at first sight disconcerting. But it could also be looked upon as an opportunity for deepening the moral responsibility of the faithful.

The Church has an invaluable contribution to make regarding the moral progress of her members and the whole of humanity. She brings a clear understanding of the dignity of the human person made in the image of God and called to share in His own life. She proclaims the sanctity of the personal conscience, where man is "alone with God, whose voice echoes in his depths." She is called upon to foster genuine human values like the sanctity of human life, to promote a common search for ethical wisdom, and to defend human rights, while at the same time drawing attention to the corresponding responsibilities.

Hence, the moral task of the pastor is, above all, to proclaim the realities concerning the dignity of man and his vocation. He has to elucidate the meaning of man's communitarian call through life in Christ by the grace of the Holy Spirit. The universal call to holiness must be taken seriously, and the artificial dichotomy between a spiritual theology meant for a few and a moral theology of minimal requirements for the rest should be abandoned.

It is the duty of the pastor to convey Christian insights regarding the person, conscience, freedom, love, law, and so forth. There is need, not only for information concerning moral matters, but, more so, for *formation* of right attitudes, discovery of ethical values, and the way toward correct decisions. The young have thus to be *initiated* gradually into Christian living.

Regarding concrete problems in areas like justice and medical ethics, the role of the pastor is, not to provide ready-made solutions to every difficulty, but to help people to form their own conscience and to find solutions to their problems in a spirit of Christian maturity. Obviously, this makes the task of the pastor as moral guide much more challenging. He has to equip himself for it by acquiring a thorough grasp of genuine Christian moral principles and of the way of educating people to moral responsibility.

However, after generations of passive acceptance of what the confessor said, it will not do now to tell the faithful suddenly, "Follow your conscience." This would mean little to those who have no idea what conscience is and how to discern its dictates. The role of the pastor is neither to say, "Follow our conscience" nor simply to solve people's problems, but to help them to solve their problems or follow their conscience. For this, the law of growth has to be taken into account. A person may not be able to reach the ideals of Christian perfection all at once. He has to strive toward it gradually, with many ups and downs, for which there is need of progressive liberation and an atmosphere of understanding and love.

The development of modern psychology has shown that mere abstract norms do not enable people to become good. The psychic inhibitions that impede moral growth and ethical response have to be handled. The findings of modern psychology, judiciously used, can be of very great help to promote moral development and resolve emotional tensions that hinder the exercise of moral responsibility. But we should beware of swinging from the excessive moralizing of the past to exclusive psychologizing. There is need for a clear understanding regarding both the distinction and the relationship between morality and psychology. It would be disastrous to overstress one to detriment of the other, or to cultivate them on parallel lines that do not meet. In pastoral practice, due importance should be given to moral values and principles on the one hand, and to the psychological conditions required for a free and responsible human life on the other.

One of the notable contributions of current moral theology is the insistence that all values implied in a moral decision should be respected as far as possible. For instance, in dealing with those who are living in an irregular marital situation, one must take into account the prophetic function of the Church in upholding the sanctity and indissolubility of the marriage covenant, and, at the same time, the call to exercise pastoral solicitude toward those who are in a difficult predicament. The effort to maintain the delicate balance required in harmonizing such apparently conflicting responsibilities must not be shirked.

The Church's mission is not only to address individual men—to save "souls," as it used to be called—but to transform human society as a whole through the saving grace of Christ. As the very life and ministry of the Church are largely conditioned by the contemporary situation, she has to analyze this situation with all available human resources and discern, in the light of faith, what she ought to do in order to help human society to realize its aspirations for fulfillment in Christ. This applies to the moral growth of each individual as well. It would not be of much use to inculcate ethical values and principles to the young if the atmosphere in which they have to live is corrupting. Of course, there is need for enlightened and strongly motivated people to change the situation. Only in this sense can we speak of an elite in the Church—an elite, not of privilege, but of vision and service.

The recognition of the fact that the "shepherds" cannot be simply and totally distinguished from the "flock" is of great significance in pastoral guidance today. Within the Church, there are not simply "shepherds" who care for passive "sheep," but every member is called upon to participate jointly in the common salvific activity of the Church, each according to his role and charism. Outside her visible boundaries, the Church has not so much to confront others who are total aliens or opponents, but to discern the workings of God's grace in them and lead them to find their fulfillment in Christ. Hence, the search for ethical values in the world today should be a joint enterprise of all Christians, all believers and all men of goodwill.

Finally, we would like to emphasize the link between genuine worship and moral life. Without the vertical dimension of true worship of the true God, moral effort will not have sufficient dynamism; also, without commitment to the transformation of the world, worship becomes an empty ritual and a contradiction in a world that is yearning for liberation. An authentic moral theology should recognize a close relationship between religion and life.

———o———

BIBLIOGRAPHY

BARCLAY William, *Ethics in a Permissive Society*, London, Collins, 1971.

BECK E.M. et alii, eds., *Moral Education*, New York, Newman Press, 1971.

BIRCH Bruce C. and RASMUSSEN Larry L., *Bible and Ethics in Christian Life*, Minneapolis, Augsburg, 1976.

BOCKLE Franz, *Fundamental Moral Theology*, New York, Pueblo, 1980.

BONHOEFFER Dietrich, *Ethics*, New York, Macmillan, 1964.

CURRAN Charles E., *Christian Morality Today*, Notre Dame, Ind., Fides, 1966.

—. *A New Look at Christian Morality*, ibid., 1968.

—. *Catholic Moral Theology in Dialogue*, University of Notre Dame Press, 1972.

—. *New Perspectives in Moral Theology*, Notre Dame, Ind., Fides, 1974.

—. *Themes in Fundamental Moral Theology*, ibid., 1977.

—. *Ongoing Revision: Studies in Moral Theology*, ibid., 1977.

—. *Transition and Tradition in Moral Theology*, ibid., 1979.

—. ed., *Absolutes in Moral Theology*, Washington, Corpus Books, 1968.

—. and McCORMICK Richard A., *Readings in Moral Theology: Moral Norms and Catholic Tradition*, New York, Pueblo, 1980.

DELHAYE Philippe, *The Christian Conscience*, New York, Desclee, 1968.

DOMINIAN Jack, *Authority*, London, Burns and Oates, 1976.

DUNSTAN G.R., *Duty and Discernment*, London, SCM Press, 1975.

EGENTER Richard and MATTUSEK Paul, *Faith, Freedom and Conscience*, Dublin, Gill & Son, 1967.

ELLUL J., *The Ethics of Freedom*, Grand Rapids, Eerdmans, 1976.

ERIKSON Erik A., *Insight and Responsibility*, New York, Norton, 1964.

—. *Identity, Youth and Crisis*, London, Faber & Faber, 1968.

FAGAN Sean, *Has Sin Changed?* Dublin, Gill & Macmillan, 1978.

FLETCHER Joseph, *Situation Ethics*, Philadelphia, Westminster Press, 1966.

—. *Christian Responsibility*, ibid., 1967.

FORD John and KELLY Gerald, *Contemporary Moral Theology*, Vol. 1, Westminster, MD., Newman Press, 1958.

FRANKENA W., *Ethics*, Englewood Cliffs, N.J., Prentice Hall, 1973.

—. and GRANROSE J., eds., *Introductory Readings in Ethics*, ibid., 1974.

FUCHS Josef, *Natural Law*, Dublin, Gill & Son, 1965.

—. *Human Values and Christian Morality*, Dublin, Gill & Macmillan, 1970.

GAFNEY, *Newness of Life; A Modern Introduction to Catholic Ethics*, New York, Paulist, 1979.

GOODPASTOR K.E., *Perspectives on Morality: Essays by William Frankena*, University of Notre Dame Press, 1976.

GRISEZ Germain G., *Contraception and the Natural Law*, Milwaukee, Bruce, 1964.

—. with SHAW R., *Beyond the New Morality*, University of Notre Dame Press, 2nd ed., 1980.

GUSTAFSON James M., *Christ and the Moral Life*, New York, Harper & Row, 1968.

—. *The Church as Decision Maker*, Philadelphia, Pilgrim, 1970.

—. *Christian Ethics and the Community*, Philadelphia, United Church Press, 1971.

—. *Can Ethics Be Christian?* Chicago and London, University of Chicago Press, 1975.

—. *Protestant and Roman Catholic Ethics*, ibid., 1978.

HAGMAIER George and GLEASON Robert H., *Moral Problems Now*, London, Sheed & Ward, 1959.

HARING Bernard, *The Law of Christ*, Vol. 1, Cork, Mercier, 1961.

—. *Morality Is for Persons*, New York, Farrar, Straus and Giroux, 1971.

—. *Sin in a Secular Age*, Slough, St. Paul Publications, 1974.

—. *Manipulation*, ibid., 1975.

—. *Free and Faithful in Christ*, Vol. 1, ibid., 1978.

HASELDEN Kyle, *Morality and the Mass Media*, Nashville, Broadman Press, 1968.

HAUERWASS Stanley, *Vision and Virtue*, Notre Dame, Ind., Fides, 1974.

—. *Character and the Christian Life*, San Antonio, Trinity University Press, 1975.

HENNESSY J.C., *Values and Moral Development*, New York, Paulist Press, 1976.

JONSEN Albert R., *Responsibility in Modern Religious Ethics*, Washington, Corpus Books, 1968.

KAY William, *Moral Development*, London, George Allen and Unwin, 1974.

KENNEDY Eugene, *A Sense of Life and a Sense of Sin*, Garden City, N.Y., Doubleday, 1975.

LEHMANN Paul, *Ethics in a Christian Context*, New York, Harper and Row, 1963.

LEPP Ignace, *The Authentic Morality*, New York, Macmillan, 1965.

LEROY Edward L., *A Survey of Christian Ethics*, New York, Oxford University Press, 1967.

LOBO George V., *Current Problems in Medical Ethics*, Allahabad, St. Paul Publications, 3rd ed., 1980.

McCABE Herbert, *Law, Love and Language*, London, Sheed and Ward, 1968.

McCORMICK Richard A., *Ambiguity in Moral Choice*, Milwaukee, Marquette University Press, 1973.

—. and RAMSEY Paul, *Doing Evil to Achieve Good*, Chicago, Loyola University Press, 1978.

McDONAGH Enda, ed., *Moral Theology Renewed*, Dublin, Gill and Son, 1965.

—. *Invitation and Response*, Dublin, Gill & Macmillan, 1972.

—. *Gift and Call*, ibid., 1975.

MACQUARRIE John, *Three Issues in Ethics*, London, SCM Press, 1970.

MACKEY J.P., ed., *Morals, Law and Authority*, ibid., 1969.

MALY Eugene H., *Sin: Biblical Perspectives*, Dayton, Pflaum, 1973.

MAY Rollo, *Love and Will*, New York, W.W. Norton, 1969.

MAY William E., *Becoming Human*, Dayton, Pflaum, 1975.

MEHL Roger, *Catholic Ethics and Protestant Ethics*, Philadelphia, Westminster Press, 1971.

MENNINGER Karl, *Whatever Became of Sin*, Hawthorn Books, 1974.

MILHAVEN John G., *Towards a New Catholic Morality*, Garden City, N.Y., Doubleday, 1973.

MONDEN Louis, *Sin, Liberty and Law*, London, Sheed and Ward, 1965.

MURRAY John G., *The Problem of Religious Freedom*, London, Chapman, 1965.

NELSON James B., *Moral Nexus*, Philadelphia, Westminster Press, 1971.

NELSON Ellis C., ed., *Conscience*, New York, Newman Press, 1973.

NIEBUHR Reinhold, *The Nature and Destiny of Man*, London, Nisbet, 1941.

NIEBUHR Richard, *The Responsible Self*, New York, Harper and Row, 1951.

O'CONNELL Timothy, *Principles for a Christian Morality*, New York, Seabury, 1976.

OUTKA Gene H. and REEDER John P., *Religion and Morality*, Garden City, N.Y., Anchor Books, 1973.

OUTKA Gene H. and RAMSEY Paul, eds., *Norm and Context in Christian Ethics*, New York, Scribner, 1968.

PESCHKE C. Henry, *Christian Ethics*, Vol. 1, Bangalore, Theological Publications in India, 1979.

PODIMATTAM Felix, *Relativity of Natural Law*, 2nd ed., Bangalore, Asian Trading Corporation, 1976.

ROBINSON John A.T., *Christian Morals Today*, London, SCM Press, 1966.

ROBINSON N.H.G., *Groundwork of Christian Ethics*, London, Collins, 1971.

RAMSEY Paul, *Deeds and Rules in Christian Ethics*, New York, Scribner, 1967.

REGAN George M., *New Trends in Moral Theology*, New York, Newman, 1975.

RICOEUR, Paul, *Freedom and Nature: The Voluntary and the Involuntary*, Evanston, North-western University Press, 1966.

SCHELKE Karl, *Theology of the New Testament*, Vol. 3, *Morality*, Collegeville, Liturgical Press, 1973.

SCHILLEBEECKX Edward, *God and Man*, New York, Sheed and Ward, 1969.

SCHILLER Herbert J., *The Mind Changers*, Boston, Beacon Press, 1973.

SCHNAKENBURG Rudolf, *The Moral Teaching of the New Testament*, London, Burns and Oates, 1965.

SCHOONENBERG Piet, *Man and Sin*, London, Sheed and Ward, 1965.

SELLERS James, *Theological Ethics*, New York, Macmillan, 1966.

SEGUNDO Juan L., *Grace and the Human Condition*, New York, Maryknoll, 1973.

—. *Evolution and Guilt*, New York, Orbis Books, 1974.

SHEA John, *What a Modern Catholic Believes About Sin*, Chicago, Thomas More, 1971.

SITTLER Joseph, *The Structure of Christian Ethics*, Baton Rouge, La., Louisiana State University Press, 1958.

SPICQ Ceslaus, *St. Paul and Christian Living*, Dublin, Gill and Son, 1964.

SPURRIER William A., *Natural Law and the Ethics of Love*, Philadelphia, Westminster Press, 1974.

THIELICKE Helmut, *Theological Ethics*, Vol. 1, *Foundations*, Philadelphia, Fortress Press, 1966.

TILLICH Paul, *Morality and Beyond*, London, Collins, 1964.

VAN DER MARCK, W.H.M., *Toward a Christian Ethic*, New York, Newman, 1969.

VAN DER POEL Cornelius J., *The Search for Human Values*, New York, Newman, 1971.

WAKIN E. and McNULTY H., *Should You Ever Feel Guilty?* New York, Paulist Press, 1978.

WOGAMAN J. Philip, *A Christian Method of Moral Judgement*, London, SCM Press, 1976.

Subject Index

Abortion, 207, 216, 302, 331, 342, 349, 351–352;
  legalizing, 263–264.
Absolutes, moral, 181, 199–219, 305, 328, 342–344, 346–347, 350–352, 357;
  solution of problem, 231–239;
  validity of, 225–230.
Act, external, 29, 344–347, 391, 398, 401;
  human, 16, 82, 88, 133, 172, 187, 214, 341–354, 403;
  moral, 18, 140, 227, 346–347.
Act-agapism, 206.
Adultery, *see* Sex, extramarital.
Advertising, 278, 370–372.
Agape, 139, 151, 157, 158, 189, 204–206, 255; *see also* Love.
Alcoholism, 364, 404.
Alienation, 95, 136, 139, 201, 261, 287, 377–378, 384, 392–393, 397, 406, 407, 411,
  417, 430.
Anointing of the sick, 136.
Anthropology, *see* Body, Man.
Antinomianism, 2, 204–205.
Anxiety, 307, 314, 318, 337, 364, 392–400.
Aristotelianism, 6, 22.
Arms race, 422.
Asceticism, 88, 118–123, 128, 418.
Authoritarianism, 245, 300, 330, 416, 420.
Authority, in the Church, 244–245, 321;
  in society, 259–261; *see also* Civil authority, Civil law.
Autonomy, 286–287, 288–289, 292–293, 295–296, 309, 313, 376, 387; *see also* Free-
  dom.

Baptism, 60, 76, 115–116, 133, 135, 143–144, 430, 433;
  in the Holy Spirit, 144;
  of desire, 348.
Beauty, 95, 294.
Behaviorism, 297–298.
Body, 86–88, 119–121, 127–131, 389.
Bourgeois ethic, 155–156.

Call, moral, 14–15, 29–32, 41, 45, 67, 69–70, 74, 93–94, 97, 99, 102–103, 104–105,
  111–114, 132–133, 187–189, 207, 281, 286–287, 325–326, 327, 329–330, 332–338,
  347–348, 386, 435.
Canon law, 8, 16, 60, 192;